Teaching in Post-Compulsory Education

2nd Edition

Also available from Continuum

Teaching in Further Education, L.B. Curzon

A to Z for Every Manager in FE, Susan Wallace and Jonathan Gravells

A to Z of Teaching in FE, Angela Steward

Everything You Need to Know About FE Policy, Yvonne Hillier

Guide to Vocational Education and Training, Christopher Winch and Terry Hyland

Reflective Teaching in Further and Adult Education, Yvonne Hillier

Readings in Post-Compulsory Education, Anne Thompson and Yvonne Hillier

Teaching in Post-Compulsory Education

2nd Edition

Skills, Standards and Lifelong Learning

Fred Fawbert
with contributions by Lyn Butcher,
Yvonne Dickman, Janet Hobley,
Liz Mayes, Dawn Norse, Margaret Postance,
Tricia Semeraz and John Wilkinson

continuum

Continuum International Publishing Group

The Tower Building   80 Maiden Lane, Suite 704
11 York Road   New York, NY 10038
London SE1 7NX

www.continuumbooks.com

First published 2003
Reprinted 2004, 2005

British Library Cataloguing-in-Publication Data
A catalogue record for this book is available from the British Library.

ISBN: 9780826490384 (paperback)

Library of Congress Cataloging-in-Publication Data
Teaching in post-compulsory education: skills, standards, and lifelong learning/[edited by] Fred Fawbert; with contributions by Lyn Butcher . . . [et al.]. — 2nd ed.
    p. cm.
  ISBN-13: 978-0-8264-9038-4 (pbk.)
  ISBN-10: 0-8264-9038-7 (pbk.)
1. College teaching. 2. Post-compulsory education. I. Fawbert, Fred. II. Butcher, Lyn.
LB2331.T398 2008
378.1'250941—dc22

                                    2007045319

Typeset by Newgen Imaging Systems Pvt Ltd, Chennai, India
Printed and bound in Great Britain by Cromwell Press, Wiltshire

Contents

Foreword

As the authors of this book have clearly demonstrated, the newly named Lifelong Learning Sector is a rapidly evolving educational provision which at last is beginning to be properly supported for the huge task that is needed in terms of vocational training. Following on from the report by Lord Leitch, which identified the skills sector as being crucial for the nation's future prosperity, other important initiatives are now in the pipeline.

The sector is now clearly emerging from its long-time role as a poor relation and is beginning to be seen as a body capable not only of delivering the promises made by policy-makers to improve the capability of our workforce so that it can effectively compete internationally, but also of responding to the needs of industry by creating bespoke courses and awards to meet particular local demands.

The Leitch report followed on from that of Sir Andrew Foster in its concern that a potentially significant national resource (the post-compulsory sector) was being under-resourced at a time when its training and educational potential was needed most. Many initiatives have flowed from these two high-profile reviews, and there is no doubt that they have raised the standing of Lifelong Learning as a credible and viable option for young people to continue learning and developing rather than face unemployment.

This is a challenging environment to enter as a new teacher, but the rewards are significant. Not just monetary (and we all agree that parity between the sectors is a long time coming!) but perhaps more importantly, in the exciting opportunity to be involved in a stimulating and important career where (you will hopefully soon discover) you have the chance to guide and encourage many bright, young students along their chosen path. If you'll forgive me for indulging in fond memories of my time as a vocational tutor in an FE college, the many instances where young people demonstrated their enjoyment of and commitment to learning are still to me a happy source of the type of fond memories which we often need to remind us just what we are supposedly all about.

Of course, the teachers entering the Lifelong Learning Sector today will be facing a much more demanding vocation than the one I faced all those years ago. However, I can confirm that there is still the same level of friendly collegiality to support them. They will, of course, be taking on a range of different roles according to their interests and experience and the type of department they enter. Many will be full-time lecturers in a particular vocational area and others will be part-time providing different levels of support. Some teachers will be working for private training providers and others may be working in adult education.

However, the sector as a whole is gradually changing for the better. For many years the DfES have been moving towards the notion of equivalence between the sectors. This would of course be tremendous for teachers in post-compulsory education who have salaries and conditions of service much inferior to their compulsory sector counterparts. However, it is obviously first of all necessary to achieve equivalence in the manner in which both sets of teachers are trained and regulated. LLUK have started to address the training through their 'professional standards', and with the establishment of its own professional body in the form of the Institute for Learning (IfL) the skills sector will register and regulate all practitioners teaching on programmes funded by the LSC. So the prospects for eventual parity have suddenly become much brighter.

If you add to the above positive developments the fact that the very successful £30 per week Education Maintenance Allowance initiative is indeed encouraging students from poorer families to continue in education, together with the recently announced coherent strategy for the education of 14–19 year olds (which has included optional vocational training from the start), you have a series of important educational initiatives which have significantly boosted the sector's profile nationally.

However, although the current ambitious plans for lifelong learning (including the possibility of raising the school leaving age to 18) are very welcome to the sector, it does mean that teachers are becoming increasingly accountable. This is to be expected because it is appropriate that the preparation and performance of teachers in the sector should gradually be brought into line with primary and secondary provision. Related to this is the manner in which the new LLUK Professional Standards have been very much influenced by Ofsted to ensure that vocational subjects have the same level of integrity as conventional curriculum subjects taught in High Schools. This will be supported in the skills sector by the appointment of Subject Mentors to monitor the development of vocational teaching.

The effects of many of the above innovations are discussed in detail within this well-informed book, which very usefully relates the traditional theories and practices of teaching and learning to the present standards and accountability processes that are evident in all educational settings today. Most important of all, it is written in an engaging and informed style, by current practitioners who enthuse about their sector of education in a manner which will confirm your decision to join them.

The changes discussed above are very far-reaching indeed and this is an exciting time to be entering Lifelong Learning. However, the demands will be considerable and developing your own values while meeting the requirements of both teacher training and your job will no doubt be difficult. Even so, remember that you will most probably be working with colleagues who are passionate about teaching and who will want you to succeed and join them in, what is for many teachers, a highly rewarding role in an environment which is ever changing and constantly rewarding. Learning alongside your learners promises to be a valuable experience you will surely enjoy.

Kathryn Ecclestone
Professor of Education
Oxford Brookes University
August 2007

Acknowledgements

The Authors

When the first edition of this book was published in 2003, we were all teachers on the University of Central Lancashire Certificate in Education/PGCE (Post-Compulsory) programme delivered by a network of partner colleges in the north-west of England. Although the Uclan Programme continues to thrive, as may be expected, many of our authors have now advanced to new posts elsewhere, and unfortunately some were unable to be involved in this new edition. However, we have been fortunate to recruit other experienced practitioners to take their place and consequently all of the team involved in this new edition are still actively involved in teacher education with the insight and commitment needed to help colleagues understand the complex nature of post-14 education.

In putting this book together, we have all drawn on our many years of practice in Cert. Ed. and PGCE programmes with the intention of providing new and intending teachers in the newly named Lifelong Learning Sector with a useful structure to help them to relate practice and theory to the national standards and to include in this guide current information about sector developments and useful references to other informative publications. To this end we have attempted to acknowledge all of our sources and we apologize if we have missed any.

Lyn Butcher, Yvonne Dickman, Fred Fawbert, Janet Hobley, Liz Mayes, Dawn Norse, Margaret Postance, Tricia Semeraz and John Wilkinson

Our sincere thanks to Kathryn Ecclestone for her Foreword to this book. Professor Ecclestone has had a long and active involvement with teacher education for the Lifelong Learning Sector and, over the years, has rightly gained a reputation for incisive analysis combined with a genuine concern for both teachers and taught. We are all indebted to her for her forthright, insightful and continuing commentary on the many aspects of provision.

TIPCET (Teachers in Post-Compulsory Education and Training) was originally formed as a forum to discuss current issues within the sector. We have developed our website **tipcet.com** to continue that debate electronically and nationally. This site also contains additional materials which we have developed to support each of the chapters in this book. Finally, because this guide was written before the new standards were actually implemented, we would like to receive feedback from any readers on the effectiveness or otherwise of this book.

We would also welcome any suggestions for improvement or recommendations about the sort of materials you would like to be added to our website.

Please email: fredfawbert@tipcet.com

Please note: For the sake of clarity, in this book we refer to 'teachers' when we are talking about teacher-trainers, 'students' when we are referring to trainee-teachers and 'learners' when we are referring to their students.

Abbreviations and Acronyms

ABSSU	Adult Basic Skills Strategy Unit
ACVE	Advanced Certificate in Vocational Education
ALLN	Adult Literacy, Language and Numeracy
AoC	Association of Colleges
APU	Assessment of Performance Unit
BSA	Basic Skills Agency
CBI	Confederation of British Industry
CEF	College Employers' Forum
CEL	Centre for Excellence in Leadership
CETTS	Centre of Excellence in Teacher Education
CIF	Common Inspection Framework
COVE	Centre of Vocational Excellence
CPD	Continuing Professional Development
CPVE	Certificate in Pre-Vocational Education
CTLLS	Certificate in Teaching in the Lifelong Learning Sector
D of E	Department of Education
DCSF	Department for Children, Schools and Families
DDA	Disability Discrimination Act
DES	Department of Education and Science
DfEE	Department for Education and Employment
DfES	Department for Education and Skills
DIUS	Department for Innovation, Universities and Skills
DTI	Department of Trade and Industry
DTLLS	Diploma in Teaching in the Lifelong Learning Sector
DWP	Department of Work and Pensions
ED	Employment Department
EMA	Education Maintenance Allowance
ERA	Education Reform Act
ESOL	English for Speakers of other Languages
E2E	Entry to Employment
FEDA	Further Education Development Agency
FEFC	Further Education Funding Council
FENTO	Further Education National Training Organisation
FEU	Further Education Unit
FfA	Framework for Achievement

GCE	General Certificate of Education
GCSE	General Certificate of Secondary Education
GNVQ	General National Vocational Qualification
HEI	Higher Education Institution
KPIs	Key Performance Indicators
LLN	Literacy, Language and Numeracy
LLUK	Lifelong Learning United Kingdom
LSC	Learning and Skills Council
LSDA	Learning and Skills Development Agency
MA	Modern Apprenticeships
MSC	Manpower Services Commission
NAFE	Non-Advanced Further Education
NAGCELL	National Advisory Group for Continuing Education and Lifelong Learning
NAO	National Audit Office
NATFHE	National Association of Teachers in Further and Higher Education
NCDS	National Child Development Survey
NCVQ	National Council for Vocational Qualifications
NEET	Not in Education, Employment or Training
NETTs	National Education and Training Targets
NIACE	National Institute for Adult and Continuing Education
NOCN	National Open College Network
NPQH	National Professional Qualifications for Headship
NRDC	National Research & Development Centre for Adult Literacy, Numeracy & ESOL
NQF	National Qualifications Framework
NTO	National Training Organisation
NVQ	National Vocational Qualification
OECD	Organization for Economic Cooperation and Development
Ofsted	Office for Standards in Education
PCET	Post Compulsory Education and Training
PCGE	Professional Certificate in Education (alternative title approved by the QAA)
PD	Personal Development File
PF	Practitioner's File
PGCE	Postgraduate Certificate in Education
PTLS	Preparing to Teach in the Lifelong Learning Sector
QAA	Quality Assurance Agency for Higher Education
QCA	Qualifications and Curriculum Authority
QIA	Qualifications Improvement Agency
QTLS	Qualified Teacher Learning and Skills
QTS	Qualified Teacher Status

RaPAL	Research and Practice in Adult Literacy
RCC	Reduced Class Contact
SENET	Skills and Education Network
SK4L	Skills for Life
SSC	Sector Skills Council
StAR	Strategic Area Review
TA	Training Agency
TEC	Training and Enterprise Council
TOPS	Training Opportunities Scheme
TUC	Trade Union Congress
TVEI	Technical and Vocational Education Initiative
UfI	University for Industry
YOPS	Youth Opportunities Scheme
YT	Youth Training
YTS	Youth Training Scheme

List of Contributors

Lyn Butcher is a Professional Development Manager within the Lancashire Education Authority Adult Learning Service.

Yvonne Dickman is a lecturer in teacher education in the School of Business and Professional Studies at Blackpool and the Fylde College, where she is also ILT Champion for teacher education.

Fred Fawbert recently retired after many years of managing a large Cert Ed/PGCE programme. He has retained his interest in education and the post-compulsory sector in particular. Still teaching part-time, he is a Fellow of the Institute for Learning, a member of the British Educational Research Association and the managing editor of the *tipcet.com* website supporting teachers in the post-compulsory Lifelong Learning sector.

Janet Hobley is the Professional Teaching Standards Facilitator within the FE Teacher Training provision at East Berkshire College.

Liz Mayes is the Curriculum Manager within the Training and Early Years Department at Furness College, Cumbria.

Dawn Norse is the Teacher Education Programme Leader at Burnley College.

Margaret Postance is the Curriculum Leader for Lifelong Learning in the Department of Education, Community and Leisure at Liverpool John Moores University.

Tricia Semeraz is the Professional Development Leader at the Ashton Community Science College, Preston and is a Professional Mentor for the University of Cumbria Graduate Teacher Programme.

John Wilkinson recently retired from the Higher Education manager's role at Burnley College, but he has continued as the Programme Leader of BA Honours Education.

Standards, Skills and Lifelong Learning

Fred Fawbert

1

Chapter Outline

Key Concepts

Access and Progression, Collaboration, Collegiality, Collegial Relationships, Domain Structure, Entitlement, Equality, Inclusiveness, Interactive Relationship, Independent Learners, Knowledge, Learner Autonomy, Learning and Teaching, Lifelong Learning, Pedagogy, Personal Development Journal, Post-Compulsory, Practice, Practitioner File, Professional Role, Professional Values and Practice, Process Justifications, Reflective Practice, Scope, Specialist Teaching and Learning, Standards, Subject Mentor.

1.1 Introduction

When undertaking any journey into new, as yet unknown territory, the first step is often the most difficult. As this book is an exploration of the process of preparing to teach in post-compulsory education, a useful first step may be to accept that becoming a good teacher, particularly within the pressurized context of the newly named Lifelong Learning Sector, is a considerable, but very worthwhile challenge. One of the most demanding processes that you will face quite early in your investigation is that of defining just what represents quality in relation to teaching. Such a definition is always elusive and those colleagues you share this journey with will each have a different interpretation. This is because such judgements are inevitably influenced by a combination of personal and institutional values which will change over the years. However, be reassured that teaching can be exciting and hugely rewarding. As you have probably anticipated, the difficulties lie in the complexity of the relationship between teacher and taught.

There are so many confounding variables within these interactions (i.e. age, gender, number and disposition of the students, etc.) that quite often the measures and evidence of success will differ for each and every learner involved. However, government legislation and accountability processes always attempt to present the situation in a positivistic and often simplistic manner, as though every interaction can have only one explanation, when in reality there may be many.

Faced with the reality of such unpredictable elements, it may be more realistic to consider teaching as an art, which many of us practise, but only on very infrequent occasions perfect. This is probably because only rarely do all the various constituents coincide to become the ideal, interactive relationship between teacher and taught. This precious interaction can promote the exciting discovery of those concepts and relationships that lead to unexpected insights into both the subject and the self, for both the teacher and the taught. Most of us have to be content with occasional, but rewarding glimpses of what might be achieved in a situation where there is the time and the opportunity to use this foundation of mutual trust and shared achievement as a basis for an exploration of the not yet known.

Despite all of the pressures, many teachers often do achieve the excitement of this shared bond with their learners, where there is a willingness by both to emerge for a time from behind physical and psychological barriers into a more open, trusting relationship. Sadly, the many pressures within most teaching situations may well diminish the value of these important teacher/pupil insights and far too often even cause them to be invisible to the participants, so that they pass by unrecognized.

Even so, because of their position, it is the teachers who must initiate these potentially mutually rewarding relationships. This requires of them a particular understanding of all the characteristics of the specific educational context in which they are working. This includes the more tangible features such as environment, subject content and assessment requirements as well as those equally important but less well-defined elements, such as the dynamics of the learning group at that particular time, the internal and external influences which bear down on their progress and the teacher's current disposition towards them and theirs towards their teacher.

Probably the least understood, simple but influential factor is timing. In any relationship there is a time to press forward and a time to hold back. Get it wrong and you may have to retreat and rebuild. This level of insightful relationship cannot be taught, let alone measured. And yet it can mean the difference between success and failure.

This book is essentially about identifying and then nurturing this relationship between learner and teacher through consciously reflective practice. Our focus is the Post-Compulsory Sector of education within the United Kingdom (which has now been renamed as the Lifelong Learning Sector) but the ideas and concepts we will discuss should have more general relevance to all teachers of students aged 14 and above, whatever their particular situation.

Teaching effectively within any context is often a hugely rewarding task but, as with all complex processes, particularly in the early stages, it can also seem to be fraught with difficulties. Sometimes learners are receptive and sometimes, of course, they are not. The reasons for this are many and varied and are usually peculiar to that setting. The same may equally be said about the dissemination of good practice, particularly to teachers. Sometimes the suggested approach seems to be significant and relevant and sometimes it appears inappropriate and trivial. Again the reason for this variation in responses is often situational. Naturally, there are times when teachers are open to new ideas and conversely, there are just as many instances where the security and familiarity of the known has much more appeal than innovation. This is particularly true when, as many of us are, the practitioner is working under pressure.

It follows then, that there will be times when this book may be seen as a welcome resource and others when it will represent only additional stress. For this reason, my colleagues and I have attempted to present this collection of ideas and approaches as a series of suggested solutions to familiar teaching problems. This is partially because we are only too aware of the connotations attached to concepts such as 'standards' or 'accountability' and wish, at the outset, to look beyond such fairly common but limited interpretations because we share the view that ultimately they can only represent prescription and compliance.

The new Professional Standards for the Lifelong Learning Sector, which form the structure of this book, were introduced in the DfES White Paper 'Further Education: Raising Skills, Improving Life Chances' 2005. Some concern had been expressed within a previous DfES publication 'Equipping Our Teachers for the Future' that the earlier FENTO Standards were not entirely appropriate to the developing skills sector which now incorporated training providers from industry, public services, and private providers as well as the Further Education sector. The new standards began to be developed by Lifelong Learning UK in April 2005 after extensive consultation with representatives of Sector Skills Councils, regulatory authorities, unions, awarding institutions and individual provider organizations.

The new draft standards were published in March 2006 and after receiving feedback at events and from advisory and development groups, the standards were reshaped and refined into their present form and were implemented from September 2007. We believe that through the establishment of these national standards for teachers within the much-enlarged post-compulsory sector, LLUK have provided us with a reasonably sound basis for professional development.

However, our stance is that all standards are merely a benchmark or a signpost, which should most definitely not be seen as a final destination. Of course, we do also realize that the real danger in articulating guidelines for performance is that those who are concerned with inspection and accountability rather than mutual development may take a damagingly instrumental approach, that focuses on simplistic measurement at the expense of the more important, subtle and holistic indicators of enhanced performance.

As suggested in the above opening comments to the chapter, our concerns are based on the simple perception that learning is not predictable and teaching is not an exact science. Treating them as though they are is not in the long term a helpful way to mark progress. So, although the content of the chapters that follow will comprehensively address the six domains of the new Professional Standards and will refer to their published, detailed specifications, the text is based on more familiar practice and theory related to each stage of the teaching and learning process.

Although we do see this book as a guided-study programme, which identifies a range of useful concepts, strategies and sources for teachers and focuses on the production of acceptable evidence of professional development, it is deliberately not assessment-led, and follows a familiar teaching/training cycle, rather than the Professional Standards' Domain structure. However the theoretical deliberations and the related practice-based activities are designed to address the Scope, Knowledge and Practice criteria indicated within the six domains of the new standards, the details of which are in Chapter 12 at the end of the book.

We have tried to anticipate some of the assessment processes of the many different teacher education programmes around the country in our suggested forms of evidence provided by such documents as a 'Personal Development Journal' and a 'Practitioner File'. These are also described in more detail in Chapter 12. However we, the authors of this book, do have some concerns that in professionalizing the sector (their term) LLUK felt that they needed to disaggregate their standards down into so many (186) different criteria. Unfortunately, if we are honest, this striving for absolute clarity has predictably been unable to avoid considerable ambiguity (is 'justify' more demanding than 'explain'?) and imprecision, because eventually, as the specifications become unwieldy, the disaggregation process has to stop before comprehensive analysis leads to total paralysis.

We do understand how this examination of the complex process of teaching may have seemed necessary in order to address the concerns of Ofsted and to support the implementation of the many national policy changes outlined by Kathryn Ecclestone in her Foreword.

However, we are left with a situation where the inherent purposes and values which are so important to the validity of educational processes (and which LLUK have stressed in their standards) may well conflict with the unavoidably high levels of prescription within their standards. Although faced with the apparent confident certainty which the specificity of the LLUK Standards is designed to generate, as teachers we must be realistic enough to accept that we cannot anticipate the special characteristics of each and every learning situation where many important educational goals cannot be precisely articulated, let alone accurately measured. However, we certainly appreciate the aim of the new Department for Innovation, Universities and Skills (DIUS) to improve vocational and skills education and the interest and optimism which these initiatives and the related funding have generated for our beleaguered sector.

The authors are all experienced teacher educators from post-compulsory education and have drawn on their work to provide appropriate examples of teaching methods and the related values and principles. This process has provided some insightful case studies that illuminate the core skills defined in the chapters that follow.

1.2 Summary of chapter themes

Although the Professional Standards are an important element within this book, we feel that a more relevant and permanent framework is the comparatively well-known teaching/ learning cycle. We have used this to structure the 12 chapters in this book and this is illustrated in Table 1.1 in the following section. Each chapter is a consecutive step in this familiar process, but we also refer to the relevant domains of the Professional Standards as we progress.

1.3 Book structure

Our starting point, provided in Chapter 2 by Janet Hobley, is an analysis of the value which a commitment to *reflective practice* has, not only when preparing to enter teaching, but also as a confirmatory process during many years of practice.

Janet also carries this debate forward in Chapter 3 by focusing on *individual learner differences* (aptitude and ability, etc.) and the ways of *identifying and responding to learner needs* (supported by appropriate theory) including *diagnostic testing, student action plans, basic skills, learning styles,* etc. Building on this knowledge of the learners, Margaret Postance provides further insights into *planning for learning* (Domain D) when she considers in Chapter 4 some of the ways of developing and planning different teaching and learning programmes and sessions within a safe, supportive, learning environment.

Following this practical application, in Chapter 5 Yvonne Dickman moves to a more theoretical consideration of teaching through an analysis of the social, cultural and emotional

Table 1.1 Chapter themes

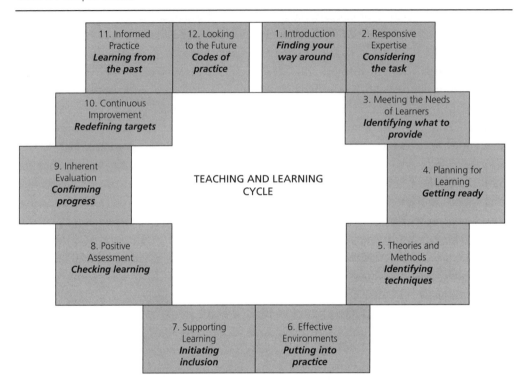

factors which affect individual and group learning. Tricia Semeraz takes this theme of the effective learning environment (setting targets, structuring learning, developing materials, and introducing basic key skills) further in Chapter 6 and also considers in more detail the work of the Subject Mentor and specialist teaching, and the various standards agencies such as the IfL and the LSC. These three chapters (4, 5 and 6) address in some detail planning for learning (Domain D), while in chapter 7 Dawn Norse and John Wilkinson investigate a student-centred approach to learner support and pastoral care. Again this entails identifying student needs, their counselling and their referral to other care agencies. Chapter 8 focuses on approaches to assessment using different measures for a range of purposes including student motivation and achievement (Domain E). Liz Mayes adds an important perspective to professional values and practice (Domain A) when she proposes in Chapter 9 that the systematic evaluation of your own performance is the basis for developing future practice to meet learner and college needs, and is an essential aspect of professional responsibility. Lyn Butcher looks at a range of quality processes in Chapter 10, which involve learning contracts, health and safety, student entitlement, access to services, information and resources, review procedures, progression and the use of unfortunate but necessarily prompt action to ensure the required level of discipline.

The background to Domain A's focus on the development of a responsible, professional teacher perspective is considered in Chapter 11, when the recent history of the Lifelong Learning Sector (previously PCET) and the range of policies which have been developed to meet changing national priorities are examined. Finally, in Chapter 12 each of the six domains of the LLUK Professional Standards are discussed together with their assessment outcomes, and these are related to a comprehensive index which identifies the suggested activities throughout the book that are designed to generate the evidence required to confirm achievement of the related LLUK standard outcome.

1.4 Chapter structure

As suggested earlier, the central purpose of this book is to support the development of teachers. However, although we have designed each chapter to progressively promote this process, we have also ensured that undertaking the suggested developmental activities within each chapter will provide practical insights into the concepts and procedures involved in a range of essential teaching and learning processes. So the central focus will be the improvement of pedagogic skills and understandings, rather than assessment. This is because it is clear that *one* actual teaching session or the analysis of particular approaches to learning is capable of generating evidence against *several* of the specified outcomes. Consequently, it would be counterproductive to structure rigidly the book around the standards. Table 1.2 below provides a summary of the common features found in each chapter.

1.5 Teacher education and educational policies

For more than ten years there has been a concern within what was the Department for Education and Skills to move towards equivalence and transferability of staff between the compulsory and (what was) the post-compulsory sectors of education. Obviously, if this is achieved and the important role of the Lifelong Learning Sector is at last recognized, it will be of significant professional and financial benefit to our teachers.

During 2003, these initiatives resulted in the DfES requesting Ofsted (the Office for Standards in Education) to carry out a review of the PCET teacher education provided by universities and colleges in order to ensure that there was also equivalence in the preparation of teachers for each sector. This review confirmed Ofsted's fears that the post-compulsory teacher education programmes (such as the Cert. Ed. and the City and Guilds 7407 certificate) were concerned with *generic* teaching abilities, rather than the dissemination of the particular *pedagogic skills* required within the range of vocational subject specialisms in the Further Education

Table 1.2 Chapter structure

Chapter Titles	Steps in the familiar teaching cycle are a basis for the titles used.
Key Concepts	Each chapter starts with a summary of the concepts to be covered.
Chapter Outline	The beginning of each chapter has a guide to the contents.
Activities	Within each chapter there is a series of activities designed to identify the sources and then develop appropriate evidence against the standards. These individual developmental activities will usually be based on reflection about a completed task. These are, of course, optional. One basic form of this evidence will be the details of teaching practice within the Practitioner's File (for more information see Chapter 12). Another of the main forms of evidence will be reflections within the suggested Personal Development Journal (PDJ) which are also explained in detail in Chapter 12.
Reading	Details about each of the references within the text are in the Bibliography.
Useful Sources	Our authors have added a short annotated list of recommended books and websites at the end of each of their chapters.
Website	Throughout the book there are references to indicate that further material on that topic is also available on our website tipcet.com. There is a small administration fee for membership of Tipcet (Teachers in Post-Compulsory Education and Training), payable when logging on for the first time.
Process Justifications	At the end of chapters 3 to 9 there are a series of simple justifications explaining why and how teachers may address the standards at the appropriate level (PTLLS, CTLLS or DTLLS), i.e. Threshold, Associate or Full Award.
Domain Specifications	A comprehensive list of the outcomes and criteria relevant to each of the six domains defined by LLUK is included in Chapter 12 together with a detailed specification of how these relate to each different level of award. There are also suggestions of where in the book each of the outcomes have been addressed and most importantly this is where the index to more than 100 relevant, detailed teacher activities which are designed to produce evidence against each of the standards may be found.
Bibliography	A full Bibliography incorporating all sources is included after the last chapter.
Index	Complete reference to issues, concepts and sources is included after the Bibliography.
List of Abbreviations and Acronyms	The full title of many of the educational organizations and terms referred to by initials throughout the text is included at the beginning of the book.

sector. The view of many in Further Education was that this situation existed because traditionally, experienced professionals from particular vocational areas had been recruited to be teachers of particular specialisms. There was also the problem of finding experienced specialists for each and every different subject in the curriculum, but most of all post-compulsory teachers point to the fact that preparing a student to teach a subject specialism within primary and secondary sectors has traditionally taken three years. Developing a Lifelong Learning Sector teacher in equally demanding subject specialisms is expected to be achieved in one year full-time or two years part-time, and currently on completion their salaries are substantially less.

However, both the DfES and Ofsted remained of the view that this area of perceived weakness should be addressed without any increase in either training time or eventual salaries. It was decided that there should be a reorganization of teacher education for the post-compulsory sector and, although the Further Education National Training Organisation (FENTO) standards were only introduced three years previously, they should be replaced by a new professional framework which would also ensure that there would be an emphasis on competence in teaching a particular area of specialism. Although the Professional Standards have much in common with the more flexible learning outcomes that have been in use by most university Certificate in Education programmes for a number of years, there is now a requirement that the teaching skills required in particular vocational areas are monitored and reviewed by a Subject Mentor. Obviously these demands have placed a considerable additional burden on the teacher education providers.

The Professional Standards for teacher education within the Lifelong Learning Sector are clearly designed for a wider audience than the traditional Certificate in Education/PGCE. Because three stages of award have been identified (Threshold, Associate and Full), the standards are flexible and applicable to the wide variety of roles that teachers, trainers, instructors, demonstrators and support workers have within the rapidly developing educational provision for the 14–19 sector. The development of standards for this widely varying group of learners was informed by the inherent values and purposes which have been identified by LLUK:

- Tutors and trainers in the Lifelong Learning Sector value all learners individually and equally. They are committed to lifelong learning and professional development and strive for continuous improvement through reflective practice.
- The key purpose of the teacher is to create effective and stimulating opportunities for learning through high-quality teaching that enables the development and progression of all learners.
- Teachers are constantly assessing the needs of learners and planning how to meet these needs.

The ability of teachers to reflect on their practice and to employ appropriate methods is therefore crucial and this programme of guided study is centred around that philosophy.

As a focus for reflection, you will be asked to develop two files during the study which are representative of the assessment vehicles which many teacher education providers will request. The first we have called the *Practitioner's File* (PF) which is a collection of evidence of practical teaching (see details in Chapter 12). The second is your *Personal Development Journal* (PDJ) which is, in effect, a reflective diary of your professional development during and beyond this programme (see Chapter 12). Teaching, studies, reflection and personal development will underpin your wider professional role as you manage the learning process, develop the curriculum and guide and support learners in partnership with others in the organization and the local community. As suggested above, the next chapter helps you to begin this process through discussion and a range of activities to promote reflective practice.

1.6 Collegiality and collaboration

Since the Education Reform Act in 1988, the post-compulsory sector has been subject to a series of new policies and radical changes (discussed more fully in Chapter 11). Consequently, for any standards to be effective within this pressurized sector, they must promote clarity, flexibility and adaptability. The role of practitioners in post-compulsory education is, by its very nature, extremely diverse and will inevitably change over time as a reflection of both the developing interests of the teacher and the changing nature of the learner.

Despite their apparent isolation in the classroom, teachers and teaching teams frequently work in partnership with external groups such as employers, parents, other members of the educational community and related agencies. They are automatically involved in different levels of practical and theoretical collaboration in order to ensure the relevance and responsiveness of their learning programmes. The purposeful development of collegial relationships is therefore an extremely important aspect of practice. From time to time during this programme it is suggested that you collaborative with colleagues during various analytical exercises and also to identify practitioners you would like to work-shadow. In addition, it is now a required element of teacher education for the Lifelong Learning Sector that you have access to a Subject Mentor (see 1.4 above, and Chapter 12) to support, review and advise on the development of teaching knowledge, skills and strategies which will enhance the delivery of that subject specialism. All of the above activities are also designed to develop the notion of collegiality and the dissemination of good practice.

1.7 Learning and learner autonomy

Another important concept promoted by LLUK is the belief that teachers and teaching teams should value the autonomy of learners, and promote the centrality of learning. By this they mean that teachers should seek to provide learners with the skills and abilities to work effectively on their own and promote an attitude to learning which views it as a lifelong process rather than the short-term acquisition of a set of specific skills. The development of a learner's key skills is an integral part of the promotion of autonomy and each of the following chapters will identify appropriate evidence against the Professional Standards.

We will summarize the requirements here for information, but more detail is contained in Chapter 12. New entrants to a teacher education programme for the Lifelong Learning Sector provided by a college, university or independent provider will be required to identify which level of award their intended area of employment will require. There are three of these levels which are defined by the role of the teacher:

1. The title of the Threshold Award is *'Preparing to Teach in the Lifelong Learning Sector'* (PTLLS) and is rated as having six Level 1 HE credits or six Level 3 or 4 NQF credits. This is an introductory award which provides a basic minimum standard for all those *entering the profession* from September 2007.

2. The title of the Associate Teacher Award is '*Certificate in Teaching in the Lifelong Learning Sector*' (CTLLS) and is rated as 24 Level 1 HE credits or 24 Level 3 or 4 NQF credits. This is an initial award for teachers who have substantial teaching, but have *not yet gained* a full teaching role and are viewed as filling an Associate teacher role. In such cases they will be teaching predominantly using pre-prepared teaching materials or packs which do not allow them full responsibility in the design of curriculum materials.

3. There are three equivalent awards with three different titles for teachers who are viewed as filling a *full teaching role*. The NQF-based award is the '*Diploma in Teaching in the Lifelong Learning Sector*' (DTLLS). The award provided by HEIs (Higher Education Institutions) is the traditional Certificate in Education (Cert. Ed.) for non-graduates and the Postgraduate Certificate in Education (PGCE) for graduates.

New teachers, who fall within any of the above three categories, have up to five years to achieve their respective award. The 30 credits gained through the completion of the Associate Teacher Award (see 2 above) will be accredited towards the Full Award. The total of 120 credits awarded for the Full Award (see 3 above) will allow the holder to progress to further qualifications (for example BA or BEd degrees) provided by HEIs and other bodies. The full-time Cert. Ed. and PGCE will usually take one year or the part-time equivalent will take two years. In summary, the Full Award involves:

- an entry requirement of a minimum NQF (or equivalent) Level 3 qualification in their own subject specialism
- an initial assessment of literacy, numeracy and ICT needs to be addressed during the programme
- a minimum of 1,200 hours of learning in total (at least 600 hours' guided learning and 600 hours' self-directed learning)
- observed teaching practice
- mentoring support (see further information in Chapter 12).

1.8 Entitlement, equality and inclusiveness

Equality of opportunity is also a basic principle within the standards as a crucial foundation upon which good teaching, learning and assessment is based. Simply put, this means optimizing the learning experience of all students because all learners should have access to appropriate educational opportunities regardless of ethnic origin, gender, age, sexual orientation or degree of learning disability and /or difficulty. Consequently, the values of entitlement, equality, and inclusiveness are seen as being of fundamental importance to teachers and teaching teams (see also Chapter 9).

1.9 The lifelong learning context

This book is designed for teachers within the Lifelong Learning Sector of education and consequently programme members may be drawn from Continuing, Further and Adult

Education as well as public service and private training providers. The values discussed previously and the main characteristics if the Lifelong Learning Sector, defined below, indicate the distinctive nature of this particular context:

- wide range of learner
- broad diversity of levels
- the emphasis upon guiding and supporting learners and the assessment of their needs
- the application of vocational knowledge and experience
- the degree of liaison with employers and of working in partnership with other agencies
- involvement in work-based assessment and learning
- the wide use of outcomes-based curricula
- the dynamic nature and complexity of the curriculum
- the emphasis on student retention and achievement
- the central role of the teacher in key skills development
- the central role of the teacher in helping people to return to learning.

The above discussion is a clear indication of the tremendously wide variety of teaching and learning which takes place within the 14–19 sector and, as Bill Rammell (the Minister of State for Lifelong Learning) pointed out when he launched the LLUK Standards:

> Six million learners every year are accessing the Lifelong Learning Sector and success rates are improving significantly from 59 per cent in 2000/01 to 75 per cent in 2004/05.
>
> (DfES 2005)

This makes Lifelong Learning the biggest provider of learning opportunities outside of the school system. Students in the 14–19 sector will range from 14 year olds involved in vocational development programmes to Higher National Diploma course members. Continuing Education prepares students for progression to higher education through A levels and vocational subjects, and Adult Education caters largely for non-vocational courses from basic crafts to theory and practice within the Arts. Other important providers within the sector include prison education, voluntary and community teachers and trainers based within various work situations. The government views the sector as extremely important and the establishment of the DfES after they won the election in May 2001 is a clear indication of their perception of the link between education, employment and the national economy. This has been further emphasized by the recent separation from the DfES of the 14–19 provision within the new organizational framework, the Department for Innovation, Universities and Skills (DIUS).

As mentioned above, during recent years there has been a drive to move towards equivalence between the sectors (i.e. Primary, Secondary and Lifelong Learning) and spearheading this is the government's determination to 'professionalize' the standard of teaching within the 14–19 sector. The principal vehicle for this process is the LLUK's Professional

Standards. The sector as a whole is discussed in further detail in Chapter 11 and the standards in Chapter 12.

1.10 Key teaching purposes

Naturally, Lifelong Learning teachers have a responsibility for ensuring high standards of teaching and learning, as well as contributing to curriculum development and the development of their subject knowledge. Good teachers will always ensure that the educational opportunities provided do meet the needs and aspirations of their learners and those learners achieve to the best of their ability. It is expected that teachers and teaching teams will play a key role in guiding and supporting their students, as well as in assessing learners' achievements. In part, the programme outlined in this book is designed to promote a student's awareness of how their subject contributes to the overall educational experience of their learners.

In essence then, this is the beginning of a career-long personal and professional development process during which our students who become teachers will take on a variety of different roles, depending upon their interests, abilities and experience. In addition to their role as teachers, they may become course leaders or subject coordinators or take up responsibility for liaison with employers, pastoral support or curriculum and subject development. Some current students may eventually move into managerial roles or specialize in other functions related to the work of their organization, such as entrepreneurial development, finance, marketing, staff development or personal management. Within such a large and developing sector, it is inevitable that at different times all staff will have to undertake CPD (Continuing Professional Development), in fact it is a required part of the process of remaining in good standing with the sector's professional body, the Institute for Learning (see Section 1.11 below).

1.11 The DfES regulations

In the 2004 White Paper 'Success for All', the DfES made it clear that in order to deliver a qualified workforce for the burgeoning Lifelong Learning Sector by 2010, a series of reforms must begin on 1 September 2007. These changes have implications for all teachers within the sector. The reforms have two major strands which have been defined by two pieces of regulation:

- Revised teaching qualifications for new teachers, including the introduction of licensed practitioner status and a means of differentiating between Full and Associate Teachers.
- Remaining in good standing as a teaching professional, including mandatory Continuing Professional Development (CPD). See Chapter 12 for further details of requirements.

1.12 Preparing for study

As this chapter closes and in preparation for what follows, we have included below two simple exercises which are designed to lay the foundation for the concepts which will be developed later in this study programme. In Activity 1a we are asking you to consider the characteristics of one of your own groups of learners and make these deliberations your first entry in your PDJ. In Activity 1b you are asked to make an assessment of your own abilities against the Professional Standards.

Activity 1a Identification of Learner Characteristics

During the following chapters you will be asked to carry out various activities in relation to your own work as a teacher. It will be helpful if you begin now to develop an analysis of the characteristics of your learners and build on this during the forthcoming tasks. Identify one particular group which you teach regularly and which could be the focus of similar activities in the chapters to come. If you do not enjoy the luxury of teaching the same group regularly, try to identify one which you have taught and find interesting. This could be a small or large group which may be easy to work with or may have particular demands that make them challenging to teach. Make this your first entry in your Personal Development Journal (PDJ). Write about 200 words in which you try to capture the nature of the group. In addition to a basic description (number, age, gender, experience of the subject, etc.), think about how they respond to you at different times and how they go about tackling the different types of work you set them.

Activity 1b Self-Assessment against the LLUK Standards

For your second entry in your PDJ, please complete the simple table below (Table 1.3) after considering your own professional development against the requirements of the standards. Bear in mind the group/s of learners you have identified in Activity 1a (above) and consider not only the standards, but also your current ability to meet their needs. As you will have seen earlier in this chapter, there are three levels of achievement – Threshold, Associate and Full Certificate/Diploma according to the teaching role you have currently achieved or are aiming for.

The details of the six Domains of Practice are provided in Chapter 12. To assess in broad general terms your current level, make an estimate of where you are regarding each of the listed domains. If you need further information, look at the details in Sections 12.12, 12.13 and 12.14 of Chapter 12. Insert a tick under the appropriate level in relation to the six domains and summarize in the right-hand column your strengths and weaknesses in this area.

Table 1.3 Self-assessment against the LLUK standards

Domains	Threshold	Associate	Full	Comment on strengths and weaknesses
A Professional Values and Practiwce				
B Learning and Teaching				
C Specialist Learning and Teaching				
D Planning for Learning				
E Assessment for Learning				
F Access and Progression				

2 Responsive Reflection

Janet Hobley

Key Concepts

Absolutist, Abstract Conceptualization, Active Experimentation, Concrete Experience, Dualistic View, Hard High Ground, Knowing in Action, Messy Swamps, Personal Construct, Poiesis, Praxis, Reflection on Action, Reflective Action, Reflective Observation, Relativist, Routine Action, Technical Rationality, Thematized Learning.

2.1 Introduction

Although it is often highly rewarding, the role of the teacher (as with other professions) does undoubtedly involve constantly coping with a range of competing demands. Within such a pressurized world there may be a temptation to think of reflective practice as the sort of luxury you can enjoy when you have time available, much as you would quiet contemplation.

Unfortunately, such an approach not only misunderstands the notion of active reflection, but may also cause a practitioner to overlook a skill that could well light a pathway to success in our very demanding world. Reflectivity is not an indulgence, but a prerequisite for effective teaching and, in fact, the new Professional Standards for the Lifelong Learning Sector require evidence that it is taking place.

The reason is relatively simple but, as you would expect, the realization takes time and conscious effort. The explanation for the value of reflective practice in today's hectic environment is premised on the fact that teachers, trainers and support workers quite often become the 'experts' within a particular learning context. Over time, your close involvement provides you with the opportunity to become better informed about the characteristics of your learners and the environment you are working in, and more aware of what may be achieved than other colleagues who have less direct contact with the group. As you become conscious of this developing ability, you become more confident, relaxed, flexible and responsive and as your students learn to trust you, they will often respond with an openness that makes the whole process easier to manage and more rewarding. Refining this highly valuable 'responsive expertise' is the purpose of reflective practice. It is the ability to identify *and prioritize* all the subtle indicators within your learning environment.

2.2 Concepts of reflection

The concept of reflective practice dates back to Plato, Aristotle and Socrates, but perhaps the most influential exponent was John Dewey. In 1938 at a time of very traditional, formal approaches such as learning by rote, Dewey was emphasizing experience, experiment, purposeful learning, freedom and progressive education. He anticipated the writings of Paulo Freire when he claimed that:

> The traditional scheme is, in essence, one of imposition from above and from outside . . . Learning here means acquisition of what is incorporated in books and in the heads of the elders.

Earlier in 1933, Dewey had contrasted '*routine action*' with '*reflective action*'. According to Dewey, routine action is the day-to-day working life, guided by factors such as tradition, habit and authority and by institutional definitions and expectations. By implication, it is relatively static and is thus unresponsive to changing priorities and circumstances. Reflective action, on the other hand, involves a willingness to engage in constant self-appraisal and development. Among other things, it implies flexibility, rigorous analysis and social awareness. For Dewey, reflective activity involves the perception of relationships and the connections between the parts of an experience. This experience may be the raw material, but it has to be processed through reflection before it can emerge as learning. It is not sufficient simply to have an experience in order to learn, because without reflection it may be forgotten and its learning potential lost. Gibbs (1988) makes the important link between theorizing and action:

> . . . it is from the feelings and thoughts emerging from this reflection that generalisations or concepts may be created. It is generalisations which enable new situations to be tackled effectively. Similarly, if it is intended that behaviour should be changed by learning, it is not sufficient simply to learn new concepts and develop new generalisations. This learning must be tested out in new situations. The learner must make the link between theory and action by planning for that action, carrying it out and then reflecting upon it, relating what happens back to the theory.

Gibbs is interpreting the experiential learning cycle developed by Kolb (1984) from the work of Lewin (1951). (See also 5.7 in Chapter 5.) This cycle moves from *concrete experience* through *reflective observation*, *abstract conceptualization*, *active experimentation* and back again to concrete experience. Kolb believes that learners may enter the cycle at any point depending upon their individual learning style, but it is important that they work around the cycle. For example, those who prefer concrete experience (doing) should be persuaded to try out their ideas in order that future hypotheses will be better informed through experience. Kolb's view is that it is not sufficient to do or to think in order to learn from experience, learners should also be aware of their own development through the testing out of their concepts and explanations.

To illustrate this process in action in the classroom, a teacher may begin (though not necessarily) with a *concrete experience* such as trying out a new teaching method or a different assessment technique. *Reflective observation* would then involve a consideration of the process and how it might be done differently and then *abstract conceptualization* would be promoted by gathering more information (reading, talking to colleagues, etc.) and forming a hypothesis as to how to be more effective.

Active experimentation would then involve trying out new ways, which may well be a synthesis of the original approach combined with new ideas gained subsequently. Summarized simply, the process consists of *doing, thinking, planning, experimenting*, and then *doing* once more. In this manner, reflective learning becomes 'whole person' learning as it involves intellectual, emotional and psychological development.

2.3 Reflections in the personal development journal

Taking the lead from Kolb, you will be encouraged throughout this book to build on your ideas and insights. At different times during this programme, you will be asked to add to the two reflections within your PDJ which you hopefully completed at the end of Chapter 1 in response to Activities 1a and 1b. These Activities will build up to form a personal analytical theme, which you can then develop further in relation to your own teaching. However, as Perry (1970) observed, many learners (particularly at first) find the process of meaningful reflection very difficult indeed and they often need guidance to move from what he calls the *absolutist* mode, where they are prepared to accept implicitly the content of a course they may be experiencing. This is because they believe that all important knowledge is 'external' to themselves, i.e. it lies with the lecturer or teacher. Perry makes the point that it is not sufficient to do or to think in order to learn from experience, learners should also be aware of their own development through the testing out of their concepts and explanations. The reflective activities within each of this book's chapters will help you to articulate your own perceptions and understandings.

Perry believes it is important to encourage learners' to conceptualize experiences and perceptions, because through this progressive development they will bring about what he calls a 'cognitive shift'. First of all, they may move to what he calls a '*relativist*' position, where they begin to perceive that the course content is manipulated by tutors, and consequently they may consider that all presented theory is ephemeral and transient and that teachers are laying assessment traps for them. Often, at this stage, the students adopt an instrumental approach using 'shallow' learning to overcome these assessment hurdles.

The final stage in this development, as outlined by Perry, is when students gain an independent commitment to an area of study. As they develop their enjoyment and involvement in the subject they become aware of their own development and begin to reflect on the process they are involved in. In relation to the subject they are studying, they often come to realize that there is not just one singular, authoritative, point of view. Through study they realize that the perspectives of teachers and authors often differ in some minor way and, in some cases, there may be a major difference of opinion. As students think about thinking (metacognition) in this way they become more ready to accept a range of different perspectives and, as a consequence, begin to place more value on their own views.

Usher (1985) shares a similar view to Perry, in that he believes that students must be persuaded to move from what he calls a dualistic view (which considers that knowledge is either true or untrue) to a perspective dependent attitude that accepts the relative merits of knowledge and is prepared to evaluate according to the context of the learning. Usher's term for this particular context is thematized learning, which has much in common with Kelly's (1955) view that each person has an individual and unique perception of events, which Kelly calls a personal construct.

Although this difficult concept is compatible with student-centred learning, it often clashes with the notion that the teacher should be seen as a 'paragon' at the centre of the learning process. However, Usher (reflecting Dewey's earlier view) believes that students who experience only teacher-centred learning so undervalue their own experience that they have great difficulty in drawing upon it. Instead they resort to anecdotal evidence without articulating the underlying principles and generalizations from their experiences. This interpretive experience is often so disappointing to them that the students (unable to see the value of the exercise) insist upon returning to the secure ground of the didactic presentation and push their teachers back into a leadership role. Usher believes that the way forward is to encourage students to make a conceptual shift to a 'thematized' (perspective dependent) view that will help them to realize that their own experiences (modified via interaction with the learning situation) are of paramount importance.

As Bain *et al.* (1999) have pointed out, in recent years student journals have been used extensively in education as a means of facilitating reflection, deepening personal understanding and stimulating critical thinking. This is particularly so in the field of teacher education where, as pointed out by Zeichner (1992) and Calderhead and Gates (1993), reflection has come to be widely recognized as a crucial element in the professional growth of teachers. Calderhead (1988) argued that the need for reflective teacher education has been justified on the grounds that it facilitates the linking of theory and practice, subjects the expertise of teachers to critical evaluation and enables them to take a more active role in their own professional accountability. Given the importance attached to the development of reflective skills and propensities, it is not surprising that a range of teaching tools for this purpose has emerged in the literature. Reflective journal writing is one such technique that has been advocated by educators in many fields as a means of stimulating reflective learning. There are examples from Counselling (Eldridge 1983); Psychology (Hettich 1990); Nursing (Landeen *et al.* 1992); Management (Leary 1981); Leadership (Walker 1985); Sociology (Wagenaar 1984) and Teaching (Yinger and Clark 1981). Ballantyne and Packer (1995) defined a Learning Journal as an *exercise in which students express in writing their understandings of, reflections on, response to or analysis of an event, experience or concept.*

Below you will find the first of this chapter's Activities (2a) to add to your two earlier reflections in your PDJ. Please take time to do these exercises, and be as thoughtful and honest

Activity 2a A Significant Learning Experience

Building on your previous reflections about your learning group and your current level of professional development, this is the third entry into your PDJ. Try to identify a 'significant learning experience' related to your own personal/professional development. This could be recent or several years ago, it may have been a positive/rewarding experience or a less enjoyable/negative event. However, it should be something you recall as being, for one reason or another, an important learning process (either formal or informal). Now, please analyse and critically reflect on that experience. You might start simply by describing the experience, but you should then go on to reflect on the event and your part in it and, finally, say what value the experience had to your own personal/professional development.

in your reflections as possible. However, don't agonize too much over your response; there isn't a right or wrong answer, and only you will be able to judge the value of your deliberations in relation to developing you own metacognition (thinking about thinking) and meta-learning (learning about your own learning).

2.4 Thinking as an educational experience

After this short bout of 'thinking' you may wish to consider Dewey's views on the importance of developing this skill which, or course, is now heavily represented within the national Key Skills. In an early book, *Democracy and Education* (1916), Dewey not only anticipated life-long learning, but also stressed the need for 'thinking' in education. Although he used the somewhat formal, stilted language of the time, the conceptual process he identifies has equal relevance today:

> . . . the important thing is that thinking is the method of an educative experience. The essentials of method are therefore identical with the essentials of reflection. They are first that the pupil has a genuine situation of experience – that there be a continuous activity in which he is interested for its own sake; secondly, that a genuine problem develop within this situation as a stimulus to thought; third, that he process the information and make the observations needed to deal with it; fourth, that suggested solutions occur to him which he shall be responsible for developing in an orderly way; fifth, that he has opportunity and occasion to test his ideas by application, to make their meaning clear and to discover for himself their validity.

Although it is a long and at times difficult quote, Dewey is making several important points about the process of student thinking and reflection, namely that they should involve:

- a real situation/experience as the focus
- an interesting and continuing activity
- problem/s
- the student developing appropriate solutions in a systematic manner
- the student testing the solutions which have been developed in order to be aware of their value.

Consider how Dewey's principles are represented in Activity 2b overleaf.

The first step is to involve the student's own experiences, this provides interest and the students will have fun comparing different food intakes. Then a problem should be set and developed in a way which presents the students with the need to process appropriate knowledge. Finally, the students should be allowed to experiment in order to test the knowledge and to view it in different ways. Using this strategy the students will be engaged in 'thinking' about the problem through reflection. It might, perhaps, be easier for the teacher to lecture them, but such a didactic approach would make it more difficult to engage the students in problem-solving *activity*.

Activity 2b Planning Teaching

A teacher is attempting to introduce students to the concept of nutrients for the first time. The teacher first asks the students to list the food they have eaten during the week on a day-to-day basis. Next the students are introduced to the five main nutrients needed for health, and the teacher asks them to see how much of each nutrient is included in their diet. The students are given food tables and begin to calculate their own values of the major nutrients from their lists. The tutor then goes on to introduce the concept of digestion, and the way that enzymes work in order to break down the food. The sessions are followed up with experiments planned by the students to test some of the theory provided by the tutor.

Can you try to analyse the teacher's approach to the sequence and activities? What steps were taken to make it interesting to the students? In what way were Dewey's ideas being used in these sessions?

A further consideration of related theory about reflective practice may help us to understand this. Building on Dewey's work in the first part of the last century. Boud *et al.* (1985) consider that:

> reflection in the context of learning is a generic term for those intellectual and affective activities in which individuals engage to explore their experiences in order to lead to new understanding and appreciations.

They note three stages during the process of reflection:

- returning to the experience
- attending to feelings during the experience
- re-evaluation of the experience.

We all have times when planned teaching and learning activities are not as successful as anticipated – to put it mildly! Although it is often painful, the earlier you are able to reflect on the problems which arose during the session, the sooner you will identify the problem and dispel those lingering anxieties. Try Activity 2c as a starting point.

Your PDJ should be starting to develop now after five entries. It may be time to start adding to these initial reflections by drawing on your own interests. You may, for instance, wish to collect interesting newspaper cuttings and add comments about the relevance to your own teaching. Moon (1999) discusses how to achieve learning through the reflexive use of journals:

> Journal writing provides a means by which learning can be upgraded – where unconnected areas of meaning cohere and a deeper meaning emerges.

Activity 2c Responding to Student Need

Consider this teaching scenario and compare it to the previous one in Activity 2b: A tutor asks a class to work through a set of instructions and to produce a desktop-published page. One student is 'trigger happy' with the mouse and makes a few 'clicks' that takes her way past the point of no return. She is then forced to ask the tutor for help. The tutor grabs the mouse, proceeds to click and move the screen about while the student looks on. The tutor then says 'You're OK now, carry on.'

How do you think the student would feel? Would she know how the tutor solved the problem? Would she be any closer to solving the problem herself? Make notes about your views on this in your PDJ.

Moon goes on to note that journals can be used to record experience, enhance other learning, develop 'critical thinking' and a whole range of extended thinking skills such as problem solving and creativity. She believes (like Dewey) that reflective activity is very powerful in allowing a novice practitioner to develop, enquire and refine practice in the light of experience. Moon uses the term 'metacognition' and the power of journal writing to develop this process of 'overviewing one's own mental functioning'. Try thinking about your own thinking as you tackle the next activity.

Activity 2d Problem Solving

Try to remember how you first went about grasping a difficult concept in a complex subject. Did you need to 'see' it from different angles? Did you try to solve it in different ways? How did you get the insight that allowed you to solve the problem? After being baffled at first, did you feel a rising sense of achievement at having found a solution? Make notes about your own particular experience.

2.5 Schon's swamp

Of course, each of us will have our own approaches to the solving of complex problems. In some situations our methods may be similar and yet, in others we will differ greatly. This will naturally be affected by the urgency of the situation, however, our preferred learning styles, personal constructs and individual needs will also have a significant bearing. These issues will be tackled in the next two chapters but, for now, let us consider the sheer inherent complexity of each educational situation. Schon (1987) manages to capture the essence of this dilemma when he metaphorically declares that:

> In the varied topography of professional practice, there is a high, hard ground overlooking a swamp. On the high ground, manageable problems lend themselves to solution through the application of

research-based theory and technique. In the swampy lowland, messy, confusing problems defy technical solution. The irony of this situation is that the problems of the high ground tend to be relatively unimportant to individuals or society at large, however great their technical interest may be; while in the swamp lie the problems of greatest concern. The practitioner must choose. Shall he remain on the high ground where he can solve relatively unimportant problems according to prevailing standards of rigor, or shall he descend to the swamp of important problems and non-rigorous inquiry?

As you will have realized, we are all working in the 'messy swamp' of complex classroom practice, but many of our managers, inspectors and evaluators measure what we are doing from the relative safety of the 'high ground'. In developing this argument Schon contrasts two differing approaches to practice. On the one hand practitioners may act as instrumental problem solvers who select technical means best suited to practical purposes. He uses the term '*technical rationality*' to describe a process of relying on formal knowledge about a profession in the manner of textbook information. In the case of teaching this would involve knowledge about lesson plans, schemes of work, learning outcomes, etc.

Schon, however, goes on to argue that professionals also use what he calls '*professional artistry*' and '*knowledge in use*' as well as propositional knowledge. He uses the example of a skill that practitioners can display in unique, uncertain and conflicting situations. According to Schon, skilled professionals can call upon a range of strategies and can think creatively in different situations. In doing so, they are using a process of reflection to produce effective action. Schon uses the phrase 'knowing in action' to describe this process of reflective thinking and uses this expression to refer to publicly observable, physical actions and private, contemplative actions. In both cases, according to Schon, the 'knowing' is in the action. To him, knowing in action is dynamic whereas rules, procedures and theories are static. So as teachers we operate within such static 'rules' as the syllabus and the time-table but knowing in action is the way that individual teachers and trainers achieve learning.

As you consider the activity below, think in terms of these twin influences on what we do.

Activity 2e Influences on Chosen Teaching and Learning Methods

Consider the teaching and the learning strategies that you currently employ. Think in terms of their usefulness and select one approach which springs to mind as being the most effective. Describe the approach and how you arrived at it and then go on to summarize what learning principles you feel underpin the method. (For example, 'always let the students know exactly what is expected of them', or perhaps 'before moving to practical applications the students must have a thorough grounding in relevant theory'.) However, remember that you should draw out the underlying principles *after* you have intuitively identified the successful teaching and learning methods.

Schon believes strongly in moving away from mere *technical rationality* in classroom practice. Teachers should primarily respond to the needs of their learners and the context in which they are working. A basic principle of this approach would be to consistently encourage different forms of feedback from students so that the teacher can be clear that they are understanding and keeping up with the development of the session. Even though you are working to a lesson plan, it is pointless ploughing on towards the intended outcomes if there are clear signs that earlier concepts are not yet understood. It would be more appropriate to return to the concept that is clearly causing some of the students problems and go through a process of recapitulation, perhaps encouraging those who have grasped the idea to articulate their understanding in their own words for the benefit of those who are still struggling. Schon would term this *knowing-in-action*.

Activity 2f Knowing-in-Action

A tutor is currently teaching a class the simple basics of ICT. He informs the class that in the future all information will be available on the VLE (see page 162). However, one brave student asks in a quiet voice, 'What's one of those?' What do you think the tutor should do now?

Of course, the tutor would explain what it is, how it works, and what it does. Now try to analyse what the tutor may have *learned* from this example?

The tutor could have ignored the question and carried on with the next topic on the lesson plan. However, if the tutor merely engaged in always delivering the same pre-planned teaching without taking into account changing variables and factors, many learning opportunities, particularly in the case of one member of his class, will be lost. Competence based only on technical knowledge would be fine if every class and every session was the same. However, as practising teachers we know they are not and one fundamental principle of teaching is that it is important not to assume knowledge just because we have it. Knowing-in-action is one way of compensating for such oversights and in this case, ensured that an unfortunate knowledge gap was addressed. At the same time, the teacher will have demonstrated to the class as a whole that, not only will they not be ignored or ridiculed for admitting to ignorance, but also that it is a very acceptable and responsible way for a member of the class to respond. As Schon points out, 'We may reflect-on-action, thinking back on what we have done in order to discover how our knowing-in-action may have contributed to an unexpected outcome.'

Activity 2g Selection of Means

Consider the example of two sessions involving the same subject, one given to a group of adults on a Thursday evening, and the other given to 16–19 year olds on Monday morning. Try to identify what differences in approach, attitude of the students, classroom management and delivery style there would be. Think also in terms of pace, questioning techniques and checking of learning.

Schon's answer would be that when practitioners recognize a situation as unique, they cannot handle it solely by applying theories or techniques derived from their store of professional knowledge. In addition, in situations of value conflict, there are no clear and self-consistent ends to guide the technical selection of means. In other words, in spite of technical expertise gained through training, the teacher needs to look beyond this in order to 'see' the situation differently. 'Reframing' is necessary to question previous constructions of practice in order to perceive things afresh with different eyes. This leads to a process that Schon describes as 'a sequence of "moments" in a process of reflection-in-action'. He believes that students cannot be 'taught' the knowledge, but should be coached towards it. 'Nobody else can see for him, and he can't see just by being *told*. However, the right kind of telling may guide his seeing and thus help him see what he wants to see.'

2.6 Principles and values

During this chapter we have discussed a number of important and sometimes difficult concepts. You may not have agreed with them all because there, in the background influencing all teaching, are the implicit values and purposes of the teacher. Concepts inevitably build into principles of operation and those that are held dear are those which form the core of not only the chosen methodology but also the underpinning ideology or fundamental beliefs.

As an example here is a principle identified by Marton (1984) from the University of Gothenburg, that may, at first, seem a simplistic statement of the obvious (principles often are), but which can provide a real insight into effective pedagogy:

> Whenever you fail to make someone understand something, it is because you have taken something for granted which you shouldn't have taken for granted.

The next exercise is about the principles of learning that are formed from the range of concepts which the practitioner feels are important within a particular context. Of course, if this programme you're reading is at all effective, these principles will inevitably change and develop during the course of it. You may find the activity to be difficult at first, but please give as much time to it as you can spare.

Activity 2h Principles of Teaching and Learning

This reflective activity builds on those you have completed previously. Consider those aspects of teaching and learning which you feel are most important. Now list (if possible in priority order) eight general principles, which you feel would apply to any teaching/learning situation (not just your own). Once again, be aware that there are no right or wrong answers to this and your views will probably change over time.

A simple example of a basic principle could be '*at the start of a session make it clear to your students what part or aspect of the subject you are going to cover with them.*' Not exactly rocket science we know, but a very important principle that is sometimes forgotten. '*Use varied and interactive teaching methods*' may have occurred to you as well as the need to '*check learning at regular intervals*'. These are some of the key principles of teaching and learning and obviously others will emerge during the chapters that follow. However, in general, principles will usually relate to the stance you take as a teacher. For example, one dimension to consider could be the question '*should education stress the importance of self or society?*' If you feel that the teacher's only responsibility is to dispense the essential knowledge and skills related to the subject, you will have a different set of principles to the practitioner who feels that a teacher's role is to facilitate the student's developing knowledge of him or herself and promote informed scepticism. These extremes may well be seen as somewhat exaggerated examples. Often a practitioner's values will move between ideological positions according to the situation they are working in.

The concept of reflective practice may be viewed as a process of moving from a subject base (and relative safety) to a more considered position of thinking about the learning process and educational issues that impact on classroom practice. It involves the tutor moving from the mechanics of imparting knowledge, through a series of personal learning experiences, to becoming a facilitator who guides students in their exploration of the subject being studied in order to develop and value their own insights. Parker (1997) notes that:

> The literature paints a picture of the reflective practitioner as one who turns her attention to the wider issues of education – its aims, its social and personal consequences, its ethics, the rationale of its methods and its curricula – and to the intimate relationship between these and the immediate reality of her classroom practice.

To support this, Parker also notes that the reflective practitioner is one 'who attempts to bring about improvement in his/her practice by applying critical thinking to her situation; an approach which is modulated by her appreciation of that situation's uniqueness and its resistance to ready-made descriptions and interpretations.'

Activity 2i Values which Underpin Approaches to Teaching

You have probably realized that your identification of learning principles during the previous reflections will inevitably have also given some indication of those aspects of teaching and learning which you most value. Please try to be more precise about your own educational values by expressing (again, if possible, in priority order) what, for you, are six important *purposes* of education. Remember, there are no right or wrong answers.

We all have certain values that we bring to the education arena which are personal and which differ from individual to individual. These values are based on our own experiences and it is these that influence what goes on in the classroom. For example, one person might think that education should involve freedom of speech and so allow all their students to discuss issues in order to develop critical thinking. Another tutor might believe that education should be about preparing for a useful role in society, which may involve a degree of conformity. The effect on students of these two differing value-bases may well be noticeable in their overt behaviour

2.7 Conclusion

It is possible that your own views on educational purposes may well develop and change during this programme. On the other hand, they may be established on such a firm value-foundation that you cannot envisage any room for manoeuvre. But how do your values equate to the teaching that you are currently doing? This is a difficult issue, and one which may well be highly political within the setting in which you work. Remember again that there are no right or wrong answers, particularly in this instance. The final reflection is designed to be a summative evaluation of your own views as expressed within all your reflective activities to this point and a consideration of how compatible these perceptions are with aspects of your current teaching: Be as honest as possible, but also be aware of the political sensitivities within your working environment.

If there are no tensions then that is excellent! However, you may have found that some of the values you believe in are compromised to some extent by the constraints within the present education system. In Chapter 10, Liz Mayes suggests how reflection may be used as a means of active self-evaluation. Chapter 12 will address many of these issues which affect the validity of education, but the plain fact is that colleges are currently under great pressure and have to make some sacrifices to survive within the present climate.

Activity 2j Relationship between Previous Reflections

Please look back through your previous reflections once more and notice how your early identification of a *significant learning experience* (2a) and your preferred approaches to *problem solving* (2d) *and teaching and learning* (2e) relate to your later articulation of *principles and values* (2h and 2i). Consider the nature of your 'significant learning experience' and your preferred 'teaching and learning styles'. Do they contain or represent any of the principles and values you identified later? In what way do your expressed values and principles relate to your present work as a teacher?

Please write between 50 and 100 words analysing each of these two aspects (summarized below):

- relationship between your own teaching and learning *approaches* and educational principles and values
- compatibility of current teaching responsibilities with educational values and principles.

To counteract this rather pessimistic note, it is worthwhile ending the chapter with a consideration of why, despite the need for technical rationality within management, teachers should continue to explore theoretical issues as well as cope with the more instrumental influences on practice. Carr (1995) introduces the concept of 'poiesis' and contrasts this with the opposing concept of 'praxis'. Carr's theoretical examination of practice has led to his identification of two approaches. The first he characterizes as 'rule-following action' (poiesis) and contrasts this with practice that is 'morally informed and morally committed action' (praxis). Praxis according to Carr is reflexive action that can 'transform the *theory* that guides it'. Poiesis, on the other hand, is seen as a non-reflexive 'know-how' that does not affect its guiding 'techne'. To Carr *techne* is a term for technical expertise and knowledge.

Kemmis (1985), a contemporary of Carr, draws heavily upon the idea of 'critical thinking' in teaching and the need for reflective practice. He, too, notes the need for 'praxis':

> [R]eflection is action-orientated, social and political. Its product is 'praxis' (informed, committed action), the most eloquent and socially significant form of human action.

In other words, teachers have the opportunity to continually reconstruct theory in response to their own praxis (active reflection). In this way they are involved with the ongoing development of knowledge related to their own practice and are not restricted to Dewey's 'routine action'. Schon's 'technical rationality' or Carr's 'poiesis'.

Knowledge is developed through practice but becomes more visible when it is illuminated by theory. Teachers who, in addition to recording events that are happening in their classroom, are also willing (through praxis) to consider *why* they are happening, are taking the first steps towards knowledge creation in contrast to routine knowledge replication. But they need the light of theory to guide them.

LLUK clearly require evidence that practitioners are becoming reflective in order to meet objective AS4 in Domain A, which states that teachers in the sector should value

> reflection and evaluation of their own practice and their continuing professional development as teachers.

Perhaps the final word on Praxis (active reflection) should go to the great Brazilian educationalist Paulo Freire (2000):

> Liberation is a praxis: the action and reflection of people upon their world in order to transform it.

2.8 Useful publications

Carr, W. (1995), *For Education: Towards Critical Educational Inquiry*, Buckingham: Open University Press.
This text is a more recent philosophical debate regarding the nature of education. Carr questions what educational practice is and raises issues such as how theory and practice are related in terms of broader educational debates. Very relevant to the ideas behind reflective practice, Carr is able to develop aspects of critical enquiry that are designed to promote a further consideration of educational values.

Dewey, J. (1916), *Democracy and Education*. A Free Press Paperback.
An old book that has set the foundations for educational discourse. Dewey's work influenced government policy changes between 1940 and 1960. Recent critics of the current accountability drive draw upon Dewey for support. A return to his problem-solving approach seems to be underpinning recent political debates.

Dewey, J. (1938), *Experience and Education*. Collier Macmillan Publishers.
Similar to the above work in a philosophical sense, but in this text Dewey draws upon student experience as a powerful learning tool and one that any educational practice should employ. Dated in some respects, but again critics of the current economic utility model of education would do well to seek it out.

Elliott, G. (1996), *Crisis and Change in Vocational Education and Training*. London: Jessica Kingsley Publishers.
An excellent text that draws upon actual research undertaken within the further education sector. Elliot uses actual practitioner comment to reflect what he sees as an escalating crisis brought about by recent government reforms in education. He questions the business-like approach to education and training and illustrates the impact of the policies on practice.

Kemmis, S. (1985), 'Action research and the politics of reflection' in D. Boud, R. Keogh and D. Walker (1985), *Reflection: Turning Experience into Practice*. London: Kogan Page.

Kemmis is well known for his opinions on education as a form of social change. This work draws upon action research for teachers as a powerful tool for liberation and social change through education. He uses examples drawn from practice that illustrate how action research can change and develop education, teaching and learning towards better practice through a cycle of reflection, analysis and evaluation.

Moon, J. (1999), *Reflection in Learning and Professional Development Theory and Practice*. London: Kogan Page.

A practical book which draws upon a range of theory to relate reflective practice to actual examples. Moon is down to earth in her approach to using reflective practice as a tool for real learning, but at the same time presents a very useful overview of the major writings on reflective practice. A very useful text on the use of journals as a powerful learning tool.

Moon, J. (1999), *Learning Journals*: *A Handbook for Academics, Students and Professional Development*. London: Kogan Page.

This book draws on the one above, but pays particular attention to the aspect of journal writing. Moon provides a powerful argument for the use of journals as a reflective vehicle to promote learning at a deeper level. She explains how journals can create metacognition through a process of reflection about one's knowledge and understanding.

Parker, S. (1997), *Reflective Teaching in the Post Modern World. A Manifesto for Education in Post-Modernity*, Buckingham: Open University Press.

A strong text on the use of reflective teaching and its place within an economic environment of education. Parker provides some useful definitions of reflective practice that places it firmly within a broader concept than that of classroom practice. His work provokes thought and challenges some concepts that have previously been taken for granted.

Schon, D. (1987), *Educating the Reflective Practitioner*. Jossey-Bass.

This very readable book is one of the 'authorities' of reflective practice. Schon uses real examples of practice to show how people move from everyday know-how through to a process of reflection and thinking about what they do. The concepts noted in this text such as knowing-in-action and technical rationality are made clear through appropriate examples.

2.9 Useful websites

There are many websites dedicated to the development of reflective practice. Below are two of the better ones, and of course the website supporting this book does have a section which encourages reflective interaction between members.

www.reflectiveteacher.com

www.gtcs.org.uk

www.tipcet.com

3 Meeting the Needs of Learners

Janet Hobley

Chapter Outline

Key Concepts

Learner Needs, Learner Skills, Practical Skills, Intellectual Skills, Interpersonal Skills, Intrapersonal Skills, Diagnostic Tests, FOG Index, Cloze Technique, Student Profiles, Deductive, Inductive, Action Plans, APL, APEL, Accreditation, Teaching Styles, Learning Cycle, Learning Styles, Learning Strategies, Holistic, Serialistic, Mediation Channels, Concrete Sequential, Concrete Random, Abstract Sequential, Abstract Random, Student Autonomy, Learner Dependence, Learner Independence.

It may be useful to check the Process Justifications (Table 3.3) *before reading this chapter.*

3.1 Introduction

Preparing for a new group of students is probably one of the most interesting aspects of teaching. Many experienced teachers will tell you that, despite having gone through the process many times before, an incoming group of learners inevitably causes the familiar tingle of an adrenalin rush. The fresh challenges that this initial process brings are exciting partially because they are, to some extent, as yet unknown. Even though you may have background information about each of the students as individuals, you cannot predict accurately how the dynamics of the newly formed group will operate. Your anxieties may be about the learners' mental, physical and social responses to your preparations. In other words you may worry about what they will think about your chosen approach, how they cope with any physical demands required of them and their reactions to each other, to you and to their new environment. Try the following activity as a starting point for this process of needs assessment:

Activity 3a Preparing for your First Meeting with New Students

Imagine that you are about to have your first meeting with a new group of learners. Make a list of any advanced information you could be given which would help you to prepare more effectively for your initial meeting. Remember, first impressions do count.

It is likely that you will be provided with a class list, but this information is only of limited value. You will then know the number of learners in the group, their gender and perhaps their age. At this stage additional advanced information that would help you to plan your first session can be summarized as follows:

Venue: The time of day and the room you are meeting in can have an effect on the outcome of the session. Facilities you may take for granted such as sufficient seating, a working overhead projector, a surface to project on, a white or blackboard, chalk or marker pen, adequate ventilation have been known to be absent. If your session is the students' second or third meeting during an induction day, it will probably affect how you approach your introduction to the topic.

Age: This information is helpful, for example, in ensuring that learners meet the requirements of a professional body and indicating whether they are a school leaver or a more mature student.

Experience: These details will let you know, for example, if they are moving to you from another education environment, are mature students with no post-school experience, have taken other programmes since leaving school, or are entering your college after or while continuing in employment.

Qualifications: You need to know if their qualifications meet the course prerequisites. These details will also give you an indication of their areas of interest/expertise and whether they are inclined towards academic or vocational study.

Special Needs: You may need to make arrangements if your incoming group contains students who require particular provision because of physical or learning difficulties.

Given some or all of the above information, you can plan the first session with much more confidence. However, as is true of each of us, you may still be caught out on the day by the unexpected, but at least you have attempted to cover the obvious eventualities.

3.2 Learner needs

Chapter 4 is concerned with teaching and learning techniques, but our concern now is to build upon the information gained in Activity 3a (above) in order to be aware of the range of needs which may exist within a particular group. You have already got together the basic data needed for you to start establishing an effective working relationship with the group. Even so, though a teacher or trainer may be very experienced within their own particular subject, they will still be faced with the need to present it in a way that will catch and hold the interest of the incoming students.

In this regard, subject expertise is valuable but it does not necessarily guarantee that the teacher will be able to convince the learners of its intrinsic worth. Any particular student group will inevitably contain a range of differing learner characteristics and knowing these qualities may help you to promote a positive teacher/student relationship. Conversely, ignoring them could well reduce the effectiveness of teacher/student and student/student interaction. Obviously, the needs of any individual will be related to the particular qualities they bring to a situation. Try the next activity as a further step forward in your learner needs analysis.

Activity 3b Learner Skills

Consider a student or trainee group (perhaps your Focus Learning Group identified in Chapter 1) with whom you are so familiar that you already have most of the information discussed in Activity 3a. Now try to identify the range of skills that individual learners bring to your sessions.

Stoker (1994) has identified the following skills which learners will possess in varying degrees:

a. Practical skills – ability to use equipment and carry out actions.
b. Intellectual skills – related to knowledge and how the learner applies this, and concerned with activities such as planning, identifying priorities, problem solving and decision making.

c. Interpersonal skills – the ability to communicate, form relationships and generally 'get on' with other people.

d. Intrapersonal skills – concerned with the learner's self-confidence, self-control and awareness of her own abilities and the effect they have on others.

Although it is clear that the level of the above skills possessed by the student/trainee will certainly affect their overall performance, information about each student's ability in each of the above areas will not necessarily be readily available. In any case, all of these skills may well vary dependent upon the context in which the student is operating. For example, if for some reason a particular environment affects their self-confidence, then (c) and (d) may well be undermined.

3.3 Diagnostic tests

Obviously, as you work with the learners over the first few weeks of the programme, you will collect more data about their skills which, in turn, will enhance your individual profiles. However, you may wish to be more systematic about your data gathering. Turning once again to Stoker's list (Activity 3b above) try the following new activity.

Activity 3c Diagnostic Tests

Suggest some of the ways you might go about identifying the levels of ability of your learners in each of Stoker's four areas – Practical, Intellectual, Interpersonal and Intrapersonal.

It is relatively easy to identify previous learning of 16 year olds with GCSE results and details from the secondary school about their abilities within the four areas. Not so easy for adult returners who have not attended an educational institution for several years, and it is harder still to identify the range of needs that individuals with communication difficulties might have. However, we must remember that the LLUK Standards do apply to *all* aspects of education and training within the Lifelong Learning Sector. Tutors must consciously develop strategies to build up a profile or picture of their own students in order to decide what teaching methods will be most appropriate for the different student needs:

- **Practical skills** – on the face of it, this is probably the most straightforward of the areas to diagnose ability. A tutor could ask students to carry out a task which contains important skills. However, in these situations it is very easy to misinterpret hesitancy on the part of the student as a lack of competence.

In fact, all manner of features within the testing situation may be quite different to those that the learner is used to and their performance may not yet reflect their true ability.

- **Intellectual skills** – most problem-solving or decision-making situations where knowledge may be applied can be used to give an indication of cognitive ability. However, it is as important to know *what* the student can do, as well as what they are unable to achieve. So the diagnosis should also provide the opportunity for the learner to demonstrate at what level *in relation to a particular task* they are able to perform within the cognitive hierarchy of behaviours (see further details in Chapter 4).
- **Interpersonal skills** – obviously, an aware teacher will be able to observe evidence of these abilities as well as collect data from student work. However, once again it is important not to jump to conclusions because although some people take longer to develop confidence in group situations, they may well be responding to and supporting their colleagues, but in a less obvious manner.
- **Intrapersonal skills** – again a difficult area to gain accurate information about true ability. Students are often influenced by factors not immediately obvious within the social setting where diagnosis is taking place. Self-esteem and self-control may differ radically dependent upon the other personalities present (see more in Chapter 4).

There are, of course, several diagnostic techniques, which can be undertaken *prior* to enrolment. Students may be interviewed and given guidance about course options and care can be taken to ensure that learners are sure about their own and their tutors' initial course decisions. This involves a process of induction and pre-course guidance that allows for arrangements to be put in place for early course changes as necessary. With this initial assessment of needs comes the use of early pre-course testing to gauge student levels and existing abilities. Examples include reading tests, mathematical tests, attitude tests and other subject specific tests that can give the tutor an insight into student ability and knowledge. These are all useful techniques that can aid course design. After all, if each of your students can already do, for example, differential equations, there is no need to spend hours teaching this. A short diagnostic test will help to determine each learner's abilities in a subject. From the results, a tutor could plan the sequence of lessons and indeed the level.

3.4 Reading and writing skills

It is easy to assume that by the time they enter further education, all students will have developed their reading skills to the required basic level, but often this isn't the case. The reading age of students who have learning difficulties will often not match their chronological age and, in a minority of cases, the problem may be more serious. By using questions that involve short answer tests, tutors may also obtain a valuable indication of the reading and writing skills of the students in order to see if extra support in these areas needs to be given. Further diagnosis may involve testing the learner's reading age using measures such as the APU Vocabulary Tests.

Simple steps which lecturers themselves can usefully take in relation to reading would be to check that the materials they are using are pitched at an appropriate reading age for their own students. Two such methods, the FOG Index and the Cloze Technique are used as the basis of the next two activities (3d and 3e).

Activity 3d FOG Index

Take a typical example of text which you have used or will use with your own students, and select a passage of 100 words which you can use to test the reading age of the material following the guidelines below.

3.4.1 FOG Index

This is a useful indicator of the reading age of written materials and is based on the notion of the number of difficult words within a passage of writing, or the 'Frequency of Gobbledegook'. For your test use extracts from appropriate textbooks or handouts. The steps are as follows:

Step One **Select a passage of 100 words**

We have selected the following extract from the beginning of *Using Video in Training* (Fawbert 1987):

The recorded image whether on film or videotape has become such a familiar part of our lives that we now treat it as we would a member of our family. In general, we enjoy its company uncritically and only when it fails us do we see it in a new light. For a brief moment we become aware of its limitations. We cannot rely too much on these accidental revelations, instructive though they may be. We must attempt to develop our awareness of these characteristics in order to be more precise when using the moving image to achieve training goals.

Step Two **Count the number of complete sentences**

In our case, the above passage has five complete sentences.

Step Three **Count the words in each of the complete sentences**

Our answer is 30, 21, 10, 14 and 25.

Step Four **Find the average sentence length (L)**

In other words, 100 words divided by 5 = 20 words on average per sentence.

Step Five **Count the number of words of three or more syllables (polysyllabic) in the 100-word sample (we will call this N)**

In our case this is 14 – recorded, videotape, familiar, family, general, company, uncritically, limitations, accidental, revelations, instructive, develop, awareness and characteristics.

Step Six **To arrive at the reading age, add L and N, multiply by 0.4 and then add 5. Written as a formula this is 0.4 (L + N) + 5. This is the reading age.**

In our case the calculations are as follows:

20 (Step 4) + 14 (Step 5) = 34

34 x 0.4 = 13.6

13.6 + 5 = 18.6 years

Obviously, if your students have a reading age of 14 years, the above passage (which has a reading age of 18+ years) is not going to be suitable. The problem is the number of words with three syllables or more, and it is a simple task to replace these polysyllabic words by rewriting the piece.

Step Seven Although the redrafting (below) has increased the number of words to 110, it has taken out the polysyllabic words and consequently the reading age has been reduced to less than 14 years:

> As we create new methods, it becomes simpler to record an image onto film or tape. These days, film and video have helped moving pictures to become so common that we tend to take them for granted. It is only when we have reason to check them with more care that we see some good and bad things about them. If we are to learn to use moving pictures well, we must also know the key rules about choosing an image. If we want to say something clearly using moving pictures, we also need to know about the effect of images and how they can help or hinder our work.

The calculations this time are as follows:
22 (Step 4) + 0 (Step 5) = 22
22 x 0.4 = 8.8
8.8 + 5 = 13.8 years

Activity 3e Cloze Technique

This test is more concerned with your students' understanding and their ability to express themselves in writing. Find another example of text that would be appropriate for your learners, and use the following test with them and then record the results.

3.4.2 The Cloze Technique

Although relatively crude, this type of test can provide some useful information about a student's level of comprehension and writing ability. If you have designed a test, or some guided study materials for example, you may wish to have an indication of how the learners will cope with it. The Cloze process is based on the Gestalt psychology notion of 'closure', which occurs when a person perceiving an incomplete communication automatically adds the missing elements, sometimes correctly and sometimes, when their understanding is poor, incorrectly.

The procedure is relatively simple. Take the material or (if it is lengthy) part of the material you wish to test and after omitting every *ninth* word give it to your students to write what they think the missing words are in the blank spaces. Allow them sufficient time to consider the alternative words carefully, but not so long that they become bored waiting for all the slowest members to complete. When it comes to marking, interpretations differ, as do the recommended intervals between the omitted words. However, a simple guide is that if a student get less than 65 per cent of the replacement words correct, then the materials are too demanding. A 65–80 per cent score indicates that they will need some guidance with terms and concepts, and any score of 80 per cent and over shows that the target group should find the materials manageable. Obviously, if you already know what the reading age is for the passage that you have used for the Cloze Test, you will also have an indication of the students reading ability as well as their level of comprehension and vocabulary.

3.5 Developing student profiles

During this opening part of the chapter we have been developing an awareness of the many and varied needs which learners will bring to your sessions. You will agree that the majority of learners attending colleges of further education have far more than just academic needs. Of course, the subject being studied is very important, but it is also crucial to understand how the student is responding to both the subject and the learning environment in which they have been placed.

The learners' life experiences will inevitably colour their perceptions of what they find when they commence their chosen learning programme. If tutors are able to develop an insight into these personal constructs, then the management of the students may well be less problematic. All that they encounter during their induction period, and often events occurring even before they attend their new place of learning, will influence the attitudes of new students. These attitudes change very rapidly and it is important that tutors are aware of the range of subtle influences that can affect the learners' attitudes, confidence and their openness to new experiences.

The essential ingredient in any positive and productive relationship is trust, and despite the fact that most of the parties involved (teachers and students) are willing to give the others the benefit of the doubt, this trusting relationship is often very difficult to achieve. It does take time and you will usually find that by the end of the term/semester the students will have moved a long way towards trusting you. However, progress in this direction does very much depend on whether or not you have intentionally or accidentally given them any reason to doubt that you have their best interests at heart. An essential feature in developing a trusting relationship is consistency. This doesn't just mean treating all members of the group equally, although that is important. It involves the difficult skill of responding in what may be called a professional manner to all eventualities. For example, although you may find that some students have naturally developed more attractive characteristics than others, you are able to avoid any inclination towards an overt demonstration of favouritism.

Another important aspect of consistency is that the learners should begin to anticipate accurately how you will respond to their performance or behaviour. In other words, they learn to understand the values that you feel strongly about and expect you to react in a particular way if these values are not respected. If your reaction to minor infringements is over the top and, on other occasions, you ignore major transgressions, the learners will inevitably be uncertain about where they stand. Students will usually respond well if they are secure in the knowledge that their teacher has established a productive learning environment which is based on values they understand so that a consistent relationship can thrive.

Try the following activity.

Activity 3f Student Trust

Think of the characteristics of a particular group of students whom you teach. Make a list of indicators (for example, changes in behaviour) that you might become aware of at the end of term, which show how the student's trust has developed since the term commenced.

Naturally, these indicators will reflect the characteristics of a particular group and so it is difficult to generalize. However, you could expect the following indications:

- Small positive signs, such as smiles, openness, shared news, etc. which show that the students are actually pleased to be there and which outweigh any negative reluctance or resentment.
- A general readiness to begin the session (and even some signs of anticipation).
- A willingness to follow a tutor-led change of direction during the ongoing discussion without signs of apprehension such as needing to know where it is leading.
- Student willingness to put forward their own views, even on unfamiliar topics.
- A concern among the learners that the teacher doesn't misunderstand them.
- A willingness to persuade reticent fellow students to contribute.
- Student acceptance of assessment results and a willingness to improve.

We have stressed that teachers need as much information as possible about their new charges. However, perhaps as an initial 'them and us' reaction, it is fairly common for a novice tutor to perceive the student group as an amorphous whole. Try the following activity as a first step in considering student/trainee learning preferences.

Activity 3g A Starting Point for Study

Imagine that you are teaching a familiar topic from your own subject area to a particular group of learners for the first time. How would you structure the session?

3.5.1 Deductive and inductive approaches

When delivering learning programmes within post-compulsory education, there is a natural tendency for trainers, teachers, learning support workers, etc. to turn to approaches that they have experienced to good effect themselves. This often involves presenting the students with the *theory* first. This theory may be in the form of rules, principles, guidelines, formulae, recipes, instructions and so on. Whatever way this essentially theoretical content is presented it will inevitably be *abstract* in nature and the learners will be involved with trying to *deduce* a conclusion from the information they have received.

A familiar example presented by Conan Doyle in the Sherlock Holmes stories is that the great detective relied on *deductive reasoning* where he ensured that the conclusions he inferred when investigating a situation were based only on the evidence that was available. Holmes established a premise (a theoretical proposition or hypothesis) and then set about collecting evidence to prove or disprove it.

When deductive approaches in teaching are used, the learners will first be given rules (the theory) and then will usually have the experience of investigating these through laboratory work, fieldwork, the real situation, etc. A simple way to represent the process is that deductive learning is 'RULE/EX', i.e. the rules followed by the experience/example.

As you would expect, a simple way to represent the alternative inductive approach to reasoning or teaching is 'EX/RULE'. Although, inductive teaching is more obvious within the primary or secondary sectors, many would suggest that it should be used more extensively in Lifelong Learning (see Chapter 5). It involves providing the learners with the experience first and then drawing the rules and principles out of the experience. Sand and water play are good examples from early years education, where children develop a range of abstract concepts from concrete experiences. These would include addition, subtraction, conservation and spatial and volume relationships. Some teachers continue this approach in a more structured manner during Year 3. For example, a walk in the countryside with the children may involve the teacher encouraging the children to identify the characteristics of different flowers or trees and then back in the classroom they will perhaps, develop through discussion the 'rules' of what characteristics a particular plant, flower or tree must have in order to belong to a specific category. So, in this way the theory is drawn out of the experience and often, because the development of the theory is based on rich, concrete experiences involving many of the senses, the learners grasp of these rules and principles is firm, long-lasting and easily recalled.

Of course, teachers in PCET will be aware that, although the inductive approach may well be successful it is also very demanding of resources, particularly time. However, given the premise that, in any given learning situation, students/trainees will have a preference for a particular learning style (even though they may not express it) it is clear that some of these learners will have real difficulty with the theory first, deductive approach. An alternative definition of inductive/experiential approaches could be building on learners' previous experience rather than basing the new learning on experience. Again this will help learners because you are starting from a basis they are familiar with and are using previous cognitive structures to develop new knowledge. Now try the following activity.

Activity 3h Group Reactions

Consider the following two examples:

1. A tutor delivers a session on *King Lear* to a GCSE group of 16-year-old males and females at 10am on a Monday morning. The session involves tutor-led readings and explanations of the key ideas of two acts, followed by a 15-minute video of a recent Stratford production. The session finishes promptly at the point that the tutor required.
2. The same tutor then attempts to deliver a similar session to a mature GCSE adult evening class consisting of 15 female students. Five minutes into the tutor's explanation of why King Lear disinherits his daughter, the class begins to argue and debate the tutor's input. At the end of the session, the tutor has only covered a quarter of the session. Try to identify the factors that have caused the change in student response.

Obviously, the time was different, but so were the students' age, sex, experience and motivation. Also, many 16 year olds find it difficult to contribute on a Monday morning, their experience of Shakespeare may well be limited and their reasons for studying GCSE will be totally different to those of the adult returners. The experience and possibly the gender of the second group would inevitably help to promote a healthy debate about the relationship between King Lear and his daughter.

It is worth remembering that within classes and between classes there will inevitably be a myriad student 'types'. It is possible that a particular student group could consist of adults who come from many different walks of life in order to study subjects that they may have missed at school, together with restless 14–19 year olds who 'need' a particular qualification in order to gain access to a particular course, and experienced people who have held down responsible jobs in industry or commerce and who are studying for pleasure and relaxation. On top of all this, the teacher may well be faced with personality clashes. For example, the extrovert who will not shut up and the introvert who remains silent throughout all discussions. In adult groups the students' ages may range from 18 to 90, and they may come from all occupations and all social classes. There are issues of gender and race as well as age, ability and self-esteem. This notion of dealing with multifaceted learners may initially be very threatening to a novice teacher even though they are very experienced in their subject area. Although you have a good awareness of how you learned your subject it very soon becomes evident that not all students learn in the same way.

It is because we are faced with this complex range of learner differences that we turn to diagnostic assessment as a vital aid to our understanding of student needs. The information gained through diagnosis can relate to several areas. Simple examples could be that it may be important if you teach a physical subject to find out the health of your students and if cookery is your subject, you may need to identify if they have any allergies to foods. We mentioned earlier student writing and reading skills and you may also need to know if they are able to add up and subtract simple numbers. The precise nature of the diagnostic tests you use will usually be directly related to the subject you teach. A useful starting point then, would be to reflect on the skills, attributes or attitudes that are needed to do well in your subject. Try the following activity.

Activity 3i Subject-specific Skills

What made you want to pursue your own subject/area of interest? Identify the skills and knowledge that would be needed to succeed in this topic. Now, identify a few questions or tasks that will identify whether or not students have these abilities and understandings. Don't forget that attitudes play a part as well. After all, hairdressing isn't just about skilfully cutting hair; a student also needs to be able to communicate effectively with customers.

3.6 Action plans

When you have developed the most effective way of obtaining basic information about your students' skills and knowledge, you need to process it in some way. This could involve producing individual action plans for each student. For example, you may have identified that one student has some difficulty in spelling and needs extra support. In this case it might be useful to suggest some form of study support to develop this aspect of performance. An individual action plan is just that, an individual prescription for a specific student. No two action plans should be the same. Take the following examples:

Action Plan 1	
Student: Judith Smith	**Course: NVQ Level 1 Hairdressing**
Skills:	Previously worked for 12 months in a children's nursery. Can already shampoo hair as a result of working for 18 months in a salon; positive comments from supervisor. Is computer literate but has no qualification in IT.
Knowledge:	Knows the theory of shampooing, but not any other techniques in hairdressing. Has Key Skills Level 1: Communication and working with others.
Diagnostic results:	Some spelling problems identified, but your essays are becoming more structured due to the implementation of essay plans.
Action:	Study support needed to improve spelling. To be entered for Clait to gain an IT qualification.

Action Plan 2	
Student: Albert Ainsworth	**Course: A-level Spanish**
Skills:	Can speak three languages already.
Knowledge:	Has GCSE Spanish, but taken 10 years ago. Has a Diploma in Management Studies.
Diagnostic results:	Other languages can get in the way of speaking Spanish. Written Spanish very poor.
Action:	Subject specific study support weekly to improve written work. To sit in on a current GCSE Spanish class alongside A-level students.

Collecting this sort of information is the first step in ensuring that, where it is needed, the right support is provided at the optimum time. Try the following action planning activity.

Activity 3j Action Planning

Using a simple format (along the lines of the above examples), construct action plans based around the known profiles of three or four of your students/trainees. Try to make your 'action' as realistic and appropriate as possible, bearing in mind the needs of the learners and the current range of provision that is available to them.

For example, in some cases the information might show that the course was not the right one for the student at that particular time. A structured induction period will identify problems early while it is still possible for students to change courses and to be placed on one that is more suitable. *For instance, an AS-level Spanish may be more suitable for Albert Ainsworth in Action Plan 2.*

What you write must be understood by all parties concerned and, like feedback, should be constructive and helpful. Try to use positive statements, clarifying what the learner has achieved. See Judith Smith's Action Plan 1 for examples. When completing the action plan, make sure tasks are clear, with definite target dates. There may be room for students to complete their own comments – and they should be encouraged to do so in order to develop their reflective skills. Timely diagnostic assessment and individual action plans can often prevent many students experiencing early failure or withdrawal.

3.7 Credit Accumulation and Transfer (CAT)

A part of identifying student needs involves a consideration of their *prior learning and experience*. Also known as APL (*the accreditation of prior learning*) or APEL (accreditation *of prior experiential learning*), Credit Accumulation and Transfer is now important as a means of ensuring that a student's previous endeavours are not only acknowledged but, where appropriate, are also translated into some form of credit within their current programme of study.

Unfortunately, the process is necessarily complicated. This is because it essentially hinges on an interpretation of equivalence and this may often be controversial. Even when accrediting a *certificated* qualification, there is sometimes disagreement about its value to the target programme and consequently what credit it should earn. Those involved talk about '*CAT Currency*' (i.e. how long ago the certificate or experience was undertaken) or relevance (i.e. what it has in common with aspects of the target programme).

However, it is important to remember that a student may enter your institution with a range of different experiences or qualifications which may not only positively influence their ability to benefit from a course (i.e. their prior learning gives them advanced standing), but in some cases make part of the course redundant because it will only be repeating what has been previously learned.

Using Albert Ainsworth from our example of an Action Plan, it might be useful to consider whether he would have any previous learning that might have influenced the way he was able to perform on his current programme of study:

Activity 3k Prior Learning

Refer back to Judith Smith and Albert Ainsworth (Action Plans 1 and 2 above) and decide if they have any knowledge or experience that could have affected their learning within their chosen programme of study.

You may have identified the value of Albert already speaking three languages. This goes some way towards indicating that this person has a natural flair for language and that he could do well on an academic study route.

With Judith Smith you may feel that she deserves some credit for her shampooing skills. It may be possible in this sort of case to give a student credit in *advance* of the course for this aspect of learning. However, as stated before, some aspects are difficult to measure. Try the following activity to investigate this further:

Activity 3l Accreditation

Given the case of Judith Smith, what information would you need to know that would convince you that this candidate really did have the skills of shampooing? If you were convinced that she had these skills, ask yourself how it would be possible to accredit them.

You would certainly need to see them in action and would probably need a witness statement of support from her employer. A tutor's role in using CAT is to collect as much data as possible about the previous learning and to assess it in the light of the new learning being undertaken. It may be that the previous learning was many years ago and did not involve current technology or techniques and is therefore redundant knowledge because it doesn't have currency. In that case, the tutor would reject the claim for the accreditation of previous learning. It may be that the previous learning is substantial both in terms of duration and level of difficulty and is equivalent to a whole unit within the current programme. Whatever the scenario, each case needs to be considered on its own merit and it is the subject tutor's role to define what is needed for a particular course and what can be accredited through previous experiences, both formal and informal. Most programmes and courses have a regulation that states what percentage of the award may be accredited on the basis of prior experience or certification.

Some courses allow *credit exemption*, which occurs when there is some CAT, which may allow the student to be exempted from parts of the programme of study. In the case of Albert Ainsworth (Action Plan 2), if he were to take a programme which includes a Management Unit, he may well be exempted from all or part of it because he holds a Diploma in Management Studies.

Some courses also allow credit transfer. This is because the CAT is directly relevant to the target programme. In Judith Smith's case, if she was entering a programme such as Childhood Studies, she may receive some credits because of her nursery nursing experience. If this was the case, the credit would be transferred directly onto the student's profile, and this will reduce the number of credits needing to be attained.

Tutors may also consider the value of CAT from another useful perspective. If, when planning a programme of learning, the lecturer takes into account any prior knowledge and experience which the learners as a group may have previously developed, it often helps to counteract any potential there may be for student disinterest or demotivation. For example, reference during teaching to any ideas, people, places or theories which are already familiar to the group will help to reduce any anxieties they may have and provide valuable shared interest and communication points which may quickly be built upon.

These mutual frameworks for the structuring of concepts and principles provide wonderful signposts or reference points which may be used over and over again during the forthcoming teaching. In simple terms, there needs to be a system integrated into the planned programme which not only credits the prior learning that has already taken place, but also values learners as a group by designing a programme which builds on their experience and meets their needs. If they are to fully achieve their potential, the tutor needs to ensure that the learner can transfer existing skills and knowledge to either a new setting or a new learning programme. Learners need to know what is to be learned so that they can make an informed choice when planning their own personal needs.

It is true that some learners do want to run before they can walk, and this may be linked to the fact that they have identified some gaps in their own learning and are eager to address these omissions. In other cases and possibly because of their previous learning experiences, some learners lack motivation. If the tutor is to help such learners to progress, the underpinning causes of demotivation need to be identified and addressed in both a confidential and empathetic manner.

One method some tutors use to obtain details about each of the individuals in a group is to use a questionnaire, which asks for specific details about each individual. This approach needs sensitivity on the part of the teacher, particularly in the wording of the questions and also in making it clear when introducing the questionnaire that it is optional. From the experience of those who use such a data collection method, the process *cannot* occur prior to the commencement of the programme, as it is human nature not to disclose personal information to an 'unknown entity' (i.e. a tutor they have yet to develop any trust in).

Practice has shown that if a carefully worded document is issued some two to three sessions into the programme and is complemented by a verbal explanation relating to the usefulness of such optional information, most students will agree to complete the questionnaire. Also, of course, students would have to be reassured that this information is for short-term use and will not be kept on a database. Some of the most useful areas to collect data about are given below, together with a rationale for obtaining this information:

- **Number and nature of dependants** – to ascertain the demands on the student's time outside of the learning context.

- **Medical conditions or learning difficulties** – that might affect learning (this may include illnesses such as asthma, diabetes and epilepsy, as well as barriers to learning such as dyslexia and colour blindness).
- **Previous related learning** – allowing the tutor to attempt to ascertain the prior experience and knowledge an individual might have, as well as academic ability with regard to the curriculum content.
- **Individual expectations of the programme** – potential insight into additional reasons why the learner has chosen to come onto the programme, e.g. raising confidence, building self-esteem, proving to themselves that they can achieve, etc.).
- **Fears of the programme** – as with previous topic, responses in this area often highlight the major concerns of the potential learner. Those who come into post-compulsory education for a 'second chance' often have a strong fear of failure. It is crucial that the tutor is aware of the strength of these concerns.

Activity 3m Individual Needs

Return to your Focus Learning Group and, without naming them, reflect on how the above sort of information would enable you to more effectively meet their needs, improve their learning experience and enhance their potential for achievement.

Provided that tutors use the data collected through the suggested questionnaire in a sensitive and confidential manner, it will often give an excellent insight into the basic needs of their learners and provide the vital knowledge necessary for an effective planning process.

3.8 Teaching and learning styles

In theory therefore, by following the above guidelines you should be able to ensure that your students have access to the most suitable course and that they will then go on to enjoy it and achieve success. However, the reality is that some students will still struggle with certain topics and in particular with certain teaching styles and methods. Try the following activity as an introduction to teaching and learning styles.

Activity 3n Solving Problems

Consider your focus group of learners and the different ways in which individuals respond to work that you set them, and how these responses may differ depending on the problem in hand and the method/s of investigating it.

It is clear that some students are able to understand a task or problem fairly quickly and others take longer, and then there are some who will ask you to explain everything several times. Intriguingly, it is not always the same students who fall into these groups and it seems that the *way you teach them* has an effect on how receptive they are and how they succeed with the task in hand. This phenomenon is at the heart of the development of what have been called 'learning styles'. Now try the following activity.

Activity 3o Starting a Task

Ask yourself whether you would read instructions first before assembling something, or whether you would prefer to get on with it and learn by trial and error.

3.8.1 The learning style imperative

We clearly differ physically and it is accepted that these differences are genetically based. What is less easily seen is that we also differ in our approaches to learning. Faced with the above problem, some would first read the instructions and others would immediately begin experimenting in order to get a feel for the task. There are many pedagogical theories related to our preferred styles of learning and this has been a growing area for research from both an educational and a psychological perspective for more than 40 years.

By the late 1990s, so convinced were influential policy-makers and educational managers that this was a way forward in improving teaching and learning within post-16 education, that in many colleges part of the induction of new students *required* the administration of a 'learning styles inventory' which was often a version of the Honey and Mumford approach (see below). The concept became so powerful by the early years of this millennium that the previous national standards for post-16 (FENTO) stressed the importance of an awareness of students' learning styles, and often it was one of the prerequisites for the funding of some college programmes. As a consequence of this, most programmes went through the process of implementing a learning styles inventory, often using computer-based administration and analysis. However, such was the pressure on lecturers, it is understandable that only a minority were realistically able to adjust their teaching styles to accommodate (according to the analysis undertaken) the range of learning styles within the average class.

3.8.2 Investigating the value of learning styles

Fortunately LLUK have *not* incorporated the use of a learning styles analysis within their assessment criteria because the value of attempting to identify a student's learning style has become a much more contentious issue since the publication of research funded by the LSRC (Learning and Skills Research Centre) and undertaken at Newcastle University by Coffield *et al.* (2004). The LSRC report on this research also stressed the complexity of the notion of individual learning styles and the possibility of teachers being able to realistically respond to them. However, the authors were predominantly concerned that the underpinning theories and the various data-gathering instruments had not been subjected to sufficient empirical examination and they posed a range of questions about the use of learning style analysis as a basis for teaching decisions within the Lifelong Learning Sector including:

1. Do students/employees receive an overview of the whole field (of Learning Styles Inventories) with an assessment of the strengths and weaknesses or the various data-collection methods?
2. Are they introduced to just one model and if so, on what grounds?
3. How knowledgeable are the tutors (who implement these questionnaires) about research on learning styles?
4. How well do learning style instruments predict attainment in post-16 learning?
5. Are students being labelled by tutors, or are they labelling themselves, or do they develop a broader repertoire of learning styles?
6. Do students and staff know how to monitor and improve their own learning via metacognition (thinking about thinking)?

A number of teachers and researchers involved in the use of learning styles analysis have also expressed serious concerns about (5) above. The researchers would like to see a rationalization, consolidation and integration of the more psychometrically robust instruments and models used to investigate learning styles, but they are concerned that there are significant pressures obstructing such a rationalization, for example:

1. Learning style instruments tend to be developed by relatively autonomous university departments with no one organization coordinating or quality controlling such research and development.
2. Fortunes are being made through the sale of inventories, manuals, videotapes, publications, workshops, etc., so the likelihood is that the development of learning style instruments will proliferate.
3. With the potential to administer, complete and score such learning style tests online, it is now a simple matter to get large groups of students to complete what may be an unreliable inventory in order to confirm or refute 'some trivial hypothesis'.

3.8.3 Proliferation without consolidation

To illustrate the concerns expressed in 3.8.1 above, one summary within the Coffield *et al.* report identifies 30 examples of dichotomies or opposites which are used as the basis for analysis. Of these, 20 are provided below to illustrate the problem of researchers moving on to new learner categories without any reference to the results of investigating previous similar dichotomies:

Table 3.1 Dichotomies used as a basis for the investigation of learning styles

activists v. reflectors	convergers v. divergers	imaginative v. analytical	organizers v. innovators
activists v. theorists	deep v. surface	initiators v. reasoners	pragmatists v. theorists
adaptors v. innovators	extroverts v. introverts	judging v. perceiving	sensing v. intuition
assimilators v. explorers	globalists v. analysts	left brainers v. right brainers	thinking v. feeling
concrete v. abstract learners	holist v. serialist	non-committers v. plungers	verbalizers v. imagers

To Coffield and his colleagues, the sheer number of dichotomies indicates a serious failure of coherence between a number of accumulated theories and the absence of well-grounded findings, tested through replication. In addition, the complexity of the learning styles field and the lack of an overarching, collaborative synthesis of the main models (or any dialogue between the leading proponents of the individual models) leads to the impression of a research area that has become so fragmented and isolated that it now appears to be ineffective as a viable educational tool.

3.8.4 Psychometric weaknesses

A set of key indicators which the Coffield *et al.* investigation used to establish the value of the various learning styles instruments was a combination of four criteria which any valid research into psychometric (measurement of mental processes) tests would need to meet:

- Internal consistency: the manner in which data is collected and processed.
- Test/retest reliability: the consistency between applications of the measure.
- Construct validity: it should test what it intended to test – no less and no more.
- Predictive validity: it should be possible to use the data collected to accurately predict outcomes and implications and consequently the test must be based on unbiased data collection and accurate measurement.

Of the four examples of learning style measurements which are discussed below, three of them only met **one** of the above criteria. Gregorc was successful with regard to *Predictive validity*, Honey and Mumford and Kolb met the *Test/retest* criteria and Entwistle met both the *Internal validity* and the *Construct validity* criteria. Coffield *et al.* believe that '. . . too much is being expected of relatively simple, self-report tests'. Kolb's LSI (Learning Style Indicators) now consists of no more than 12 sets of four words to choose from. Even if all the difficulties associated with self-report (i.e. the inability to categorize one's own behaviour accurately or objectively, giving socially desirable responses, etc.), are put to one side, other problems remain. For example, some of the questionnaires, such as Honey and Mumford's, force respondents to agree or disagree with 80 items such as 'People often find me insensitive to their feelings'. Richardson (1990) has pointed to a number of problems with this approach:

> [T]he respondents are highly constrained by the predetermined format of any particular questionnaire and this means that they are unable to calibrate their understanding of the individual items

against the meanings that were intended by the person who devised the questionnaire or by the person who actually administers it to them.

3.8.5 Examples of learning styles inventories

In view of the very real concerns expressed above by Coffield *et al.* it may seem pointless for us to provide examples of four models which promote the use of learning styles. However, the research above condemns the methodology and the assumptions made rather than the analytical perspective. Each of the four methods described below have been rightly criticized, but they are also valuable strategies that can be used to get an insight into how particular students approach particular problems and how they may be encouraged to use these insights to extend their methods of learning. Please try to view the examples below with an open mind, and remember that the categorizations suggested by the different methods are merely ways of looking at various learning processes and are not permanent labels.

(a) Honey and Mumford – pragmatist, activist, reflector and theorist

Building on the earlier theories of Lewin and Kolb (see previous chapter), these two researchers have identified four basic learning styles – pragmatist, activist, reflector and theorist. To Honey and Mumford (1982) a pragmatist would take a planning approach, activists like doing things, reflectors enjoy thinking about issues and experiences and the theorists enjoy analysis as a means of explaining things. Although these styles seem widely different, many teachers believe that it is possible for a teacher to plan a session which does accommodate to varying extents each of the above styles. Try the following activity.

Activity 3p Different Learning Styles

Focusing on your own teaching subject, reflect on how you might plan one of your sessions to include learning activities which appeal to each of Honey and Mumford's styles.

A simple approach would be for the tutor to present a problem (theorist), follow this with a practical (activist), then ask the students to identify another situation where the process which they are discussing would be relevant (reflector) and then plan how the process might best be implemented in that situation (pragmatist). Of course, this teaching process can very easily be carried out in a different order. Now attempt to apply the above approach to your own teaching situation by carrying out the following activity.

Activity 3q Accommodating Learning Styles Within your own Teaching

Take the above simple explanation of Honey and Mumford's approach and apply it to one of your lessons. Use the strategy suggested above in any order which is appropriate, and then give details of how each activity in turn addresses a particular learning style.

One example of a teacher's attempt to accommodate the different learning styles within an English Literature class would be to first show a video extract from *King Lear*, followed by a series of questions related to the scenes shown and then a group discussion on various aspects of the scenes and their relation to the main plot. So far, the tutor has addressed the styles of reflectors and theorists (thinking and analysing). The next part of the session may involve planning a role-play exercise related to the play that will involve all the class and then carrying it out. The pragmatists will relate well to the planning and organization of this activity and the actual role play is very appropriate for activists.

However, although these sessions will probably be well received by the learners, it is timely to add a word of caution at this point. If a tutor allows the reflector to continue reflecting and the pragmatist to continue to plan, etc., the students may still not learn a great deal despite the appropriateness of the activities. We will introduce the teaching and learning cycle here as a way of explaining this apparent contradiction. You may notice its similarities to our 'Book Structure' in Table 1.1 in Chapter 1.

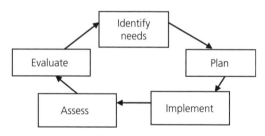

Teaching and learning cycle

3.8.6 Teaching and learning cycle

The above is a simple but useful model in which, first of all, the teacher identifies the needs of the learners. This is basically what this chapter has been about and as you know, we have already looked at the use of diagnostic assessment and the use of the resultant individual action plans. We have also considered ways of identifying our students' learning styles using such techniques as learning style questionnaires. Hopefully then, we are now in a position to plan a structured lesson based on these identified needs.

Following the above model, we next deliver the planned session, check student learning using appropriate assessment techniques, evaluate how the process went and then (armed with this knowledge) start the process off again. This time, our experience of delivering the planned session and our evaluation of the result, will usually have changed our perception of the *actual* needs of the learners.

It is worth pointing out that as teachers and trainers, we, too, notionally have particular preferred learning styles and we may well be very effective in some aspects of the above teaching and learning process, but not as good in other areas. This may be illustrated by adding Honey and Mumford's categories to our teaching and learning model:

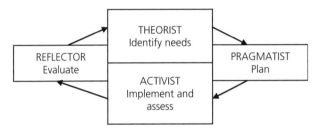

Teaching and learning model with learning styles added

Obviously, in order to optimize your development as a teacher or trainer, it will be necessary for you to improve in those areas which might not necessarily come naturally to you. If you are good at planning but not as effective in delivering, then you will know you must improve in that active area. Alternatively you may be totally comfortable with the actual teaching process, but are reluctant to reflect on the process. Kolb (1984), Honey and Mumford (1982), Gibbs (1988), etc., would all say that in order to maximize development you must be willing to push yourself round the above cycle. This is also true of your learners. Teaching and learning involves encouraging the learner to progress from their 'comfortable/ familiar' position on the cycle and carry on round until they complete the full circuit. Only then can the learners reflect on their own experiences and actions. In this way, we develop Schon's (1987) 'knowing-in-action' as discussed in the previous chapter.

Therefore, although as an essentially practical person, the *activist* may be more inclined to move immediately on to the next task, he or she needs to *reflect* about the implications of what has taken place, before the subtle signs and meanings are forgotten. Similarly, even though he or she may be unwilling, the *reflector* needs to be persuaded to *develop a theory*, which will enable the fruits of his or her contemplation to be applied.

This is one of the more difficult aspects of teaching and this is where the skills of planning a session become most significant. The tutor needs to consider activities and exercises that will move each learner through the cycle, so that each one can become aware of and further develop the important skills which lie in areas that their natural inclinations may have led them to neglect. So the *theorist* should be encouraged to *apply* his or her ideas to practice, and the *pragmatist* should move on from merely planning to becoming *actively involved* in the task.

Consider ways of moving your own learners on by trying the following activity.

Activity 3r Moving Round the Cycle

Take the above simple explanation of Honey and Mumford's approach and apply it to one of your lessons. Use the strategy suggested above (in any order that is appropriate) and then give details of how each activity would, in turn, address a particular learning style.

As we said earlier in this chapter (Section 3.5.1) a well-used starting point for FE and HE teaching is to begin with the exposition of a theory (the deductive approach). You then need to consider how you could introduce some activities based on the theory in order to develop an understanding of the key concepts. You could encourage your students to become engaged in a planning process such as applying the theory in a particular situation (e.g. surveying students using theodolites to measure a road junction). You might choose to start with a practical exercise (the inductive approach) such as applying the concepts to be learned within a given context (e.g. students learning a foreign language asking for directions to a particular destination). You may then decide to follow this up by involving the learners in some sort of experimentation (e.g. using a key concept in another way as when catering students move from making bread to baking pastry). Problem solving could be used as a means of reintroducing the theory (e.g. asking accountancy students to analyse an annual financial report in order to identify the main features of the particular company's performance). The final stage may involve some sort of evaluation where you could ask the students to report on their perception of the learning process and say how it could be changed or improved.

(b) Gordon Pask – Holist v Serialist

Pask (1976) built on the above notions of learners adopting a preferred approach to understanding. He identified *two* strategies that students adopt when learning. The first of these he called the **Holist Strategy,** and he identified particular attributes as common to those students/trainees who predominantly used that approach to learning. Such learners preferred a **broad, global approach to learning** and were by nature idiosyncratic and intuitive. In addition, they were impatient of rules, structures and details. During their learning, they liked to jump in anywhere and to work from a big picture back to detail. This type of learner may well demonstrate the following familiar characteristics:

Holist Strategy Characteristics	
Flexible and creative	Good visual memory
Good at improvisation	Inspired
Good at problem solving	Risk taker
Lateral thinker	Good in discussions
Able to have a good overview	Able to make unusual connections

Pask's second type of learning approach is the **Serialist Strategy,** and he noted that this type of learner likes a **step-by-step approach** with a narrow focus. In contrast to a holistic slant, this type of trainee/student enjoys rules and structures. They build their learning around steps or stages and can deal with these either in order or separately in isolation and will work towards the bigger picture through a series of small steps. Pask also noted that they were logical rather than intuitive and factual rather than using their own experience. Characteristics which this group demonstrate include:

Serialist Strategy Characteristics	
Good sequential memory	Good reading and writing skills
Clear concept of boundaries	Good logical thinking
Achievement of steady measurable progress	Ordered and organized

Now try the following activity.

Activity 3s Holistic or Serialist Learners

Write about some examples of your students demonstrating the two learning strategies identified by Gordon Pask.

Perhaps you have someone who likes to have an overview of a topic in relation to previous learning. Maybe there are students who can only deal with small amounts of learning at a time, while others want to know it all at once.

Although this identification of preferred strategies will give you some insight into Pask's theories, take care not to place your learners into overly rigid categories. Remember that students do respond to the situation they are in, and their learning can be affected by many different factors. Learning theories are there to give you an insight into student needs and should not be treated simply as a set of rules. Use the following activity to summarize your reaction to the styles considered so far.

Activity 3t Responding to Learning Style Theory

Reflect on the learning styles covered so far and decide how, why and if these theories are important to teaching and learning. If they are, what are the implications for practice? If you accept the notion of learners being individual and often idiosyncratic, how should a teacher respond in the reality of the practice setting?

One practical thing you can do when you commence a programme is to provide the learners with an overview. This will make clear to the learner what will be taking place over the coming weeks. For example, you might tell them that:

> This programme will consist of a series of taught sessions that consist of a one-hour input by subject specialists. Following this hour, students could be put into groups to discuss the issue under study. Following the group sessions, students will be expected to present their findings to their peers and to accept questions. Topics covered will include the following . . .

Given this information, a holistic learner would probably search out information on the unfamiliar subjects, while a serialist would be comfortable in the knowledge that programme members are expected to research topics at regular intervals. In addition, the tutor can provide a more detailed week-by-week breakdown of activities and topics that will be covered over the course. This allows a more seralistic learner to plan and order their readings, research, etc. in a structured way. Using a framework such as this allows the student to either break down the programme into manageable slices, or for them to research the entire course at once. Their learning style will influence what they do, but it is their choice, you provide the framework that they as individuals can use according to their needs.

(c) Anthony Gregorc – left brain/right brain

Gregorc (1984) developed a further model of learning which has some similarities to Pask's, but is founded on the concept that there are *two* channels through which the mind receives and interprets information. This is closely related to theories about the way in which the two hemispheres of the brain process information. However, Gregorc calls his pathways '*media-tion channels*' and considers that they are primarily involved with the *perception* and *ordering* of information.

Considering first the process of perception, Gregorc claims that some people like to deal with thoughts, concepts and feelings in a reflective and theoretical manner and defines this as *abstract thought*. He claims that other people prefer to deal with a 'real' world that they can sense and experience. This type has a *concrete* or more solid sense of perception.

Within the 'ordering' mediation channel, Gregorc has noted other differences between individuals. He believes that some individuals like to think sequentially and in a linear manner, while others prefer to think in a random and non-logical fashion. He identifies the following characteristics:

- **concrete sequential:** very practical and ordered, preferring to work with facts and reality
- **concrete random:** more experimental than ordered, but still fairly practical
- **abstract sequential:** logical and rational, preferring concepts and patterns
- **abstract random:** more concerned with feeling and emotions, good at 'insight' into problems.

In order to build on this model, try the following activity.

Activity 3u Feelings and Rationality

Assume that you are teaching your own subject to a group of learners and you wish them all to undertake a task which will give them an insight into a particular process. Then consider how best you could present the task to a student/trainee who, being primarily concerned with feelings, falls into Gregorc's *abstract random* category. Next, think how you might come at the same task from a different angle in order to encourage another learner, who is very practical and who prefers to operate with facts in an orderly manner (*concrete sequential*), to tackle the exercise.

As a simple, hypothetical approach to the above fairly complex analysis we will take as an example the familiar process of changing a wheel on a car. Although essentially practical, this task does require some understanding of simple theory, for example in relation to gaining effective leverage, safely securing and supporting the vehicle while the wheel is taken off, or ensuring the even distribution of pressure when tightening up the wheel nuts.

As the process of changing a wheel is essentially sequential and practical, learners who prefer an *abstract random* approach will probably present a particular challenge to a tutor attempting, in their own interests, to persuade them to conform to a particular safety regime. However, in setting the context of the task, the teacher can deliberately introduce a number of elements which can be tackled in an imaginative or creative way, before the learner gets down to the prescribed procedure (in this case changing the wheel) which must be done carefully in a particular order.

For example, the time of day, weather or situation (e.g. motorway hard shoulder) may add unexpected problems which must be addressed to ensure the safety of the passengers and the person changing the wheel.

The *concrete sequential* learners will be comfortable with following the structure of an established routine and with the practical processes involved. However, it may be good to challenge them by suggesting an unusual context.

Coping with an unusual situation will be a welcome challenge to the *concrete random* student but their inclination to experiment would be challenged by the need to follow a precise order.

Finally, the *abstract sequential* learner would enjoy exploring how the various concepts involved in the process (i.e. leverage, pressure, distribution) build into rules and procedures to be followed. They may be surprised to be confronted with practical difficulties such as a tight wheel nut or the need to chock the wheels.

(d) Marton et al. (1984) – surface or deep learning

This framework was designed for HE students and its most important element is that data should be collected directly from learners themselves through self-reports and interviews. Furthermore, the content and setting should be those actually involved in learning. Research based upon this phenomenological approach was designed to examine students' experiences and discovered their attitudes, motivations and purposes in relation to learning. Coffield *et al.* (2004) felt it to be

> a sound basis for discussing effective and ineffective strategies for learning and for diagnosing students' existing approaches, orientations and strategies.

However, they felt that it would need to be redesigned for use in such contexts as 14–19 provision and stressed that the model should not be divorced from the central process which involves a complex inventory of attitudes and dispositions. They also stressed that students should not be labelled as 'deep' or 'surface' learners, as has happened in some research projects using similar methodologies.

3.9 Student learning strategies

Marton *et al.*'s (1984) investigation (above) of student strategies for learning does of course indicate a serious concern which many teachers and educational researchers have, in these times of finance-driven accountability regimes within colleges and schools. Any educational process should have the ultimate aim of developing learner independence in relation to the subject they are studying, so that they will eventually be able to function effectively and independently without the support of their teachers. However, it is often the case that teachers and their departments who are seriously concerned about inspection-related funding, will condone 'teaching to the test', which narrows not only the students' focus but also their breadth of study, and will inevitably lead to a type of 'surface' learning. This approach does not promote independence as it often leads to impoverished learning involving replication rather than the development of an individual perspective.

Activity 3v Emancipation or Dependence?

List some of the ways in which teachers may, either deliberately or unconsciously, encourage learner dependence.

To teachers under serious pressure to ensure high levels of student achievement, the above may seem to be an exaggerated interpretation of the present educational climate. However, if these views are placed in the context of the beginning of this chapter, where we discussed how learners might be encouraged to trust their tutors, it is a consistent philosophy. Teachers should always have the interests of their learners at heart, and spoon-feeding to ensure good results is not in their best interests. It does encourage 'surface' learning and it does develop, at the very least, prolonged dependence on the teacher. It may not be achievable with all students, but the aim should be to encourage the development of what may be called 'informed scepticism' where students are willing to ask questions and are reluctant to take anything at face value.

As discussed above, at the present time teachers have to operative within a climate of strict accountability and are only too aware that they (and their department or institution) will be judged by their students' performance. Under these circumstances, it is only natural for teachers to monitor student progress systematically, and to apply remedial teaching as soon as there is a hint of failure. Although it may be argued that this is the responsible thing to do, too much supervision often encourages learner dependence and the adoption by students of surface learning strategies in order to meet the assessment requirements. We will discuss these relationships in more detail in the following chapters, but it is worth noting here that cognitive learning is often enhanced when students are allowed to make and then correct their own mistakes. For now we will raise the issue by introducing the continuum below as an indication of the various ways in which a teacher's good intentions may well be counterproductive.

Our consideration of the different *models* of learning theories has indicated that it is useful for tutors to understand the ways in which their students prefer to learn so that they are able to accommodate their preferences within their sessions. These may involve simple processes, such as using interactive exchanges to build up and check understandings, or they could be more demanding such as using computer-based dissemination or deductive approaches.

Table 3.2 Learner perspective and teaching styles

Encouraging learner dependence	Encouraging learner independence
Encourage instrumental learning which addresses only the defined assessment requirements.	Get students into the habit of consolidating learning, correcting mistakes and developing new skills and a deeper interest in the subject.
Set tasks which are too easy or too difficult.	Set tasks which build appropriately on previous experience.
Explain task in great detail in order to eliminate student questions.	Don't always break things down in order to make learning easy; students encouraged to do this themselves.
Repeat things many times.	Don't always give the complete, definitive answer to students, merely hint at a way to arrive at a solution and let them know that they have to work it out.
Carry out difficult part of the exercise for the students.	Get students to discuss how they intend to go about learning something.
Belittle student attempts and compare them unfavourably with others.	Make students aware that they have a contribution to make and take notice of their views.
Supervise students to ensure they don't make mistakes.	Students allowed to work things out for themselves.
Merely mark assessed work right or wrong.	Get students to check their own work and to assess the standard attained.
Give unrealistic feedback that contains undue praise or criticism.	Give accurate feedback, which doesn't merely confirm what they have achieved but identifies how learners may progress.

It is often true that groups of students do collectively and individually develop preferences for particular teaching and learning approaches, and these may well be revealed through simple diagnostic assessment, which will in turn promote more student/student and teacher/student interaction and openness to different approaches. The ability to adapt and respond within teaching and learning situations is valuable and inevitably teaching does become an amalgamation of several styles. At all costs, resist the temptation to label students as this is a crude and damaging way to develop relationships which often results in inaccurate assumptions and crude generalizations which undermine the very purpose of teaching. After all, as a teacher you are about promoting learning and development and not permanent pigeon-holing. Tutors need to know and recognize traits in their students so that they can build on and then help these learners to develop a range of abilities that will be required for successful lifelong learning.

However, because our deliberations in this chapter clearly touch on assessment as well as structured learning, it might be useful at this point to consider how interrelated the whole teaching and learning process is and how significant the choices which teachers make about approaches, methods and styles are in relation to ultimate success.

Activity 3w Which Comes First?

Consider, once again, your own particular subject and your focus group of learners. The success of your teaching could be said to depend upon

1. your intended aims and objectives
2. the selected content
3. your chosen delivery style
4. the assessment methods
5. how effectively you evaluate your success.

Select a starting point from the above five aspects of practice and give a reason for your choice.

The teaching and learning process is cyclical, and each time you complete a cycle and prepare for the next you should consider the evaluative data and then identify possible areas for improvement. It seems obvious then that, if evaluation comes last, the above *order* must be correct. However, we stressed earlier that teaching and learning should be treated as an essentially holistic process, so we should consider the effect which each of the parts have on each other and on the whole (i.e. the total student experience). For example, although the learning outcomes identified and tested during the *assessment* stage should reflect the aims and objectives of the curriculum, sometimes assessment is defined first and may heavily influence the whole process. In other cases, some of the implicit intentions of the teaching are difficult to observe and measure. It is because of these and other significant variables that we need to hold on to a view of the whole, rather than concentrating exclusively on the disaggregated parts.

Activity 3x Purposeful Learning Environment

For the final activity of this chapter, we will look ahead to preparing evidence against the LLUK Standards which are considered in detail in Chapter 12. Within the 'Practice' component of Domain B *'Learning and Teaching'* is the following outcome:

> BP1.1 'Establish a purposeful learning environment where learners feel safe, secure, confident and valued'

Consider your Learning Focus Group identified in Chapter 1, and make an entry in your PDJ of about 200 words discussing what makes students feel 'safe, secure, confident and valued'.

3.10 Useful publications

Gregorc, A. (1984), *An Adult's Guide to Style*. New York: Harper & Row.

Gregorc writes about learning types and notes in this article that there are either concrete or abstract learners. He refers to the way that individuals think and order information in order to make sense of it. He draws on the idea that in addition learners can think in a random or ordered fashion. This gives rise to the idea that there are four different types of learner. Gregorc provides a useful questionnaire that allows the reader to determine his or her own learning style. He goes on to provide educational ideas that relate to teaching and learning in accordance with these types of styles.

Honey, P. and Mumford, A. (1982), *The Manual of Learning Styles*. Maidenhead: Peter Honey.

This is a very popular reader for educational teacher training teams. Honey and Mumford are pioneers of the concept of learning styles and this book provides a detailed account of the main learning styles that are attributed to Honey and Mumford. These are activists, pragmatists, reflectors and theorists. Each type is described in detail and a questionnaire provided which allows the reader to determine his or her own style. Aimed at teacher trainers it allows teachers to determine their own student profile, and the book indicates how this information can inform and develop teaching strategies in order to maximize learning.

Pask, G. (1976), 'Styles and Strategies of Learning'. *British Journal of Educational Psychology*, 46, 128–48.

This article provides a different concept of learning styles and this relates to the idea that individuals think either in terms of a whole, or in small pieces and in a serialist fashion. Pask gives an academic account that is based on psychological theory and describes the underlying reasons for these types of thinking pattern. He provides an educational rationale for the development of these styles of thought and this has been an influential book on educational practice.

3.11 Useful websites

www.brains.org

A good site for learning styles.

www.csrnet.org/csrnet/articles/student-learning-styles.html

Applying what we know: student learning styles.

www.demos.co.uk/publications//aboutlearning

David Hargreaves's site.

www.edwdebono.com

Edward de Bono's site.

www.lsda.org.uk/

Learning and Skills Development Agency.

www.pzweb.harvard.edu/Pls/HG.htm

Project Zero which details Howard Gardner's work.

Table 3.3 Process justifications for assessing learners' needs

FAQs at the stage of:	Threshold award	Associate certificate	Full award
Why do it?	The essential starting point for effective teaching is to know your students. To help anyone to learn you need to find out about their current knowledge, ability, aptitudes and motivations	To make your assessment of the needs of learners more accurate you need to develop appropriate techniques. You should aim to accommodate individual learning styles, needs and preferences and be aware of the ways in which the physical and social environment will influence and motivate learning.	In order to effectively reflect on your ability to assess the needs of learners you need to be sure that you have really understood the individual characteristics of your learners, and the manner in which they are influenced and motivated by the total learning context.
Where are we going?	You are attempting to optimize the provision for your particular learners. This will involve recognizing and valuing, and helping them to recognize and value, their previous learning.	You are moving towards an understanding of each group of learners and how their individual characteristics influence the interactions and responses of the whole group.	You are evaluating your own performance in order to become more precise in the way you identify the very subtle variations in each situation which affect the quality of student experience.
How do we get there?	Begin to move beyond intuitive decisions (as valuable as they may be on occasion) towards deliberately collecting and analysing appropriate data about your learners without infringing data-collection guidelines. Use any information provided by the institution about their previous performance, their expectations or their preferred learning styles.	Collate information on previous educational background. Test for literacy/numeracy and other key skills. Test for subject specific skills/knowledge. Use induction exercises, 'ice-breakers', progress reviews, student attitude surveys, counselling sessions, tutorials, etc. in order to gain more useful and varied knowledge. Support the learners as they settle in and respond to their new environment.	All of your judgements and actions related to optimizing student learning should be evaluated in terms of their appropriateness, flexibility, timing, accuracy, breadth, depth, etc., in order to continually improve your provision.
Is this the best way?	You need to remain aware of all indicators of your learners' needs, rather than accepting all provided data at face value. Talk to the students, consider their progress and their evaluations of the work they have been doing.	College or departmental procedures may well be adequate, but you may need to improve your own access to general information, or to set up your own diagnostic or monitoring systems. Confirm that you have a flexible system for recording students' prior learning and achievement and for diagnosing student needs. You will need to effectively monitor student progress and identify potential problems.	Confirm that all of the information is available and accessible. Check if there are problems balancing accessibility and confidentiality. Find out if students are given opportunities to talk about their needs. Consider whether your record system is too paper bound and if IT could help with record keeping. Ensure that you take the initiative in identifying student need. Evaluate how sensitive your systems of identifying and recording needs are.

When is the right time?	Check if you have appropriate information before you meet the students. Confirm what (if anything) has been done during induction.	Consider the stage at which you achieved all of the valuable information which helped you to diagnose student needs. Inevitably some would have been more valuable if it had been received earlier – how do you rectify that next time round?
	Check if reviews are used at fixed points during a programme. Confirm how progress is monitored and how you should deal effectively with diagnosed problems. Make sure you know at which point a student is considered to have failed and the ways in which they can recover from this and try again.	Confirm that the order of gathering data was the most appropriate. For example, would it be more motivating to the learners if possible APL/APEL had been identified earlier?
Who needs to know?	Initially, you and the students.	Obviously, the students themselves and then the various support appropriate agencies both within the department/faculty, the college, and externally.
	Confirm how information about students is shared and whether this information is passed on adequately to the students themselves, and to teaching and support colleagues, educational managers, parents, employers, etc.	
How do we know when we've got there?	When you feel that you know enough about your students to make reasonably well-informed decisions about what is appropriate teaching, learning and assessment.	Evaluate how effective the dissemination of information about student needs is. For example, does vital information reach support staff early enough?
	Check student satisfaction, student retention, pass rates, grades, progression, survey results, employment statistics.	
Has everyone had a fair chance?	Consider the information you have gathered on which you have based your decisions. Does the data adequately represent their experience, needs, ambitions and constraints?	Reflect on the 'value added' achieved and think not only of the outcomes gained but the distance travelled. Consider equally the less obvious learning achievements such as social abilities, improved confidence, trust, openness, etc.
	Confirm that you are asking the right questions, that your procedures are adequate to identify differences in need arising from age, sex, class, ethnicity or disability.	

4 Planning for Learning
Margaret Postance

Key Concepts

Planning, Preparation, Syllabus, Curriculum, Programme, Diversity, Awarding Bodies, Key Dates, Scheme of Work, Topics, Holistic View, Topic Order, Prioritizing, Additionality, Layout, Programme Aims, Behavioural, Non-Behavioural, Objectives, Cognitive, Affective, Psychomotor, Prerequisites.

Before you begin this chapter you may wish to check the Process Justifications (Table 4.6)

4.1 Introduction

In Chapter 1 we discussed the drive to improve standards within all sectors of education. The focus for this accountability process is, as you would expect, the quality of the learners' experience, be it during classroom teaching, fieldwork, laboratory experiments, workshop sessions, gymnasium exercises, etc. However, always underpinning these various delivery processes will be the effectiveness of the planning and preparation carried out by the teacher or trainer.

We have also stressed the individual nature of each teaching and learning situation and the importance of taking a holistic view of these complex relationships. We will further develop these themes during this chapter by stressing the need for the practitioner to not only understand the particular characteristics of these contexts, but also to effectively respond to them during the planning process.

In addition to the familiar subject specialisms, teachers must be aware of their responsibility for the incorporation into any scheme of work of a range of generic requirements, such as:

- key skill implementation
- basic skills initiatives
- ICT and ILT (information learning technology) strategies
- work-based learning
- inclusive learning
- widening participation
- lifelong learning.

4.2 Approaches to planning

Although the above more general requirements have been introduced at this early stage because it is important to bear them in mind during planning, the predominant influencing factor will always be the syllabus or programme. This may be provided by the awarding body in the form of study units, competence statements or learning outcomes and sometimes just a syllabus. Naturally, practitioners will respond in varying ways to these central prerequisites as they will be aware of the needs of their particular groups of learners (see previous chapter), their own skills and, inevitably, the demands of the host institution.

It has often been said that *if you fail to plan, then you plan to fail*. Never has this old adage been truer than it currently is within all sectors of education. Systematic planning is crucial if the delivered curriculum is to meet both the needs of the learners, the other issues previously mentioned and the various accountability processes.

However, students within the Lifelong Learning Sector share a significant, distinguishing characteristic. In no other sector is the range of learners so diverse. It is possible for a learning group to contain members from the age of 14 to 90+. Recent policy discussions (see Chapter 11) are seriously considering raising the school-leaving age to 18, and it is likely that many of these young learners will follow a vocational route. If this does happen, then the whole of the Lifelong Learning Sector will have to be prepared for some radical changes. Also, because very often in the skills sector a programme will have broad entry requirements, there may be graduates alongside those who have no prior academic achievements. In addition, a learning group may well contain people who are extremely well motivated, as well as those who feel they have to some extent been coerced into attendance.

Another familiar characteristic encountered among students in this sector are those learners who, for any number of reasons, are taking a 'second chance' to return to study and whose first experience of education was sufficiently unsupportive to leave them anxious about the whole process. It is also very possible that there will be individuals who, because of their learning difficulties, have previously been working in discrete groups separate from the mainstream.

At this point, you may well be asking whether it is possible for a teacher to effectively plan to meet the extremely varied needs of such groups of learners while, at the same time, grappling with the ever-increasing curricular demands and quality targets. Castling (1996) points the way forward:

> Planning is the bridge between your identification of learners' needs and the learning activities they undertake. It is a vital stage in the teaching/training cycle and deserves your full attention whether you are planning whole programmes, courses or single sessions. Planning is the process of making decisions about the directions that learners will take and the activities they will engage in to help them meet their long- and short-term goals. It may involve negotiation with learners and other staff, and will need to be followed up by thorough planning.

4.3 Defining the curriculum

One of the first tasks which a teacher must carry out is the thorough review of the curriculum content that is being offered. Initially, the teacher will commence this task by completing a comprehensive interpretation of either the syllabus or the criteria indicated by the awarding body. Daines and Graham (1997) suggest that:

> You may be working to an external syllabus and feel that you are compelled to teach all the content it specifies. If you find out what your students already know, and what they feel they need, you should be able to select what material is essential, what is peripheral, and what they already know sufficiently well for you to be able to move on. Syllabuses rarely indicate the structure and emphases to be placed on particular topics, nor do they usually specify the approach that should be taken. You are quite at liberty to decide, in consultation with your group, how the topic is to be tackled. There is probably much greater freedom to select and prioritize the content defined by a syllabus than would first appear. Syllabuses are as much guides as directives.

Activity 4a Syllabus or Curriculum?

We may seem at times to be using the terms 'syllabus' and 'curriculum' as though they are interchangeable. Discuss briefly how, in your experience, the two differ.

The *syllabus* is really a list or an indicative content that is usually provided by the awarding body. This may come in alternative or additional forms such as competence statements, programmes of study, directives, learning outcomes, bibliographies, etc. It is essentially static and is brought alive by the teacher's interpretation, whereupon it begins to become a *curriculum*. The curriculum is dynamic, and incorporates the whole of the learners' experience, both formal and informal. As a starting point for your planning, try Activity 4b below.

Activity 4b Moving Towards a Curriculum

Obtain a copy of your own awarding body's specifications that will be in the form of a syllabus, competence statements, directives, etc. Familiarize yourself with the content before you carry out the activities which follow.

Having studied the awarding body's guidelines, how comfortable do you feel about interpreting the content and translating it into learning experiences for your students? Is there a clear, coherent, developmental sequence identifiable in the way it is presented? Are there ambiguities, which may be difficult to resolve? Most of all, is the syllabus deliverable within the time frame specified by your institution? Additionally, do you feel that your own subject expertise is sufficient to effectively inform the curriculum and session content?

4.4 Particular needs

One of the shared goals held by the majority of learners is the need to learn and achieve. As we highlighted in the previous chapter, learners attending further education establishments also possess their own learning agendas, as well as their own preferred learning styles. Clearly, if the learning is to be considered 'effective', the planning process carried out by the tutor has to take account not only all of the above, but also the personal perceptions of the tutor in respect of their role, and their own personal style of delivery. Armitage *et al.* (1999) support this complex task by stating:

> No teaching takes place in a vacuum. Even though we may see teaching as a partly planned and partly spontaneous act, our approach to it, our interpretation of our role, our attitude to our students and our view of what we should be teaching are shaped by a variety of factors. These include our personal belief system, our own experience of being taught, our personality and our theoretical understanding of the teaching and learning process.

Activity 4c Identifying Needs

Bearing in mind your awarding body's specifications, make a list of the range of needs which must be taken into account when planning a programme of study. The list should include the institutional as well as the personal needs of the learners and the teachers. Give a brief justification for the needs that you feel should be considered, and an indication of the ways in which you might address them.

First of all, we must take into account the expected standards articulated by the awarding body in their document. These include subject coverage and the expected achievement by the learners. These are often, but not always, expressed as learning outcomes, which we will discuss in more detail below. As a lead in to this, first try Activity 4d below.

Activity 4d Awarding Body Requirements

Summarize the range of awarding body requirements that you are aware of, and indicate how you would expect to meet these.

The learners' needs will usually include new skills and knowledge, but they will also seek reassurance in relation to other areas because most learners within post-compulsory education have far more than academic needs. For many who attend our establishments, life experiences colour their perception of what they find when commencing their chosen learning programme. Tutors need to consider these characteristics and how they may respond to them. Above all, learners need to feel valued if they are to fully achieve their goals. The tutor should ensure that the learner can transfer existing skills and knowledge to either a new setting or a new learning programme. Learners need to know what is to be learned so that they can make an informed choice when planning their own personal approach. Many learners will wish to run before they can walk because, often for the first time in their lives, they have had assistance in systematically identifying gaps in their own learning and now urgently wish to fill them.

Other learners may lack motivation, possibly because previous learning experiences have not been successful. If the tutor is to help such learners to progress, the underpinning causes of their anxiety need to be elicited and addressed in both a confidential and empathetic manner.

Activity 4e Learners' Needs

As we develop our scheme of work, the next few activities will focus on your learners. To establish consistency and for the process to be developmental, you should use the same familiar learning group during these tasks. Identify which of your student cohorts you will use and then summarize the particular needs of these learners. Think in terms of both their personal and practical requirements.

Finally, there will be a number of institutional needs, which should be taken into account. The obvious ones are timetabling, key dates and use of resources:

- Most teaching providers are obliged to operate fairly complex systems to ensure that teaching sessions occur at the required time and in the designated venue. Nothing upsets new students more than being unable to find their class at the published time because it isn't being held in the room advertised. Often there are good reasons for this, but it still makes the student feel inadequate or frustrated, and if the experience is repeated it will have a serious effect on retention.
- The planning of a programme must also take into account the important dates that have been previously decided by the institution or the awarding body. These dates may be rigidly set in order to accommodate examinations, internal/external verification, submission of results, award ceremonies, etc.
- Many courses require access to institutional resources that are in great demand and so there must be an effective allocation system. One obvious example is the library, but there are many others including ILT, directed study materials, sports facilities, laboratories, workshops, etc.

Activity 4f Institutional Needs

Consider the above bullet points as you summarize the institutional needs, but also remember such requirements as enrolment, retention, inclusive learning, widening participation, etc.

4.5 Schemes of work

Now, having developed an understanding of the needs within your own learning context, you can begin to move your 'plan' towards fruition in the form of a scheme of work. This is essentially a strategy for turning the static nature of a prescribed syllabus into an active, living curriculum composed of relevant and beneficial, formal and informal student experiences.

We should consider the following important 'component parts' when beginning our design of a scheme of work:

- the course/programme aims
- the learning outcomes/objectives
- the content (subject matter)
- the teaching and learning strategies (methods)
- ways of monitoring and reviewing learning
- methods of assessing achievement
- approaches to course/programme evaluation.

It is worth remembering at this stage that schemes of work (which may well have been perceived by many in the past as merely a 'paper exercise'), while remaining a significant tool in the process of successful and effective planning, have also moved to a key position within the quality framework.

The scheme of work should identify the *topics* to be covered within the programme under study. Simply put, a topic is an aspect of the subject being taught which can be presented as a separate learning focus. In practical terms, you may decide to use a particular topic for each session, or a topic may span a number of sessions. Of course, we must remember that, in the new sector, the delivery of a curriculum and the sessions within it may well change to be quite unique. This may be particularly so in industry and business centres, where the training might need to be block-delivered or taught at weekends in order to avoid disruption to the day-to-day work of the establishment. Try the following activity.

Activity 4g Topic Identification

Identify the topics that a syllabus you are familiar with may be usefully broken down into for the benefit of a particular group of learners (preferably the learning group you identified earlier).

Of course, you would expect each teacher to disaggregate a study programme into topics in a different way to his or her colleagues. This is because you will be looking for learning entities, i.e. topics that can stand alone as a basis for teaching which are appropriate to your particular learners. This is always, in a sense, an artificial process because understanding much of what is contained in a syllabus is dependent upon having a grasp of other parts of the learning process, or developing a holistic view. However, because learning is delivered in digestible 'chunks' the separation into topics is an unavoidable process. Some teachers will feel that the syllabus naturally falls into themes, each of which contains selected topics. Others will perceive it as a series of developing concepts or a linear progression. Topic identification will often reflect a preferred teaching style, but it is important to remember that the resulting curriculum should also respond to the students' preferred learning styles (see Chapter 3). Once identified, the topics will be presented in a particular order and it is important to consider the learners as you grapple with this structure. There may be times when you deliberately use a more 'inductive' teaching approach by introducing your learners to something new without prior warning in order to develop their skills and confidence in tackling the unknown. However, generally it is important that the learning process moves the student from the 'known to the unknown', so that learning is perceived by them to be logical and sequential. This systematic process of development will often help to successfully nurture the skills of retention, recall and application. Now try the following activity.

Activity 4h Sequencing

Using your previously developed list of topics, develop a notional order for your programme of study. Remember to also consider how the order you select will fit in with such institutional imperatives as key assessment deadlines, venue availability, vacations, etc.

Obviously, the manner in which you sequence a programme is extremely important. However, there are so many variables involved in each of these difficult curricular decisions that, during its implementation, some parts will, inevitably, be more successful than others. Even so, the next time you deliver the programme, other areas that have previously gone well may cause you problems. This can be extremely frustrating, but unfortunately, the cumulative effect of such factors as student group dynamics, your own performance, institutional pressures etc. cannot be predicted with absolute certainty.

The following suggestions may be helpful, but please avoid treating them as definitive rules. As you would expect, the most useful guidance will come from your learners themselves in the form of formal and informal, evaluative feedback (see Chapter 9).

- *Start with the easiest topics first* – this will help to reduce any threat which the learners may perceive, and will give them the opportunity of being motivated by some achievement before progressing to more difficult and challenging topics.

- *Logical sequence* – in many subjects there will be a clear order for the topics which learners need to progress through and understand before moving on to more complex learning, i.e. 'known to the unknown'.
- *Timing* – clearly the length of time a particular topic will take to deliver may influence its position within your scheme. It is unwise to commence a topic if it cannot be completed before a vacation. Timing can also apply to those curricular areas where there might be seasonal considerations, e.g. catering, floristry and horticulture. Here, the availability of materials, or the production of specific items may be related to or governed by the time of the year.
- *Commence with topics which you will enjoy teaching* – remember, moving from the known to the unknown applies to tutors as well as learners! Teachers are far more intrinsically motivated when delivering a learning session they know well and have had success with in previous programmes. Conveniently, this approach will also give you more time to consider the less-familiar topics and prepare an approach which most effectively meets the needs of the learning group.
- *Meet the assessment schedules* – many of the current awarding bodies have pre-set dates within their programmes by which time the learners need to complete various forms of assessment (see also Chapter 9). If this is the case, it is particularly important that the order of scheme topics is compatible with the specified assessment dates.

Activity 4i Confirming the Order

Revisit the session order you devised for Activity 4h and see if your notional plan does the following:

1. plays to your strengths
2. allows for awarding body requirements
3. still has a logical order if the above bullet points were implemented.

In addition to sequencing, the planning of learning must also take into account the *quantity* of topics to be covered. Realistically speaking, it is generally true that most syllabi have more information contained within them than there is time to effectively deliver. Consequently, another difficult task for the tutor is the development of a system of prioritization, which will ensure that the most important content is delivered.

Activity 4j Prioritizing

Look again at the topic order you have developed. Have you already excluded some areas of the curriculum, which you feel you haven't time to deliver? Have you a clear idea of what you would omit if any internal or external college influences brought further pressure to bear on the teaching time available? Try to indicate those areas, which are, regrettably, the most expendable.

There will obviously be particular institutional requirements, which impinge on teaching time and cannot be identified here. However, the following guidelines may help you to develop a policy for prioritizing curriculum topics and activities. Include topics which the learners:

- *MUST know* – if these areas are omitted it will cause serious damage to the overall learning experience and may possibly lead to non-achievement of learning outcomes and even the target award.
- *SHOULD know* – these are the areas which really need to be included in the programme in order for the learners to have as full an understanding of the content as possible.
- *COULD know* – these are the topics which might offer 'additionality' to the programme. These areas are clearly related to the subject, but should they be omitted, they would not be detrimental to the students' successful completion of the programme. This then is the 'flexible' section of the scheme which will include topics that may be cut should one or more of the above 'must' and 'should' areas take longer than originally planned.

Activity 4k Flexible Content

Looking back at your evolving curriculum, identify those topics, which you may have omitted because you felt they were less essential and also those you may have included, but which you felt were marginal to the students' ultimate goal. Use these topics to structure potential additionality should, for some reason or other, the currently available time resources be increased.

The scheme of work is the first, very important step to the effective management of teaching and learning. If you are a member of a team, each of whom is teaching the same or similar subjects, then obviously it would be very beneficial for this group of tutors to work collaboratively to ensure that the final content represents, as well as is possible, each of the member's preferences.

In a lot of Lifelong Learning establishments, the schemes of work are required to be passed to a line or quality manager in order to ensure that both the document and its content meet the standards set by both the LLUK and the employing institution. Writing a scheme of work can be tedious, but, providing that you use a thorough, holistic approach that considers all of the aspects suggested above, it will pay dividends throughout the delivery of the programme. Clearly, it is important to remember that a scheme of work is a flexible document, which should not be perceived as being set in 'tablets of stone'. Throughout the delivery of the programme it is important that you should monitor the progress of the students to ensure that their learning experiences are beneficial and that the curriculum is progressing at a suitable pace and pitch (see Chapter 10 for further information about evaluation). As we discussed in Chapter 2, effective teachers are consciously reflective practitioners who develop the habit of continuously questioning themselves about the purpose of their actions. With regard to planning and preparation, Minton (1991) suggests that we should ask ourselves the following useful questions:

WHO?

Who am I going to teach?

What age are they? What is their background?

Why are they in this class?

What do they want, or what do they need to learn?

Why do they need to learn it?

What are they going to learn?

What do they know? Or what can they do already?

What are they expecting of me?

What are they going to learn?

What do they have to do in order to learn that?

What do they need in order to do that?

What are they going to learn with?

What do I have to do in order to provide that?

What do I have to do to help them learn?

WHERE?

Where are they going to learn? Or where am I going to teach?

What kind of help and support will they find there?

What kind of difficulties are they likely to find there?

What equipment can they and I use?

How do I get hold of it, set it up, find out how to use it?

What reorganization and preparation must I do?

WHEN?

How much time have I and they got for each class? And for the programme?

What time of day will it happen?

How often will they meet?

What might be the effects of time of day or frequency?

HOW?

Where are they starting from? Where should I start?

How are they going to learn?

How am I going to teach? What pace of learning?

How will we agree a learning goal?

How will I get them working and committed?

Can I assume that they will want to learn what I teach?

How do I engage them in the learning?

What kind of problems are they likely to have in learning?

What can I do to make it easier to do?

How can I anticipate these problems and make it easier?

How shall I know whether they are learning – and what?

How shall I get feedback, and how shall I use it?

How should I adapt what I do to what they need?

How flexible should my learning/teaching programme be?

Having used Minton's checklist to confirm that your intended scheme of work is complete, you now need to find an appropriate presentation format. You will probably be required, by your institution or by the awarding body, to incorporate considerable administrative information in addition to the topics to be covered. Some information that may be required could include:

- the venue
- the academic year
- the group to be 'taught'
- the proposed number of learners
- the person/s responsible for the scheme design
- general aims of the programme
- assessment strategies for the programme
- application of key skill areas; minimum core inclusion; resource-based learning/ICT (information communication technology)/ILT (information learning technology).

Activity 4I Scheme of Work Layout

You should now be in a position to gather together the information you have developed and present it as a Scheme of Work. Most establishments will have an in-house pro forma, which they use for this. A completed first page of an imaginary scheme of work is included as an example overleaf. If you wish to use this layout, you will find a blank pro forma on the **tipcet.com** website.

SCHEME OF WORK EXAMPLE

Title of learning programme: Introduction to humour	No of weeks in scheme: Thirteen – (13)	Venue: Lecture room 3
Academic year: 2007/2008	Start date: W/c 17.09.07	Name(s) of scheme designer: Ivor Funnybone
Semester/term: One	Finish date: W/c 14.12.07	Date scheme written: July 2007 (Scheme must be updated at least every two years)

Aims of the programme:	Specific learning outcomes of the Unit/Module	Individual learning needs will be met by:
<ul><li>To promote an understanding of the role and value of humour.</li><li>To develop awareness of the historical origins of humour.</li><li>To identify different forms of humour within present-day society.</li><li>To evaluate the role of humour in communication.</li><li>To identify explicit and implicit barriers to using humour.</li><li>To understand cultural differences in comedic expression.</li></ul>	On completion of this module, students will be able to:<ul><li>Identify examples of humour within at least five contemporary forms of communication media.</li><li>Describe three traditional forms of humour still evident in society today.</li><li>Analyse the purposes of humour evident in four examples of popular media.</li><li>Describe the cultural differences between two major examples of popular comedy.</li></ul>	<ul><li>The provision of a full spectrum of delivery strategies.</li><li>Regular positive and constructive feedback at all levels of programme assessment.</li><li>Provision of self-study materials.</li><li>Support being offered on an individual basis via a supportive tutorial system.</li></ul>

Week number	Date	General objectives (or objective reference number where applicable)	Teaching and learning activities (in outline including resources to be used)	Assessment strategies
1	17.9.07	• Participate in an icebreaker exercise. • Complete the college induction procedure. • View 15-minute video extract from a popular comedy programme. • Work in groups to identify how script, direction, acting, set and music contribute to the overall humour within the video example. • Discuss in groups photocopies of cartoons. • Collect other examples of cartoons before next session.	• Welcome to the college/module verbal/Q & A. • Introduce module and portfolio assessment. • Work in groups to identify how script, direction, acting, set and music contribute to the overall humour within the video example. • Present video extract. • Working with groups to produce flip charp summaries of sources of humour in video extract. • Provide photocopies of cartoons. • Discuss and ask class to collect examples for next week.	• Group flip-chart summaries. • Q & A. • Discussion.
2	24.9.07	• Consider examples of cartoons collected by class. • View exemplar cartoons (British, American, European) from last 100 years. • Discuss humour, politics and culture. • Group work on humour and political purposes. • Consider three topical verbal jokes. • Collect other jokes on identified themes for next week.	• Introduce examples of cartoons collected by class. • Show exemplar cartoons (British, American, European) from last 100 years. • Initiate discussion on humour in politics and cultural influences. • Work with groups on use of humour. • Provide three topical jokes and ask group to collect jokes for next week.	• Q & A. • Discussion. • Developing portfolio on examples of humour.
3	01.10.07	• Consider descriptions and illustrations of clowns from the Greek Theatre and Contemporary Circus. • Relate collected to the role of the medieval clown. • Consider humour, incongruity and narrative. • Working in groups to identify morality tales. • Collect gender-based humour examples for next week.	• Introduce examples of cartoons collected by class. • Show exemplar cartoons (British, American, European) from last 100 years. • Initiate discussion on humour in politics and cultural influences. • Work with groups on use of humour.	• Q & A. • Discussion. • Developing portfolio on examples of humour.

4.6 Writing aims, objectives and learning outcomes

You will be aware that, in writing this chapter, we have assumed that either the awarding body or your establishment will be providing you with the syllabus and the defined outcomes of the learning. As you become more experienced, it is quite likely that you will be given the responsibility of designing the curriculum, which involves important decisions about content and outcomes. This is further referred to in Chapter 12.

However, even though at this stage it is likely that the programmes you are involved with may be carefully prescribed, you will still be required to write outcomes for each of the topics or segments that you have disaggregated the provided syllabus into. These will form the core of each of your session plans, which will be a more fully developed presentation of the teaching and learning activities summarized for each of the separate weeks in the scheme of work above.

For obvious reasons, it is important that you consider the aims and objectives of any learning session. As discussed earlier in this chapter, the planning of the curriculum will encompass the requirements of the syllabus in terms of the distribution of the underpinning content, the appropriateness of the selected level and the needs of the target learners. Depending upon their particular conventions, the educational establishment involved may require the tutor to write aims and objectives for both the scheme of work and the constituent sessions. However, it is more often the case that *only* the scheme of work will include aims and objectives. The more detailed session plans will concentrate on specific behavioural objectives or defined learning outcomes. As a lead into this process, try the following activity within your PDJ.

Activity 4m Aims and Objectives

If you have completed the earlier exercises you should by now have attempted to draw up a scheme of work for at least part of your syllabus and this scheme should include the aims of the programme and the general objectives. Look back at your plan and try to explain how your defined aims differ from your objectives.

4.6.1 Aims

An aim is a general statement of the overall direction of the course. It indicates what the teacher intends to achieve. It does *not* indicate how it is to be achieved – this is what the tutor decides during the planning process. Aims will usually be first specified for the whole course or programme, and then for the individual parts of it (sessions, for example). The scheme aims tend to be *long-term, broad statements* which need to be translated into more immediate intentions. Here are two examples:

• to prepare learners for a role in the travel and tourism industry
• to enable learners to familiarize themselves with the structure, functions and applications of a range of ICT.

Activity 4n Defining Programme Aims

Revisit your scheme of work and ensure that your aims are long-term, overarching statements. If you have only written one, try to add a second aim to develop the breadth of the programme.

As you will be aware, the *programme aims* that you have defined are, in effect, only 'sign-posts' and lack a detailed description of your destination. To achieve this, you now need to break down this general concept into definitions of the more precise *intentions* of the course or programme. As within our previously discussed scheme of work, these intended outcomes will be represented within each of the session plans. Although not quite as overarching, individual *session aims* are still quite broad and are based on what the teacher intends to do. Some examples are:

- to revise mathematical conversions relating to binary and decimal systems
- to highlight the causes of food poisoning and indicate the methods of prevention
- to demonstrate and give practice in techniques of subjective examination for patients with musculo-skeletal disorders.

Activity 4o Identifying Session Aims

Consider now the Session Aims you have defined for your scheme of work. Do they adequately represent the curriculum indicated by the Programme Aims, or do they need adding to? Remember, you are still working at a general level and are not yet considering the *detailed* objectives or learning outcomes, which are typical of a session plan.

An aim then, is a generalized statement of intent, often encompassing broad areas of the planned curriculum. An aim is not measurable, but highlights what it is that the syllabus (and tutor) wishes to cover. As an example, if we apply this concept of a broad, umbrella statement to a teacher education programme, one example of an appropriate aim could be

To promote an understanding of the learning theories underpinning effective teaching and learning.

or

To encourage learners to develop an awareness of the diversity of students' needs.

Both of these statements would be difficult for anyone to 'measure', but are acceptable as broad terms used to explain the primary purposes of a teacher education programme. Discussing aims, Petty (2004) stresses their importance as guiding signposts:

Aims are like compass directions, indicating the general direction in which the teacher wishes to travel. As such they are vital; but they are not specific enough to help the teacher pick learning activities, or assess whether learning has taken place. There is no general agreement about how to decide aims and objectives, or precisely how they should be written. But there is an agreement that aims are vitally important.

The aims then provide a general understanding of the conceptual area from which the more specific objectives will be drawn.

4.6.2 Behavioural objectives

It is their more precise nature that makes objectives a subgroup of the original devised aim. We are moving now from the broad intentions of the programme to the specific requirements actually placed on learners during the teaching/training session itself. Each facet of their expected performance is stated as an objective, for example 'the students will be able to list the qualities of a good leader'.

Verbs such as *list, explain, justify, evaluate*, etc. are used to define *behavioural objectives*. In other words, the students are able to demonstrate their learning by doing something (in one of the above cases, *listing*) that can be observed and measured.

It is obvious that, in encouraging the learners to develop the skills of listing, selecting, rejecting, etc., the tutor will be also helping them to practise *non-behavioural objectives* such as *thinking, appreciating and understanding*. Although they remain a central part of learning and development, non-behavioural objectives are much less specific and cannot be observed or precisely measured in the way that behavioural outcomes can.

Activity 4p Differentiating between Objectives

Look back at the aims and objectives you defined within the scheme of work that you developed earlier. It should be easy to identify the behavioural objectives from the above description. However, also see if you can identify *non-behavioural outcomes* (i.e. those that will be difficult to express as an observable behaviour), which are either within the aims of the programme or are implicit within the defined objectives.

Within our current educational climate where there is such an emphasis on standards and accountability, it is to be expected that teachers delivering learning sessions will focus on the actual, measurable progress being made by individual learners as well as developing and enhancing their subject knowledge and expertise. This is most effectively achieved by checking them against specific behavioural objectives or defined learning outcomes.

Educational Objectives were developed by Bloom and his colleagues (1956) when they developed their taxonomies for the Cognitive (thinking), Affective (feeling) and Psychomotor (doing) areas of learning. They are essentially hierarchies of behaviours, which the authors referred to as 'Domains' and which attempt to articulate an ascending, progressive development. So, for example, within the cognitive domain, Bloom defined behaviours which became more complex and demanding as they moved from Knowledge through Comprehension, Application, Analysis and Synthesis to Evaluation (see also Chapter 9).

However, although behavioural objectives are undoubtedly useful as a means of making educational purposes more transparent, the complex processes involved within the higher levels of learning are sometimes impossible to capture sufficiently accurately when using only behavioural objectives, and often the overall aim of a programme will be expressed in non-behavioural terms. Cohen and Manion (1989) rightly point out that although the present currency is certainly behavioural, there is a useful place for both methods of expressing the intentions of a curriculum:

> Behavioural objectives might well be most effective when the subject matter and intended learning is skill-based and can be demonstrated easily, or where overt writing or speaking can demonstrate appropriate levels of learning, or where learners need small, behavioural stages brought into the subject matter to provide clear, attainable targets. Non-behavioural objectives might be best used when the intended learning is more complex or less specific, is developmental and almost impossible to view in terms of behaviour without reducing the learning to an absurd level.

4.6.3 Curriculum theories

Two major curriculum paradigms have dominated education during the last 50 years. Perhaps the most familiar one was introduced by Tyler (1949) as the *aims and objectives* model.

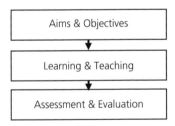

Aims and Objectives Model

This simple design, which is clearly influenced by behaviourist approaches, is the forerunner of our present teaching and learning cycle. Tyler proposed that our starting point in curriculum design must always be the aims and objectives, which, of course, are based on the values and purposes of the educational provider. Next, when stated precisely, the aims and objectives will indicate what teaching and learning methods will be the most effective in achieving these outcomes. Finally, student assessment and course evaluation will indicate how effective the implementation of the design has been. Using this information, it may be necessary to adjust parts of the framework to improve future provision.

Developed partially as a reaction to the behaviourist, deductive approach promoted by Tyler, Lawrence Stenhouse (1975) proposed the *process model* in order to focus less on pre-scribed outcomes and more on inductive development.

The essence of Stenhouse's approach is that teachers are able to design significant, beneficial experiences for learners without being constrained by defined outcomes. It is the teachers' expertise which allows them to identify holistic, learning processes, which aspects to give priority to, and the most effective means of consolidating this procedure.

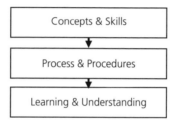

Holistic Learning Process

4.6.4 Designing objectives

The Common Inspection Framework, which is now the basis of the accountability processes implemented by Ofsted together with the management of the sector through the Learning and Skills Council has, as you might expect, been based on the Tyler approach rather than that of Stenhouse. However, the central concern is still the *quality of the learning experience* enjoyed by each individual within Lifelong Learning Sector sessions. As the effective planning of these learning experiences depends very much on the range and value of the objectives devised by teachers, it is clear that it is important for tutors to develop the skill of articulating intended outcomes.

The first step when defining behavioural outcomes is to write an opening statement, which makes clear just what you wish to achieve. For example:

> At the end of this session (or unit/module) the students/learners will be able to:

Remember, your intention is to *achieve* the objectives which follow the statement, so you do not need to qualify these intended outcomes by using 'should' in preference to 'will'.

Also, the objectives provide an indication of how much each individual has progressed against the expressed measure during each learning session. We can take it therefore, that:

> If the objectives commence with a verb, then this usually ensures that the resulting evidence is 'measurable'.

In an educational context, objectives are precise descriptions of how you wish the learner to behave as a result of the successful learning. So it follows from our opening statement, that objectives should always be expressed from the *point of view of the learner.*

> State clearly what the learner will be able to do

The following are examples of this approach:

> *describe* the binary system
> *convert* binary numbers to decimal
> *explain* the need for such conversions in practice
> *put* the client at his or her ease before questioning
> *question* in a logical sequence
> *record* the client's responses during questioning.

Activity 4q Objective Characteristics
Analyse briefly the major common characteristics which the above six objectives share.

It is clear that each of the objectives:

- begin with a verb
- are specific
- refer to an activity which can be seen/heard and measured
- use simple sentence structure and plain language (the exception could be specialist terms, the understanding of which are, of course, part of the learners' curriculum)
- link into the key areas for assessment – informal or formal
- set targets for learners to achieve
- provide the teacher with evidence of learning
- help the teacher to evaluate the effectiveness of their teaching – i.e. has the lesson helped the learners to achieve their targets?

It is evident from these examples that objectives are easy to specify for all kinds of subject areas and provide a good guide to the content of the sessions, to the tutor's choice of teaching/learning strategies and to the assessment vehicle. Now try the following activity.

Activity 4r Writing Objectives

Bearing in mind our discussion above, write down two objectives to match each of the short-term session aims you considered in Activity 4o previously.

Referring back to our (fictional) specific learning objectives in the example of a Scheme of Work (Activity 4l above), it will help us to illustrate a point here. They were:

- *identify* examples of humour within at least five contemporary forms of communication media
- *describe* three traditional forms of humour still evident in society today
- *analyse* the purposes of humour evident in four examples of popular media
- *describe* the cultural differences between two major examples of popular comedy.

As you will have realized, the *evidence* from each of the above assessment activities meets the important characteristics we defined above (i.e. can be observed by the tutor). In order to clarify this still further, some *incorrect* objectives for that same 'humour' context might be:

- *know* examples of humour within communication
- *appreciate* forms of humour evident in society today
- *value* the purposes of humour evident in the media
- *understand* the differences between major examples of comedy.

Use the above examples as a basis for Activity 4s, below.

Activity 4s Ensuring Achievement

Would the learner have a clear idea of how much evidence is required and the type of information needed? Would the tutor have any evidence to be absolutely sure that the objectives had been achieved by the learners?

Unfortunately, despite the fact that the above objectives are worthy, they are non-behavioural and so would not generate the evidence required by most of our assessment processes. Also we have taken out the descriptors, which clarify how much work is expected of the student (i.e. 'four examples of media').

The problems associated with such omissions are identified by Petty (2004) when he states that:

specific objectives should

- specify precisely and in concrete terms what the student should be able to do
- be written in such a way that it is possible to determine whether or not the objective has been achieved
- usually be short term
- be drawn up by the teacher to suit the resources, the teacher and the students
- optionally, define the circumstances under which the objective is to be demonstrated and/or what constitutes an achievement.

4.7 Session plans

Having designed the scheme of work, the next task is for the tutor to plan the delivery of learning in the form of the individual sessions. Each of the particular sessions will be free-standing but must build on earlier sessions and prepare the way for what follows. It is, of course, necessary for the objectives set out in the scheme of work to be covered in the session plans and for there to be a particular progression in terms of content and conceptual understanding. Table 4.1 overleaf shows some of the many aspects that must be considered.

4.7.1 Depth and breadth in learning

So far in this chapter, we have mainly discussed the accuracy of the defined outcomes we use in order to plan our programmes. Despite the importance of these considerations, if we didn't look a little beyond them, we could end up with precisely written outcomes which meet the observable and measurable requirements, but which also, unfortunately, are so undemanding as to be virtually useless. Learning is directed towards many different situations and purposes and some of these are simple and fairly straightforward, while others are much more complex and have to be achieved over time.

Gronlund (1985) discussed the fact that quite often it is necessary to achieve lower level objectives before moving on to more demanding development:

Learning outcomes that are considered *minimum essentials* are typically low-level outcomes that can be rather easily achieved by students and that serve *as prerequisites* to further learning in the area. Those outcomes at the *developmental level* represent goals toward which students may show different degrees of progress but which they never fully achieve. The ability to *understand*, to *apply*, to *interpret*, and to *think critically*, for example, typically depend on an extended period of development. Their *complete* attainment is not expected in any given course.

Gronlund is making the point that many curriculum designers and teachers tend to treat all objectives as minimum essentials, which must be achieved. If this approach is taken, the outcomes tend to be written to cater for the lowest common denominator and the quality of the total student experience is diminished. On the other hand, if the more demanding

Table 4.1 Session planning considerations

Topic to be covered:
You may decide to have some variety in the way you distribute the different topics to be covered, or you may wish to develop a topic over a number of weeks, drawing the various strands together at appropriate intervals.

Number of learners in the group:
Naturally, small-group teaching can be quite different to the approaches you need to take with a larger group. Generally speaking, interaction with the learners will decrease as the group size becomes larger.

Length of session:
Approaches will be quite different for one-hour sessions (where some steps are more urgent) when compared, for example, to half-day or full-day programmes.

Previous session/topic covered:
Obviously, the success of the previous session in achieving the desired outcomes will have a significant bearing on at least the opening of the following session.

Special knowledge of the learners:
If the learners have a similar understanding of the subject, it is easier to design the learning than if the students have widely differing levels of ability. It may be useful to develop separate learning groups for some parts of the session.

Main teaching and learning methods envisaged:
It is clear that the methods which you intend to implement during the session need to be carefully considered in advance in order to ensure that you are familiar with the content and, most importantly, how you will deliver the key content in a successful manner.

Learning environment:
It may be that certain facilities are needed for a particular topic and these are only available on certain dates. Or the arranged venue may have particular characteristics which must be considered.

Age of the learners:
If there is a wide age mix, you will need to provide appropriate compensation and stimulation in order to hold the interest of all the learners. If they are roughly the same age, you will need to try to differentiate.

Time of day of the session:
Sessions immediately after lunch (on a Friday in particular) will need to be approached in a way which takes account of the learners' disposition and uses appropriate strategies to counteract any lethargy.

Next session/topic to be covered:
It is often useful to prime the learners about what will be discussed at the next session and, where possible, to encourage them to prepare for it in some way.

Significant learning needs:
If your learning group contains students with particular physical or emotional needs, you will obviously have to plan your methods of sustaining inclusion carefully. This could include gaining the cooperation of the other learners in advance of the session.

Resources and teaching/learning aids required/available:
You need to know, for example, not just that there is an overhead projector in the venue, but that it is working and that the projection surface is acceptable. Designing particular aids to learning can make the difference between a moderately successful session and a memorable one.

Nature and composition of the student cohorts:
The learning characteristics of the group will influence your planning. For example, group dynamics, learning styles or level of ability could each have an effect on student interaction and the progress of the learning.

Maturity of the learners – both socially and emotionally:
Naturally, you will respond to the levels of responsibility that your students are able to accept and this may be affected by group dynamics.

Desired outcome/s of the session:
The objectives to be achieved will, of course, be a central consideration when deciding on the teaching and learning methods to employ. As a simple example, it is easier to get students to learn rules of operation than decision making.

General knowledge of the learners:
In placing a subject in the context of the students' level of experience, it is valuable to know to which areas of general knowledge you can rely on them being able to respond.

Constraints and difficulties anticipated:
Planning sessions usually involves negotiating some problem or other. This could relate to the venue, to the timing, to activities taking place near to your session, etc. General awareness of establishment-wide developments and commitments is needed.

How the session will be evaluated:
Even though the evaluation processes you employ may be just an informal Q & A exchange, you should have a clear idea before the session, of the areas on which you need information in order to improve your practice and how best to get it. A clumsily managed evaluation can easily do more harm than good. You should also know if you need formative or summative information.

development-level objectives are the only focus, the students may not be sufficiently versed in the knowledge and skills, which are prerequisites for higher-level learning.

Bloom (1956) made the ascending developmental stages that all learners must go through very clear in his description of the Cognitive Domain, and Gronlund (*op. cit.*) provides a very useful summary of this hierarchy:

Table 4.2 Major categories in the cognitive domain

1. Knowledge	Knowledge is defined as remembering of previously learned material. This may involve the recall of a wide range of material, from specific facts to complete theories, but all that is required is the bringing to mind of the appropriate information. Knowledge represents the lowest level of learning outcomes in the cognitive domain.
2. Comprehension	Comprehension is defined as the ability to grasp the meaning of material. This may be shown by translating material from one form to another (words to numbers), by interpreting material (explaining or summarizing) and by estimating future trends (predicting consequences or effects). These learning outcomes go one step beyond the simple remembering of material, and represent the lowest level of understanding.
3. Application	Application refers to the ability to use learned material in new and concrete situations. This may include the application of such things as rules, methods, concepts, principles, laws and theories. Learning outcomes in this area require a higher level of understanding than those under comprehension.
4. Analysis	Analysis refers to the ability to break down material into its component parts so that its organizational structure may be understood. This may include the identification of the parts, analysis of the relationships between parts and recognition of the organizational principles involved. Learning outcomes here represent a higher intellectual level than comprehension and application because they require an understanding of both the content and the structural form of the material.
5. Synthesis	Synthesis refers to the ability to put parts together to form a new whole. This may involve the production of a unique communication (theme or speech), a plan of operations (research proposal), or a set of abstract relations (scheme for classifying information). Learning outcomes in this area stress creative behaviours, with major emphasis on the formulation of *new* patterns or structures.
6. Evaluation	Evaluation is concerned with the ability to judge the value of material (statement, novel, poem, research report) for a given purpose. The judgements are to be based on definite criteria. These may be internal criteria (organization) or external criteria (relevance to the purpose) and the student may determine the criteria or be given them. Learning outcomes in this area are the highest in the cognitive hierarchy because they contain elements of all of the other categories, plus conscious value judgements based on clearly defined criteria.

Activity 4t Defining Levels

Consider your developing session plan and look again at the *levels* of the outcomes you have written, referring to Bloom's Cognitive Domain above. Are many of your objectives concerned only with knowledge?

It is possible that you may think that your learners are not yet at a stage to develop beyond application, yet many apparently simple tasks also involve analysis, synthesis and evaluation.

If we examine a very fundamental process such a shopping, you will see below that the learners very quickly move beyond the mere comprehension and application levels.

Table 4.3 Possible cognitive levels demonstrated during shopping through the learner being able to:

Knowledge	**List** items intending to purchase. **Name** the stores that may hold the required commodities. **Justify** the amount of money which is available for the intended goods.
Comprehension	**Explain** the characteristics of the items to be purchased. Give **examples** of categories of goods. **Defend** the range of products identified as necessary purchases.
Application	**Relate** the choice of goods in one store with those available elsewhere. **Change** the order of priority within the shopping list. **Discover** previously unconsidered possibilities.
Analysis	**Relate** available goods to original shopping list. **Identify** good value. **Differentiate** between two competing choices. **Separate** imperative buys from possible purchases.
Synthesis	**Recognize** how intended purchases will relate to goods already owned. **Plan** to delay the purchase of some of the items in favour of more desirable goods. **Revise** shopping list.
Evaluation	**Appraise** the final list of possible choices. **Discriminate** between two similar items. **Justify** a final short list. **Conclude** the process with appropriate purchases.

Of course, our debate above is focused only on the Cognitive Domain but, as we stressed earlier, we feel that it is very important to promote holistic learning which involves more than just thinking. There are basic physical skills to be developed (the Psychomotor Domain) and most learning is also about the development of values or feelings (the Affective Domain).

Activity 4u Moving beyond Knowledge

Revisit your defined session objectives once again and consider what psychomotor and affective skills will also be learned by your students as they grapple with the cognitive element of their programme.

The following summaries of the Affective Domain, taken from Krathwohl (1964) and the Psychomotor Domain, taken from Simpson (1972), provide a useful hierarchy of behaviours and related learner actions which indicate how objectives at each level may be expressed – see Table 4.4 below. Remember when planning a curriculum or a range of assessment tasks that there are other important outcomes in addition to cognitive objectives. You need to achieve a balance of *Cognitive*, *Affective* and *Psychomotor* outcomes set at appropriately *demanding levels*.

Table 4.4 Affective and psychomotor behaviours and appropriate objectives

Affective (Krathwohl 1964)		Psychomotor (Simpson 1972)	
Receiving stimuli	Listens attentively. Shows awareness. Accepts differences. Attends closely.	*Perception of sensory stimulation*	Relates the taste of food to the need for seasoning. Detects differences in temperature. Differentiates between stimuli.
Responding	Shows interest. Accepts school rules. Participates in discussion. Completes homework. Enjoys helping others.	*Mental, physical and emotional set*	Knows sequence of steps in a particular process. Demonstrates correct stance for a physical activity. Responds with interest to a particular opportunity.
Valuing	Appreciates good literature/art/music. Shows concern for the welfare of others. Demonstrates belief in the democratic process.	*Guided response*	Imitates actions demonstrated by an instructor. Uses trial and error to develop a technique. Determines best sequence for optimum effect.
Organizing	Accepts responsibility for own behaviour. Understands and accepts own strengths and limitations. Recognizes the need for balance between freedom and responsibility.	*Mechanism of performance*	Writes smoothly and legibly. Is able to touch-type when operating keyboard.
		Complex overt response	Automatically takes up correct position during ball games. Plays from music.
Characterizing by a value	Begins to develop own value system. Demonstrates self-reliance. Behaves in a consistent and predictable manner.	*Adaptation*	Adjusts play to counteract opponent. Modifies use of machine to allow for unusual conditions.
		Origination	Creates an original dance step. Develops a new style of painting. Uses established procedure for a new purpose.

Activity 4v Developing More Rounded Learners

Continue to think holistically about your students' development. Consider not just the knowledge, skills and values you wish them to acquire, but also their stance in relation to study, work and relationships. Are you encouraging gradual independence, or is your over-supportive approach prolonging their dependence?

Our previous discussion has been concentrating on the development of depth (i.e. *concern for levels*) and breadth (i.e. *holistic concerns*) when writing objectives, by consciously incorporating variable outcomes related to feeling and doing in addition to thinking. It is clear that, even more important than precision in the writing of outcomes, is our ability to ensure that we stimulate the learners' interest and enthusiasm for the subject, by stretching them in terms of the range and complexity of the abilities they develop. As Rogers (1994) stresses when talking about the education of adults:

> If we have a narrow objective, aiming at some specific competency or externally moderated achievement, we will tend to lay greater stress on the part played by the teacher than on the learners' activities. If, on the other hand, we set our sights more on the growth of the individual, then the emphasis of our programme will rely more on the activities engaged in by the participants, less on the work of the teacher.

Rogers is pointing out one of the serious problems of systems that are heavily dependent on closely prescribed outcomes. Such a process inevitably leads to 'teaching to the test', which limits both the teaching and the learning to the inevitably limited objectives (because language cannot encompass all the nuances of learning) and students become concerned more with knowledge replication, rather than knowledge creation. Rogers also indicates a further implication of such an approach. The teacher assumes a dominant role as the holder of the knowledge and the assessor of the defined outcomes, which leads to the learners accepting a passive role as the receivers of the prescribed knowledge and the subjects of the assessment demands. It is difficult for the potentially rewarding learning partnership between teacher and student to flourish during such a relationship because the implication to the learners is that the really valuable knowledge is external to themselves.

It may seem incongruous that we have introduced these imprecise notions of breadth of study and shared responsibility towards the end of a chapter, which has been so concerned with systematic planning. However, as we pointed out at the start of this book, although the need for accountability is accepted, we believe teaching to be more of an art than a science. We accept that some accountability is necessary in order to ensure consistency of standards, but believe that there must be room for student flair and teacher judgement.

4.7.2 Session plan layout

Table 4.5 is an example of a possible way of laying out a session plan. It is based on the *second* session of the imaginary scheme of work that we used in Activity 4l. You will note that:

- the teacher has a notional timing for the session (although this is open to adjustment depending on how the students respond to each of the intended activities).
- the four defined learning outcomes are identified clearly at the top of the session plan.
- the defined learning outcomes are related in column 2 to each of the teacher activities. This establishes clearly that the identified learning outcomes are covered during the session.
- although this may be a non-vocational programme, the student achievement is assessed in various ways throughout the module. The tutor makes clear the assessment approaches.

Table 4.5 Session plan

Date:	18th September 2007		Time of session:	19.00 to 21.00 hours
Venue:	Lecture room 3			
Programme:	Adult non-voc. Leisure class		Unit:	Introduction to humour
Group:	Part-time evening		Topic:	Purposes of humour in cultural contexts
Session aims:	Promote an understanding of humour			
Learning outcomes:	a) Extract humorous and subject themes from collected cartoons		c) Identify how humour is used for cultural and political purposes	
	b) Identify the historical origins of present-day humour		d) Analyse topical verbal jokes to identify themes	

Time	Outcomes	Teacher activity	Learner activity	Resources	Assessment method	Comments
19.00	a)	Discuss cartoons collected by class	Bring in collected cartoons	Collected cartoons	Informal	Formative assessment used to accredit student contribution
19.15	b)	Present examples of historical cartoons	Viewing presentation	Power Point presentations and laptop	None	
19.35	b)	Establish groups to discuss cultural and political humorous themes from cartoons	Form groups to discuss humour and politics	Group experiences	Q & A	
19.45	a) & b)	Describe discussion task during break	Receiving directions	None	None	
19.50	None	Break	Break	None	None	
20.00	a) & b)	Instigate continuation of discussion	Discussion	Group experiences	Observation	
20.15	a) & b)	Coordinate feedback from discussion groups	Feeding back	Group experiences	Observation	More formal summative assessment to be used at the end of the module
20.25	c)	Encourage groups to identify topical verbal jokes	Discussing current jokes and selecting three	Group experiences	Observation and Q & A	
20.40	c) & d)	Organize presentation of three jokes by each group	Helping with presentation	Group preparation	Observation and Q & A	
20.50	c) & d)	Themes and purposes identified	Analysing jokes for themes	Previous presentation	Observation and Q & A	
20.55	a), b), c) & d)	Summary and encouragement of groups to collect verbal jokes on identified themes for next week.	Noting requirements for following week.	Earlier cartoons. Summary of historical presentations and topical jokes.	None.	

4.8 Conclusion

In generalized terms, the planning of teaching sessions may seem to be a straightforward, uncomplicated process. However, as this chapter has indicated, in reality the teacher must achieve the difficult balance between, on the one hand, being overly prescriptive and, on the other, allowing disorganized classroom chaos which demotivates all of the learners, and most likely the teacher as well! The planning must, of course, produce a clear framework, which articulates exactly what the teacher wishes to achieve. On the other hand, it is imperative that the teacher's planning should allow for the unexpected in the various possible ways the learners may respond to the teaching.

Because of all the reasons we have so far discussed, teaching and learning are not predictable. The teacher who pushes ahead with a planned session, despite all the indications that the learners are not receiving the message, is doing nobody a service. Sticking to the planned session and continuing to fire didactic missiles when it is clear they are not reaching their target, is clearly not effective teaching. Keeping to a notional timing in such a situation is, in fact, wasting everybody's time.

Even so, becoming reflective and responsive does not mean that planning becomes redundant. Reflecting on practice and developing strategies that have the appropriate teacher response ready to hand demand considerable prior thought and organization.

However, the key to the whole process is *resonance* rather than prescription. In these stressful days it is undoubtedly difficult to retain the ability *and the willingness* to respond positively to our students. To do this successfully, we need to spend time getting to know the learners well and attuning ourselves to their wavelength so that we are able to understand most of the subtle signals that are transmitted between the students and the teacher and between student and student.

Once we have the ability and the motivation to accurately read how the majority of our learners are receiving both the taught material *and the manner in which it is being presented*, our planning and preparation will inevitably begin to have much greater accuracy and meaning.

Rather than preparing ourselves to fail because we fail to prepare, we must plan to prevail by becoming more aware of even our smallest weaknesses. Mapping our failures is often very difficult and uncomfortable, but it is the most reliable way of illuminating the path to learning success.

4.9 Useful publications

Armitage A. (ed.) (1999), *Teaching and Training in Post-Compulsory Education*. Buckingham: Open University Press.
   This book looks at what it is like to teach in the Further Education sector. Chapters include teaching and learning, resources, assessment, course design and developments in the post-compulsory sector. This is a good all-round introduction for the new FE teacher.

Daines, J. and B. Graham (1997), *Adult Learning, Adult Teaching*. Nottingham: Continuing Education Press.

A useful handbook for teachers who are new to teaching adults. It begins by identifying the characteristics of adult learners and explores planning for learning, teaching methods and reviewing learning.

Reece, I. and S. Walker (2007), *Teaching, Training and Learning* (5th edn). Business Education Publishers Ltd.

Nine chapters full of detail about teaching and learning. Strong on the role of the teacher and a good attempt has been made to relate methods and theory to the LLUK Standards and although these tend to be threaded throughout the book, the relationship is not always entirely clear.

4.10 Useful websites

There are many websites dedicated to the planning of learning. The following two are examples:

www.educause.edu/library

www.tipcet.com

Table 4.6 Process justifications – planning for learning

FAQs at the level of	Threshold certificate	Associate award	Cert. Ed./PGCE/Diploma
Why do it?	You are involved in delivering learning which will help your students achieve specified outcomes and the less you leave to chance, the more likely you are to meet your targets within the resource limitations which every programme must acknowledge.	To facilitate effective learning many factors need to be considered in addition to the immediate problem of delivering identified content to particular learners. If important factors (ability, learning styles, etc.) are ignored all your efforts may be in vain.	You need to evaluate your curriculum planning in order to identify to what extent it is affecting the quality of student experience and achievement. Future planning will improve as you learn to take account of the range of variables.
Where are we going?	You need to be clear about what you wish to achieve within a particular lesson/unit/course. Your destination will be clearly indicated by the aims and objectives of the programme you are involved in and often more precisely spelt out within the defined learning outcomes that your students must achieve. You should have begun to plan appropriate diagnostic tests.	You could express the intended outcomes as objectives or competences or as a process you wish to take the learners through, but you must know the purpose of the educational experience you are planning. Don't forget to include goals from the affective (feeling) and psychomotor (doing) category, as well as the obvious cognitive (thinking) domain. Be aware of the development of key skills.	You are developing the ability to actively reflect on curriculum processes in order to identify the range of intended and unintended influences which are affecting the learning outcomes. You are moving towards a planning approach which is supported, but not constrained, by an appropriate structure while remaining able to respond effectively to the needs of learners.
How do we get there?	Consider carefully any information you have been given such as a scheme of work, syllabus or curriculum. Identify the key content that the learners must gain an understanding of and plan a realistic progression to these learning outcomes. Identify your assessment strategy and don't forget to take into account the times when important assessment must take place.	An obvious beginning is the content of syllabus. Use your experience and intuition to prioritize the major themes/points you wish to include and also an appropriate introduction which will enable your students to build on earlier ideas and draw out from the experiences you provide the key concepts and principles they will need later.	Start by reflecting on the more obvious aspects of teaching and learning such as achievement of defined outcomes, student interest and motivation, management of time, etc. Consider later the more subtle influences of planning such as teaching and learning styles, physical environment, timetable position in relation to other subjects, etc.
Is this the best way?	Look again at what you intend to do and try to separate content that is essential from that which would be your ideal. Allow extra time in the early stages for learners to get used to your delivery and aspects of the learning environment. Keep an ongoing record of effectiveness and use this formative evaluation to consider if any modification is needed in later sessions.	Examine what you have planned objectively. Ensure you have selected the optimal order and allow time for remedial work whenever necessary. Check that you haven't included too much, and that what you have selected is relevant to your defined outcomes and the agreed assessment strategy. Beware of self-indulgence when planning the syllabus.	Confirm that the lesson plan/scheme of work has a linking coherence and development. Ensure variety of presentational methods and planned student experiences. Confirm that learners are able to see the value of your intended provision. Check underpinning values and purposes as well as planning, delivery and assessment.

(Continued)

Table 4.6—cont'd.

FAQs at the level of	Threshold certificate	Associate award	Cert. Ed./PGCE/Diploma
When is the right time?	You have to accept that you will only rarely have enough time, but obviously the earlier you start planning and preparing the better. Remember to plan some form of induction into the programme for the learners and think of appropriate ice-breaker exercises to promote group cohesion.	Be aware of the timing of significant events/experiences and inputs so that you allow the students time to absorb these important ideas before being expected to develop and build on them. Watch out for key events such as visits/field trips, availability of resources/guest speakers and assessment deadlines.	Evaluate and modify your approach during the teaching (i.e. formative) in order to correct any problems encountered in the delivery of teaching or the development of learning. It may be too late to correct student misunderstandings or teaching ambiguities at the end of the process.
Who needs to know?	Obviously, the students need to know about the intended schedule. Check that the library and the learning resource centre have been told about the needs of your programme. Confirm that your teaching room is adequate for the intended session, that you have ordered any specific audio/visual/IT hardware/ software. Ensure that what you have organized will not disrupt other classes held during, before or after your session.	The detail of your planning will obviously be influenced by the success of your earlier teaching, particularly with the target group. If you can, build on their earlier learning and use familiar terms and references to help them develop a mental 'set' in relation to the learning to come. Do you need a translator, or an interpreter? Perhaps you need to arrange access or learning support for students with specific learning difficulties.	The analysis of the effectiveness of planning will affect present and future students but it will also inevitably affect colleagues involved directly in that provision or indirectly in terms of support, use of resources and changes in department culture, etc. Managers will also need to know if there are resource implications or if a particular problem such as retention is being addressed.
How do we know when we've got there?	Your planning has been effective when the majority of your students have enjoyed the programme and have achieved the learning outcomes. Obviously, it is important to consider the retention data. However, the reasons for drop-out are often complex, so do not immediately think that you are automatically at fault if some students stop attending.

As noted in the previous chapter, meeting the particular needs of every student is extremely difficult. Start by considering whether such broad aims as the provision of an appropriate, orderly environment where the views of individuals are respected and where learning is a common goal are met. | All the key aspects of the curriculum have been incorporated and the delivery is varied and interesting. The planned sessions are manageable and although the content is challenging, the teaching is not over-demanding on the students and you and your colleagues. Where necessary, there is time for remedial work with the students before the assessment processes take place.

Ensure that your intended strategy doesn't discriminate in some way against some members of the group. Think about how the less able will be able to cope. Check that the high-fliers will be able to demonstrate their range of skills adequately and will be fully occupied during the class. | Analyse how effective the planning has been in terms of the allocation of resources and time to the key stages. Ensure that preferred student learning styles have been accommodated and that you and your colleagues are comfortable with the designed teaching and learning strategies and are confident that they will achieve the desired learning outcomes.

Reflect on your response to perceived student need and confirm that you have made optimum use of available resources. Consider if your teaching strategies could be detrimentally affecting students' perception of their own abilities and autonomy as learners. |

Theories, Methods and Learning

Yvonne Dickman

Key Concepts

Accretion, Advanced Organizer, Andragogy, Behaviourist, Cognitive Dissonance, Comrades in Adversity, Conceptual Structure, Conditions of Learning, Controversy, Cooperative and Competitive Learning, Disinhibition, Dual Professionalism, Dynamics and Roles, Eclectic Approaches, Experiential Learning, Exposition, Group Learning, Higher-Level Thinking, Iconic and Symbolic Learning, Individual Accountability, Inhibition, Instrumental Conceptualism, Internal and External Knowledge, Mental Set, Metacognition, Multiple Intelligences, Positive Interdependence, Positive Reinforcer, Respondent and Operant Behaviour, Restructuring, Self-Concept, Self-Directed Learner, Self-Esteem, Significant Others, Social Constructivism, Successful Sessions, Surface Learning, Teacher Actions, Theory, Threat to the Self, Verbal Intelligence, Whole Person Learning.

5.1 Introduction

The Lifelong Learning Sector covers a wide range of diverse learning environments and situations and there are increasing demands made on practitioners within these varied settings. So that we can make informed decisions in order to use techniques which we can be reasonably confident will be successful, it may be useful to start by considering the learning process. Most competently taught sessions will usually be based on models and underlying principles that have been developed by practitioners over the years. Although intuition does play a significant part in the way we respond to our learners, there is considerable value and insight to be gained through an examination of some of the more useful theories relating to the planning, organization and presentation of motivational learning experiences. It's an old cliché I know, but there is, after all, no point in reinventing the wheel.

Unfortunately, it is also often the case that a relatively new teacher who has found an approach to session design which is relatively successful may then be reluctant to move from this familiar and 'safe' teaching method to any sort of innovation or further development. However, as we have mentioned before in previous chapters, the context of teaching is inevitably an ever changing and challenging environment with many new pressures and influences each and every day. Continuing success does depend on learning to 'read' these situations, and have within your portfolio of methods a range of appropriate approaches and solutions which you can turn to and apply almost without thinking about it.

It is this process of identifying and successfully adapting to the many variables and different organizational requirements which makes teaching so potentially fascinating. Faced by students with unfamiliar learning styles or behaviour, or taking on new subjects or curriculum areas often require us to re-evaluate our teaching techniques. The requirement to introduce more flexible delivery methods and new technologies, such as computer-based learning, internet research sources and communication tools, also places demands on us to continuously update and re-skill.

As practitioners we must be responsive to the challenge of difficult situations but continue to promote learning based on established principles and concepts. With the confidence of having an extensive and varied range of teaching and assessment methods to hand and an overarching concern to provide rewarding educational experiences for our students, our work can be exciting and fulfilling. However, as you would expect, developing such a receptive, flexible disposition is a lot to ask of the teacher and requires an open mind, rather than an intransigent determination to remain within the secure environment of the known and familiar.

Different learners, courses of study, environmental and organizational demands and the requirements of awarding bodies, all necessitate flexibility, if not from individual tutors, then from the teams who have responsibility for the delivery of learning. Also, as we observed earlier, education within the learning and skills sector is concerned with such a variety of learners within so many diverse educational contexts that, inevitably, each teacher will draw on many different theories in order to develop an appropriate method of organizing and delivering learning.

The study of learning theories may initially be viewed as peripheral to your teaching sessions and your specialist knowledge of the subject being taught may at times be your immediate priority. It can be tempting to dismiss the use of learning theories as being *abstract*, *irrelevant* or *separate* to the process of learning how to teach. As a novice practitioner you may find that you simply imitate the techniques of more experienced staff, without appreciating the principles (or lack of) that underpin their use.

In this chapter we will introduce a range of educational theories and relate these to individual, group and experiential learning. As a starting point it may be useful to consider some of the key questions that arise when we consider the value of *learning theory* and how this relates to the development of teaching and learning techniques.

Activity 5a Why Consider Theory?

Reflect on the value of learning theory to a busy practitioner who is coping well in the present situation by using familiar methods and adopting departmental practices.

You may well have raised some of the following questions:

- How will my learners benefit?
- How will I benefit?
- If it isn't broken – why fix it? My students already have a reasonable learning experience.
- Why change? I am comfortable with the range of methods I already use.

Despite their obvious competence in the classroom (or perhaps because of it) many teachers are hesitant about entering into theoretical discussions about pedagogy. This reluctance may be related to a perception that the pressurized realities of the chalkface are a million miles from the vague, abstract world of academia.

However, it is worth remembering that the actual *source* of most, if not all, knowledge is *practical endeavour* and not the reflections of erudite academics. Yet their scholarly activity is of some value, because it is through their analysis and eventual synthesis that they identify the validity and wider implications of the new knowledge. Eventually, through the integration of these interpretations within evolving theories, the generalizability of these practices to other settings is achieved. Over time, as the theories are refined during testing within actual practice, they gain acceptance, thus allowing new knowledge to emerge and the cyclical process to continue. If we bear this process in mind as we return to our rightly sceptical questions, perhaps the following simple responses may indicate the value of alternative points of view:

a. **Finding the problem.** Try comparing teaching to something familiar, such as owning and driving a car. In the early days, we often copy other styles which have been taught or observed and this may well be successful for a time. However, should that practice become less successful, it is often useful if your analysis of the problem is informed by theory. For example, if this problem is in teaching, it could be related to the effect of group dynamics. In the car analogy, the problem could be problems in starting the engine on a winter's morning. It is very possible that both difficulties will be solved more quickly if our analysis is informed by theory.

b. **Justifying the methods.** Within current inspection frameworks, we may well be asked to justify our chosen approach and obviously arguments based on established theories will provide useful support for any rationale.

c. **Repeating our success.** If we are to usefully evaluate the success of our methods, the analysis should rely as much on theory as intuition. In order to repeat successful performance we need to know what we did that was effective. If we are to evaluate the success of our methods usefully, the analysis should rely as much on theory as intuition.

The central fact is that there are extremely valuable basic principles which have been developed by the theorists and assimilated by we practitioners over the years. In this chapter we will explore these theories and relate them to the accepted and conventional teaching strategies with which we are all fairly familiar. You are not expected to become an expert in the range of methods discussed, only to develop an awareness of them and thus make informed choices about their application, validity and usefulness.

The following discussion falls naturally into two parts – learners and teachers and their particular characteristics and relationships. We hope you will be able to be able to identify and extract from each area some theoretical ideas which may have general application and from these principles be able to arrive at guidelines for the organization of successful learning within post-compulsory education. Through the development of your competence in the classroom, your practitioner skills will evolve gradually into an individual style and your professional development is advanced through a combination of analysis of your own experience and your reflection on wider issues and theories.

This recognition of the value and use of theories forms part of your self-development into a 'dual *professional*' role. Robson (1998) described this as being a developing consciousness of the process of learning how to teach, in addition to your subject development and knowledge. The process of knowing and understanding, where the 'how' something is taught becomes as essential to the planning as 'what' is taught. This self-development can form part of the study of learning theories. As practitioners we may find that our study of theory leads into an unsettling experience described by Festinger (1957) as 'cognitive dissonance'. This disturbing experience occurs when you find that you are obliged to integrate new ideas into what you already know or believe. If this new learning appears to contradict or conflict with your previously held beliefs, resistance and tension can heighten. The way in which we deal with any inconsistencies between our already held preconceived ideas and new knowledge can be instrumental in changing our attitudes. Consequently as practitioners, if we dismiss the study of learning theories because of possible subconscious conflict, it may also become a way of avoiding the need to change as well as instinctively resisting contradictions.

5.2 Learner self-esteem

Of all the characteristics that affect a learner's achievements within post-compulsory education, it is perhaps their level of *self-esteem*, which is the most influential. Learning and performance is significantly affected by the students' views of their own self-worth, and this predisposition towards achievement or failure will already have been established long before they arrive in your classroom. Interaction with parents, friends, peers and previous teachers, each of whom have offered differing levels of interest, acceptance and love, will have helped to shape how positively or negatively they regard themselves.

Activity 5b Self-Concept Summaries

Identify some examples which you are aware of, where learners have been positively and negatively affected by parents, friends, peers, employers, previous teachers, etc.

This group of 'significant others' are a valued reference group who have helped to shape the student's view of him or herself. Cooley (1912) introduced the theory of the 'looking-glass self' suggesting that one's self-concept is significantly influenced by what the individual believes others think of him. Tomatsu Shibutani (1971) considers that deliberately, intuitively or unconsciously, each of us performs for some kind of audience, not actual but conceptual. Although this influential audience may not be actually present, our conduct is oriented towards certain people whose judgement we see as important. Bruner (1966) agrees:

> Human beings fall into a pattern that is required by the goals and activities of the social group in which they find themselves.

Mead (1934) reinforces the fact that when we adopt the behaviours that we feel our 'significant others' would accept, we are recognizing and sharing the meanings which this audience has attributed to us. This performance helps us to define ourselves as a specific role player in a given relationship.

The humanistic theory of learning stresses the individual nature of every learner and includes strong emphasis on the need for our learners to become more than simply receivers of knowledge and skills but rather to become active participants in the process for themselves.

Part of the development of this concept of self-directed learning is the promotion of learner independence, where learners develop this personal self-concept through the fulfilment of their own potential. Here the emphasis is on self-motivation and the use of teacher skills in 'helping people to learn'. In adult learners this is typically referred to as andragogy. Knowles (1984) based his theory of andragogy on four assumptions:

- mature learners are more self-directed, preferring to discover things by themselves with guidance where necessary
- their past history can form part of experiential learning with resources from previous experiences and skills
- they are motivated by more relevant learning and will respond to learning that they feel has immediate relevance, for example, in problem solving
- this learning should be of immediate application in the form of task-related activities.

Principles within the development of andragogy stress that the involvement of your learners is central to their learning process and that their learned knowledge is required to have immediate relevance for their needs and problems in order to be effective. Your role as a teacher in this model is to encourage the learner to take control and to encourage and facilitate rather than being the authority figure. Learners who have developed this 'self-direction' themselves may resist attempts to impose what could be viewed as irrelevant tasks or demands, leading to possible confrontational or non-cooperation situations.

Mead (1934) reinforces the fact that when we adopt the behaviours that we feel our 'significant others' would accept, we are recognizing and sharing the meanings which this audience has attributed to us. This performance helps us to define ourselves as a specific role player in a given relationship within the learning environment and our own position and influence within the social group. Within the post-compulsory sector learners arrive in the classroom, or increasingly, other places of learning having had previous educational learning experiences that affect their entry behaviour and characteristics. These shape their individual concept of their own potential and expectations and at times barriers are created which contribute to negative attitudes to learning and difficult social behaviour.

This contributes to the view of self-identity or 'personal construct psychology' devised by Kelly (1955), which examined the ways in which learners use their past experiences, or 'life events' to form their expectations of experiences and the way these affect the learner's anticipation of their own success or failure. This expectation is often established well before the learner begins a course of study, and will contribute to their attitudes and behaviour as they attempt to establish their own individuality within a new setting.

Activity 5c Significant Teachers

Of all the 'significant others' we have mentioned who influence a students' self-esteem, teachers are perhaps the most influential of them all. Think in terms of your own educational experience and situation, then comment on whether you think this is so, and why it should be.

It is important to note that of the three predominant groups of 'significant others' (parents, peers and teachers), only the teacher is in a *formal, systematic, institutionalized, evaluative role* during which they produce *recorded assessments* of the learner. Outside of the educational situation we can avoid assessments or rationalize them away, but once inside a formal establishment, they become official.

Where previously, should the learner prefer not to risk any damage to her or his self-esteem by becoming involved in an exposed situation where public evaluation can take place, then there would usually be available appropriate strategies to minimize involvement.

James (1890), a founder of research into self-concept formation, wisely pointed out:

> . . . with no attempt there can be no failure, with no failure no humiliation. So our feeling in this world depends entirely on what we back ourselves to be and do.

Consequently lecturers in post-compulsory education are in an extremely responsible position (as are all we teachers) where they may promote or destroy the self-esteem of each of their students according to the way they either involve or neglect them during the learning process.

We will discuss further these attribution aspects of lecturers' responses in the next section. For now we will continue to concentrate on the novice learners whose previously established attitudes will considerably influence how they perceive their teachers, colleagues and the demands of the learning within their new college.

Activity 5d Coping Learners

Consider some of the ways in which learners who have a relatively secure self-esteem cope with the various college demands and requirements.

Learners with high levels of self-esteem will usually have the advantage of being able to see these important aspects of their educational situation in a positive manner and to cope with them adequately, despite the fact that they themselves may not be competent in *all* of the areas they are studying. After an initial period of evaluation they will begin to respond to their new teachers in a context specific way, which they feel is appropriate. With formal teachers they may demonstrate the required 'academic' norms, with less formal teachers they will often establish a productive relationship and take advantage of the more flexible situation.

Activity 5e Low Self-Worth Responses

Now compare the coping strategies of those who have less confidence in their self-worth.

The students with a relatively low self-esteem are less likely to be as effective in the early decisions they make about the qualities of different teachers and will often treat them uniformly. Because they find it difficult to differentiate between them, their response to each teacher is not necessarily always appropriate. Also, as some students grow to accept this more passive role as 'receivers' of whatever their tutors wish to present to them, they are more likely to see worthwhile and desirable knowledge as *external* to themselves. They often perceive the learning they value as being possessed and dispensed verbally by 'respected academics'. Burns (1982) again observed that:

> In traditional classrooms verbal intelligence has generally been recognized as the major, if not the sole basis for determining who is capable and likely to succeed. Teachers in these classrooms have generally failed to teach children to recognize, use and value their other skills and abilities. Consequently, many children who are not in the top quarter in verbal intelligence feel that they are incapable and are virtually doomed to failure.

Although Burns is referring to the compulsory sector of education, his comments apply equally to post-compulsory education, where many less academic students are marginalized, despite their high levels of commitment and range of vocational skills, because of their limited verbal communication.

Gardner (1993) also stressed the importance of 'linguistic intelligence' when, as part of his study of 'multiple intelligences' he initially identified seven types of intelligence. He observed that teachers valued most highly linguistic and mathematical intelligence, and felt that the tendency to exclusively concentrate on these two types of intelligence while neglecting a broader understanding of how people learn in the other categories, is a serious criticism of traditional education.

Gardner's next three original listings are those generally associated with the arts and the final two are the personal intelligences described as interpersonal (understanding and being able to work effectively with others) and intrapersonal (the capacity to understand oneself). To recap, Gardner's initial seven intelligences were:

- linguistic word intelligence
- logical/mathematical intelligence, dealing with numbers and reasoning
- spatial/visual or pictorial intelligence
- bodily/kinesthetic intelligence, physical coordination
- musical intelligence
- interpersonal intelligence, understanding other people
- intrapersonal intelligence, self-understanding.

These different types of intelligence are not considered to be absolute and learners will possess a 'blend' of intelligences that work together to form their own individual combination. Gardner also suggests a relationship between the identified intelligence types that connects them to career choices and preferences made by learners.

Related to this is the use by confident students of the *surface* approach to learning. Whereas the less confident learners may be committed to learning the knowledge 'prescribed' by their teachers because they see that as the authoritative version that they must master, the securely confident students adopt an instrumental, surface learning approach dedicated to a replication of 'prescribed' knowledge, because they see this as the simplest route to examination success.

Activity 5f Surface Approaches

Try to identify among your students those learners who stand out as being able to use 'surface' approaches to learning. Reflect on the ways in which they differ from other learners who do not use surface approaches.

A key point here is that the students with high self-esteem are able to select the most effective route to success, while those with less confidence are not aware of the alternatives. All students should be encouraged to develop their cognitive skills to reflect on particular processes and concepts and, to do this, they need to be able to take an objective stance and to question fundamental, widely held beliefs and practices. This requires considerable confidence and independence that very often learners with low self-concepts have not been encouraged to develop. In order to encourage a conceptual shift from the passive, absolute acceptance of 'external' knowledge to a more questioning, reflective, evaluative mode of operation, learners must be persuaded to believe more in themselves and less in those established processes of education which create physical and psychological barriers to their personal development (see also Section 3 in Chapter 3).

Activity 5g Developing Self-Esteem

Summarize some ideas of how students with less confidence in their abilities, may be persuaded to value their contribution more?

Usher (1985) believes that we need to encourage the less-confident students to move to a view that it is their *experience* of education which is of paramount importance, rather than the 'often sterile academic input'. It is our task to persuade them that reflection and the *awareness of the process of learning* have equal importance to the product and we must show that we value their prior formal and experiential learning.

The views of George Kelly and Carl Rogers have much in common with the above concerns for the learners' self-esteem and the importance of individual interpretation. Rogers (1983) is concerned with student-centred, experiential development based upon 'whole person' learning, that is intellectual, emotional and psychological. This is dependent upon the creation of an appropriate ethos characterized by friendliness and informality and a spirit of mutuality between teachers and students. The teacher here acts more as a facilitator providing regular and supportive feedback sessions in order to promote a conscious evaluation of the processes and indicating that learners' experiences are valued. Rogers' aim is to reduce any threat to the learner's self, so that the student is able to develop the skill to judge the value of the learning experience that has been provided. Only when learners can perceive experience in this differentiated fashion and relate it to their own needs will effective learning be achieved.

Kelly's (1979) constructivist view of learning often echoes the humanistic perspective of Rogers as both share a focus on the individual and believe in active interaction with the environment as a means of structuring knowledge as a response to experience. Kelly also shares a holistic view of learning and considers that the development of knowledge is not so much a process of 'accretion' (i.e. merely adding to previous knowledge), but, more importantly, is the process of *restructuring* previous knowledge as a consequence of learning received during a new experience. Rogers and Kelly also believe that existing concepts should be challenged by planned experiences so that new and more appropriate ideas may be developed.

Activity 5h Challenging Experiences

Consider one of your areas of teaching and think about the stereotypical notions which many students bring to their studies. Take one such perspective and consider what sort of educational experience you could plan which would challenge their preconceptions and make them reconsider their present ideas.

The ideas of 'self-directed learners' that were developed by Knowles (1984) clearly relate to the work of Kelly and Rogers. Knowles compared andragogy (adult learning) with the more familiar pedagogy which, in his view, places too much of the responsibility for learning with the teacher or the institution, i.e. setting goals, determining the curriculum and using more authoritarian and didactic teaching methods. Knowles preferred andragogical methods where responsibility is shared and the role of the teacher is more facilitative and, as a consequence, the learners are more responsive and participative. Knowles had a considerable influence on adult education and the current development and use of 'learner contracts' owes a great deal to his push towards increasing learner autonomy.

Our examination so far of the relationship between the individual person and learning does have obvious limitations as it is biased towards a humanist/constructivist standpoint and seriously neglects a *behaviourist* perspective. However, we may usefully draw from the above, brief discussion the following *five principles*, which we will add to during this chapter, so that we may arrive at a composite review of the implications for post-compulsory education of relevant learning theory. Practitioners should ensure that:

1. each learner's prior learning and experience is valued.
2. where possible, any threat to the learner's self-esteem is removed.
3. the purpose of the provided learning is understood by the learners.
4. students are encouraged to become aware of their own learning processes.
5. the development of independent thinking by the learner is encouraged.

5.3 Teachers teaching

Often practitioners have a predilection for teaching in a style similar to the way they themselves were taught and their chosen approach will usually have a bias towards either student or teacher-centredness.

Rogers (*op. cit.*) points out that often the self-esteem held by a teacher will influence how they will teach, and those with a self-perception of relatively low worth will find security in an authoritarian style. Those with more confidence will allow the learners increasing participation in the organization and evaluation of learning experiences.

Rogers, along with Kelly, emphasizes repeatedly the importance of providing learning experiences that allow the students to develop their own concepts through the construction of their own interpretations, which will be related to their own needs. Bruner and Gagne would also stress a real consideration of the learner's conceptual development, but Gagne's theories would be more at home within a didactic approach than an experiential mode.

Humanist theorists believe that learning is an emotional process and regard the experience of learning and the learner's development of their own 'self-concept' as central to their perception of the learning process. The influence of feelings on the learning process is considered to be of particular importance to each individual's response to learning, and the way in which they view their own capabilities and potential. Rogers believed that meaningful learning was experiential in nature and that the teacher's role in this case is more that of a 'facilitator' to assist learning. The issue of 'self-regard' and personality is seen to have specific relevance to the adult learner who needs to be encouraged and assisted to take control of their own self-initiated learning.

Gagne (1985) groups together all factors influencing learning through his discussion on the 'conditions of learning' where he states that the changes brought about by learning are related to the situations in which they occur. He divides these conditions into two types. First, there are the conditions *internal* to the learner and he suggests that we find evidence of these from studying his or her existing capabilities. Second are the *external* conditions, which he considers to be any exterior factors that may influence or initiate learning.

For us as teachers, the establishment of a supportive environment involves planning to create a focused and purposeful atmosphere which meets our learners' needs for self-esteem and self-respect. The establishing of ground rules and appropriate behaviour within the learning environment is central to the promotion and development of a supportive atmosphere between peers. By using modelled behaviour and respect for learners to create a safe and secure environment for learning we can have a positive effect on the interaction of individual learners and the development of the social confidence necessary to learning.

Gagne provides a taxonomy of learning in the form of a hierarchy moving from attitudes through motor skills, verbal information and cognitive strategies to intellectual skills including discriminations, formal concepts and developing rules. He analyses each learning category in detail and suggests appropriate learning methods, however he does not say that a given learning task can be related to one of his categories. He believes that the task itself must be analysed into steps to reveal its procedural characteristics, which are a series of subtasks that must be performed in a particular order. This process produces a number of instructional objectives, which represent the whole task.

Activity 5i Procedural Analysis

Take one reasonably small learning task which you use in your teaching and analyse it into subtasks as suggested by Gagne. Place these in order of completion and identify the instructional objectives which you must achieve to ensure the student is able to understand the whole task.

Bigge (1982), summarizing Gagne's approach to teaching, states that:

instruction means arranging the proper conditions of learning that are external to the learner. These proper external conditions include the teacher communicating verbally with the student to inform him of what he is to achieve, reminding him of what he already knows, directing his attention and actions and guiding his thinking along certain lines.

A further three principles may be drawn from Gagne's work:

Practitioners should ensure that

6. learners are stimulated to recall previously learned capabilities.
7. the desired mental sets of the learner are activated.
8. the learner receives appropriate feedback from the teacher.

Bigge believes that Gagne is not sympathetic to experiential learning as he proposes *providing* student problems rather than allowing their negotiation and development and Bigge notes that:

the discussion class is not primarily concerned with learning at all, but with the transfer (generalizing) of what has already been learned . . . To get learning to happen is still the basic problem. The conditions that bring learning about are not those of the discussion class.

Although Gagne has much in common with Bruner with regards to the importance of developing the appropriate mental 'sets', they differ considerably with regard to the experimental dimension.

Bruner (1966) sees learning as involving three almost simultaneous processes. First, there is the acquisition of new information, which could either be the refinement of existing knowledge, or perhaps it may run totally counter to current beliefs. The second characteristic Bruner proposes is the transformation of knowledge, which takes place when learners manipulate what is known in order to address new problems. In this way the student goes beyond what is known in a creative manner making assumptions about untried situations by extrapolating from accepted knowledge. The final stage takes place when the learner checks the 'pertinence and adequacy' of gained information through an evaluation of its usefulness in relation to the current problem or task. This cognitive growth Bruner labels 'instrumental conceptualism' and is based on two tenets:

a. a person's knowledge of the world is based on his constructed models of reality
b. such models are first adopted from one's culture, then they are adapted to one's individual use.

During the perceptual process, a learner will form a hypothesis as to what the incoming stimulus is. This process is based on previous experience and involves making an inferential leap. Bruner believes that the process of learning involves *enactive, iconic* and *symbolic* modes of representation. A learner's representations collectively constitute his model of reality. The *enactive mode* occurs when a learner does not require imagery or words to represent learning, but achieves it through motor responses. For example, a child *enactively* knows how to ride a bike or tie a knot. *Iconic* representation takes place when a learner uses internal imagery to represent categories of events and Bruner believes that this mode of representation is usually at its height when a child is between the ages of five and seven, and is extremely dependent upon personal sensory images.

The final mode of representation, the *symbolic*, is the most relevant to post-compulsory education. Approaching and during adolescence, language becomes increasingly important and gradually the learner moves from a preference for sensory imagery to an increasing use of *symbolic representation*. Language, the most used of these abstract forms, enables a person to manipulate real or imagined concepts, to solve problems and to evaluate. This is the basis for reflective thought mentioned earlier in this essay during the discussion on self-concept.

Bruner, too, places great importance on the negative effect of weakened self-images in students:

> [T]he one most pervasive thing that prevents man from reaching his full potential is a lack of confidence not only in his own capacities but also in the ability to develop them further.

Bruner believes that, in order to improve their confidence, students should be encouraged to see the value of their own perceptual ability. Bruner also sees great value in developing students' *problem-solving skills* through their ability to transfer acquired knowledge to new situations. Through their own manipulation of these phenomena the students become more independent learners and develop their own value system through understanding when they are right and when they are wrong. This independence and self-appraisal demands intellectual honesty. Bruner believes that this development may be promoted through experiential learning:

> [D]iscovery, whether by a schoolboy going through it on his own or by a scientist cultivating the growing edge of his field, is in its essence a matter of rearranging or transforming evidence in such a way that one is enabled to go beyond the evidence . . . to new additional insights.

From Bruner's writings the following further four principles may be extracted:

Practitioners should ensure that

9. they share the process of learning with learners in order to reduce the effects of cultural-based resistance.
10. learning is organized in order to build on previous learning (e.g. the spiral curriculum).
11. learning is clearly structured to show relationships and continuity.
12. problem-solving techniques are used to challenge previous perceptions.

Ausubel (1965) shares with Bruner the view that it is important that teachers promote conceptual structures, but he does not agree with any overemphasis on discovery learning. Ausubel argues that much instruction, particularly at higher levels of education is (and always has been) successfully performed by the process of exposition leading to meaningful reception learning. He is concerned with the value of didactic methods, arguing that it is not possible for a learner to have the time to rediscover the whole of the intended curriculum and that, in any case, experiential learning does involve reception learning – it is merely the style of presentation which differs.

Ausubel believes that proponents of discovery learning often confuse reception learning with rote learning and discovery learning with meaningful learning. The popular misconception, he believes, is that discovery learning is automatically meaningful and that reception learning automatically involves rote methods. Ausubel agrees that rote learning is *not* a route to understanding and because of the discrete, compartmentalized nature often results in a lack of retention. He believes that long-term learning is often achieved through presentational style methods, which are appropriate to meaningful reception learning. This involves relating new material to previous conceptual structures, and Ausubel feels that only up to the age of 11 or 12 is experiential learning necessary in order to build up these schemata.

Ausubel has much in common with Bruner in his views that subsequently learners begin to move to a more symbolic means of representation where they are increasingly able to manipulate abstract concepts. Ausubel stresses the importance of using 'advance organizers' to facilitate the reception of related concepts and principles. These organizers are substantive structures or schemata, which are stable and discernible from related conceptual systems.

These organisers are introduced in advance of the learning material itself, are formulated in terms that are already familiar to the learner, and are also presented at a higher level of abstractness, generality and inclusiveness.

Activity 5j Advance Organizer

Identify a discrete area of learning which you present to your students and plan a structure which would help them to see the relationship between the component parts, for example a 'tree' of ideas or steps in a process.

Ausubel explains in detail how a well-designed organizer acts as a 'subsumer' in that it is able to subsume a great number of related concepts or principles. It is this 'tree' of understanding on which many concepts are hung that enables the learner to successfully manipulate abstract hypotheses on the way to solving related problems. As problems are solved, new concepts emerge, related rules of operation are developed and that particular 'tree' is enlarged.

Ausubel is highly critical of curriculum designers and authors who, despite this psychological evidence, structure content in discrete categories which do not draw out their relationship to the gestalt of the overarching conceptual system. From Ausubel's discussion, three additional principles may be added to our list:

> Practitioners should ensure that
>
> 13. meaningful reception learning is used in order to develop existing conceptual systems.
> 14. teaching is organized around concepts and principles which potentially have the widest explanatory power, inclusiveness, generalizability and reliability to the chosen content.
> 15. a sequence of presentation is selected which best illustrates the characteristics of the chosen cognitive structure in terms of clarity, stability and integratedness.

Although Ausubel is primarily concerned with cognitive processes he does often use behaviourist explanations for the process of learning. The behaviourists, on the other hand, consider the structure of internal thinking and learning processes as irrelevant to the process of instruction. Their concern, as exemplified by Skinner (1938), is for the structuring of the environment in such a way as to maximize the probability of the desired new behaviour being learned. These desired behaviours are taught by a series of successive approximations, which begin with an already established behaviour and work towards the learning objective.

The process is based on the principle of reinforcement expounded by Skinner which was a more precise restatement of Thorndike's (1931) law of effect. This law of effect states the observed phenomenon that behaviour, which produces desirable or pleasant effects, tends to be repeated. Skinner helped to develop this classical conditioning theory relating to voluntary behaviour and recognized two different kinds of learning:

> Respondent behaviour is elicited by specific stimuli and given that stimulus the required response occurs automatically. This follows the pattern of classical conditioning where a new stimulus is paired with the one that already elicits the response and after a number of such pairings the new stimulus comes to elicit the response.

A simple example of an existing stimulus would be an animal salivating at the sight or smell of food. If this is deliberately paired with the sound of a bell, eventually the animal will salivate on hearing the sound. However, Skinner maintained that most behaviour is of a different sort, which he refers to as:

> operant behaviour. The characteristic which differentiates operant behaviour from respondent behaviour is that it operates on the environment to secure particular consequences. There is no specific stimulus that can be identified which will consistently elicit an operant response.

Skinner speaks of operant behaviour as being emitted by the person or organism rather than elicited by stimuli. Most behaviour is of this sort – walking, talking, working and playing are all made up of operant responses. Skinner does not mean to say that operant behaviour is not influenced by stimuli and, as we know, much of his analysis of behaviour is concerned with the controlling influence of stimuli. However, his point is that in relation to operant behaviour, such control is only partial and conditional. For example, the operant response of reaching for food is not simply elicited by the sight of food; it also depends on hunger, social circumstances and a variety of other stimulus conditions.

Because of this distinction, Skinner does not consider it useful to think of operant behaviour as made up of specific stimulus-response connections in the sense that respondent behaviour is. He concentrates instead on the fact that if an operant response (sometimes referred to just as an operant) occurs and is followed by reinforcement, its probability of occurring again increases. So even though the actual stimulus or stimuli for an operant is uncertain, if it is followed by a reward it is likely that the response will occur again.

Operant behaviour and the resulting patterns of learning are Skinner's chief concern. Series of operants become organized into a chain, for example a person rising from an armchair to switch on the television set. Each of the steps in the process may be seen as individual operants but the whole may be considered to be a single operant because it is the chain of responses, which will be reinforced by the reward of sitting back and enjoying a television programme. This would be considered to be positive reinforcement. If, however, the television programme should have some kind of irritating content (perhaps a poor presenter), then the viewer will often switch off the set. This removal of the irritant (a negative reinforcer) could be considered to be a reward.

Thus a response can be reinforced either by presenting a *positive reinforcer* (the enjoyment of television viewing) or by removing a negative one (the irritating content). Both types of reinforcers may be conditioned. If a stimulus occurs repeatedly with a positive reinforcer, that reinforcer tends itself to acquire the capacity to reinforce behaviour and this is called a conditioned positive reinforcer. For example, the title of a previously enjoyed television programme in a newspaper schedule of the evening's entertainment would be associated with pleasure and would lend to an anticipation of switching on the television in readiness for the broadcast. Conversely, the description of a disliked programme would lead to avoidance and is acting as a *conditioned negative reinforcer*.

Activity 5k Positive and Negative Reinforcers

Identify a student behaviour you wish to encourage and then suggest both a positive and a negative reinforcer that it would be appropriate to use to stimulate this behavioural response. Add your own comments on the relative value of these suggested reinforcers.

Skinner believes that a learner will rarely perform the target behaviour without having to be trained towards it. The teacher must gradually mould the students' behaviour to the desired learning outcome. This is done by the teacher's employing *shaping*, through reinforcing that behaviour which successively approximates toward the desired outcome. Behaviour that is not reinforced gradually stops. This is known as *extinction*. From these behaviourist concepts a further five principles may be drawn.

Practitioners should ensure that

16. learning is regularly rewarded during the early stages, which should consist of short steps. In later stages variable reinforcement is preferable in order to avoid extinction.
17. reward quickly follows the appropriate response. Motivation is increased by immediate feedback.
18. desirable behaviour is reinforced and unwanted behaviour is, as far as possible, ignored (since attention can often be a strong reinforcer). Emphasis should be on praising and encouraging desirable behaviour and not on punishing undesirable behaviour. Undesirable behaviour should, as far as possible, be extinguished.
19. negative reinforcement is used with care even though it is preferable to punishment. Punishment should not be used since it often has emotional side effects (anxiety inhibits learning) and will produce avoidance behaviour (learners start missing lessons).
20. lessons are carefully planned in order to encourage desired behaviours by eliciting necessary responses through appropriate reinforcers.

Behaviourist approaches have proved to be extremely valuable to education and training over the past 50 years, and are still very much in evidence within the many national standards we have today. However, some critics would point out that, when we attempt to disaggregate more sophisticated skills into behavioural outcomes, it often proves impossible to articulate clearly the nuances of the range of complex outcomes that are involved. Also, when several psychomotor responses are occurring simultaneously (such as learning to drive a car) it is difficult (and even dangerous) to attempt to shape them using Skinnerian procedures. As Bigge points out:

Reinforcing the learner for each successive approximation to the final correct use of each of the controls would not only be maddeningly slow, it would also give little assurance that the learner would survive the training course, considering how a person would be likely to drive who had achieved only a first approximation to mastery of the steering wheel and brake!

The fact that a learner can observe and imitate an experienced practitioner who is also providing verbal instructions and interpretations greatly increases the speed of learning. Bandura and Walters (1963) expanded this concept of modelling (which is, in fact, a sophisticated form of imitation) and discussed the process of 'identification', where the learner is trying as well as possible to be the other person. Bandura and Walters talk about two other forms of imitation, *inhibition* or *disinhibition* of already learned responses and the eliciting of an already learned response.

In the case of inhibition, a learner sees from observing others that a learned response is not appropriate in that context and conversely disinhibition involves a situation where a learner, who has understood from previous experience that certain behaviour is not acceptable, now sees others exhibiting that previously unacceptable behaviour and realizes that constraints have been removed. Teachers hope that inhibition by observation will take place when they reprimand a student for being disruptive and then other students will also learn what the desired behaviour is. Disruption occurs where the disruptive student persuades others to abandon their previous inhibitions and become disruptive.

Activity 5I Inhibitive Action

Discuss a situation where you have tried to inhibit undesirable behaviour by reprimanding an individual student. Comment on the success or otherwise of your strategy and suggest how you might develop this process.

The third manner in which imitation can operate is through the eliciting of an already learned response. This occurs in a situation where the observation of a model of behaviour (such as painting) creates a positive desire in others to join in the activity. Depending on how the teacher responds to the displaying of particular behaviour, vicarious reinforcement will take place. The giving of rewards (i.e. displaying the resultant work of art) will increase the likelihood of the observer imitating the behaviour and the handing out of punishment will make it more likely that the observer will refrain from imitation.

A great deal of social behaviour is learned through modelling or reciprocal interaction with the teacher and students operating as personal, behavioural and environmental determinants of one another's behaviours. Bandura has lent a cognitive focus to behaviourist principles through the notion of vicarious reinforcement, and has included humanist concerns by stressing the importance of a learner's self-efficacy. Bandura's work provides another three principles:

Practitioners should ensure that

21. behaviours and tasks which the students are expected to learn are modelled, preferably by them. For example, being punctual, showing enthusiasm or taking a critically reflective stance.
22. students are aware that desirable behaviour is being reinforced.
23. students are also used as models. For example, during group work, pair the confident, successful students with those who are less successful and try to build a mutually supportive relationship.

5.4 Group learning

Learning is often a group experience, with interaction between learners forming part of the learning process as well as that with the teacher. The connection making and interpretation of new knowledge does not take place by individuals in isolation. Known as social constructivism, the recognition that learning is a social process was strongly influenced by Lev Vygotsky (1997). In social constructivist theory, learning does not take place in the classroom only but extends to all other areas of social interaction, particularly in language-based situations. Activities such as group learning and engagement with other learners during tasks allow learners to refine their construction of new knowledge and ideas and this allows individuals to 'test' their connections against the thinking of others. Working in collaboration with other learners in group tasks and presentations engages the 'finding out' process and encourages discussion and questioning and the challenging of preconceptions.

The idea of learning as a socially collaborative function extends to the concept of 'situated learning' (Lave and Wenger, 1991), where the learning is related to situations such as in the workplace, and where learners are subject to influences and ideas from everyday work practice. The development of interaction and socialization in which learners participate is instrumental in developing and becoming part of 'communities of practice' in which the knowledge is contextualized within situations where learning takes place.

Activity 5m Rich Learning Experiences

Try to identify a rewarding group learning experience and summarize all the details you can recall about the situation and the nature of the learning. Say why you think this incident has remained so clearly in your memory.

Usually a group of people gathered together for a particular purpose will very quickly develop characteristics of its own as, through the initial interactions, the members begin to evolve a role which they feel comfortable with. Our discussions earlier in this chapter about the 'significant other' and levels of self-esteem have important parts to play in this process. The dynamics of this process are themselves fascinating and a great deal of research has analysed these interactions and the range of roles which members assume or which are ascribed to them.

5.5 Group dynamics

Belbin (1981) suggested *eight* different roles that individuals can identify with and, given the opportunity, would choose for themselves. Belbin's conceptualization of group processes has much relevance to education and his role descriptions give an insight into the complexity *and the potential for learning* of the dynamics existing within most groups.

Each group role within Belbin's categories has a different function to perform which is compatible with the individual's abilities, and their current disposition towards the task in hand and the other members. Belbin argued that a successful team must contain many, if not all, of these contributors:

- **Company worker.** This team member is practical, organized and reliable and has the capacity to turn ideas into actions and see them carried out. **Characteristics**: practical, methodical, organized, not easily discouraged, but may flounder in times of change.
- **Team worker.** This person is sensitive, sociable and supporting and brings to a group the capacity to foster team spirit by supporting other members. **Characteristics**: helps communication, builds on ideas, counters friction, likeable and popular, dislikes personal confrontation, but may seem 'soft' to some members.
- **Chairperson.** This person is seen as calm, self-controlled and self-confident. They strive to get the team working together to produce results. **Characteristics**: clarifies, coordinates, is disciplined, probes, listens, brings out the best in people, but is not particularly creative or innovative.
- **Plant.** This person may be unorthodox, serious and individualistic as they suggest new ideas and strategies to solve problems. **Characteristics**: innovative, imaginative, creative thinker, pays special attention to major issues, may be radical at times, but can make careless mistakes on detail and may respond poorly to criticism.
- **Completer/Finisher.** This member is conscientious, detail conscious and delivers on time. Will take care that details are not overlooked and that pace is maintained. **Characteristics**: checks detail, meets deadlines, relentlessly follows through, dislikes a vague approach, but can get 'bogged down'.
- **Monitor/Evaluator.** This team member is highly analytical and objective. Using judgement to evaluate team ideas, analyse problems arising and critique contributions. **Characteristics**: analytical, 'feet on the ground', good judgement, assimilates and assesses data, but can lack tact and fail to accept new ideas.
- **Resource Investigator.** This member is enthusiastic and curious. Often an extrovert who is externally orientated which allows him/her to create and develop outside contracts to help the team progress. **Characteristics**: energetic and positive, has masses of contacts, follows interests, goes outside of the team for information and ideas, but may be poor on follow through and can be elusive.

- **Shaper.** This person is outgoing and dynamic and seeks to direct the team and get the desired results. *Characteristics*: dominant and extrovert they challenge and respond to challenge. They give shape to a discussion, but can be seen as arrogant and abrasive, impulsive or impatient.

Activity 5n Group Roles

Think of a fairly well-established group that you teach and try to identify where members have taken on one of the roles described by Belbin. Are there other roles that members have assumed in addition to Belbin's categories?

It is often useful to look at the composition of the groups that you work with and also to consider the type of person you are yourself in relation to the groups that you function within. As a member of a course team, do you have preferred functions or particular characteristics, which either suggest you for a role or let you slip into one? In addition to showing how various roles may contribute to successful outcomes for the group, Belbin was also able to identify how potential characteristics have significant disadvantages that may inhibit the progress of the group.

Activity 5o Counterproductive Characteristics

At the end of most of his role descriptions above, Belbin has added a qualification which identifies potential weaknesses or problems with that particular role characteristic. Give some examples of such problems which you have encountered and how you have dealt with them.

Of course, this aspect of group dynamics is both the strength and the potential weakness of collective operation, for as well as their positive qualities, members will usually also have areas where their performance could be stronger. For example, the person in the role Belbin describes as 'Plant' is good at innovative thinking, but careless when dealing with detail. These characteristics may well create internal dispute when the group is working under stress.

Part of your responsibility will be to encourage your learner group members to 'play to their strengths' and in so doing, compensate for those less proficient in this particular role. In this way, the collective has more resources than the individual.

5.6 Group productivity

Given that a group has more potential for achievement than an individual learner, it is important that the achievement of this performance is monitored. Douglas (1992) examined groups from a *performance* point of view and suggested a number of activities which he feels groups perform more successfully than individuals:

- tasks requiring a division of labour
- producing a *range* of solutions to a problem
- using resources efficiently
- social motivation
- increased productivity
- arriving at superior judgements during tasks involving random error
- sustaining tenacity of purpose
- providing involvement, participation and a high level of commitment.

However, the group's *social* processes may well inhibit the group's *potential* productivity, creating what Steiner termed '*group deficit*'. This occurs because groups are very seldom able to utilize their resources to the full because there are often losses due to processes within the group, which impede the group's maximum attainment.

Activity 5p Facilitating Group Productivity

Again consider your own group of students, which you identified in Activity 5n above, and identify the social interactions and processes that may affect the total performance of the group.

It can be argued that groups exist on two levels: *the task for which the group comes together* and *the hidden tasks and activities* or the social relationships which are an integral part of everyday group interaction. The quality of verbal and non-verbal interactions will help to determine the effectiveness of the group, but members will need to spend as much time listening as they spend talking. As you can imagine, for some this is a serious challenge! Being sensitive to the feelings of others is also crucial during the development of a collaborative climate and will be one of the determinants when establishing the norms of acceptable behaviour.

Another key dimension is 'crowd behaviour'. Individuals should not become so overwhelmed by more dominant members that they are unable to express themselves and so relinquish the power to make decisions to others, consequently forgoing their own individual rights and responsibilities. Obviously, if a person's role is diminished in this way it will create ongoing resentment, which may fester for a while before erupting in angry confrontation.

Activity 5q Managing Conflict

Similar conflicts to the above can arise from the personal differences of individuals and from different role expectation. Identify ways that your groups manage this sort of conflict themselves and the situations where you need to use your skills to manage it on their behalf.

Addressing such problems, Hackman and Morris (1978) and other theorists concerned with group processes believe that group 'deficit' (i.e. not achieving their potential) occurs when groups are left to work 'spontaneously' through a task. In other words, insufficient attempts have been made to improve the *facilitatory* processes such as effective communication, decision making and action planning. Obviously, facilitating the optimum performance from a group of learners is the responsibility of the practitioner or support worker. Commonly conflict may be dealt with through:

- avoidance – redirecting the focus of the situation to more positive aspects, i.e. what **has** been achieved
- defusion – reducing the cause of the problem, i.e. indicating misunderstandings or taking responsibility for part of the confusion
- confrontation – challenging consistently inappropriate behaviour or malicious practice, i.e. as a last resort when all other forms of persuasion have been to no avail.

For a group to function effectively its members must agree on mutual roles and norms of behaviour. Each member needs to contribute and, although individual members will subordinate their own needs to those of the group, this should not result in these needs being totally submerged. Other factors which affect interpersonal interaction in groups are:

- *distractions* – both internal and external, psychological and physical
- *irrelevant topics* – learners can easily wander, or be drawn into topics which are irrelevant or out of context
- *domination* – group members who are over-dominating can affect the behaviour and performance of others within the group
- *reluctance* – a reluctant learner can bring with them a set of issues which cause disruption and need to be addressed.

Belbin's concepts and those of Hackman and Morris add two more principles to add to our list:

Practitioners should ensure that

24. when forming learning groups they are aware of the personal characteristics of members and their influence on the dynamics of the group.
25. effective group operation is facilitated by developing or providing skills and resources.

5.7 Experiential learning

Because, by its very nature group learning is *experiential*, our previous discussion has led us into our penultimate teaching and learning technique of this chapter. Traditionally within post-compulsory education the balance between theory and practice has been heavily influenced by the predominant educational context. Within workshops, laboratories, etc., learning has been essentially 'on-the-job', practical and experiential in nature, while in the classroom learning would often be related to theory taught in a didactic manner.

These two approaches are not mutually exclusive and represent either end of the spectrum of learning processes. The teacher/facilitator would settle at a point along this continuum that satisfied both personal preferences and the demands of the learning situation. Usually, the introduction of theory would be followed by appropriate opportunities for application and practical experience would be accompanied by reference to underlying concepts and principles. However, the present concern to promote more active learning across all subjects does not depend as it once did, upon the nature of the task in hand or the actual *content* of the curriculum. Previously, in most cases, academic theory would automatically be presented through lectures, seminars and tutorials and practical skills through demonstration, drill and practice. Both of these delivery methods would be directed towards an audience who, although receptive, would also usually be quite passive.

Activity 5r Attitudes to Learning

Summarize how students' attitudes to learning may be affected by sessions delivered in the conventional, didactic manner described above.

As we discussed earlier (see 2.3 in Chapter 2) learners receiving a conventional, didactic presentation will respond in what Perry (1970) describes as either the 'absolutist' or the 'relativist' mode, that is either believing implicitly in the content, or considering *all* theory to be ephemeral and transient and therefore not worth the trouble of learning.

These attitudes would usually lead to either rote or surface learning designed only to meet the needs of assessment. Very few students would progress to what Perry describes as 'commitment', where learners develop their own values which allows them to make judgements about the relative worth of the expert view compared to their own active participation.

On the other hand, students involved in the development of practical skills would often not be encouraged to reflect on their learning or to consider how processes could be developed and their skills transferred to other areas.

Activity 5s Experiential Implementation

Describe how you could move from the traditional instructional approach you analysed in Activity 5s to a more experiential approach.

The purpose of experiential learning is to transcend the limitations discussed above. It is equally concerned with theoretical and practical subjects and can successfully address learner development within each of the hierarchies defined by Bloom and his colleagues – the cognitive, affective and psychomotor.

This approach has been derived from the work of Lewin (1951), who had a considerable influence on post-war group psychology. 'Experience' is stressed in the name given to his perspective of learning, partially to highlight its link to the work of Dewey and Piaget but also, as Kolb (1984) explained:

> to emphasize the central role that experience plays in the learning process. This differentiates experiential learning theory from rationalist and other cognitive theories of learning that tend to give primary emphasis to acquisition, manipulation and recall of abstract symbols, and from behavioural learning theories that deny any role for consciousness and subjective experience in the learning process.

Kolb stresses that experiential learning is a holist, integrated perspective. It is essentially student-centred involving the intellectual, emotional and psychological development of the learner.

The recognition that people learn in different ways is a significant stage in the development of a skilled and professional practitioner. The use of independent learning tasks necessitate that your learners themselves also need to consider how their own learning takes place. Rogers (1983) believed personal involvement in learning could change attitudes, behaviour and even the personality of the learner. Involving your learners in thinking about their own planning and encouraging them to take control of their own cognitive processes is beneficial in developing awareness and affecting progress in a positive way. The concept of metacognition or 'thinking about thinking' came from the cognitive psychology field and refers to the process in which learners are encouraged to take active control over their own thinking and to learn how they can best meet their goals through using planning procedures. Some of your learners may already use similar techniques to plan their approach to tasks and activities, others may not. You can encourage your learners through the use of journals, action planning and debriefing after activities to plan around their personal preferences and strengths.

Flavell (1979) developed one of the first formal models of metacognition and his example included four categories:

- Metacognitive knowledge – beliefs about themselves and how they learn, recognizing their individual preferred ways and styles.
- Metacognitive experiences – how the individual feels and responds to experiences, in particular new tasks and what motivates them.
- Metacognitive goals and tasks – identifying the desired outcomes or results of an activity, setting targets.
- Metacognitive strategies – the behaviour and strategies needed to complete the goals including timescales.

Instruction and guidance in using metacognition techniques and planning can be a useful aid to motivation for learners, encouraging them to set their own goals and formulate their own strategies for achievement. Training learners how to use information about their own cognitive processes to control, evaluate and monitor learning through metacognitive techniques has been identified as improving successful achievement. One of the better-known methods of developing individual learner's metacognition abilities is the use of mapping techniques. Mind Mapping, developed into a popular technique by Buzan (1993), can be used as a memory aid, as a record of discussions or as a brainstorming technique. Mind maps have topics arranged around a central core with grouped themes and subject matter, often in the form of a chart or pictorial representation. An alternative mapping method, Concept Mapping as described by Novak (1983), uses a hierarchical structure that illustrates the constructivist concept where new information is linked to existing knowledge in a consequential format in which the relationships, or connections, between different concepts are illustrated visually through links such as arrows or headings. This can be useful as a means of avoiding incorrect connections and confirming that the learning is meaningful.

This need to not only learn about the learning process, but also for learners to take on the responsibility for their own learning is graphically captured in Lewin's (1951) experiential model, which has since been further developed by Honey and Mumford (1982) and Kolb (1984).

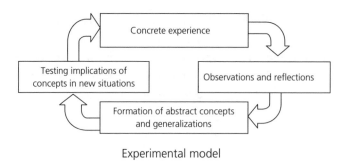

Experimental model

An important feature of the Lewinian model is that there is an emphasis on current, *concrete experiences* as a basis for the assimilation of later more abstract concepts. This immediately places value on the internal, personal experience of the learner and reduces the traditional classroom focus on the knowledge of the 'expert' (teacher or textbook) which, because it is external to the learner, may affect their perception of their role, moving it from an active involvement in the development of knowledge to a passive acceptance of the knowledge provided by others.

In addition, the cycle of operation provides the opportunity for *feedback* on the concrete experience, first from observations, which are reflected on in order to develop theories. These are then tested so as to identify new approaches and experiences. Simply put, the learner, having done something, reviews its effectiveness, develops ideas on how to do it better, and then tries out the modified approach.

The important point made by Lewin and Kolb is that many people have experiences and do not learn from them. It is the reflective processes that enable the memorizing and the learning that are so important. From these metacognitive deliberations emerge concepts and generalizations, which allow the ideas to be developed and transferred to other contexts. Similarly, it would not be sufficient to merely learn concepts and generalize them in the abstract. These theories must be tested out in the actual situation to enable the learner to establish the links between theory and practice by working through the cycle of theory, experiment, experience and reflection.

Activity 5t The Importance of Experience

Given the above explanations of the importance of the experiential cycle, relate the cycle of theory/experiment/experience/reflection to your own subject and your own learners. Make notes about how you can use this process to help the students to respond in an active manner, owning the learning rather than responding passively to tutor input.

Of course, one of the problems of introducing experiential approaches within an educational culture which is primarily concerned with the achievement of accountability outcomes is that it is difficult to create the opportunity for students to explore and understand the value of learning about how and why particular learning experiences lead to different forms of *conceptualization*. The metacognitive processing which leads to a developing awareness of learning *quality* is heavily dependent upon the context in which it takes place. For example, surface learning (which can be successfully employed to achieve good assessment results) may not lead to the deeper levels of personal and academic insights which can be so satisfying and long-lasting.

Obviously, not all experiences will be conducive or relevant to learning and consequently, as teachers we are responsible for the selection and organization of appropriate learner activities. Ideally the learner should have some involvement in this planning process but, because they will not always have the prior learning necessary to make informed decisions, it will often be a shared activity between facilitator and learner. Knowles (1970) made the point that:

> The function of planning consists of translating diagnosed needs into specific educational objectives (or dimensions of growth), designing and conducting learning experiences to achieve these objectives, and evaluating the extent to which these objectives have been accomplished. In andragogy, responsibility for performing this function is a mutual one between the learners and the teacher.

Learning from experience may be gained through learner interaction in the context of group processes organized around such activities as buzz groups, fish-bowl exercises, shout-outs, syndicates, encounter groups, etc. (see also Chapter 6). Even more elaborate interaction-based learning exercises using designed materials and equipment could involve role play, simulations and games.

Activity 5u Learning for Life

Although the above activities do create group interaction, how effective do you feel that they can be in encouraging students to develop the ability to transfer their learning to other situations, perhaps even beyond the classroom?

The type of activities we have suggested above may be seen as 'active' learning which is an improvement on passive, receptive learning. Even so, Revans (1980), the inventor of 'action learning', would have concerns that, although simulations do allow learners to run through various important interactions, they lack the crucial dimension of responsibility that is inevitably present in *real* experiences. Revans promoted the concept of 'comrades in adversity', which occurs when colleagues faced with difficulty within a work situation, solve the problem collaboratively and stressed that taking responsibility in this way, developed crucial context-based learning which is not present when the issue is solved, either by an authoritarian management decision or by the employment of an external consultant.

The theories of Lewin, Kolb and Revans add three more to our principle categories:

Practitioners should ensure that

26. the learners' previous experiences are valued.
27. no matter at which point they commence, students should move through each step of the learning cycle.
28. students should be encouraged to take responsibility for their own learning.

Experiential education is not merely about learning by doing, but is essentially about the learner identifying the need to develop and then taking on responsibility for their own learning to meet a particular objective. This brings us to this chapter's final example of theory in practice, 'collaborative learning', which is another challenging aspect of the same experiential debate.

5.8 Group collaboration

Johnson and Johnson (1990), who have carried out extensive and detailed research into the relationship between learning and cognition in *cooperative* and *competitive* educational environments, have shown absolutely categorically that collaborative learning is by far the superior method. Their findings raise serious questions about our preference for competitive arrangements within both education and the workplace. To Johnson and Johnson, *cooperative learning* involves small groups of students working together to maximize their own and each other's learning. Within such groups, students are given *two* responsibilities – to learn the required material and to make sure that *all* other members of the group do likewise. The success of individual students is measured by their *own* achievement and the achievements of *all* other group members.

The researchers believe that simply placing students in groups and instructing them to work together does not, in itself, promote higher achievement or higher-level reasoning because there are many different ways in which the learning can fail. In order to be productive, cooperative learning groups must be structured to include the essential elements of *positive interdependence*, i.e. each member can succeed only if all members succeed. The positive interdependence is facilitated by *face-to-face interaction* during which learners assist and support each other's efforts to achieve *individual accountability*, which ensures that all members do their fair share of the work.

In addition, Johnson and Johnson facilitate the development of the *interpersonal and small group skills* which are required to work cooperatively with others and the *group processing awareness,* which helps members to reflect on how well they are working together and how their effectiveness as a group may be improved.

It is useful to compare these collaborative learning processes with what Johnson and Johnson term *individualistic* learning. In a *competitive* learning situation, individual students work against each other to achieve grades that only a few students can attain and consequently within such a situation students seek an outcome which is *personally* beneficial and ignore as irrelevant the efforts and achievements of other students. Crucially, according to the theories of Johnson and Johnson, the *interpersonal interactions* that promote cognition and metacognition (thinking about thinking) *do not take place.*

In many hundreds of studies which have taken place in the USA and elsewhere during the last 20 years, cooperative learning experiences have promoted *higher achievement* than competitive and individualistic learning. Achievements which indicated this success are the quality of reasoning strategies, the generation of new ideas and solutions and the transfer of what is learned to other situations. This research has demonstrated that the more conceptual the task, the more problem solving is required, the more creative the answers need to be, and the more long-term retention is desired, the greater the superiority of cooperation over competitive and individualistic learning.

Within performance situations where considerable advantage is given to learners who

a. engage in critical, higher-level thinking
b. know what thinking strategies they are using
c. modify their strategies to perform better in different situations.

the following reasons are given by Johnson and Johnson for the success of cooperative learning strategies:

1. The expectation among learners that they will have to summarize, explain and teach what they are learning has a direct effect on the learning processes they use. Students conceptualize material and organize it cognitively differently when they are learning material in order to teach it to others, than if they are only learning for their own benefit.
2. Discussion within cooperative learning situations promotes on the part of the learners more frequent oral summarizing, explaining and elaborating of what one knows. This oral rehearsal promotes long-term retention.
3. Cooperative learning groups thrive on the heterogeneity of group members. As they accommodate themselves to each other's perspectives, strategies and approaches to completing their assignments, divergent and creative thinking are stimulated. This is especially so the more divergent the group members are.
4. In most cooperative learning situations, students with incomplete information interact with others who have different perspectives and facts. In order to understand all the relevant information gained by everyone involved, students must actively attempt to understand the content being presented and the cognitive and affective perspectives of the person presenting it. They must also at the same time evaluate the relationship of these ideas to their own and other's beliefs. It is their ability to understand other perspectives which enables the use of the wide range of information available.

5. Cooperative learning group members must externalize their ideas and reasoning for critical examination by their peers. As a result, there is often significant monitoring and regulation of learner's thinking and reasoning.

6. Within cooperative learning groups members give each other continuous feedback regarding the quality and relevance of their contributions and how performance may be improved.

7. Participation in cooperative learning groups inevitably produces conflicts among the ideas, opinions, conclusions, theories and information of members, i.e. controversy. Johnson and Johnson (1979) consider that the promotion of controversy is one of the most important routes to learning. In summary, because controversies are resolved by engaging in the discussion of the advantages and disadvantages of proposed actions and theories aimed at synthesizing novel solutions, there is an advocacy and challenging of each participant's position which is based on the synthesis of both perspectives. When managed constructively, controversy promotes uncertainty about the correctness of one's views, an active search for new information, a reconceptualization of one's knowledge and conclusions and as a consequence, increased motivation to achieve and retain deeper understanding.

Activity 5v Collaborative Learning

Try to design a learning activity for your students based on Johnson and Johnson's seven concepts. Remember, each group has a responsibility to ensure that each member not only achieves the assigned task, but is also able to explain and defend their point of view in relation to the learned content.

Johnson and Johnson's theories help us to add two final principles to complete our list.

Practitioners should ensure that

29. through enabling the interpersonal interactions of group members, they develop learner awareness of group processes.
30. once cooperative learning has been established, they deliberately stimulate intellectual conflict by structuring academic controversies.

5.9 Becoming eclectic

So, as a basis for our eclectic approach, we have now selected 30 principles from the fields of humanist, cognitive and behaviourist learning theory. Of course, this is not a definitive list; we have selected these principles for their generic nature and relevance to post-compulsory education. Many related principles from each of these fields, which have more currency within the compulsory sector, have been ignored. Nor have we presented any critical discussion on the relative merits of each of the psychological theories. Instead they have been left to stand alongside each other, and a review of the list does not now seem to present any discordant contradictions. True, there are different areas of focus but none of the principles selected create problems of congruence in relation to others in the list. There are many areas of overlap, more notably between the humanist and the cognitive fields, which can be tightened up in our final set of guidelines to successful lessons in post-compulsory education.

First of all, in order to help us arrive at a notional order, we have summarized in the following table each of the principles discussed previously and related them to the sort of action a teacher may take in order to implement them. Of course, this is only a convenient device to illustrate how principles underpin many of our routine processes. We realize that our simplistic interpretation of these complex principles will not be universally accepted in the abridged form that is presented here and in the session guide that follows. However, although many of the principles also underpin other teaching processes that have not been included, we feel that, on the whole, the exercise does illustrate good practice.

In Table 5.1 below, each of the 30 principles which have been discussed above is summarized and, by way of illustration, an example is given of how it may be implemented in practice. As pointed out previously, this table presents a limited number of implementations of a particular theory; there will be many others within each different context.

5.10 Successful sessions framework

The eclectic set of principles which we have collected together in Table 5.1 and presented as a summary guide to successful sessions in Table 5.2 could just as easily have been obtained, almost intuitively, from many experienced teachers without resorting to the survey of psychological theory contained in this chapter. However, the exercise has helped to identify the research behind many empirically tested and now accepted methods of delivering learning and it does indicate that a study of one particular field of psychology does not necessarily undermine principles drawn from another. As a consequence of the many variables within a teaching and learning relationship, each area of study does of necessity focus upon a particular facet.

The resulting guidelines for the teaching of sessions are by no means definitive, but they do contain a set of useful, generic and heuristic principles for practitioners, which represent a reasonably balanced approach to teaching. Certainly, most teaching will be improved through their inclusion.

Table 5.2 contains a summary of one approach to teaching or training which draws on established principles that have been incorporated into a generic session framework in a particular order. Of course, the purpose of the various methods can be achieved in many other ways, in a different order or in a range of contexts. This is merely an illustration and should be used as an example rather than a rigid prescription. Our emphasis, as always, is on responsive teaching which has been informed through practice and theory.

Table 5.1 Summary of theoretical principles translated into teacher actions

	Practitioners ensure that:	Theoretical sources	Relevant teacher action:
1.	Each students' prior learning and experience is valued.	Bruner, J. (1966) Kelly, G. (1989) Rogers, C. (1983) Ausubel, D. (1965)	Be aware of student entry behaviour; use experiential methods where appropriate.
2.	Where possible, any threat to the learners' self-esteem is removed.	Cooley, C.H. (1912) James, W. (1890) Mead, G.H. (1934) Rogers, C. (1983) Shibutani, T. (1971)	Create a supportive learning environment.
3.	The purpose of provided learning is understood by the learners.	Burns, R. (1982) Kelly, G. (1989) Rogers, C. (1983) Skinner, B.F. (1938)	Set clear, achievable objectives.
4.	Students are encouraged to become aware of their own learning processes.	Perry, W. (1970) Usher, R.S. (1985) Ausubel, D. (1965), Flavell, J. (1979)	Adjust pace according to elicited student responses, encourage thinking about thinking.
5.	The development of learner independence is encouraged.	Knowles, M. (1984) Kelly, G. (1989) Rogers, C. (1983)	Avoid prescription; encourage learner independent thinking.
6.	Learners are stimulated to recall previously learned capabilities.	Gagne, R.M. (1985) Perry, W. (1970) Usher, R.S. (1985)	Consider student responses in order to evaluate understanding.
7.	The desired mental sets of the learner are activated.	Gagne, R.M. (1985) Bruner, J. (1966) Ausubel, D. (1965) Rogers, C. (1983)	Use probing, high-order questioning; promote consolidation/transfer.
8.	The learner receives appropriate feedback from the teacher.	Gagne, R.M. (1985) Perry, W. (1970) Usher, R.S. (1985) Skinner, B.F. (1938)	Provide appropriate feedback to support students.
9.	Teachers share the process of learning with learners in order to reduce the effects of culturally based resistance.	Bruner, J. (1966)	Encourage and consider carefully student feedback with a view to improving future teaching and learning.
10.	Learning is organized in order to build on previous learning (e.g. the spiral curriculum).	Ausubel, D. (1965) Bruner, J. (1966)	Relate new knowledge to previous learning.

(Continued)

11.	Learning is clearly structured to show relationships and continuity.	Ausubel, D. (1965) Bruner, J. (1966)	Plan the session – the individual parts should be clearly related to each other and previous learning in an appropriate way. Break the skills or knowledge down into a logical sequence. Form a link to the next session.
12.	Problem-solving techniques are used to challenge previous perceptions.	Ausubel, D. (1965) Bruner, J. (1966)	Challenge learners to solve problems.
13.	Meaningful reception learning is used in order to develop existing conceptual systems.	Ausubel, D. (1965) Bruner, J. (1966)	Identify definite stages and relationships to the whole. Use aids competently. Stress key words and essential stages.
14.	Teaching is organized around concepts and principles which potentially have the widest explanatory power, inclusiveness, reliability and generalizability to the chosen content.	Ausubel, D. (1965) Bruner, J. (1966)	Provide successful closure – major purposes, principles and constructs are summarized to form a cognitive link between past knowledge and current achievement.
15.	A sequence of presentation is selected which best illustrates the characteristics of the chosen cognitive structure in terms of clarity, stability and integratedness.	Ausubel, D. (1965) Skinner, B.F. (1938)	Provide a statement of objectives, explanation, purpose, relevance of topic, process to be followed, etc. Use presentational approaches where appropriate.
16.	Learning is regularly rewarded during the early stages, that should consist of short steps. In later stages variable reinforcement is preferable in order to avoid extinction.	Ausubel, D. (1965) Skinner, B.F. (1938) Thorndike, E.L. (1931)	Break skills or knowledge down into a logical sequence; reinforce behaviours.
17.	Reward quickly follows the appropriate response. Motivation is increased by immediate feedback.	Skinner, B.F. (1938) Thorndike, E.L. (1931)	Use appropriate motivators and incentives; provide appropriate feedback to support student development.
18.	Desirable behaviour is reinforced and unwanted behaviour is, as far as possible, ignored (since attention can often be a strong reinforcer). Emphasis should be on praising and encouraging desirable behaviour and not on punishing undesirable behaviour. Undesirable behaviour should, as far as possible, be extinguished.	Skinner, B.F. (1938); Thorndike, E.L. (1931) Bandura, A. and Walter, R.H. (1963)	Use positive reinforcement to reward desired student behaviour.

(Continued)

Table 5.1—cont'd.

Practitioners ensure that:	Theoretical sources	Relevant teacher action:
19.	Negative reinforcement is used with care even though it is preferable to punishment. Punishment should not be used since it often has emotional side effects (anxiety inhibits learning) and will produce avoidance behaviour (learners start missing lessons).	Skinner, B.F. (1938) Thorndike, E.L. (1931)	Use voice, manner, language and personal characteristics to reassure learners and facilitate learning.
20.	Lessons are carefully planned in order to encourage de-sired behaviours by eliciting necessary responses through appropriate reinforcers.	Skinner, B.F. (1938) Bandura, A. and Walter, R.H. (1963)	Stimulate interest/attention using a variety of verbal and non-verbal techniques.
21.	Behaviours and tasks which the students are expected to learn are modelled, preferably by the tutors. For example, being punctual, showing enthusiasm or taking a critically reflective stance.	Skinner, B.F. (1938) Bandura, A. and Walter, R.H. (1963)	Communicate clearly; maintain eye contact; model behaviours.
22.	Students are aware that desirable behaviour is being reinforced.	Bandura, A. and Walter, R.H. (1963)	Demonstrate subject expertise and enthusiasm and encourage students to respond.
23.	Students are also used as models. For example, during group work, pair the confident, successful students with those who are less successful and try to build a mutually supportive relationship.	Bandura, A. and Walter, R.H. (1963) Vygotsky (1978)	Encourage student rapport and interaction; encourage sharing through discussion.
24.	When forming learning groups teachers are aware of the personal characteristics of members and their influence on the dynamics of the group.	Belbin (1981) and Hackman, J.R. and Morris, C.G. (1978) Gardner (1983)	Form viable learning groups; structure activities for a 'blend' of intelligences.
25.	Effective group operation is facilitated by developing or providing skills and resources.	Belbin (1981) and Hackman, J.R. and Morris, C.G. (1978)	Facilitate effective group operation.

(Continued)

26.	The learners' previous experiences are valued.	Kolb, D.A. (1984) Lewin, K. (1951) Revans, R. (1980) Kelly, G. (1989) Rogers, C. (1983)	Move learners through cycle but allow to start at different points according to their preferred learning style;
27.	No matter at which point they commence, students should move through each step of the learning cycle.	Kolb, D.A. (1984), Lewin, K. (1951), Revans, R. (1980) Knowles, M. (1984)	Promote learner independence and self-direction.
28.	Students should be encouraged to take responsibility for their own learning.	Knowles, M. (1984) Johnson, D.W. and Johnson, R.T. (1989)	Develop student awareness of group dynamics and processes.
29.	Teachers encourage collaboration by making learning a collective responsibility.	Johnson & Johnson (1989)	Establish collaborative learning groups.
30.	Once cooperative learning has been established, teachers deliberately stimulate intellectual conflict by structuring academic controversies.	Johnson & Johnson (1989)	Structure learning activities which encourage students to explain, defend and challenge ideas.

Table 5.2 A suggested framework for successful sessions

1. Preparation

1.1	Be aware of student entry behaviour and build on learner's previous experience (1 Rogers, 12 Ausubel 26 Knowles, Kelly, Rogers).
1.2	Set clear achievable objectives (14 Ausubel, 19 Skinner).
	Plan lesson – the individual parts should be clearly related to each other and previous learning in an appropriate way (9 Bruner).
1.3	Create a supportive learning environment (4 Rogers).
1.4	Form viable learning groups (24 Belbin, Hackman & Morris, Gardner).
1.5	Structure learning activities which encourage students to explain, defend and challenge ideas (30 Johnson & Johnson).
1.6	Develop student awareness of group dynamics and processes (29 Johnson & Johnson).

2. Introduction (Short opening period)

2.1	Stimulate interest/attention using a variety of verbal and non-verbal techniques (20 Bandura).
2.2	Use voice, manner, language and personal characteristics to reassure learners and facilitate learning (4 Rogers).
2.3	Provide a statement of objectives, explanation, purpose, relevance of topic, process to be followed etc. (2, 3 Rogers, 13 Ausubel, 8, 10 Bruner, 6 Gagne).
2.4	Relate new knowledge to previous learning (1 Rogers, 5 Gagne, 9 Bruner, 12 Ausubel).
2.5	Communicate clearly, maintain eye contact (20 Bandura).

3. Development (Major period)

3.1	Demonstrate subject expertise, enthusiasm (20 Bandura).
3.2	Break skills or knowledge down into logical sequence (10 Bruner, 14 Ausubel).
3.3	Identification of definite stages and relationship to whole (13, 14 Ausubel).
3.4	Competent use of appropriate learning aids (19 Skinner).
3.5	Use suitable, probing, high-order questions (3 Rogers, 5 Gagne, 11 Bruner, 14 Ausubel).

3.6   Consider student responses in order to evaluate understanding (12 Ausubel, 6 Gagne).

3.7   Adjust pace according to elicited responses (12 Ausubel).

3.8   Use appropriate motivators and incentives (15 Skinner).

3.9   Use presentational approaches where appropriate (12 Ausubel).

3.10   User experiential methods where appropriate to move learners through theory, experiment, experience and reflection cycle (3 Rogers, 11 Bruner, 26, 27 Lewin, Kolb, Revans).

3.11   Use positive reinforcement to reward desired student behaviour (15,16,17 Skinner, 21 Bandura).

3.12   Facilitate effective group operation (25 Hackman & Morris, Vygotsky).

3.13   Promote learner independence (28 Lewin, Kolb & Revans).

4. Closure (Short, closing period)

4.1   Provide successful closure – major purposes, principles and constructs are summarized to form a cognitive link between past knowledge and current achievements (13 Ausubel, 10 Bruner).

4.2   Stress key words and essential stages (15 Skinner, 14 Ausubel).

4.3   Promote consolidation/transfer (6 Gagne, 10 Bruner, 14 Ausubel).

4.4   Make any assessment relevant to objectives (11 Bruner).

4.5   Form a link to next session (14 Ausubel, 10 Bruner).

4.6   Promote and consider student feedback with a view to improving future teaching and learning (1 Rogers, 9 Bruner, 14 Ausubel, Flavell).

5.11 Conclusion

As is so often the case when considering national standards, the overlap between professional areas of practice becomes apparent. Taking into account the needs of learners, supporting, planning and assessing them, all have their part to play in informing our selection from the range of appropriate teaching and learning methods available for particular student groups.

What seems clear is that, even when teachers have established a preferred approach, they must also be willing to consider new methods from the increasing variety which are available, in order to ensure that they are taking the necessary steps to promote the growth of all their learners.

It is important to point out that the means of delivering any of the above concepts has deliberately *not* been discussed because the available media and potential emphasis are developing and changing daily and will inevitably be different in every situation and consequently the options available in specific educational situations cannot be predicted.

Although the teacher's 'tool kit' that we have presented may seem overly complex, many of its conceptual devices will be appropriate only in particular contexts and for specific purposes. However, although we all grow to rely on our favourite methods, the better we are informed the more quickly we will be able to select the optimum approach when faced with new or difficult situations.

5.12 Useful publications

Bigge, M. (1982), *Learning Theories for Teachers*. New York: Harper & Row.
  Quite a 'weighty' book which does explain in detail the main learning theories and identifies how theorists such as Bandura, Gagne, Bruner, Bloom and Skinner impact on the classroom. There is a tendency by the author to assume an existing knowledge of basic psychological schools of thought.

Buzan, T. (1993), *The Mind Map Book: Radiant Thinking*. London: BBC Books.
  One of a series of books by Tony Buzan. They are all very easy to read and tend to prompt the reader into thought and reflection rather than presenting theory in a formal way. Hints and suggestions about ways to improve the thinking process and memory. A good read to supplement some of the more academic publications available.

Berryman, J. (1991), *Psychology and You*. London: British Psychological Society.
  A good introduction to psychology and theories about the human personality. Highly readable with two particularly useful chapters on memory and learning and thinking. Small and portable and a good book to 'dip into'.

Dryden, G. and J. Vos (1994), *The Learning Revolution*. Accelerated Learning Systems.
  This book looks at ways to use your mind to enable you to learn as much as possible as quickly as possible. It is very much a 'fun' text which should be read with an open, but critical mind.

Shaffer, D. (1999), *Developmental Psychology* (5th edn). US: Brooks/Cole.
  A detailed psychological text which looks at childhood and adolescence. It contains useful chapters on learning and thinking, information processing and intelligence. The section on the development of 'self' is also relevant when considering motivating factors in education. All major theorists are discussed and most learning theories are examined.

5.13 Useful websites

www.emtech.net/learning_theories.htm
Learning theories.
www.gse.buffalo.edu/fas/shuell/cep564/Metacog.htm
Metacognition: an overview, by Jennifer A. Livingston.
www.infed.org/biblio/b-learn.htm
Learning theory.
http://tip.psychology.org/
Explorations in learning and instruction: theory into practice database.
www.tipcet.com
Additional materials related to teaching and learning.

6 Effective Environments
Tricia Semeraz

Chapter Outline

Key Concepts

Assignments, Buzz Groups, Constructivist, Demonstrations, Effective e-Learning, Environment, Entry Characteristics, Formal teaching, Hierarchy of Needs, Ice-Breaking, Instructivist, Keeping Track, Learner's Agreement, Learners as a Resource. Learning Contracts, Learning Resources, Lecturer-Centred, Lectures, Motivation, Projects, Resonate, Role Play, Search, Self-Concept, Seminars, Sensory Experience, Session Management, Simulation, Games, Small-Group Tutorials, Student-Centred, Syndicates, Team-Teaching, Values and Attitudes, Virtual Learning Environments.

6.1 Introduction

As you know, the earlier chapters have introduced you to the Professional Standards, Reflection, Student Needs Planning and Educational Theories, and we are only halfway through the book. Unfortunately, it has been necessary to separate the many constituent parts of Lifelong Learning in this way, but we are concious of the dangers of disaggregating down such a complex process. Although we are very aware of the various processes and the interacting relationships which make up a teaching and learning provision, it is also important to be aware of how the whole, total environment that we have necessarily created impacts on our learners, both on entering our colleges and as they begin to become more familiar with what we are trying to achieve. For it is the *totality* of the learners' experience which is our primary concern and the effect of the various components on this intricate amalgamation of interacting parts can be difficult to predict. However, as teachers this is our task and it is, after all, what makes education and training so difficult, fascinating and, ultimately (when we finally get it right) so richly rewarding.

There is, of course, some value in separately addressing each of the parts which make up the whole. This disaggregated view invariably helps in our analysis because the whole is often so intimidatingly complex that it defies examination. Even so, it is only after we have taken an informed *holistic* overview, that we will become aware of the role and importance of some of the less obvious components and can begin to appreciate the extent of the influence for good or bad, which just one part of the system can have. This point is relevant because this chapter is addressing the *learning environment, learning activities* and *learning resources*, each of which is dependent upon the success of the others.

In exploring these areas we are helping to address two domains of the LLUK Professional Standards: B, '*Learning and Teaching*' and C, '*Specialist Teaching*'. Obviously each of these discrete areas is related, but there is also considerable overlap. First we will consider the more general of the two topics and then later discuss how the work of the Subject Mentor relates to this general area of operation. Then, in Chapter 10, we will discuss *reviewing learning, working relationships* and *effective communication with learners*. It is our intention, as you consider how each of these six facets are related to your own practice, to try to sustain a sense of the totality of what, in fact, are management practices plus the importance of the interconnectedness of each of the component parts which form the two chapters.

6.2 The learning environment

I'm sure we are all aware that effective teaching is not a haphazard process whereby the eagerly awaiting students automatically consume any knowledge or skill that might be presented to them. Previous chapters have discussed how we increase the likelihood of effectiveness by purposefully planning our teaching, taking into account the learner and subject characteristics. However, this interaction takes place within a particular environment or setting which may well have its own characteristics that can significantly affect the quality of the ensuing interactions.

Activity 6a First Impressions

Imagine that a new group of learners have entered for the first time the learning environment that you manage. Consider what the students may be feeling as they arrive for the first time, the nature of their apprehensions and the range of attitudes they may adopt. What practical steps can you take to encourage them to react positively?

Naturally, the learners will be looking for any explicit or implicit indications that the experience they are about to take part in will be positive, enhancing, non-threatening, enjoyable, rewarding, challenging, organized, entertaining, cool, surprising, etc. These hopes and aspirations will, of course, differ from student to student and you will *not* be able to predict or change the attitudes they bring to the session. However, there are many things that you can do to reassure them, whatever their needs are, that you and the environment you have created, will be positively responsive. Try simple things, such as:

- ensure that the setting looks cared for, decorate with colourful pictures, play music
- minimize authoritarian notices or instructions, use humorous, interesting displays
- smile, reassure, explain, use their names as soon as possible
- encourage questioning and respond sincerely as a facilitator
- inform the students, provide choice
- emphasize success, use upbeat language, avoid stressful references
- trigger positive emotions, suggest targets they can achieve, introduce hope
- find something about each of them to like.

Activity 6b Building on Good Beginnings

As the students settle in, their questions will become more specific and personal to them. Reflect on the sort of anxieties they may have and the questions these attitudes will generate.

Naturally, students need to feel that their contribution to the learning is valued. These needs challenge the teacher to manage the learning process in a way that may provide answers to the following notional questions students may ask themselves regarding whether the teacher will

1. provide opportunities for me to be involved and motivated?
2. know who I am?
3. know what I'm doing?
4. explain to me what I should be doing?
5. provide varied, appropriate and interesting sessions?
6. facilitate my success on this learning programme?

These six fundamental questions may be used to evaluate the success of your chosen approach for whatever learning group you may be working with. The answers will provide a good guide as to how conducive to learning your learners themselves *perceive* the environment to be. We will use these questions as a basis for our investigation of an effective learning environment.

6.3 Motivation

The above questions indicate an essentially humanistic approach, which we discussed briefly in the previous chapter. During the development of these ideas more than 50 years ago, Rogers (1983[1951]) and Maslow (1970[1962]) were concerned with the individual's willingness to accept and participate actively in his or her environment. This aptitude is very much dependent upon their own self-concept and related levels of motivation or 'self-actualization'. This, in turn, affects their perception of their learning environment as something that they can *affect and manipulate* or something they must *accept as unchangeable.* Maslow believed that self-actualization was a human need, which he placed at the top of his notional hierarchy, as he believed that other needs must be met *before* this ultimate level of fulfilment could be achieved.

Table 6.1 Maslow's hierarchy of needs

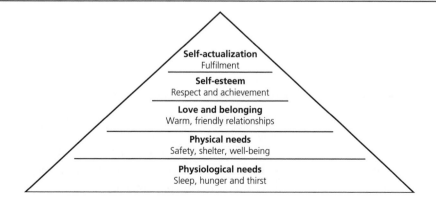

The ascending order of needs identified by Maslow begins at the bottom with basic physiological demands (*hunger, thirst,* etc.) that require satisfying before moving up to comfort requirements such as *safety and shelter. Love and belonging* helps to establish *self-esteem* needs (pride), which provide a platform for the cognitive and conceptual needs of *self-actualization.* Thus physical survival needs must be satisfied in order for people to concentrate on higher needs. Maslow believed that the final self-actualization level may only be achieved by some people and then perhaps only for a short time. However, this higher level of fulfilment, which is mainly experienced on a conceptual level, may take many different forms and is open to all of us.

Activity 6c Hierarchy of Needs

Consider Maslow's theory that the lower need must be satisfied before moving on to a higher need and then relate it to your particular learners. Is it true, for example, that the motivation related to the establishment of self-esteem cannot be achieved without gaining love and belonging first?

It is true that if students are made to feel comfortable and involved in their learning they will be much more likely to succeed. Even so, sources of motivation take many forms within a whole range of different human activities and often lead to surprising levels of learning and achievement, which enhance the individual self-esteem of people who do not appear to be endowed with a well-developed sense of belonging. Their motivation is often a powerful but intrinsic force.

Activity 6d A Motivational Structure

In your PDJ, develop a list of practical ways in which you could improve the motivation of your particular group of students. Give a brief explanation of why you feel that each particular method would work with your learners.

Of course, as we have stressed several times, each learner group will be motivated by *different* things and many of the motivational forces will be *specific* to your own particular context (e.g. competing with another group, bettering previous performances, helping other learners). However, the following are some more generic approaches, which are often successful (notice the importance of assessment, feedback and evaluation):

a. Set clear objectives at the beginning of the session so that you and the learners have expectations of what they should be able to achieve by the end of the session. *This helps to encourage the learners to establish a positive mental 'set'.*

b. Try to develop differentiated objectives. *These cater for the range of abilities within the group. In this way, the outcomes are more appropriate and learners will feel either less patronized (by easily achieved objectives) or less stressed (by being presented with overly difficult targets).*

c. Ensure that, although there will inevitably be a spread of marks, everyone should be able achieve a reasonable result. *This may seem patronizing, but if you develop the skill of devising an appropriate assessment that the learners know is a challenge, but during which they also anticipate that, if they do the work, they will be able to do reasonably well, they will find it reassuring, motivating and rewarding.*

d. During all classroom activities your students should be encouraged to feel that, should there be anything that they are unsure of, it is *expected* they will seek clarification. *Try to **avoid** putting the onus for any lack of understanding on them. Try asking 'Have I explained everything clearly?' rather than 'Is there anything you don't understand?' which will often result in silence as they do not wish to appear to be the only one with a problem.*

e. All contributions should be acknowledged and, where appropriate, praised. *Resist the temptation to make jokes at the learners' expense.*

f. Try to use a range of techniques to make the session interesting, involving and stimulating. *Think in terms of **varying compatible methods**, rather than an all singing and dancing extravaganza.*

g. Where possible, provide an opportunity for *formative* assessment so that students know that they are on the right track. *The earlier they are aware of any misunderstandings, the more time they have to correct them.*

h. Try to make feedback constructive with clear points for development. *The learners need to know how to recover if they have made serious errors. Sometimes it isn't very helpful to receive only **confirmatory** feedback (i.e. 'you have listed all the components correctly'). Because your students need to know about any potential way forward, always try to ensure that the feedback is also **developmental**.*

i. Take steps to demonstrate to the students the *relevance* of the session to the syllabus *as a whole. They need to see the total problem to appreciate the function and value of the parts. This provision of a 'gestalt' or whole view helps to develop a level of understanding that often cannot be achieved through a study of the parts.*

j. Ensure that your final assessment of the learners' work incorporates *summative* comments, which look back at what has been covered, together with *constructive* comments, which help to prepare the student for the next piece of assessment. *It is often possible to incorporate into assessment feedback acknowledgement or praise together with suggestions of how particular elements can be developed further within the next piece of coursework.*

k. Don't forget that the intention is to develop *independent* learners, so try to suggest ways forward which are not overly prescriptive. *Let the student make choices and decisions by suggesting a **number** of ways, rather than stipulating what you consider to be the 'proper' or 'ideal' method.*

6.4 Self-concept

We included a lengthy discussion about the theories of group dynamics and the effect on learning in the previous chapter. The implications were that, *only a very limited number of people* within a typical learning environment, *wish to remain anonymous.* Most want their fellow learners to be aware of their interests, experiences and needs and usually they also wish to know about their peers. Very often, even individual learning is promoted by the security of a group of fellow students who are sharing the same experiences and difficulties. An important part of this security is the knowledge that their teacher or trainer not only knows them, but also is concerned for their well-being. Try to think of a means of informally getting to know more about your learners by completing the following activity.

Activity 6e Getting to Know the Learners

Think again about a particular group of learners you know well and suggest an enjoyable, less formal activity which will not only encourage the class members to get to know more about each other, but will also let them know that you (the teacher/trainer) are getting to know them and allowing them to know more about you.

There are many interesting 'ice-breaking' exercises and we have suggested two of these below. As you would expect, it is essential when undertaking such exchanges that the learners are not embarrassed by interactions they cannot handle, or that they do not become stressed by exercises they have difficulty completing.

- *Presenting*: One simple way is to allow groups of two or three students to talk to each other for about ten minutes in order to discover as much as possible about each other and what their reason was for joining the particular class. In turn, they will then introduce their 'interviewee' to the rest of the class, providing as much detail as they have managed to glean.
- *Signatures*: A second method would be to organize an 'autograph hunt' by finding as many different questions (or signatures) as there are people in the group, including yourself. Get the class to help you find out who:

  1. speaks more than one language
  2. has bathed a baby this week
  3. has a younger brother or sister
  4. has a relative who lives abroad
  5. is new to this area.

Activity 6f Interactive Activity

When you have tried one of these interactive 'getting to know you' exercises with your learners, reflect on the process. Consider if and how they helped you. Reflect on the usefulness of this type of interactive activity. For example, would it have been just as effective if you had just told everyone the name of each group member? Would it work for all learners, at any time, in any setting? What influences this?

6.5 Keeping track

You will probably realize that, even though you have spent time building up the trust of your students through various interactive activities, you can easily damage this very precious relationship. Your careful nurturing of them towards independence can be undermined should they suddenly realize that *you* don't really appreciate all of the different ways in which they are developing. Students can be extremely disappointed to find that a tutor, whom they believed to be attuned to their interests and achievements, is not in fact, aware of the strides they have recently made. Nevertheless, teachers are extremely busy and cannot be expected to be aware of every development which is taking place in learning environments other than their own.

Activity 6g Significant Student Development

How can you possibly keep abreast of student development? Summarize the ways in which you can remain aware of significant development being achieved by each learner.

6.5.1 Learning contracts, agreements and journals

One obvious device which would allow you to keep abreast of your learners' developing areas of interest and exploration would be to encourage them to keep a reflective log or learning diary/journal (see guidance in Chapter 2). An occasional review of this record, together with the student, will allow them to explain their interests and how they wish to develop further.

A more formal approach, which effectively places some of the responsibility on the learners themselves, is the use of *learning contracts* or *learning agreements*. This device may seem to be merely 'passing the buck' but, if implemented with integrity, the process can be a vehicle for the genuine sharing of the learning process between tutor and student, where progressively the formal *teacher/taught* relationship is replaced with the notion of a learning partnership or community. This process clearly embraces philosophies of learner-centred learning, by encouraging individuals to articulate and then realize their own goals. Along the way they are helped to identify more clearly the abilities, potential and progress which they have already achieved and those that they will achieve as they proceed through their chosen programme of study.

A simple definition of any contract is 'a written or spoken agreement'. It is important that this agreement should make explicit what the expectations of both the learners and the tutors are within the particular establishment context.

Activity 6h Developing a Learning Contract

Again take your own learners within your own establishment as your focus. Summarize the things that you feel it would be important to include in any learning contract. Think of the separate and the shared responsibilities of the parties involved. Remember that this is essentially a mutual agreement between equals, rather than a formal, legally binding contract characterized by authority and compliance.

The contract should focus on the *process* of learning, rather than solely on the product of the learning process. You will probably be concerned to ensure that not only should the achievement at the end of the programme be important, but also the quality of each individual learner's journey to the selected goal. The 'value added' will not only be quantitative (i.e. the award achieved) but also qualitative (the range of subtle experiences along the way).

Dart and Clarke (1991) believe that a learning contract will help learners to develop habits related to lifelong learning. The current educational processes for many of today's learners encourage, and indeed expect, them to be autonomous individuals in charge of their own learning, and the use of contracts fosters that autonomy. The ownership of learning becomes a reality and individual learning is the result.

6.5.2 Learning agreements

Table 6.2 shows some typical statements that we have gathered together from a Learning Agreement which you may consider including in your own learning contract/agreement. You will note that the responsibilities of both the learner and the educational institution are made clear to both parties.

Activity 6i Learning Agreement Details

Compare the contract/agreement you have designed with the example in Table 6.2 and make any adjustments you may consider appropriate.

McAllister (1996) made the point that this focus on what is to be achieved is an essential part of education today:

> [T]eachers should not deny their teaching and learning expertise and so should continue to advise, guide and encourage students to meet their learning objectives. If such an approach is not integral within the planning process, it may well be difficult, if not impossible to attempt to 'change' once a programme is being delivered.

Table 6.2 Learning agreement

between (*Full name of programme member*) and (*Full name of institution/establishment*)

Institutional/establishment commitment:

On the .... programme, the (*name of establishment*) undertakes to provide:

a. teaching by suitably qualified and experienced staff
b. adequate accommodation to meet the demands of the course
c. an opportunity to negotiate a learning programme
d. a system for the accreditation of prior learning
e. a programme tutor and a personal tutorial system
f. a validated system of assessments and accreditation
g. access to appropriate equipment and facilities
h. access to college-based library resources
i. access to appropriate services, e.g. student services, counselling, health support
j. a formative review system
k. an understanding that it may be necessary for a member to leave the programme if continued attendance would not appear to be in her/his best interests or the interests of other members
l. an appeals procedure.

Programme member's commitment:

Following enrolment onto the .... programme and after initial assessment and guidance, I undertake to:

a. follow an agreed programme of learning, which can only be amended after negotiation with personal tutor/course tutor
b. attend all sessions/activities as required in the agreed programme and provide written explanations in the case of absences
c. make appropriate contact with the programme during any 15 working-day (3-week) period
d. cooperate in all administrative matters covering enrolments, attendance, assessment and programme evaluation
e. provide a Learning Agreement for any programme being undertaken at another institution
f. where I have indicated that a sponsor will pay my fees, if for any reason the sponsor does not pay, I will be liable for the debt
g. in signing this form I agree to comply with the College Learner Agreement and Code of Conduct, details of which can be found in the Student Handbook.

I accept the commitments stated above:

Student Name: ....………… Signature: ....……….. Date: ....

I accept the commitments stated above on behalf of: (*Institution/Establishment Name*) ....

Programme Leader Name: ....….............. Signature: ....……. Date ....…......

By signing this form, you are agreeing that the College is entitled to use the information provided both on this form and for your student memebership card, for purposes connected with the college as an educational institution, including publicity and marketing. The information collected will be stored on the college computerized student record system. Some or all of the data may be supplied to other organizations, as described in our registration under the Act. The information you provide on this form will be passed to the Learning and Skills Council, which is registered under the Data Protection Act 1998. The registration is primarily for the collection and analysis of statistical data but it also allows the council to share information with other organizations for the purpose of detecting fraud. Further information about data confidentiality is available by written request to the Central Administration Unit.

The teacher's task is inevitably demanding. Not only is it important to plan a purposeful lesson, but also it is equally important to be able to manage the lesson to meet the varying needs of the students so that they are motivated to learn. The four important steps in structuring this process may be remembered through the acronym REAL:

Resonate This simply means that before you can initiate any learning, you need to get on the same 'wavelength' as your students. You must develop strategies that ensure that your input is being received and understood.

Educate Having established two-way transactional communication, you can now introduce your key concepts to the group.

Activate Don't leave the learners sitting there merely receiving information for too long. Get them more involved through relevant activities.

Liberate Think about how, through your teaching, you are going to start to gradually move your students towards *independent operation*. You should begin these small steps towards autonomy as soon as possible because the longer they remain dependent upon you to provide all of the answers, the more difficult they will find it to stand on their own two feet.

Activity 6j Getting REAL

Observe an experienced teacher and analyse how they operate these important concepts of classroom management. Compare this to your own methods and reflect on how you might improve the students' engagement with the learning process and reduce poor motivation

---

A device which might help during this developmental/analytical process is the checklist in Table 6.3 which suggests some ways of developing our REAL concepts. You may use this as a planning sheet, as a way of recording for yourself key incidents during an observed session, or as a framework for giving feedback to a practitioner after an observed session (this pro forma is available on the **tipcet.com** website).

6.6 Establishing an effective learning environment

Perhaps the most essential feature of an effective learning relationship is that students always know exactly what they should be doing. Admittedly, it is difficult to consistently achieve this ideal state. However, the establishment of an ethos where learners are consistently

Table 6.3 Session planning or observation sheet

Steps:	Comments:
1. Resonate • Ice-breaking or introductory phase – getting to know them again • Show the learners respect; know their names, interests, etc. brief overview of the session using familiar terminology • Link to previous learning identifying intended learning outcomes • Earn their trust by trying to understand and meet their needs • Stimulate interest through glimpses of what each of them can achieve • Challenge by passing to them some responsibility • Differentiate by setting individual targets.	
2. Educate • Provide information using a range of appropriate methods • Communicate clearly • Use open, directed questioning • Deliberately develop their understanding and skills • Avoid spoon-feeding or unnecessary repetition.	
3. Activate • Vary the pace; introduce activities • Get the learners to summarize what they have learned • Facilitator learning wherever possible, instead of lecturing • Use collaborative learning exercises • Help learners to appreciate and share your enthusiasms • Don't let them lapse into a passive/receptive mode.	
4. Liberate • Let the students summarize what has been learned • Share understandings • Discuss how they arrived at their conceptualization of key points • Identify areas of concern and let others suggest ways forward • Revisit targets and stress their achievability • Suggest how their learning will be developed further in subsequent sessions • Let them bring ideas to the next session.	

encouraged to become informed, independent and motivated, will often depend on setting certain ground rules for both staff and students. Obviously many of these guidelines will be specific to the actual educational context and are difficult to generalize about, but some possible examples of these prerequisites might be:

- all tutors should support the underpinning values of the programme
- learning should be active and student-centred
- high expectations of learner performance should be demonstrated by setting challenging but achievable targets.

Activity 6k Underpinning Programme Values and Attitudes

Consider what you would expect of colleagues who are teaching on a programme you manage. What would be their core values and how would they be expressed in their interactions with your learners?

Good tutors show that they care about students. They engage with them and take responsibility for dealing with problems. They have high expectations, ensure good attendance, homework completion and achievement. They follow up students when they fall behind required standards and they inspire students and communicate their own enthusiasm about their subject to them.

The above is a summary of some fairly basic principles, which also set good examples for students. These first steps begin the gradual process of developing student independence (which eventually will encourage them to take on more responsibility) and may be further broken down into the following activities:

- try to get to know learners as quickly as possible so that you can address them by name
- remember what it is like to be a beginner learning a new skill
- where possible, make use of the students' knowledge and experience
- spend time finding out about their background, culture and reasons for doing the course
- set high standards at the start of the course, for example 100 per cent pass rates
- generate enthusiasm and thus a positive work ethic by allowing students to see your own genuine delight in their achievements
- praise students' success and encourage them when they encounter difficulties
- communicate non-verbally as well as verbally
- use metaphors and real examples to provide insight into difficult problems
- remember that teaching and learning is a two-way process, you can learn new skills and ideas from your students
- occasionally provide something special, such as a trip or a guest speaker.

6.6.1 Session management

It is fairly obvious that very little positive learning will take place during our teaching sessions if we do not achieve an effective management of the proceedings. That is not to say that we must impose strict controls over each of the learning processes; that would be far too heavy handed, particularly for more mature students.

However, as teachers, the activities and interactions *are* our responsibility and, as we stressed earlier, planning for success is essential even if we find the need to modify our approach in the light of the learner's initial response. Ironically, this is even more true of a laissez-faire, experiential session where the outcomes are deliberately kept vague or unknown. In such a situation, a whole range of variables will need to be anticipated and planned for if we are to avoid unproductive chaos.

Most learners will enter our taught sessions wishing to achieve a positive outcome, and we have a responsibility to establish an environment where they may use the strategies they feel comfortable with to achieve that success. Students must be encouraged to respect fellow learners and this includes trying to ensure that their behaviour is not intrusive to others.

As tutors, we will find if difficult to manage learning effectively if students are not attentive or able to concentrate on the session. We have the responsibility of establishing an environment which is conducive to the learning of those present and to do this we need to establish clear ground rules for the behaviour of all members:

1. be punctual and expect your students to be punctual: start session on time
2. develop respect between the student and the teacher
3. discourage disruptive behaviour which distracts others, such as chatting while you are teaching
4. use positive reinforcement, good humour and a pleasant disposition as your key session management strategies
5. support college rules and procedures
6. adhere to breaks in long sessions
7. begin with and maintain a friendly, approachable authority in your dealings with students
8. take immediate action to challenge abusive, sexist or racist language and comments
9. always check up on absences
10. ask students to turn off mobile phones
11. make sure that students have work to be going on with
12. ensure that productive work is being done when tasks are set in groups or pairs.

Activity 6I Managing Group Work

Imagine that you have a large group of students with varying abilities and personalities. You find that a group of more capable students prefer to sit together and object to being separated and placed in preselected groups on the grounds that, while they may well each be able to contribute a great deal to the overall group performance, they will individually gain very little because they will not find the experience sufficiently challenging. How would you manage this situation?

Compromise will be the keynote here. The high-flyers do work well together and always remain focused on the task. The rest of the class seem to prefer to have the composition of the group changed with each new activity as they enjoy exchanging learning with as many others as possible.

Obviously, the class should not be exposed to any sense of elitism in their midst since our aim is to make all students feel equally valued. However, at the same time we should give equal recognition to the needs of all students, taking account of their widely differing abilities, aptitudes and learning styles.

A solution could be for the tutor to continue to organize the groups, but to discreetly arrange different patterns of membership according to the task at hand. For example, where the activity is to investigate what has been learned, the problem group will stay together and will, in this way, benefit from peer pressure at their own level of learning. When they feed back during a plenary, the rest of the class will benefit from their ideas. When the group activity involves practical implementation of earlier learning or revision exercises, then the more capable students will join other groups so that eventually all learners have the opportunity to work with each other.

6.7 Teaching and learning methods

Earlier chapters have discussed the planning of sessions and the theories of learning which should underpin these plans. Using broader terms, a teacher has a limited number of choices to make when deciding what are appropriate methods to use. True, when planning a session, it is important to be aware of the range of student learning styles or particular needs which will be present in the class. However, a major choice, which will affect other decisions, is between *lecturer-centred delivery* and *student-centred processes*. Even though the specific learning activities will inevitably vary, most sessions will be a combination of these two strategies. At some stages, the lecturer's input will be have a more crucial bearing on the learner's development and during others it will be more important that the learners' active involvement predominates.

Activity 6m Selecting a Teaching Approach

Take one of your planned sessions and look at the balance between teacher-centred and learner-centred activities. Adjust the strategies if you wish and then provide a brief justification for the balance you have achieved.

As you would expect there is a range of different approaches, which may be considered in three simple categories. The first and most commonly used method involves various forms of *presentation* and as you would expect these are essentially teacher-centred. *Search* approaches are more focused around the learners' exploration of sources and the third strategy, *interaction,* is again learner-centred and experiential but will often involve much more student collaboration. As a basic reference, in Table 6.4.1, Table 6.4.2 and Table 6.4.3 we have listed these different models of learning, together with a list of advantages and disadvantages.

6.8 Learning resources

Johann Amos Comenius, a seventeenth-century philosopher and one of the founders of modern educational theory, stressed that:

> to exercise the senses well about the right perceiving of the differences of things will be to lay the grounds for all wisdom and wise discourse.

More than 300 years ago he was providing an insight into teaching and learning which, despite all the resources of modern technology, we still often ignore within our classrooms today. We cannot claim to be 'exercising our senses well' if our preferred methods (i.e. formal teaching) continue to be predominantly dependent upon communication through *hearing*, a sense which provides us with less than 20 per cent of the information we gain through sight, as we try to understand the world around us.

As you know, the models of learning presented in Table 6.4.1, Table 6.4.2 and Table 6.4.3 are designed to promote different aspects of learner development according to the aims of the particular session. However, choosing the most appropriate teaching strategy is only the first step. The selected method may, in turn, be communicated and supported using a range of resources to provide a learning experience, which is sufficiently rich to be compatible with the learners' needs. If well designed, this approach should be reasonably appropriate to most learner characteristics. The range of learning resources currently available to teachers is so many and varied that ignoring it and relying entirely on the spoken word is perverse and inexcusable. However, because the choice is so wide, it isn't always easy to decide what is appropriate. As an introduction and in order to develop some basic principles, we have gathered various educational media together in Table 6.5.

Activity 6n Learning Aid Principles

Again, take a particular session you have planned for a specific group of learners and (using Table 6.5) suggest how you might enhance the process by including particular learning resources. Remember to consider any information about the group's learning styles, which you may have collected earlier.

Table 6.4.1 Presentation (teacher-centred models)

	Purpose	Characteristics	Qualities	Limitations
Lecturers	For use with large groups of learners, where participation is limited because of time constraints or student numbers.	Didactic delivery, usually with a minimum of audience interaction.	The transfer of large amounts of information in a limited time which lends itself to Ausubel's theories of meaningful reception learning (see Chapter 5).	Passive learning due to lack of learner participation.
Formal teaching	Again, the transfer of large amounts of information during a limited period of time.	Again, an essentially deductive approach, but may use a range of techniques and allow questions and debate.	Charismatic presentations remain memorable and lend themselves to the use of 'advance organizers' to enable the formation of cognitive structures.	One-way communication, so the teacher has little idea of how the various concepts are being received.
Demonstrations	The transfer of skills but this often requires follow-up practice.	The 'unpacking' of a particular skill or process and the provision of an insight into specific expertise.	The more difficult aspects of a process may be highlighted through the disaggregation of the whole into constituent parts. However, learner errors or bad babits must be addressed early in the process before they become learnt.	Without the aid of projected images via PowerPoint or DVDs, etc., this process will usually be directed at relatively small groups and the lack of 'hands-on' experience may limit the extent of the learning.
Individual/small group tutorials	A more personal exchange of opinion and feedback, often on a one-to-one basis.	Useful for reviewing progress and discussing specific assignments and projects; an opportunity to provide individual guidance and counselling.	A more direct one-to-one exchange of views and interpretations between tutor and taught often provides insights into the source of misconceptions and areas which may be causing unnecessary concern for the learner, which a few words of explanation from the tutor can resolve.	The development of competence-based education and training with its highly individualized approach requires tutors to spend more time coaching individual learners, helping with study problems, negotiating and re-negotiating targets and generally providing guidance and support on an individual basis.

Table 6.4.2 Search (learner-centred models)

Method	Purpose	Characteristics	Qualities	Limitations
Projects and assignments	Important aspects of coursework, which are often integrated activities – involving more than one subject (i.e. cross-curricular).	Promotes student-initiated investigations of subjects either identified by them or selected from a range of possibilities suggested by the tutor.	The breadth of the study and the extended range of sources often motivates students to produce excellent, original work which has involved the development of many new skills and understandings.	Demands a high level of organization and preparation because of the cross-institutional contacts. Can be difficult to monitor standards, plagiarism, etc.
Case studies	A history of an event or set of circumstances where the learners examine the relevant details. These fall into two broad types: 1. Those in which the learners diagnose the causes of a particular problem. 2. Those in which the learners set out to solve a particular problem.	Particularly suitable where a cool look at a problem or set of circumstances, free from the pressures of the actual event, is beneficial. A useful opportunity to exchange ideas about solutions to common work problems.	Learners may not realize that decisions taken in the training situation are different from those which have to be made 'on the spot' in a live situation.	Courses focusing on human behaviour. Training in decision making (management). Diagnostic work in any subject area.
Search or discovery	Learners are placed in situations requiring self-directed learning under the tutor's general guidance. Exercises, tasks or games are used – enabling learners to make their own discoveries.	Allows learners to demonstrate and develop a wide range of skills and personal qualities. These include the ability to show initiative, to take responsibility and plan, to solve problems, make decisions and communicate effectively. A highly active and participative form of learning. Opportunity for involvement may encourage poorly motivated learners.	Promotes collaborative learning and the learners' ability to take responsibility for their chosen methods and to develop the ability to present and defend their findings. It may also encourage them to support the learning of other group members.	Poorly motivated learners may regard the freedom of learner-centred strategies as an opportunity to do very little.
Seminars	To disseminate ideas and good practice by allowing individuals or small groups to investigate a topic, report back to the main seminar group and lead a discussion around the topic.	Student/s collect information, about a chosen or designated topic, sufficiently well to be able to prepare a presentation around the subject and then lead the discussion afterwards.	Often stimulating and challenging to students. Helps to develop the learners' ability to craft and present a case. To be able to learn something sufficiently well to be able to inform others is a rewarding experience.	Some students need considerable support and guidance, as leading a seminar can be a very intimidating experience.

Table 6.4.3 Interaction (learner-centred models)

Method	Purpose	Characteristics	Qualities	Limitations
Buzz group/ word shower/ callouts	The generation of solutions to a problem through a concentrated period of free responses from this collective process. (The term 'brainstorming' is less used now because of the unfortunate connotations with epilepsy.)	A small group is given a topic or question and for five or ten minutes members say anything that occurs to them in connection with it. A recorder writes up anything that is said (no matter how irrelevant, silly or perverse) on a board or flip chart. Members then evaluate the ideas and develop selected ones.	A good way of introducing a topic and helps to make everyone feel involved and valued as a contributor. It promotes creative thinking, which often provides new or unexpected perspectives on the topic. It is useful to establish simple ground rules, e.g. the ideas should be called out in any order without giving or seeking explanations, justifications or comment.	Requires good management because a few members can dominate the session and others will often hold back on good ideas because they feel that they may be too radical.
Small groups or syndicates	Groups of learners are split into smaller subgroups to work (sometimes in competition with the other groups) on related problems/issues.	Provides an opportunity for learners to show initiative. Can be highly motivating.	Provision of sufficient basic information is essential. Group-work activity must be well planned and prepared, and seen to be relevant.	Management training. In-service training. Often used in conjunction with simulation exercises where groups work concurrently on the same (or different) lifelike problems.
Simulation	Learners may be asked to undertake a particular task, such as solving a problem, using the same procedures as those which operate in a real-life situation. Simulation often involves a practice session or a test of knowledge acquired prior to the exercise.	A highly active form of learning particularly suitable for any situation where learners need to practise making choices and following through the implications of their choices. Frequently used instead of formal tests to find out how much learners have assimilated and how well they can apply new skills.	Teaching practice: personal selection; courses for armed forces and 'emergency' services – police, first-aid, fire; in-service training in industry and commercial/public sector organizations.	Must be realistic and the expected result reasonably attainable by all learners. May be expensive and time-consuming to prepare.

Games or ice-breakers	Games take all kinds of forms, but often involve competition (and cooperation), teams, point-scoring, etc. They are often used to simulate real-life situations and allow learners to experience roles where they are required to make decisions and present a case. Ice-breakers can be used when a group first meets, to establish a good rapport quickly, enable learners to get to know each other and help diffuse possible tensions. Or they may be used at the beginning of regular sessions, to establish an appropriate group atmosphere.	Similar to role plays. Allows participation by learners of varying ability. Adds variety, assists in problem solving and in understanding inter-personal relationships. Used to introduce competition (or promote cooperation) and provide motivation.	Can be used to good effect in most subject areas – but must be used tactfully and skilfully in appropriate situations.	If badly handled they can 'fall flat', embarrassing or even alienating and antagonizing learners.
Discussion	Knowledge, ideas and opinions on particular subjects are freely exchanged among the tutor and learners.	Particularly suitable where the content involves matters of opinion or tutors are aiming to change attitudes. Useful for obtaining feedback about the learners' level of understanding and ability to apply knowledge.	To follow up a visit or a talk by a visiting speaker or the showing of a film or video. Of course, many of the best discussions are spontaneous and unplanned.	Learners may stray from the subject matter or fail to discuss it usefully – whole session may be unfocused and woolly. Learners may become entrenched in their attitudes. Group leader may talk too much and intervene too readily to fill silences.
Role play	Learners practise being in particular roles by acting out a face-to-face situation that represents real-life – a work situation for instance. Each participant should have sufficient background information to allow a proper understanding of the part to be played.	Learners can practise and receive advice and criticism in the safety of a learning situation. Practice in role play provides guidelines for future behaviour. Insight into the motives and attitudes of others is gained in this active learning experience in which learners can draw their own conclusions and formulate their own ideas.	The training of social workers, managers and other involved in personal relationships; the training of tutors, through micro-teaching.	Learners may be embarrassed, suffer loss of confidence and not take the role play seriously.

(Continued)

Table 6.4.3—cont'd.

Method	Purpose	Characteristics	Qualities	Limitations
Open learning	Open learning is the term used to describe any form of learning in which the provider enables individual choice over any one or more of a number of aspects of learning. It frequently involves the use of materials developed specially to allow independent learning. The tutor's role is usually a combination of 'resource-manager', guide and advisor.	Particularly useful where access to conventional courses is restricted (e.g. for domestic, work or geographical reasons). Learners can work through open learning materials at their own pace (at home or during quiet times at work) although the materials may also be used in a college-based workshop. An individual approach is being embodied in the move towards competence-based education and training and the introduction of National Vocational Qualifications. This is likely to lead to increasing use of open learning in educational mainstream classes.	Where learners are well-motivated and willing to work independently for significant periods of time.	Open learning requires investment in high-quality materials and in training tutorial and administrative staff to adopt a more flexible, learner-centred role. Where such investment is lacking learners can rapidly become demotivated, especially where there are repeated problems.

Table 6.5 Learning media characteristics

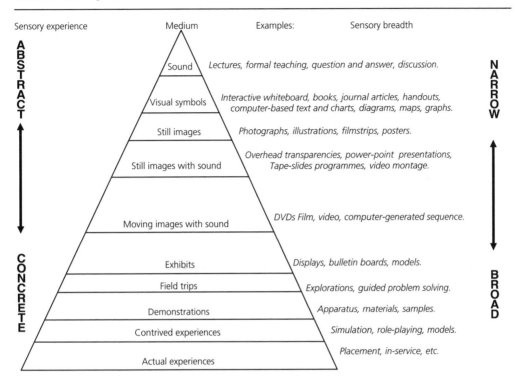

Of course the first principle is that the addition of a learning resource should *enhance* the previously unaided presentation. If it adds nothing to the session, then it isn't worth including. Secondly, as you will see, Table 6.5 contains two important dimensions. From the narrow top of the diagram to the broader bottom line, there is a gradual increase in the *number* of the learners' senses, which the particular medium engages. This indicates another basic principle, which is that when more of our senses are used, the communication and the related learning will generally be richer and more effective.

Next we should consider the *nature* of the sensory experience and point out (at the apex of the diagram) that the use of auditory language and visual symbols (i.e. letters and words) involves presenting material in an *abstract* form. We considered earlier in Chapter 3 the ways in which particular, individual, learning styles either promote or inhibit learning. Learners who respond better to concrete experiences will find the rich sensory media towards the bottom of the diagram much more rewarding.

For some learners who are adept at abstract conceptualization, the use of sound (i.e. formal teaching) will be effective even though communication is primarily through hearing, which is a less informative sensory path than sight. With these learners, good progress can be made with a minimum of resources.

However, even gifted learners often find that broader, experiential learning is more productive because they simultaneously receive information through more of their senses and this allows them to use this range of memories (i.e. touch, smell and taste in addition to hearing and sight) to recall more accurately the knowledge and skills they have gained. It becomes richer, kinesthetic learning. We can also clearly see from Table 6.5 that the teacher's toolkit contains more than a pen, paper and extensive subject knowledge and it is good practice to have a bank of resources available to you. These aids could include flip-chart paper and marker pens, dry wipe pens (remember not to confuse the two!) for use with the whiteboard, sticky tack, craft materials, postcards, post-it notes, coloured pens and paper. You may also need to know how to access TVs/DVD players, cassette recorders or video cameras, computers and digital projectors, or an interactive whiteboard. Most importantly if you are not technically proficient with the equipment you must remember who and where the technical support can be found, should you need help and DVDs, CDs, film and batteries, etc.

Activity 6o Selecting Learning Resources

Following on from Activity 6n and having considered some basic principles, try to identify the selection criteria which you might use when you are considering developing learning resources for your students. Think in terms of the steps in the process.

Remember that learning resources may be used to promote any of the stages within the learning processes outlined in this and earlier chapters. For example, if we use again our REAL acronym, resources may be used to facilitate *Resonance* between tutor and learners, i.e. establish communication through humour, common experiences, shared aims, etc.

All forms of *Education* may be facilitated and supported through resources and *Active* rather than passive learning may be stimulated by using search and interactive exercises based around simple resources such as library use. Finally, *Learner autonomy* can be promoted through resource-based simulations, field trips and role-playing.

Following our familiar learning cycle, your learning resource selection criteria would need to address the following questions:

- **Target audience:** *Who are the resources for?* As in our earlier session planning exercises, the more you know about your learners, the more appropriate will be your choice of supporting resources. For example, the images, references and language which you might use will be different for a group of 16-year-old modern apprentices from what it would be for non-vocational adult learners.
- **Content:** *What is the subject or topic?* Consider the subject or topic to get an indication of the cognitive, affective and psychomotor aspects of the syllabus that would benefit from the additional support of resources.

- **Learning outcomes:** *What should the resources achieve?* Resources can be used to address any aspect of the learning cycle. They may, for example, be used to motivate, as metaphors to introduce difficult concepts or to break down the steps in a complex process. Resources can also provide an excellent means of differentiating learning to address diverse and individual needs.
- **Delivery:** *How will these resources be provided to the learner?* You need to decide how best the programme learning experiences and materials can be brought to the learner at the optimum period in the programme. For example, you may wish to have reference material constantly available or, at the other extreme, you may feel that providing an impact at a crucial point in the learners' development will be more important.
- **Media:** *What learning media are available to you?* You need to know exactly what learning resources you can utilize and which of them are appropriate for the defined objectives, content and delivery methods.
- **Constraints:** *What restrictions and pressures will you have to cope with?* You will have to consider such things as current budget, deadlines, preferred learning styles, expectations, health and safety requirements, etc.

6.8.1 ICT and e-Learning

Perhaps the most influential of the resources currently in use in schools and colleges during the last ten years have been *Information and Communication Technology* and *e-Learning*. A DfES consultation document 'Towards a Unified e-Learning Strategy' (2005) provided the following definition:

> If someone is learning in a way that uses information and communication technologies (ICTs), they are using e-learning. They could be a pre-school child playing an interactive game; they could be a group of pupils collaborating on a history project with pupils in another country via the Internet; they could be geography students watching an animated diagram of a volcanic eruption their lecturer has just downloaded; they could be a nurse taking her driving theory test online with a reading aid to help her dyslexia – it all counts as e-learning.

In the government's White Paper '21st Century Skills, Realizing Our Potential' it acknowledged that ICT was a 'skill for life' that ranked alongside literacy and numeracy and in the DfES 'Harnessing Technology' (2005), Ruth Kelly saw the huge potential of the computer for education:

> I am particularly excited by the idea of giving every student and learner online learning space where they can store their own course materials and assignments in digital form, and record their achievements.

Although this is another of the former Secretary of State for Education's ambitions which we haven't yet achieved, certainly at every level of education the investment in computer technology has been huge. Of course, the educational uses of such a powerful resource as a computer are many and varied ranging from access to online encyclopaedias such as 'Wikipedia', language translation facilities, and online searches using engines such as 'Google', all of which contribute to the whole range of curriculum subjects. Add to this the notion suggested by Ruth Kelly of online journals or 'blogs' and the range of specialist sites designed to exchange creative work in music, art and literature which are available and you have a fascinating treasury of material relevant to every aspect of a college curriculum. A final point well worth making is that almost all of our learners in the Lifelong Learning Sector have grown up with computer technology and want to utilize it.

However, with access to the wealth of material on the internet comes the inherent problem of students gaining access to sites which contain material which may be potentially pornographic, violent or disturbing and every educational establishment using such technology does need to ensure that they have in place filter systems which refuse the students access to restricted sites. Even with these dangers, the benefits far outweigh the drawbacks and the following is a brief summary of the many benefits of e-Learning:

- It is able to improve the variety of teaching methods and resources used, inside and outside the classroom.
- It can be used to work with a range of learning styles and preferences.
- It can promote learner autonomy in personal research and speed of learning and widen the situations in which learning takes place: home, library, etc.
- Teachers can use visual/audio learning: videos, sound, film clips.
- It can assist in the sharing of good practice within organizations and also globally.
- There is an abundance of ideas and available resources online that are free to teachers.
- Interactivity can be built into individual work for learners, such as quizzes, webquests, etc.
- The use of forums and discussion boards can encourage communication through discussion, group interaction and contributions from learners.
- There can be more social interaction and the development of a course identity, particularly when learners are not physically present at a learning centre.
- VLEs – Virtual Learning Environments allow 'joined up' working; they can integrate learner records and results as well as materials and resources and can be used to create a 'house style'.

However, with such tremendous technological advances come the inevitable problems:

- Support must be available for the technology and must be available quickly when needed, because nothing is more dispiriting for a class to hear than 'Sorry, the server is down!'
- Expensive resources can quickly become obsolete and often organizations are not sure when to 'buy in'.
- Staff training, support and enthusiasm can be very variable.
- E-Learning is still often seen as a specialist area embraced by a few, and as being 'technology for the sake of it' and removed from the normal class situation.
- Resource accessibility could often be better and in line with Web Accessibility Guidelines.
- The time needed to create original learning activities using e-Learning is often greater than planning for traditional delivery.
- Learners and teaching staff need training and induction into the technology so they are comfortable using it.
- Equal access issues involve the cost of hardware and software (learners may not be able to afford their own computers), etc.
- The wealth of available material is a considerable plus, but plagiarism when doing coursework is a constant problem.

- There is a tendency to use VLEs and intranets only as a depository for materials that were designed as handouts, etc. Quantity rather than quality becomes the measure.
- Management views of e-Learning are sometimes not well informed, leading to the belief that it can be a useful cost-cutting method, allowing for delivery without teaching staff needing to be present.

In summary then, e-Learning resources are only just beginning to realize their potential in education, but we need to beware that the technology doesn't take place at the expense of learning and therefore becomes technology-led rather than learning-led. Although e-Learning theory and pedagogy is developing with increasing speed, the comparative value in relation to conventional teaching has not yet been adequately researched.

Even so, there appear to be emerging two different approaches to e-Learning techniques. First there is what has been termed the '*instructivist*' mode where students are instructed to follow a series of regulated steps and there is little discussion to consolidate the learning. Alternatively, there is the '*constructivist*' mode which uses a combination of interaction with the electronic learning material that is then moderated through an exploration of the various concepts and principles involved in the topic.

Activity 6p Modes of e-Learning

Considering the last points above, discuss in your PDJ how you might teach some aspect of your subject using e-Learning and which of the two modes you would use.

6.8.2 Learners as a resource

Remember that your various learning groups are themselves a most valuable resource. As discussed in the previous chapter, the members of any large group of people will have within their ranks significant intellectual, practical, organizational and creative skills. Not only that, most of these learners will enjoy being allowed to share their particular skills with their colleagues.

Activity 6q Resourceful Learners

Discuss how the learners within one of your groups or classes have provided or could provide a valuable resource for the other group members. Consider how you may develop this and in what ways you need to lend your support.

As we know, each teaching situation has its own particular demands, but with a little will and organization it is very possible to systematically draw on the strengths of a group of learners. Even more rewarding, as the class start to realize that they have particular qualities, a group identity will often begin to emerge. Many teachers talk with pride about groups of their learners who continue to meet regularly years after their programmes have been completed.

Naturally, the establishment of such unified, collaborative learners will not happen if there are constraints within their classes that restrict the essential opportunities for group interaction. The promotion of such processes isn't always easy, because often the more dominant members do not realize how they are inhibiting the contributions of less confident members. Such situations require careful and sensitive management.

6.9 Conclusion

In this chapter we have explored some of the significant aspects of managing the learning process and during this discussion it has become clear that when we break such complex relationships down into constituent parts for the sake of analysis, we often create difficulties for ourselves. In actual fact, student experience within any educational setting is an amalgam of aspects of the environment, learning activities and the supporting resources.

When you add to these the three topics covered in Chapter 7 (reviewing learning, working relationships and effective communication), you begin to appreciate the rich range of experiences provided by most educational establishments. It also becomes clear that one of our key responsibilities as managers of learning is to sustain this seamless web of educational opportunity where students are implicitly encouraged to accept the notion of lifelong learning.

It is important that we allow the disaggregated parts to merge back into one another in order to provide an environment that is consistently conducive to learning, but as managers we have to remain aware of how the various parts may influence the whole.

6.10 Useful publications

Kyriacou, C. (1998), *Essential Teaching Skills*. Gloucester: Stanley Thornes.
   This is a very reader-friendly book about teaching which could apply to all sectors. It has lots of practical advice and incorporates cartoons and blackboard summaries of each chapter. The second edition has been updated to include current teaching and learning styles and aspects of mentoring and portfolio assessment.
Walkin, L. (1990), *Teaching and Learning in Further and Adult Education*. Gloucester: Stanley Thornes.
   A very good all-round book on the principles of learning. The characteristics of different kinds of learners are identified. Equally he goes to great lengths to identify the many

roles of the teacher. Curriculum development, assessment and reviewing are dealt with in detail.

Elliot, G. (1996), *Crisis and Change in Vocational Education and Training*. London: Jessica Kingsley Publishers.

A good chapter on being a reflective practitioner and wider implications for managers and college organizations.

Jarvis, P., J. Holford and C. Griffin (1999), *The Theory and Practice of Learning*. London: Kogan Page.

An excellent first chapter on Lifelong Learning and a very readable general book about how people learn.

Coulthard, M. (1992), *Advances in Spoken Discourse Analysis*. London: Routledge.

An interesting read to make one realize how much the teacher talks in the classroom compared to the students. It makes one realize the importance of planning the learning for students so that they are engaged in the learning and not just passive listeners.

Fairclough, N. (1989), *Language and Power*. Harlow: Longman.

This is worth dipping into to realize the importance of using the appropriate language in the classroom.

Halliday, M.A.K. (1978), *Language as a Social Semiotic: Social Interpretation of Language and Meaning*. London: Arnold.

This book again is a good source of material on the importance of understanding not only the language but also the culture of your learners. Teachers can upset their students without even realizing that what they have said is being misunderstood.

The following publications are all useful in relation to e-Learning:

Gillespie, H., H. Boulton, J. Hramiak and R. Williamson (2007), *Learning and Teaching with Virtual Learning Environments*. Learning Matters.

Hill, C. (2003), *Teaching Using Information and Learning Technology in Further Education*. Learning Matters.

Stevens, J. and D. (2001), *Web-based Learning*. London: Kogan Page.

Laurillard, D. (2002), *Rethinking University Teaching: A Conversational Framework for the Effective Use of Learning Technologies*. London: Routledge Falmer.

Salmon, G. (2002), *E-Moderating: The Key to Teaching and Learning Online*. London: Routledge Falmer.

Salmon, G. (2000), *E-tivities: The Key to Active Online Learning*. London: Routledge Falmer.

Thorne, K. (2002), *Blended Learning: How to Integrate Online and Traditional Learning*. London: Kogan Page.

6.11 Useful websites

http://ferl.becta.org.uk/

An advice and guidance service supporting individuals and organizations in making effective use of ILT within post-compulsory education.

www.jisc.ac.uk/

The Joint Information Systems Committee (JISC) provides world-class leadership in the innovative use of information and communications technology to support education and research.

www.w3.org/WAI/

WAI: Strategies, guidelines and resources to make the web accessible to people with disabilities.

Supporting Learning

Dawn Norse and John Wilkinson

Chapter Outline

Key Concepts

Alienating Learners, Cinderella Sector, Deviant Subculture Groups, Disability Discrimination Act, Disability Equality Duty, Disclosure, Efficient or Effective, Empathy, Eradicating Racism, Ethos, Gender Genuineness, Holistic Approach, Inclusive Learning, Inclusive Resources, Institutional Induction, Ladder of Failure, Learner Contracts, Learners Matter, Lifelong Skills, Listening Skills, Managing Support, Ownership of Future, Personalization of Services, Personalized Teaching and Learning, Respect, Self-Concepts, Skills for Life, Situational Context, Technical Efficiency, Unknown Factors.

Before you begin this chapter you may wish to check the Process Justifications (Table 7.1)

7.1 Introduction

We will explore in this chapter the many ways in which we can provide support for our learners in the Lifelong Learning Sector. This support differs as we, as well as our learners, move through the continuum from 'novice' to 'expert' and as we progress our perceptions of our role and the influences that affect us begin to change.

Initially, at the introductory phase of our own learning (*Professional Standards: Threshold Award*, see Chapters 1 and 12), it is likely that we will focus on ourselves and the skills we require to pass our subject specific knowledge on to our learners. During this stage we will be establishing our own technical efficiency at achieving predetermined teaching and learning goals. Much of our energy and planning time will be taken up preparing for the teaching process and creating resources to achieve the goals of the sessions we are teaching. It is also likely that, during this stage, our focus on 'supporting' learners will be based around the very personal relationship we are building between the learners in our classroom and ourselves. We may even feel *responsible* for our learners and attempt to 'sort out' and 'solve' many of their needs for them.

The *Professional Standards: Associate Certificate* may well correspond to a developing maturity as a teacher and, with our fundamental teaching skills in place, we begin to explore and become aware of the situational context in which we teach and how this impacts upon our teaching approach.

As we have discussed in earlier chapters, this 'situation' will embrace a range of influences, including our values and beliefs about teaching and learning, the culture and the structure of the organization we work in, the characteristics of learners and our growing awareness of the teaching process. During this stage, we may well refocus our ideas about 'supporting learners' and look more widely into the type of support offered within our establishment as a whole. We may be involved in processes that help to match the support offered to the needs of individual students. We may begin to see support as part of the learning process and engage in recording that process for each learner and ourselves. We may also come to recognize the areas of support we are responsible for and the associated skills we require to carry out these functions.

Later, at some point in our own development, our knowledge of teaching increases in sophistication, depth and breadth. Also, moral and ethical considerations of teaching and education begin to formulate. We may start to focus more on the 'external influences' that impact on the teaching process we are engaged in, and relate these to contemporary educational issues in government policy and our own growing awareness of our varied teaching roles and our students' learning processes.

Such developing awareness approximates to *Professional Standards: Cert. Ed./PGCE/Diploma* and helps us to see support in a much wider way. We may start by looking at where the instigation for the support came from, how it is funded, ethical issues, point of focus and how we, as teachers, play a part in its provision to learners.

At whatever stage you are at in your own development now, providing learners with support will be relevant to you. During this chapter we will explore aspects of support and the effect this has on both teacher and learner. As a starting point, we are going to consider two notional case studies that identify two separate approaches which provide completely different experiences for the 'giver' and the 'receiver' of learning support.

7.2 Approaches to learner support

In educational establishment 'A' the management team, in line with government initiatives, have set up learning support for all students to access. The establishment has lots of 'support' systems in place and has them ready for the learner should they be required. This institution 'sees' itself as making support available to those who need it and 'gives' support through its staff and services to identified learners as they progress through the establishment. Emerging at the other end with their all their qualificatory aims met, the learners have 'taken' all they need to achieve their set goals.

In this establishment its teaching and support staff 'give' and the learner 'receives'. The responsibility for the support process sits firmly with the institution and its staff and the learner expects the right to 'purchase' support along with access to their programme. As with any situation where one side is always giving and the other taking, sometimes in this establishment, support 'runs out'. Teachers get tired and exhausted with carrying the weight of the support; resources and services get used up and funding disappears, leaving support needs unmet. When this happens (just as in any giver and receiver scenario) the receiver gets angry when what is perceived as a right and entitlement has gone and will demand that this be returned. At the same time, the giver is blamed for not 'managing the support' successfully and being unable to meet the learners' needs.

An alternative to this approach may be found in establishment 'B'. Here, the management team have also established support systems in line with government policy but, in this case, there is a subtle difference.

A central aim of the learning process in establishment 'B' is the development of both independent and interdependent learners through the development of individual empowerment. This institution not only 'offers' learning experiences and support and takes responsibility for this provision, but also expects its learners to contribute to both aspects and take responsibility (with the help of the providers) for *supporting themselves*. However, in situation 'B' the institution is not simply the 'provider' because here many learners become able to support themselves (a liberating experience), while those who require constant support for a range of personal reasons can have time and resources allocated to them to meet their needs.

Of course, establishments such as that in the second example are by no means perfect. Institution 'B' will still run out of money, some learners will still get angry and the establishment will still get 'blamed' for not doing things better. Even so, teaching there will 'feel' different, and it is this difference that we focus on for the first activity in this chapter.

Activity 7a Differences in Ethos

Consider the contrasting effects which the two different approaches to learner support may have in the two establishments in the case study above. Focus in particular on how the learners in 'A' may react as compared to those in institution 'B'. Please summarize your views as an entry in your PDJ.

In the first example, establishment 'A' *takes* responsibility and *gives* the necessary support provision. As a consequence, their learners are encouraged to *surrender* responsibility and *accept* the support provided. This establishment is meeting its targets and appears 'efficient' in the way it offers support.

In the second example, establishment 'B' also offers appropriate support, but their concept of the learner is different. This institution has a vision of the learner as being able, given the right conditions, to take *responsibility* for their own learning. The learner becomes an active player in the relationship and this more empowered role encourages them 'to do' for themselves. The establishment accepts that it has a responsibility to learners, but it stops *taking* responsibility for them. By allowing them to become responsible for themselves, the institution is 'efficient' in the support it offers, but more importantly it is also 'effective'.

This difference between being 'efficient' and 'effective' is one of the most important within the whole teaching cycle. In establishment 'B' we can see the initiation of a process which encourages learners to take responsibility for supporting themselves. As a consequence, the learners move from a position of passive acceptance (where they assume that they will be 'spoon-fed' throughout their course) to an active, responsive stance, which views teachers and support staff as a valuable resource that enables them to learn to support themselves. In this way, important lifelong skills are developed and the self-esteem and confidence of all participants is enhanced.

Learning Support means just that. Supporting learners does *not* mean doing it for them. It is about empowering someone to take action and assume responsibility for themselves by providing at the right time the appropriate human and material resources for this to happen.

Activity 7b Type of Learner Support

Consider in your PDJ whether you feel it is always necessary to support learners on a one-to-one basis. Give reasons for your views.

Wherever you are in your own development at this moment in time, providing learners with support will be relevant to you and other key questions to consider are:

- What effect may group support have on the learning process?
- How will we know that learning has been effective?
- Will our learners always require the same support or will it change?
- Will the rate of change be different for each individual learner?
- How can we improve the support we offer?
- Will the time come to pass our learners on to a different type of support offered by other colleagues?
- How do we know when we are stretched to our own limits and when do we stop and request 'expert' help?

Activity 7c Extent of Learner Support

As an entry in your PDJ, respond briefly to the above questions in relation to your particular teaching situation and where possible give some reasons for your answers.

7.3 Every learner matters

Despite the government's intention to continue in schools and colleges the strict account-ability processes built around league tables and inspection programmes, they began to be persuaded in 2003 that the present educational system was failing many young learners when Mike Tomlinson, the ex-Chief Inspector of Schools called on them to address the 'ladder of failure' which was producing highly depressing results. It was found that 17 per cent of students did not achieve Key Stage (KS) 1, 25 per cent did not achieve KS2 (*these are the figures relevant to the 14–19 sector*), 33 per cent did not achieve KS3 and a massive 50 per cent did not achieve KS4. Of course since then, Tomlinson has been instrumental in the development of more appropriate provision for those 14–19 year olds who may more appropriately be following vocational programmes. Yet still the situation persists where teachers at all levels are obliged, because of accountability regimes, to focus their efforts on those learners who are capable of providing the results which will enhance the position of the teachers, the schools/colleges and the county in the continuing ratings war.

Within this climate of 'teaching to the test', 'setting' and coaching the achieving students, it is little wonder that increasing numbers of disaffected learners find ways of boosting their self-esteem through local deviant subculture groups. And so the vicious circle of disadvantage grinds on. One northern local authority's figures for 2005 show disturbing statistics regarding their young people under the age of 19:

- 22 per cent live in one-parent households
- 18 per cent live in poverty (Indices of Deprivation 2004)
- 29 per cent of detected crime is committed by them and the rate of reoffending is over 30 per cent.

However, the government *did* respond in 2005, first with the new Ofsted 'framework' which identifies '*how the inspectorates will judge the contribution of services to improving outcomes*'. Some of the criteria which these 'outcomes framework' assessments are based on, include:

2.3 – the incidence of child abuse and neglect is minimized
2.6 – action is taken to avoid children and young people having to be looked after
3.2 – early years provision promotes children's development and well-being and helps them meet early learning goals
3.3 – action is taken to ensure that educational provision 5–16 is of good quality
3.4 – children and young people are enabled and encouraged to attend and enjoy school and to achieve highly
5.1 – action is taken by partners to support families in maximizing their economic well-being.

The first impression of this list of outcomes is that it is worthy but predictable. However, if any of the above goals are considered in isolation, they do start to seem simplistic and naïve. In the case of 3.2 the proposals are misguided according to the precepts of Froebel, Steiner, Montessori and other highly regarded child educators. According to these authorities, the educational requirements of young children are significantly different to the needs of older children and adults. Informed later by the psychological insights of Bruner and Piaget, the progressive nursery educationalist believed in a 'holistic' approach, which considered the educational, social and physical development of children was the only acceptable methodology, and in different ways they each stressed that it was essential to start from where the child actually is. In other words, to develop from current skills, understandings, attitudes, needs and interests, rather than planning the learning solely around future objectives. To have four-year-old children in nursery education being coached towards KS1 targets is ignoring the respected advice of these great educators, who view 'play' to be the most effective component of pre-school education.

The DfES also produced their White Paper in 2005, 'Every Child Matters' and 'Youth Matters: Next Steps' in 2006. 'Every Child Matters' identifies four themes: 'Being healthy, staying safe', 'Enjoying and achieving', 'Making a positive contribution' and 'Economic well-being'. 'Youth Matters' describes the *personalization* of services, and the offer of greater choice to young people. The role of the teacher will be to ensure that learners are made aware of the types of support available.

Although the sentiments underpinning the 'matters movement' are laudable, the reality for teachers within the Lifelong Learning Sector is quite different. FE colleges have been supporting students who have failed GCSEs at local High Schools for many years and their role (despite the above rhetoric) has, in fact, been to try to reduce the long-term damage caused by the so-called 'standards movement' and the way in which the 'driving up of standards' has created so many casualties through the process of alienating learners. This process often begins in infant school when the self-concepts of very young children are seriously bruised when they begin to understand the implications of being placed with less-developed youngsters at the 'red table'. Ten years later, many will have become alienated before they arrive at a local FE college or training provider.

Within further education colleges now placed within the new Lifelong Learning Sector (a more familiar name is the Cinderella sector), successes *have* been achieved when compared to schools and higher education. The low level of funding received by mainstream FECs does put their learners at a disadvantage and decisions relating to the levels of possible support are often determined by external factors, with the Learning and Skills Council (LSC) playing a key role. Many colleges offer a range of programmes aiming to cater for full-time and part-time students, vocational and non-vocational, 14–16 year olds and adult students, 'Skills for Life' and full degree programmes. In a truly comprehensive college with limited funding an equitable policy for all learners may not be possible.

Activity 7d Do Teachers Matter?

Nobody disagrees with the long-term ambitions of the Learners Matter initiative. However, educational managers face difficult 'opportunity cost' decisions, i.e. if they spend money on one sort of provision, then another will have to be neglected. Teachers are in the middle (often with a commitment to particular groups of learners) and recently, sudden changes in LSC funding have meant that one group of learners either faced a cut in provision or a substantial increase in course fees. Give your views on these dilemmas in your PDJ.

Further questions arise about how well equipped our teachers are to provide appropriate support to such a wide range of learners. Teachers in colleges in most cases have not received training to work with the 'new client' groups e.g. 14–19 year olds, undergraduates and the adult unemployed. Many teachers in the sector will need to undertake relevant staff development to enable them to effectively support these learners.

7.4 Teaching processes

Each group of learners has its own priorities and learning goals and consequently different strategies may well have to be applied when working with adults or with young people.

Adults may have to fit in study around other demands such as family and work obligations. Hayes (2006) echoes Montessori when he suggests that we take a *holistic* approach to supporting learners. Such an approach considers the whole experience of the student and that we need to provide practical and emotional support to help them during their period of study.

On a practical level it is vital that specific support needs are identified as early as possible as it can sometimes take several weeks for the appropriate support mechanisms to be put into place.

Although adult students benefit from meeting key people, many are flexible enough to take advantage of the internet and the intranet to access a multitude of sources, in addition to essentials such as course notes, assignment briefs, etc. It must also be recognized that in many institutions there are 'workshop' sessions to assist adult students with such things as assignment writing skills. Learners are encouraged to 'buddy up' with at least one other member in the group. This is especially useful if they have missed a session.

Many years ago the Open University advocated the formulation of 'self help' groups outside of class time, and traditionally such groups met in a café, bar, restaurant or even at someone's house, but now it may be that they discuss the course via inter- or intranet technology. Adults, of course, may well be parents and the National Institute of Adult and Continuing Education (NIACE) works to encourage more and different adults to engage in learning of all kinds. Also, as we have mentioned above, the 'Every Child Matters' movement has recognized that only by putting parents and families at the heart of its reforms can the desired outcomes be achieved. NIACE research shows that a broad range of learning opportunities is most successful at engaging parents and families in building commitment to learning over time. Once parents have been engaged, a high level of support should be provided (e.g. quality childcare and transport as well as support on learning issues such as help with basic skills or study skills). Every learner does have a unique learning history and family context that requires individual attention.

Activity 7e Supporting Learners

Thinking of your Focus Group of Learners, discuss in your PDJ the type and levels of support which your learners would benefit from.

7.5 Inducting learners into the organization

Within a 'funding driven' culture such as ours, the financial security of educational establishments is dependent upon our learners accessing the appropriate course for their needs, remaining on that course and developing both subject specific knowledge and 'lifelong learning skills' while arriving at a successful outcome in terms of achievement. This does not happen by chance. It happens because considerable care is given to the recruitment, selection and placement of learners onto our programmes.

Formalized induction is very much a part of this process. Within our classrooms, we as teachers have a responsibility to enable all of our learners to maximize their learning experiences. This means that we need to ease them into the group they will share their learning with, find out about them as 'learners', identify their individual learning needs and begin the process of establishing the 'boundaries' of the teaching and learning situation.

For most of our learners, induction will happen in two significantly different ways and depending on the role you have as a teacher, you will be involved in this process at differing levels.

Institutional induction usually happens at the very beginning of the learners' programme. Some establishments have induction programmes that span the first six weeks of the first term. During this time learners are encouraged to take part in a range of activities to enable them to find out about the organization, its facilities and services, programmes of study and the systems and procedures they will be part of. At the end of this period, learners should feel 'at home' in the establishment, be able to 'find their way round', feel 'safe' in their new environment and recognize that they are on the right programme and at the right level for them to be able to achieve a successful outcome. Induction should not be an endless round of boring and tiring visits where the learners sit and receive information that may or may not be valuable to them.

Activity 7f Well-Inducted

Obviously, the above outcomes are what we all desire for our learners. In your PDJ, briefly consider how you would make these things happen for a particular group of your own learners within your own particular educational establishment.

This becomes even more important when we consider some of the safety aspects that most students will need to be aware of as they enter a particular institution. It is not enough to be told about the Health and Safety at Work Act or Fire Regulations, First Aid Procedures or specific regulations that apply to some programmes. As with all learning, the student needs to 'see' the importance and relevance of the information and be able to access it in a way that makes it 'real' for them. Planning a good induction programme is being 'efficient'. However, being 'effective' involves not only meeting the perceived needs of new learners, but also making induction alive, real, relevant and useful to the learner.

As opposed to 'formal induction' the second type of induction will usually be directly under the control of a programme tutor and will have a different focus to the institution-wide induction.

At this level, tutors will identify different outcomes that they wish to achieve with a particular group of learners and the planning of this induction is no different to the preparation of any other educational session which we may provide. We will still require specific objectives that are achievable through a range of predetermined activities. These activities, as always, will need to address a range of learning styles and allow learners to work both independently and collegially during the session. The objectives, as always, will need to be assessed (informally and unobtrusively) and then the whole process evaluated.

Ice-breaking activities designed to help the group to get to know each other and to feel more at ease are useful and purposeful activities during this type of induction. Using ice-breakers allows you to get to know your learners and their names quickly, attempting to build a more personalized relationship with them and allowing you to recognize any experiences or knowledge that can be drawn upon as a resource.

However, this is no easy task. Your group of learners are unlikely to be a homogenous group with the same life experiences, past experiences of learning and present learning needs. Instead, your learners will inevitably be a group of contrasting individuals, each with their own needs and expectations. At this point, during the initial stages of induction, it is likely that you don't know a great deal about your learners, such as their expectations of the course or programme, how they relate to other members of the group, their level of confidence and preferred learning styles.

Activity 7g Unidentified Factors

Think about your Focus Learning Group and in your PDJ describe the range of 'unknown factors' which they presented when first you met them, and what special arrangements you have had to make to accommodate these idiosyncrasies.

It is often the case when a new group of learners enrol onto a programme that the teacher will initially have some immediate learning to do. Perhaps one of the most controversial 'unidentified factors' you may encounter as a teacher, trainer or tutor is low self-esteem.

The New Labour government supports the view that low self-esteem is one of the most destructive causes and effects of social deprivation and social exclusion. Low self-esteem undoubtedly is an obstacle that prevents many people of all ages not only engaging in education but in other forms of valuable activity such as employment, leisure interests and being part of a social group. Given that low self-esteem frequently triggers a desire for change, people who return to learning in adulthood, especially those who have struggled to overcome a number of barriers to learning, often speak of increased self-esteem as a major gain from learning. Therefore, it is vital that as tutors we have some degree of empathy and understanding and this should be reflected in the support we are able to provide for our learners. However, as we develop in our role as a teacher we should become more advanced in how we are able to support our learners and be able to more readily distinguish between the role of a supportive teacher and recognizing when and who to refer to for specialized support.

Activity 7h Getting to Know your Learners

Use your Focus Learning Group and discuss in your PDJ:

1. How much information did you have about the learners before your first session with them?
2. How did this impact on your planning for the initial session with them?
3. What strategies for initial assessment, if any, did you incorporate into your lesson plan for this first session with the learner group?
4. Do you feel that you had sufficient information about your learner group to make decisions about their learning needs?
5. What other information do we need about learners if we are to be as effective as possible in helping them to learn?

The purpose of this type of induction is to initiate a learner's feeling of ownership of future learning and to excite them regarding the content of future sessions. It is also a time to explore the expectations and hopes we have for ourselves (teachers and learners) and each other, to establish the working practice of the group and recognize accepted patterns of behaviour towards each other. It is also a good time to look at equal opportunities and inclusive learning and to allow the group to establish their own 'rules' which ensure ownership for all members.

This is also a good time to identify how learners like to learn best. The usual mechanism adopted by many post-compulsory institutions is through a learning styles questionnaire. However, we need to ensure that we don't do students a serious disservice by simply 'labelling' them, implying they have only one learning style, rather than a flexible repertoire from which to choose (see Chapter 3 for a further discussion on this).

Programme induction is about getting to know both each other and the programme. We will establish how we will interact together and anticipate what we are all aiming to achieve. However, quite often when teachers are working under pressure, they wish to 'get on' with the real teaching and never allow their groups to take part in this important process. This is very unfortunate because other tutors, who do manage to go through this familiarization procedure, usually find that it considerably enriches the overall group learning experience.

During the induction period many different things are happening that allow us to ensure that the learner is on the right programme and that we can successfully meet their needs. The learners' level of knowledge and skills on entering the course or programme of learning is assessed through what are often referred to as initial assessments, initial diagnostic assessments, prior assessment of learners or assessment of entry behaviour. Assessing learners prior to them commencing their chosen programme of learning helps to identify whether they will require ongoing additional support in coping with the demands of the programme, or initial support to 'bridge' the gap between their current skills and knowledge and those required to start their chosen programme of learning.

This kind of initial support is often what adult learners who are returning to study find extremely valuable, for example, how to structure an assignment, note-taking or how to prepare a presentation. Initial assessments will help to identify a range of support needs (both personal and academic) while also exploring how learners like to learn and focusing on identifiable strengths and areas for development. The initial assessment activity need not be an intrusive test or exam. All kinds of classroom activities should be able to be adapted to create a suitable assessment activity that can be used to plan strategies for learner support – formal support from experts can be requested and budgeted for.

At the beginning of the learning programme, 'Learner Contracts' (see Chapter 10) can be established which can have a range of purposes. Some contracts or agreements are more formal arrangements, between learner and provider, which set out the terms and conditions of the relationship and the formal support the college will provide. Others can be more open arrangements established between the individual learners, their group and the teacher, which set out boundaries within which all parties will operate.

Fundamental to all this, however, is the belief that learners are valued as individuals and this valuing is expressed through the culture of the classroom. With these values in place, learners can grow in confidence and ability as they are enabled to maximize their potential. A philosophy of inclusiveness is therefore at the heart of both learning support and the humanistic approach to teaching and learning.

7.6 Inclusive learning

The importance of learning support has been nationally emphasized since the FFEC Learning Difficulties/Disabilities Committee produced their report 'Inclusive Learning' in 1996 under the chairmanship of Professor John Tomlinson. Although the central concern of the report is equality of opportunity, Tomlinson and his colleagues emphasized the importance of optimizing the learning of *all* students, rather than focusing on special needs provision in isolation. Thus the proposals set out the improvements necessary to establish a policy of *inclusive learning* which would require all staff to make the needs of all their students their priority.

This 'inclusive approach' deliberately distances itself from those strategies which leave the learners to their own devices as a 'strategy' for encouraging independence. Instead inclusion means developing a way of working which responds to each individual learner's particular needs by providing a sensitive, responsive and supportive learning environment. The taking on by the learning organization of the onus for the implementation of an agreed inclusive policy is a radical concept which has considerable implications. First of all, it is an acceptance that the policy will be applied to all learners in the establishment and not just those who have been previously labelled as having some identifiable difficulty. Initially, it also implies that we have to clearly identify who our learners are, what support needs they have and how we can design teaching, learning and assessment to enable learners to succeed while meeting these needs.

The Disability Discrimination Act, which was passed in 2005, replaced the Special Educational Needs Disability Act of 2001 and aims to end discrimination against disabled people in specific areas of life, including education. This Act is far wider reaching than previous legislation and makes it very clear what is expected within educational establishments. In essence the Act means that legally, the providers of education (schools, colleges, universities and providers of adult education) must not treat disabled students less favourably than their non-disabled peers. Providers must make necessary adjustments to ensure that their students are not disadvantaged; indeed the guidance states that the provider may even have to treat some learners more favourably than others, to ensure that there is equality of access to learning:

1. Options open to the Lifelong Learning Sector students attending a college could be a mix of home and college study to meet the needs of those who find it hard to get to college because of their disability. For the first time within recent legislation, the DDA addresses the wider needs of the learner with mental health problems. It states that these disabilities would include mental illnesses such as depression, schizophrenia, eating disorders and some self-harming behaviours.

In effect the DDA covers three particular and important areas of legislation with reference to disability, race and gender. An important development under the heading of disability was the introduction of the 'Disability Equality Duty'. The legislation contains six clear areas of responsibility for public authorities:

1. promote equality of opportunity between disabled people and other people
2. eliminate unlawful discrimination
3. eliminate disability-related harassment
4. promote positive attitudes towards disabled people

5. encourage participation by disabled people in public life
6. take steps to meet disabled peoples needs, even if this requires more favourable treatment.

In addition there are specific duties that apply to *all education providers*, including the publication of a Disability Equality Scheme. Colleges must have a transparent and fair process for decision making, they must encourage disclosure, actively seek to extend access (not just physical access) and carry out appropriate staff training and awareness training. Overall the process should be one where the institution considers and takes account of the needs of those with disabilities as part of everything they do.

As with any new legislation related to public authorities, it affects both the teachers and their educational organizations. 'Disclosure' is a major issue as evidence from the Disability Rights Commission (2006) suggests that 52 per cent of those who come under the Act do not consider themselves disabled and would not wish to be labelled in this way. Others, who might not be opposed to disclosure, do fear that they may receive unfavourable/special treatment.

Whatever the extent of disclosure, it is clear that there will be a resources issue for the additional support that will be needed. Many teachers are concerned about the implications of the legislation because they are anxious about doing the wrong thing and/or causing embarrassment. There are other possible anxieties which occur when teachers are supporting learners whose impairment is not immediately obvious, as in the case where students may have mental health problems.

Your starting point as a teacher will be to embody good practice, i.e. listening to learners, planning and delivery to meet individual, alongside group, needs. It is also your duty to make 'reasonable' adjustments and obviously to seek advice or help when you do not know or are unsure.

The Gender Equality Duty (GED) is a legal obligation which came into force in April 2007 and it requires public authorities to promote gender equality and eliminate sex discrimination. Unfortunately, 30 years after the Sex Discrimination Act there is still discrimination. Under the DDA organizations will have to promote equality. There will obviously be issues when women or men are put off using a service because of lack of childcare or an unsafe or unwelcoming environment. For example, if a young mother wants to attend college on a plumbing course, she may not be able to take the course if the childcare at the college is not available at the time of her course. Most colleges will find it difficult to have all of the resources available to meet the needs of students with caring responsibilities, particularly in this case because plumbing is likely to be a male-dominated course. This could also affect men, as they too may benefit from childcare facilities.

The Equality Act of 2006 requires organizations to have due regard to the need

- to eliminate unlawful discrimination
- to eliminate harassment
- to promote equality of opportunity between men and women.

To many colleges, the key issues which they now face are when:

- career and course choice continues to reflect gender stereotypes
- young men continue to underachieve and remain disaffected from the mainstream
- there are gender differences in the achievement of the 'Every Child Matters' outcomes.

Activity 7i Gender Inequalities

Consider in your PDJ how we can, as teachers and colleagues, help to support our learners in the area of gender inequalities.

We could, for example, increase the involvement of young women in sports and fitness activities and of young men in health awareness activities. Further strategies could include:

- personalized teaching and learning
- providing special support to students making non-traditional course choices
- ensuring resources do not encourage gender stereotyping
- using careers education programmes to address gender inequality
- having identified barriers to employment in relation to gender, take appropriate steps to address these
- ensuring the safety of all of our learners on all of our sites – particularly in the evenings
- effective use of childcare support
- working closely with feeder schools, particularly single sex schools in addressing gender stereotyping.

Education has a key role to play in eradicating racism and valuing diversity. The government's acceptance of the recommendations of the Stephen Lawrence Inquiry Report, published in 1999, reinforces this responsibility for all educational establishments. Colleges have a vital role to play in preparing people for life in Britain's diverse and multi-ethnic society. Our learners are likely to encounter many different cultures and backgrounds, wherever they live, work and study.

We are obliged to make arrangements to prevent racial discrimination, for example by monitoring student performance and the ethnic composition of different courses so that all students have the opportunity to achieve their full educational potential. As teachers we need to acknowledge the ethnic cultural and religious backgrounds of all students and make sure these are reflected in our resources, curriculum and activities of the institute generally.

A partnership approach will be necessary to support our learners i.e. a partnership with other institutions, community groups, parents, Students Union and governors. In short, we need to establish clear policies that enable our learners to study in an environment free of racial harassment.

Activity 7j Promoting Inclusion

List in your PDJ some of the ways of promoting inclusion within your own college. Please give some reasons for the strategies you suggest.

As teachers in the Lifelong Learning Sector, it is important to look at the ways in which we can work towards an inclusive approach in our classrooms and identify the benefits this will bring to all of our learners. For inclusion to be successful, it needs to start at the beginning of the learning process, even before the learner has entered our establishments. Successful organizations are part of the wider social context that they represent and they will have built a relationship with that community which allows them to meet their present and future needs.

Learning provision is one measure of an institution's close identification with the needs of a community. A more obvious one is the actual design and structure of the buildings. Feeling included within an organization should be evident from first entering the door. Ask yourself if access is easy for everyone concerned. Establish whether wheelchair users or mothers with prams are able to use the same entrance as everyone else. Could you reach the reception desk if you are sitting in a wheelchair, are doors automatic and do they open to the side? Check if there are sufficient notices (including symbols as well as text) at appropriate heights for all people to find their way round.

Activity 7k Inclusive Resources

Consider some of the resources colleges need to have in order to move towards more inclusive approaches. How does this affect equality of opportunity issues, particularly when you are teaching learners who have been at work all day?

The thought that goes into an 'inclusive' building is considerable. At the planning stage we would need to consider ease of access, availability of all services to learners in wheelchairs, those who are physically and mentally challenged and learners who have visual and auditory difficulties. It is essential that the initial feeling for all learners on entering the building and using the facilities, must be welcoming. If this fails and learners, for whatever reason, feel isolated and segregated, then the chance of turning this into a positive, inclusive experience will most certainly have been damaged, if not lost altogether.

As equally important as the physical resources are the human ones, such as the teachers and the many different support workers. Inevitably, these human resources rapidly gain more value as they develop into *inclusive* facilitators of learning. From the very beginning of the relationship we really need to recognize that all learners are valued and respected for what they bring with them into the classroom. Having identified their individual needs and learning styles, we then need to develop our teaching to allow the learners in our group to equally access the learning we provide. This process of managing diversity (rather than trying to make everyone the same) is at the heart of inclusive learning. In practical ways this may mean us developing teaching materials that are differentiated at a range of levels, appeal to different learner's learning styles and allow access to concepts and ideas in a range of ways. In order to optimize our teaching, we will also need to consider the different approaches we may take with learners, using a range of methods, some practical and creative, some requiring individual and group involvement and some experiential and didactic. The most important aspect for us to deal with is to ensure that we teach in a way which enables our learners to access and enjoy the learning experience. This will inevitably be much more effective than merely falling back on methods which are comfortable and familiar to us. A humanistic approach – as advocated by educationalists such as Carl Rogers when making choices about learning strategies, should be to always put the student at the centre of the decision-making process. While we are teaching we also need to confirm individual learner success and progress in a positive and critical way, in order to establish what it is they need to do in order to continue to succeed. Positive, constructive, regular feedback to all learners is therefore an important part of working inclusively in the classroom and feedback should always be given as soon as possible.

Being diverse and responsive when planning teaching and learning must also include the assessment of our learners. To ensure an inclusive approach, we need to carefully consider whether our choice of assessment method is as appropriate to the learners as the defined learning outcomes. Offering a range of assessment opportunities does not imply a reduction in the quality of the assessment process. It is an attempt to ensure that the assessment process is 'fit for purpose' by making it appropriate not only to the subject but also the particular students.

Having assessed in as valid a way as possible, our valuing of the learners will also be evident in the quality of feedback we provide. Rather than being concerned about their clearance of assessment 'obstacles', we will be focusing on their progression after the hurdle. This will be achieved through accurate, fair and informative feedback, which promotes development and growth. Recognizing achievement in this way should be followed by the identification (with our learners) of where they want to move on to next. Understanding the progression routes, both across and up the qualification framework, is essential if we are to provide the motivation for lifelong learning that inclusiveness suggests.

In summary, at the heart of inclusiveness is the acceptance that all of our learners have equal access to fair and accurate initial assessment, informed advice and guidance, and appropriate support to meet their identified needs. At the same time this is enhanced by a classroom environment that encourages diversity and is responsive to our students' changing needs through the creation of learning situations which are challenging and varied in delivery and assessment. For the final unit of this chapter we will revisit some earlier ideas, including the concepts of an inclusive and humanistic student-centred approach to learners and learning.

7.7 Providing personal support

The humanistic approach to teaching which developed mainly from the work of Carl Rogers and Abraham Maslow has since been embraced by many other educators. At the heart of this approach is the belief that learners are valued for who they are and are empowered to become the autonomous and self-actualizing individuals they are capable of being. This philosophy embraces the values of inclusiveness because it applies to all learners, regardless of their characteristics or individual needs and sees the diversity of all humans as strength on which to build. Rogers believed that in order to support learners to achieve to their maximum potential, three conditions needed to be in place within the learning environment. He called these conditions the 'Core Conditions' and recognized that they are special to any supporting or helping relationship and used them as a central theme within his Person Centred Counselling Theory. Put simply, as a teacher you need to first *Respect* your learner, second, have *Empathy* with what they are experiencing and feeling, and third, be real and *Genuine* when you are relating to them. An examination of these concepts is perhaps, an appropriate way to end this chapter.

7.7.1 Respect

Respect in the classroom will have real implications for both the teacher and learner. As a teacher you can demonstrate respect for learners in many different ways, which will, in turn, encourage the learners to respect you. As you would expect, the key question is how do we show respect to the learners in our groups?

The strategies are very simple but, because of all the current pressures in teaching, are not always so easy to achieve. Some simply ways in which we can show respect are to:

- Always know our learners' names and use them when we are working with our groups, especially when giving feedback.
- Enable learners to have a voice in our classrooms and give them time to speak and develop their ideas. This can often be a challenge to the teacher, as we may want to move things on.
- Listen to our learners and this requires that the teacher and the group be silent when someone is speaking. This may be one of the 'rules' which you might like to establish during induction when the group is deciding how they will work together.

- Allow learners to work at their own pace and recognize that this may not always be our pace. This acknowledges where the learner is in their own learning process. Again, this may be difficult when we have a syllabus to cover within a particular time.
- Be on time. The use of time is an important way to show respect to others. For example, handing marked work back on time and valuing the time you spend together with your group.

When we show respect for our learners, what usually happens is that we are modelling a process for them which makes them feel good about themselves in their learning situation. The result of this is that, given time, the learner starts to respect us and the group they work with and this gives us a real foundation on which to build very positive future learning experiences.

7.7.2 Empathy

Empathy is often described as being 'as if you are walking in another person's shoes'. The important consideration here is the 'as if'. In empathy, we are not *being the other person* but are trying, through listening, to understand how they are experiencing events, and what their understanding of the situation is for themselves. We don't need to become the other person to be empathic with them, but we do need to recognize how they are feeling and (remembering 'respect') to accept that, for them, this is the truth and a real description of what it is like.

So if our learners tell us that they are frightened about writing an assignment, telling them to pull themselves together and get on with it, or that everyone feels frightened when they start an assignment so not to worry, is neither respecting how they feel nor empathizing with them. A much better response would be to take this feeling seriously and check out what is 'frightening' for them, and work through strategies to make the overall task become more achievable. This approach allows us to be really supportive of our learners and at the same time helps them to feel valued and respected, reinforcing that their feelings and perceptions matter.

Another important part of being empathic is to avoid the temptation to say '*Oh yes that's just how I feel too, and this is what I do to help me*'. When we are being both respectful and empathic and offering support, how *we* feel is not that important. Our aim in supporting the learner is to help them find ways through us, or other support agencies, to solve issues for themselves. Telling the learner what we would do in the same situation is like putting a plaster on both their problem and their feelings about it. It renders them helpless and will not promote self-respect or personal value. Enabling learners to work with you or others to find a suitable solution for themselves recognizes both how they feel and the action they want to take. This is empowering and promotes real feelings of achievement and personal worth.

7.7.3 Genuineness

Genuineness is simply about being the 'real' you. A real person listening to what your learner is saying as opposed to a 'teacher' or 'parent', or someone in authority over them. The reality of the teacher/learner relationship is that, unless your learners already perceive you as a genuine person they can relate to, respecting them for who they are and understanding their point of view, they will not ask for your support and help in the first place. This answers the obvious, age-old question many of us ask of colleagues who are involved in a difficult relationship:

> Q: 'Why don't you go to and talk this through with X?'
> A: 'Because they won't understand, or they will make me do something I don't want to do'.

The first rule then, in providing personal support to learners seems to be that we must offer all of our learners (no exceptions here please) the three conditions identified as respect, empathy and genuineness, and then we can be effective in our relationship with our learner groups.

7.7.4 Listening skills

To help us create these conditions there are some very simple listening and non-verbal communication skills we can use in the classroom. We need to be aware of our bodily posture. The way we sit or stand when we are listening to and supporting our learners is often more significant than the things we say. Think of a time in the past when someone told you off, or made you feel uncomfortable. It is likely they stood or sat directly in front of you, looked you straight in the eye and had a formal body language, which communicated to you that they were in control. In a supporting relationship this is the opposite of what we want to achieve. If we stand or sit to the side of the person we are supporting, they will feel equal to us and we will not be able to stare them straight in the eyes. We can look relaxed and interested in them and by giving space and time for them to do the talking we will help them to have control. These very simple steps when added to the tone of our voice, plus really hearing what they are saying, will reinforce those valuable three conditions we discussed earlier. We can also use some very basic listening skills to demonstrate to our learners that we have heard what they have said. We can identify what is said by repeating to the learner their own words, reflecting back to them the main content of what is said to show our understanding. We can identify the content of the discussion and also a little of the feelings the learner is demonstrating. We can also clarify what we understand and check this out with the learner to make sure we have not got the wrong end of the stick. Doing all of the above will help the learner to see that we understand exactly what is being conveyed to us and, rather than interpreting what we think the problems and issues are, we should allow the learner to tell us what they really are for themselves. If this happens, you can see for yourself that the learner and teacher will develop a trusting relationship upon which a lot of support and learner empowerment can be built.

7.8 Conclusion

We have already discussed the Tomlinson Report and further legislation and inclusive learning approaches which have developed from it. We will conclude this chapter by considering briefly a report launched by Helena Kennedy on 2 July 1997 entitled 'Learning Works'. The main focus of the report was to call on the government to put further education at the heart of its post–16 agenda, and it also recognized that the *motivation of learners* was central to widening participation and that it should recognize in its aims the responsibility to work with others to encourage and promote a demand for learning. Widening participation is still prevalent today: almost ten years later the government continues to promote agendas and policy developments that are focused on the motivation of learners, such as 'Every Learner Matters' and personalized approaches to learning. Also within Lifelong Learning we are, through the use of 'Learner Voice', providing opportunities for learners to have their voice heard, and in this way are promoting higher levels of motivation, better relationships between students and teachers and encouraging learners to become more actively involved in what they learn and the way in which they learn.

'Every Child Matters' is a government policy that has led to the philosophy of 'Every Learner Matters'. While we would all agree with the notion at the heart of the government's Change for Children agenda, focused on giving every learner the support they require, whatever their needs, abilities, background or circumstances, at all levels throughout their education, it is often far more difficult to put it into practice within the further education or training sector at the desired level we would like to. As outlined earlier in the chapter, the post-compulsory sector operates at a financial disadvantage compared to schools and we work with a greater variety of client groups.

The prevailing attitude within most UK education is to treat it as a 'marketable commodity' which those involved must sell as you would any other product. At an institutional level, we are obliged to focus on current 'market groups' of learners who do not yet use our services. Having identified gaps in our current provision, we have been creative in designing programmes of study to meet their individual needs. In many institutions, a 'stepped curriculum' has been put into place, which allows learners to access at an appropriate level and progress.

This stepped curriculum notion also allows transfer across curriculum areas with initial programmes having such a broad perspective that they are almost a 'taster' menu of a range of courses, which can be used as a base to move on to more specialist programmes of study.

The impact on provision has been positive as it allows new curriculum combinations to be explored. To achieve this, staff must be willing to teach on a range of associated programmes from 'foundation' level through to HE, which are linked to a particular curriculum area.

As a result of these new initiatives, we have attracted 'new' learners at 'foundation' and 'introductory' levels, who often have no formal qualifications. Consequently, they need significant support to help them develop intrinsic motivation and to encourage confidence and personal growth before they can develop the skills of independent study. As a result, we are involved with teaching both our subject content and also the processes of learning. Learners at this level can feel very dependent on us and do require our constant feedback, intervention and support. As we have discussed earlier (when looking at Maslow's hierarchy of needs in Chapter 6), with correct teaching strategies and sufficient support, these learners can become self-motivated and independent.

In addition to these new 'clients', we may simultaneously be involved in the teaching of more traditional groups (for example, A-level students) who are already independent and equally demanding. This teaching requires a different type of support, possibly resource-based. With the provision of these wider resource bases, plus their greater depth of subject knowledge, these learners will have the opportunity and the means to research their subjects. However, the precise nature of the prescribed curricula and the pressures on time will inevitably demand that they also have close and expert support if they are to succeed.

Throughout this chapter we have emphasized that the individual learner is at the centre of the teaching and learning process. Everything that we do as teachers has an impact on whether we are providing the best possible support for our learners. It is vitally important that we establish as much information about our learners as we possibly can and that the teaching and learning activities, the resources and the assessment methods used are based on a sound understanding of the needs of our learners. However, as we develop as teachers we should become more sophisticated in how we support our learners, and in particular know when and who to refer to for specialized support.

Earlier in the chapter we raised some key questions which it would be worth referring back to now and clarifying your thoughts about these questions. From this simple picture we can identify the diverse teaching approaches required and the different levels of support which each type of learner will demand. Alongside this, we also need to be aware that the widening of participation has inevitably raised serious issues of 'age', 'social class', 'gender' and 'disability', which have forced institutions to address the equality of provision and access across their community.

In many post-compulsory establishments we are now enrolling learners between the ages of 14 and 80 on a range of programmes at many different levels. The qualification framework offers anything from pre-GCSE through to undergraduate study, 'taster' sessions for adult education programmes and residential and short course provision. There is also Vocational Training from initial access through to NVQs at Level 3 and 4. This massive framework also includes professional qualifications and tailor-made awards that are developed to meet the needs of individual businesses in the local area. The whole philosophy of 'widening participation' has encouraged educational providers in the post-compulsory sector to be proactive and responsive to the needs of an ever-growing range of 'customers'.

The effect of widening provision is also felt in the venues in which teaching and learning now takes place. To be able to meet more learners, we have expanded the institutional environment into areas well beyond our college's jurisdiction. Some of these new venues work well, but others less so. Teachers are now running programmes in the community using school and church premises, in local business centres and public buildings. You may also find yourself teaching in a prison or in other regulated settings, and even in the homes of learners.

Although this has certainly widened the client group within the Lifelong Learning Sector, it also places more stress upon the teacher. In the light of all these developments, you may find it useful to consider the points raised by our final chapter activity.

Activity 7I The Cost of Widening Participation

Consider in your PDJ the range of different skills you need to teach 'off-site' and how this will affect your approach to the different types of classes. Think about the need in these situations to transport your own materials, if there are no support services for either student or teacher.

As we explore the widening of participation we can see that it has had a profound effect on institutions, teachers and learners. The walls of our establishments have become invisible and teaching/training is no longer confined to a known space. The skills required to teach at a range of levels to a wide range of abilities with various personal needs may all be required of one teacher, and learners may find themselves working in very mixed groups in terms of ability and experience.

All of these factors place considerable stress on the organization, the teacher and the learner alike and the support that we can offer and is offered to us in this constantly changing situation is critical to our healthy survival.

Widening participation has also focused on groups previously under-represented in formal PCET environments. These may include learners who carry a statement of 'Special Educational Needs', those with learning or physical difficulties, learners from ethnic minority and disadvantaged groups, learners whose first language is not English and those who have a learning impairment due to visual or auditory difficulties. In many cases this may mean that as teachers we are working in our classrooms, workshops and laboratories, alongside support staff, interpreters and note-takers.

Changes in legislation in recent times have promoted the move towards inclusive learning particularly through the Equality Duty. There are both general and specific duties and the key areas relate to disability, gender and race. Our organizations and ourselves as teachers have a duty to eradicate discrimination wherever it occurs.

In this chapter we have suggested strategies for addressing these duties and recognizing that while the physical environment is important, equally so are the teachers and all those other people who provide support to learners. In summary, we have identified that a range of factors will influence the support offered to our learners. Some of these factors will be personal to us and some related to the organization we are working in. We have recognized that our own development as teachers will relate to the type of support we can offer and the focus of that support. Support also relates to the educational journey our learners take with us, from recruitment to achievement. How we visualize that support places the learner as either a consumer of our services or the central player in an individual process of learning. Key factors in this strategy are two simple ideas of being 'efficient' in what we do and being 'effective' in how we perceive our purposes and values.

We have advocated the adoption of a humanistic approach where we respect our learners, empathize with them and show ourselves to be genuine. Our listening skills are a vital component in providing support to our learners. At the very heart of all the support we offer, be it inclusive learning or widening participation, there is a core, irreducible tenet. Give our learners respect, empathy and genuine people to relate to, plus appropriate support to meet their individual and changing needs and we will empower them to achieve to their highest potential.

Carl Rogers (1983) succinctly summarized this philosophy of efficiency allied to effectiveness when he said:

> Learning should involve the student as a whole person; at an emotional and personal as well as at an intellectual level, learning should be pleasurable and relevant.

7.9 Useful publications

Sanders, P. (1996), *First Steps in Counselling*. London: PCCS Books.

An introduction to basic counselling and listening skills that will support you in working with both students and colleagues. This book also gives an overview of behavioural, cognitive and humanistic theories and how these relate to approaches we may take. Although the discussion is centred around counselling it is directly transferable into the classroom.

Rogers, C. (1980), *A Way of Being*. New York: Houghton Miffin.

Another classic from Carl Rogers which provides more insight into humanistic theory.

Cotton, A. (ed) (1998), *Thinking about Teaching*. London: Hodder & Stroughton.

Read and enjoy Tony Cotton's review of eight teachers reflecting on their development which provides great insight and advice on practice.

7.10 Useful websites

www.british-learning.com
www.elearning.ac.uk/innoprac/institution/supporting
www.lifelonglearning.co.uk
www.ltscotland.org.uk/inclusiveeducation/findresources/supportinglearners
www.tipcet.com

Table 7.1 Process justifications for supporting learning

FAQs at the stage of:	Threshold award	Associate certificate	Cert. Ed./PGCE/Diploma
Why do it?	For one reason or another, many learners are anxious about their ability to meet the demands of formal educational situations. Our responsibility is to help them overcome these anxieties so that they can make the best of the learning opportunities we are providing. Assessing the range of differing learner needs is a firm foundation for a successful teacher/student relationship.	It is the teachers' responsibility to provide effective support for learners and give them guidance on current and future opportunities and requirements. This level of support will enable learners to maximize their learning potential and overcome problems which could cause them to underachieve, fail or withdraw from a course.	Analysing the support received by your learners will allow you to evaluate its effectiveness. You may then find it necessary to enhance certain aspects or to reduce provision which is underused.
Where are we going?	You are developing a real understanding of the learners you are responsible for. These understandings will be at many levels and across a wide variety of interests, aspirations, needs and concerns.	You are attempting to ensure that all learners have equality of opportunity in the sense of access to learning support, appropriate teaching, an effective learning environment and supportive assessment feedback.	To be effective, learner support must be responsive to the needs of particular groups of students. Reflecting on the nature and extent of support provision will allow you to ensure that support addresses particular identified needs.
How do we get there?	You are in an ideal position to become an 'authority' on the characteristics of your particular groups of learners. Your role will encourage most of your class members to express their fears and hopes because they will usually have come into education in order to succeed. However, there will be those who have difficulty articulating their needs and it will be your task to help them identify any problems.	The first requirement is to ensure that students are recruited with integrity. Secondly, you should encourage the learners to express any doubts or anxieties they may have about the learning process. You need to be aware of the range of facilities and opportunities that are available for learners so that you can refer them to appropriate support processes if the problem exceeds your resources.	You will need to develop systems of evaluation and analysis which give you details of support provision and how this relates to identified needs. Obviously, the more clearly you understand student need the more specific you can be about the type of support needed.
Is this the best way?	There are formal processes of needs analysis (see Chapter 3), but often the initial identification of student need is gained through informal discussion. The success of this process will depend on you adopting an appropriately confident manner, while remaining supportive and empathetic.	You need to monitor the progress of students so that you will receive an early indication of potential failure or withdrawal. Don't attempt counselling if you are not qualified or sufficiently experienced. If in doubt always refer to an experienced colleague.	Collect data on the effectiveness of support and confirm that it is available at the right time, in the right place and addresses the identified need.

(Continued)

Table 7.1—cont'd.

FAQs at the stage of:	Threshold award	Associate certificate	Cert. Ed./PGCE/Diploma
When is the right time?	The most important times when learning support is needed often occur during the early days of a programme, when the new students are slowly coming to terms with their new environment and the demands of the programme and the institution. There will also be anxieties later as assessment or progression begins to loom on the horizon. We also need to be aware of small signs of concern which may be initiated simply by a misunderstanding of the processes.	Learners need support at all times, but there are key periods when there may be greater potential for a crisis of confidence that may lead to problems. These more difficult times are often related to periods of stress for both students and staff such as during enrolment, assessment or progression. If you can gain the confidence of learners early in their programme they are more likely to give you some indication of problems before it is too late to act.	Analyse how different needs occur at different stages of a student's programme. Consider how these differing needs are interrelated and whether there is a common cause (e.g. low confidence/self-esteem) which may itself be tackled.
Who needs to know?	If you have concerns about any aspect of your learning situation, you should discuss it in the first instance with your line manager. You may then decide between you to provide formal learning support. Or you may prefer initially to tackle the problem in a more low key manner.	Obviously, this depends on how serious the need for support may be. Teacher colleagues and other students are an obvious choice but do not neglect to inform the support services and specialist professionals and where appropriate parents, employers and carers.	Reflect on the support services as a whole and whether information is disseminated effectively.
How do we know when we've got there?	Groups of learners who are enjoying the experience usually become self-supporting and will let you know when there are problems you hadn't been aware of. This collaborative ethos is the ideal situation, but be aware that it may take some considerable time to achieve. Until you get there, you must continue to promote a conducive learning environment which is supportive without being overly intrusive.	It is the nature of the work that you are never completely free of students requiring support, but there is considerable satisfaction when a less-confident or difficult student achieves and progresses, particularly if this is contrary to expectations of the student themselves and other stakeholders.	It is difficult to analyse the ongoing effectiveness of such a responsive provision as student support. Obviously, each new learner brings different demands and in some cases the support given is excellent and in others, because of shortage of resources, the support provided is only minimal. A crucial aspect is the collection of accurate feedback from the learners themselves.
Has everyone had a fair chance?	Inevitably, you will experience the disappointment of a learner who, for one reason or another, is unable to fulfil the potential you have identified. All you can do is leave the door open for them to return and learn something from the process.	This is a difficult question when applied to support because there is always a nagging doubt about whether or not a failing student could have been helped more. Consistent standards and professionalism will help to minimize these ever-present difficulties.	Carry out an evaluation of the support given to a group of learners and identify the strengths and weaknesses of provision.

Positive Assessment

Fred Fawbert

8

Key Concepts

Appraisal, Assessment, Balance, Choosing Answers, Controlled Response, Convergent, Criterion Referencing, Distractor, Divergent, Evaluation, Fit for Purpose, Formal, Formative, Ipsative, Free Response, Giving Value, Informal, Key, Learning Outcomes, Making Answers, Measuring Performance, Methods, Moderation, Modes, Multiple Choice, Normal Referencing, Objective Tests, Practical Tests, Process, Product, Reliability, Scheme, Specifications, Stem, Sufficient and Fair, Summative, Validity, Written Answers.

Before you begin this chapter you may wish to check the Process Justifications (Table 8.9)

8.1 Introduction

The assessment of learners' achievements has such a high profile within our present quality procedures that it has become in effect also an assessment of organizations, departments, teachers, trainers and support staff. However, despite its undoubted significance in the life of teachers and their students, there is, ironically, a temptation to mentally relegate assessment to the status of a demanding end of term chore which will get done when the time comes. It can easily be seen as something to be considered after all the hard work of teaching and learning has been completed.

In fact, the opposite is true. Assessment is not only a core activity which impinges on all other aspects of teaching and learning; it is also a means of promoting or denying learner achievement and autonomy. As mentioned in Chapter 4, when planning teaching and learning, assessment should be one of the *first* things we consider, not the last. We need to understand not only the associated concepts and principles, but also the intended and unintended consequences of assessment practices. In order to achieve this, during this chapter we will discuss approaches to assessment and the conditions in which it may be used to promote learning and the situations where it may have the undesired opposite effect.

8.2 The characteristics of assessment

A good starting point for this discussion is the *educational* meaning of the word 'assessment'. As you know, in conventional conversation, the terms evaluation, appraisal and assessment seem to be interchangeable and basically mean to make a judgement about the worth of something. However, within education these words seem to be used almost exclusively to distinguish between three different forms of judgement making:

- assessment – judge a learner's performance against identified criteria
- appraisal – judge a member of staff's contribution towards achieving the organization's mission
- evaluation – judge the success of a unit of teaching (i.e. session, programme or course) in achieving its aims and objectives.

Of course, we are concerned here with the first of these definitions, 'assessment'. Evaluation is discussed in more detail in chapters 9 and 10.

These days assessment in one form or another has become familiar to us all. Most members of our society have become used to having their performance measured and the ways in which data is collected about our abilities are many and various. For example, we are assessed if we wish to:

- drive on public roads
- get a job
- obtain a prescription for a pair of glasses.

As a starting point for this chapter try the following activity.

Activity 8a Approaches to Assessment

Discuss how each of the three assessments above are carried out and what, in your view, are the strengths and weaknesses of these methods.

---

a. The practical 'driving' part of the driving test is based around learning outcomes, and is a confirmation of practical skills within a real situation. The related theory paper checks out knowledge of the Highway Code and how it may be interpreted and these tests ensure that all qualified drivers on our roads have reached a national standard of acceptable performance. The actual driving is within an environment, which cannot be controlled or predicted, and the driver's performance may be adversely affected by stress brought about by the test situation itself.

b. By testing the oral skills of applicants within an artificial situation, the job interview is used to select the most suitable candidate for employment. This interview allows the employer to probe the various levels of experience and ability of the applicant, but the amount of useful information gleaned may depend entirely on the verbal abilities of the candidate.

c. The eye test is a physiological examination against precisely defined criteria in order to establish a diagnosis as a basis for the technical prescription of a pair of spectacles or contact lenses. This close examination allows the optician to be aware of any eye defects or diseases, and to use the prescribed lenses to correct any impairment in vision. Much of the test is based on the patient giving oral responses when comparing the effect of different lenses on each eye. These judgements can be very difficult and to some extent, are always subjective decisions.

The above brief review of a range of fairly familiar testing strategies does give us some indication of the general characteristics of assessment. We can confirm that effective assessment is:

1. concerned with measuring aspects of performance and attitude in a particular context (in other words, it has a clear purpose)
2. a means of giving value
3. carried out using appropriate modes and methods
4. sufficient and fair
5. valid and reliable
6. fit for its purpose.

The above are clearly six key criteria in relation to most assessment and are discussed further below.

8.3 Assessment purposes

Assessment will have differing goals. The above three examples which we have provided are designed to a) qualify a candidate to drive on our roads, b) reveal the characteristics of applicants for the same vacancy, promotion or course, so that judgements can be made, and c) arrive at the specification for glasses or contact lenses to meet the needs of a particular patient. These goals represent the three broad categories of all educational assessment, namely:

- *Qualification*
  The confirmation of achievement through certificated qualifications is now extremely important within Lifelong Learning. It allows student progression to employment or other programmes of study where certificated credit transfer may be a means of accrediting earlier learning towards another award. It provides a 'transparent' public record of the institution's achievement, which may be used in national league tables to inform customer choice. We are concerned here with present attainment.
- *Selection*
  Most schools, colleges and universities will use assessment to select learners for admission and their criteria may not always be made public. Most employers will have devised criteria for joining their company and many professions have entry qualifications. The focus here is differentiation to provide data, which will better inform judgements.
- *Diagnosis*
  When students are entering the Lifelong Learning Sector, most establishments will use diagnostic appraisal in order to decide appropriate levels and programmes, be aware of learning characteristics, and understand support needs and student expectations (see also chapters 4 and 7). We are concerned here as much with potential and aptitude as with previous achievement.

8.4 Assessment aims

The concept of 'giving value' introduced above, is a good starting point for a discussion about the aims of assessment. In other words, the formal assessment process has added value to the recorded profile of abilities of each of the individuals involved. Compared to a popular perspective that assessment is a series of hurdles prepared by teachers to trip up unsuspecting students, the addition of value is a much more positive and motivating perspective for all those concerned. Even so, we shouldn't forget our discussion in Chapter 5 when we suggested that the same process, which gives value to one group of learners, might be seen as a threat to others.

> ### Activity 8b The Threat of Assessment
> Discuss how a formal assessment process may seem threatening to some of your students and what you may do to counteract that.

Learners with low levels of self-esteem can manage to rationalize away the criticisms and jibes of family and friends, or may seek the security of a subcultural, social group of like-minded peers. However, a systematic system of assessment where there is the potential that recorded data will be passed on to other teachers and assessors, cannot be so easily dismissed. The support processes suggested previously in Chapter 7 must be in place to counter these fears before the burden of assessment becomes too great.

To return to our debate about adding value. As a result of the qualificatory, selection and diagnosis examples of assessment above, the following values can be attributed to the learners involved:

- *Driving test* – ability to drive a car safely on roads and motorway and the disposition to show respect to other road users.
- *Job interview* – competence in work-related skills, working with others, meeting the company's employee regulations, self-motivation and ability to contribute to the mission statement.
- *Eye test* – the comparative and combined performance of each of the patient's eyes.

We have discussed briefly how the above assessments were carried out and their strengths and weaknesses. We now need to look beyond these to a range of other strategies.

8.5 Assessment modes

The *mode* or style of assessment is the overall approach. The choice of mode by the assessors will usually make their intentions clear, which in turn will provide an insight into their underpinning values. The *methods* used within these modes (see 8.6 below) will be more narrowly concerned with the range of techniques they employ and are not affected by the mode chosen.

The most familiar descriptors of *modes* that we use in assessment are *formal* or *informal*:

- **Formal assessment** involves methods such as examinations, written tests, essays, multiple-choice questions, etc. It may also include situational tests, continuous assessment and student profiles.
- **Informal assessment** is mainly concerned with observing and questioning the learner during course-related activities. Such unobtrusive techniques as consulting records and monitoring behaviour will often indicate, not only what the student is able to do, but also what the student is *willing* to do.

At some time or another we may all *informally* assess our learners. This may, for example, be based on the way they dress or talk or write.

Activity 8c Informal Assessment

Thinking about a group of your own students, discuss how you may informally assess them and consider the potential value of this and some of the problems with this technique.

As you would expect, the use of informal assessment *must be approached with caution*. Such approaches usually imply that the students will not know the criteria they are being assessed against or even that an assessment is taking place. Also, more often than not, they will not be aware of the outcomes of the judgement or how it will affect their progress. In other words, informal assessment will often be ethically suspect, particularly if the results of that assessment may have a bearing on the student's final achievement. The possible implications of this type of 'labelling' and the self-fulfilling prophecy notion will be referred to again towards the end of the chapter.

However, despite the obvious dangers, there are situations where, when properly used, informal assessment may be helpful to a teacher or support worker who is concerned about how a particular student is coping with some of the more demanding aspects of their programme of study. This may take the form of observation or discreet questioning and may be indirectly related to time-keeping, personal hygiene, bullying, etc. Any information gained this way should be treated as a private means of confirming or rejecting specific concerns and if any fears are aroused, a more formal, recorded process should be undertaken.

8.5.1 Referencing assessment

Another important choice of modes, which an assessor will either make or will be prescribed by the awarding body, is between *norm, criterion* and *personal referencing*.

a. *Norm referencing* is simply a mode of assessment used when the assessor wishes to compare the performance of learners against a particular 'reference' group, which may be:

- class or group members
- local, regional or national groups of students taking the same assessment
- students in the same age group
- professional groups.

This comparative approach to assessment is designed to facilitate forms of *selection* through the *ranking* of candidates and to promote internal and external quality procedures which demonstrate the *relative performance* of students, departments, institutions and local authorities over time.

b. *Criterion referencing* in contrast, is concerned with the achievement of defined objectives and is not concerned with comparing student performances. To be effective, the criteria aimed at by the learners and referred to by the assessors must be as explicit as possible (see 8.6.6 'Learning Outcomes' below). Ideally, the information provided by such assessment will then make clear:

- the *level, range* and *type* of performance expected of the learner
- the specific details of the learners' achievement when they have satisfactorily completed the assessment
- to internal and external assessors and verifiers, the learners', teachers' and establishments' performance

- the relationship of the learners' achievements to other external, formal examinations and standards
- the effectiveness of the current curriculum design during any later evaluation processes.

Activity 8d The Implications of Referencing

Discuss how the use of the above norm- and criterion-referenced modes may affect the achievement and progression of a group of your learners.

During the last decade there has been a gradual move at all levels of education from norm referencing towards the use of specific criteria. Learning outcomes are now so dominant within educational assessment that the remaining norm-referenced systems (such as those used in some A-level examinations and university degree classifications) are continually under fire. However, there are still pressures from employers, admissions tutors, etc. to have simple systems of grading which facilitate selection. Such political pressures can lead to a less than satisfactory, hybrid assessment process. For example:

a. In recent years within the traditionally *norm-referenced higher education* assessment practices, there has been a drive towards articulating assessment in terms of learning outcomes. In some situations, the specificity of these assessment targets does allow students to meet targets in such an unambiguous way that norm-referencing criteria are compromised. This process has the effect of apparently driving up student performance levels.

b. The opposite situation exists in some further education programmes where there have been attempts to *provide simple graded outcomes* to facilitate various selection procedures. As a consequence, the familiar, criterion-referenced, competence-based systems may now also include norm-referenced grading often based on portfolios or written examinations. We have included below a simple representation of the mark distribution typical of each system. The vertical line on the left of each graph would represent the number of assessment candidates and the horizontal line shows the mark distribution, with the marks increasing from left to right in each example.

   Many lecturers in higher education will defend the traditional *norm-referenced approach* shown in our example on the left. Their view is that only a minority should gain a first-class degree and the

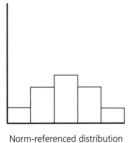

Norm-referenced distribution

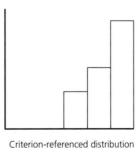

Criterion-referenced distribution

majority will lie in the 2:1 or 2:2 classification categories. These attitudes and their preferred processes usually result in assessment scores being grouped together in the central range (i.e. few candidates receive a mark below 40 per cent or above 70 per cent). However, because of the development in both FE and HE of a *criterion-referenced approach* through the imposition of precise learning outcomes, the curve of distribution should be moving towards the example on the right.

In contrast, the criterion-reference systems pioneered particularly within NCF vocational programmes should produce a distribution similar to the one on the right, because the majority of learners will achieve the defined learning outcomes. However, in an attempt to facilitate selection through the use of a simple grade, some assessment processes are now incorporating a norm-referenced system (shown on the left above) within a criterion-based, learning outcome framework.

c. Personal Referencing has previously been used primarily in Adult and Community Education and such ipsative or self-referenced assessment is now being used in both post-compulsory and higher education. This personal referencing may be based on the students' previous attainment or simply the outcomes that the students identify for themselves (or negotiate with a tutor) within say, a student-initiated module or within a dissertation. Strictly speaking this is a form of criterion-based assessment, but again, it may well lie within a norm-referenced system. More importantly, the development of ipsative assessment approaches (where learners have developed the ability to make informed judgements about their own abilities and performances) lies at the heart of the promotion of formative assessment as the increasingly important way forward towards improving educational practice at every level (see 8.5.2 below).

These examples taken from contemporary educational situations may show that, across education, assessment processes are gradually moving to a position where the best use is made of both the norm- and criterion-referenced approaches. However, an alternative view could be that, despite attempts to achieve 'transparency' of assessment through the use of defined learning outcomes (see 8.8 below), the difficulties involved in achieving the unambiguous specification of outcomes, plus political pressures for simple, often crude grading in order to establish quality and selection procedures which allow easy comparisons, will always leave us in situations where we have to cope with difficult methodological compromises.

8.5.2 Formative and summative assessment

Assessment information may also be gathered in different ways. Using different techniques we may wish to collect data during a course, so that we are continuously assessing our learners or we may wish to use a final assessment, which summarizes their achievement. Obviously, we need to make a decision about which of these two systems to use.

Activity 8e Formative or Summative?

Summarize the advantages and disadvantages for you and your learners of using either the formative and summative modes of assessment. Think not only about when you need information about learners' ability, but also the effect of assessment on their performance.

---

a. *Formative assessment* is essentially an integral part of the learning process, which takes place throughout the learning. Used in this way, the chosen assessment methods not only provide us with information about our learner's progress, they may also provide teachers with the means to encourage and motivate them. At a basic level formative assessment does provide teachers with regular feedback on their learners' progress and this enables them to adjust programmes to address any shortfall they may discover in student achievement. However a much more important argument was developed by Black and William (1998) when they pointed out that the average classroom is treated as a 'Black Box' where people are very aware of the input (i.e. teaching strategies and national educational initiatives) and the output (i.e. national accountability targets and education's performance against them) but know little about how learners (particularly those learners who, because of continual failure have rejected the system as a whole) process the complex barrage of information which they receive in the average classroom and even less about methods to motivate those who have become disengaged from the process. After a huge amount of research (funded by the Nuffield Foundation) into links between assessment and learning, Black and William's report makes it clear that improving learning through assessment depends on five, simple key factors:

- *the provision of effective feedback to learners about aspects of their performance*
- *the active involvement of students in their own learning*
- *adjusting teaching to take account of the results of assessment*
- *a recognition of the profound influence which assessment has on the motivation and self-esteem of learners*
- *the need for students to be able to assess themselves and understand how to improve.*

b. *Summative assessment*, as the name suggests, provides a final summary of the learner's achievement and this traditional approach to assessment in the form of end of year examinations, was the norm in most areas of education up until the 1970s. Although the advent of continuous assessment procedures has reduced reliance on the summative approach, it is still used in many areas of education and training because it meets the needs of stakeholders other than our students. Quality managers, parents, employers and the public in general attach great importance to summative results and, as we indicated in Chapter 4, often the assessment stipulated by external awarding bodies will effectively define the curriculum that is followed.

Activity 8f Assessment Focus

Consider some assessment that you are responsible for and analyse which aspects of student performance are given priority. Discuss how important you feel the process is when compared to the product. In other words the manner in which students approach the task (planning, organizing, designing) as compared to what they produce (assignment, action plan, artefact or performance).

8.5.3 Process or product

Another mode decision when planning assessment is the relative importance of *process* when compared to *product* when writing or interpreting criteria. In some cases, the end product may only be a relatively small part of the whole assessment process. In other cases, the final product is a good basis for the majority of the assessment. However, be aware that many final products, particularly at the end of a programme of vocational training, will not necessarily make it possible for the assessor to be certain how effectively the earlier stages have been carried out in order to award a grade.

8.5.4 Convergent or divergent

Our final mode decision will be to identify whether it is appropriate for our assessment to focus on *one* correct answer or for there to be a range of possible solutions. A typical *convergent* approach would be the use of multiple-choice questions (see 8.6.1 Objective Tests below), which have only one correct answer. Specific, competence-based assessments are also looking for a limited range of answers within a particular context.

However, it may be important when assessing the creative abilities of your students to encourage a range of solutions to a given problem.

Activity 8g Divergent Mode

In relation to your own learners, consider those situations where is may be necessary to encourage a more divergent response to assessment problems.

Assessment, which is designed to assess divergent thinking, will be appropriate in those situations where there is no unique, correct solution. Obviously this will occur frequently within creative subjects such as fine art or drama, but it is also valuable within other subjects where it is important that students look at a range of alternatives.

8.6 Assessment methods

There are many methods of assessment available to teachers and, although their value will not usually be affected by the mode, these methods may well reflect some of the mode's characteristics. For example a simple way of defining our methods is whether or not they encourage a *free* response or a *controlled* response.

A *controlled* assessment task is one where a one-word answer or a short sentence is appropriate and this would be congruent with the convergent mode where the assessor is concerned to achieve a precise outcome. A *free* response may well be an essay question that, although encouraging some specific content in the answer, is also expecting the students to be more individually creative or wide-ranging in their interpretations.

Of course, in many vocational education situations, assessment will be a combination of both *written answers* and *practical tests*. We have listed below the various techniques used within these two approaches.

8.6.1 Objective tests

We have called our first *Written Test* category 'Choosing and Constructing Answers', which, in effect, is an objective test. These items are written so that there is only one right answer and this facilitates objective marking, as they do not require the assessor to make subjective interpretations of the candidate response. The advantages of objective tests are that:

- the marking is *consistent*, regardless of who is marking the test and is not affected by the 'halo' effect produced by the candidate's ability in written expression (i.e. this also helps the marking to be more *reliable*).
- the testing is *efficient* because answers are restricted to the questions asked, and this enables quicker marking and more speedy feedback of the results.
- this method is *effective* because objective tests are able to test a wide range of knowledge and comprehension.

Table 8.1 Assessment methods

Written tests		Practical tests	
Choosing and con-structing 'answers'	Making answers	Active – Hands on (knowing and doing) focusing on:	Passive – Hands off (knowing only) focusing on:
Recall/completion	Sentence completion	Process being tested	Recognition (use of photographs, diagrams, etc.)
Matching	Explanatory paragraph	Product of the process	Interview
Multiple choice	Essay/assignment/dissertation (open)	Process and product (job observation)	Tape-recording answers
True/false	Essay writing (structured)	On-the-job fault diagnosis (problem solving)	Separate from job fault diagnosis (problem solving)
Sequencing	Summary paragraph	Situational role play	Imaginary role play
Multiple response	Listing	Games and Simulations	ICT
ICT based self-assessment	Advantages/disadvantages Process application (e.g. calculations) Project Open-book Seen paper exam Self-assessment	Project	Profile/portfolio

---

Activity 8h Objective Test Development and Evaluation

Focusing on an area of subject assessment that you are familiar with, design an objective test consisting of ten questions and then check your design against some of the criteria discussed below.

For objective tests and other types of assessment, it is important to first produce an assessment specification (see 8.7 below) which indicates syllabus coverage, abilities and skills to be tested, etc. Before writing the items, it is important to decide which format you are using. Obviously, it is easier to produce short answer/sentence completion questions than those involving multiple choice. A multiple-choice question will consist of three components:

- *the stem* which is the part that *asks* the question
- *the key* which is the *correct answer,* chosen from several possibilities
- *the distractors* which are the remaining possible answers.

Stems may be direct questions or incomplete statements. *Keys* must be indicated in such a way that only students with the necessary knowledge can see them. *Distractors* are incorrect answers, which appear correct to those who do not have the knowledge.

When writing items

1. the stem should be presented clearly and unambiguously
2. the stem should be correct in all respects
3. there should be no clues to the key
4. options should be grammatically consistent with the stem
5. items should be as concise as possible
6. negatives are not recommended as distractors (i.e. 'none of these')
7. negatives in the stem should be used sparingly (i.e. 'not', 'never')
8. items should focus on important content, not trivia
9. items should be set out clearly.

After writing an objective test, it should be reviewed and then pre-tested/piloted. There are many formulae for evaluating the effectiveness of an objective test and a good example is a method of checking on the difficulty of the test.

Facility (Difficulty) Index

$$\frac{CSAQ}{TC} \times \frac{100}{1} = \text{Facility Value} \qquad \text{e.g: } \frac{40}{50} \times \frac{100}{1} = 80\% \text{ Facility Value}$$

CSAQ = Candidates Successfully Answering Question, TC = Total Candidates.
Over 70% = Fairly easy, 30–70% Moderately Difficult, Below 30% = Fairly Difficult.

Table 8.2 Examples of objective test types

Recall/completion	a. What is the capital city of Spain?
	b. Who invented the telephone?
	c. The chemical symbol for water is . . .?

Matching   d. For each of the national dishes in List B, select from list A its area of origin:

List A		List B	
Austria	North Africa	Paella	Pecan Pie
Denmark	North America	Apple Strudel	Shish Kebab
France	Russia	Sauerkraut	Tagliatelle
Germany	Spain	Borsch	Fondue
Greece	Switzerland	Moussaka	
Italy	Turkey	Bouillabaisse	

Multiple choice	e. Which of the following is the world's longest river?
	1. Nile, 2. Amazon, 3. Mississippi, 4. Zambesi.

True/false   f. The mean of a set of scores is:

i. The same as the average.	True/False
ii. Calculated by dividing the sum of the scores by the number of scores.	True/False
iii. The score of the person halfway down the rank order.	True/False

Sequencing	g. Place the following in the correct sequence:
	1. depress the accelerator and move away; 2. turn the ignition key;
	3. check the rear view mirror; 4. adjust seat and mirrors; 5. release handbrake;
	6. lift clutch; 7. place in correct gear; 8. depress clutch; 9. depress brake.
Multiple response	h. Which of the following are thought to be factors involved in heart disease?
	i. smoking; ii. high blood pressure; iii. intake of surplus vitamins;
	iv. high cholesterol level in the blood; v. stress.

The Facility Index can be used to check if the distractors within multiple-choice items are appropriate or *too* distracting. A distractor should normally attract about 5 per cent, any less and it is not successful. If a distractor is gaining more responses than the key, it is *too* successful, probably because it is too close to the right answer.

8.6.2 Free response assessment

One of the most popular assessment methods is the *free response* type of test, which is encouraged through essays, assignments and dissertations. We have called these 'Making Answers' in our Assessment Methods table above (Table 8.1). An effectively designed free response assessment will allow the 'high-flyers' to express a range of views and carry out an in-depth analysis of situations and processes. It will also allow the less-able students to demonstrate their particular interests and strengths. When compared to the objective test, a free-response assessment will be high on validity and low on reliability (see 8.7 below). In other words, even though they are *subject experts*, the range of possible interpretations by different assessors (even when they are marking the same piece of work) will often produce a range of marks which differ considerably.

This is why it is important to *moderate* the marking of essays, assignments and (especially) dissertations. Moderation involves a number of markers reviewing each other's assessments and (where there are differences) presenting a justification for their own interpretation/mark.

Activity 8i Moderation

Consider the methods you use to ensure that there is a consistency of marking within your team. Discuss the advantages of the chosen approach and also the difficulties in arriving at a process which ensures that assessment is not only consistent but also addresses the identified criteria.

It is very common for different markers of free response types of assessment (essays or assignments for example) to assess student answers differently and it is essential that the moderation processes move the team of markers towards an accepted consensus where a particular interpretation is agreed as acceptable.

Using a 'meeting halfway' approach to moderation is *not good practice*, because it is often the result of one or more of the assessors marking less efficiently than the others and, because the difference in their values and views are not discussed, the markers do not have the opportunity to develop their judgement through debate and comparison. The values of teachers which become evident during marking will undoubtedly also be present in their teaching and so it is probable that the students will have understood one thing and will be marked against another.

There is an example of an objective test style of *recall/completion* in Table 8.2. If a *free response* approach is preferred, it could be something along the lines of '*My three reasons for and against capital punishment are . . .*'

A structured essay is a halfway house between objective and subjective approaches, where the learners will be asked to write about a particular subject but their answer will be constrained by detailed instructions about what must be included in their work. In essays, candidates are required to address particular issues, processes or periods, whereas in more crude examples, the students may be asked to incorporate particular words, which can be ticked off by the assessor.

8.6.3 Practical tests

The assessment of practical skills within vocational areas does inevitably present the assessor with particular problems, which need to be addressed in order to sustain reliability and validity.

What is to be tested?

As we suggested earlier, the first step is to achieve an appropriate balance between process and product. This isn't always easy, because in many cases, that vocational area is defined by the quality of its product (catering, for example) and in focusing on the product some important requirements in the process of production could be overlooked. A good starting point would be to clarify the:

- *objectives* to be achieved and key skills to be demonstrated
- *quality* of performance (i.e. what criteria will be used to ensure that the candidate has reached the required standard)
- *relative* importance (i.e. *weighting*) of each task/skill/objective.

The next consideration is at what stage should the assessment take place? Every process has a key period when the learner has to manage important events and this crucial time is not necessarily at the end.

When to test?

Sometimes, particularly when measuring value added, it is important to be aware of the levels of skill, understanding and experience which the learner brings to the programme. We need to decide:

- whether or not to measure the abilities of learners on entry to the programme (i.e. *pre-test*).
- if it will be useful to use a series of *formative* assessment strategies during the programme or just use summative assessment on completion.

What assessment strategy to use for practical subjects?

Good assessment is a fusion of timing, modes, methods and marking processes (see also 8.10 below). Often we develop an appropriate strategy through a series of adjustments and modifications to make what we are doing compatible with the environment in which we are working. We need to check:

- whether it is important to test understanding separately from the practical skills and if so decide how to do this (e.g. multiple-choice, structured questions, problem solving).
- what proportion of the total marks will be allocated to the testing of understanding?
- the best method of assessing the practical aspects (i.e. do you set one piece of work per task, or select a task which will show proficiency in a number of skills?).
- what proportion of the total marks will be allocated to the testing of practical skills?

How to assess performance?

Again, the accurate marking of performance requires a fine balance between process and product. We should agree:

- how the practical aspects of performance will be marked, e.g. using checklists about stages in the process, rating scales applied to the finished product, or a comparison to other work
- how to identify satisfactory performance
- whether we need to moderate the marks as our judgements may be very subjective
- the way in which those who fail to meet the standards are able to recover.

How to arrange assessments?

The implementation of assessment is always a stressful time for both the tutors and the learners. If there is a breakdown in communication between the responsible parties, it can create a range of tensions which will continue well beyond the period of assessment. To reduce problems we should:

- confirm that the instructions about what the learners being assessed need to do is clear, that the time allocated is appropriate and that the arrangements (e.g. the mark allocation) is known to those being tested
- ensure that sufficient equipment and materials are available to those being assessed
- identify who will benefit from the information gained through assessment from among the learners, teachers, employers and others
- agree how the results will be presented – i.e. individual, aggregate, profile.

8.6.4 Competence-based assessment

Since the launch of the National Council for Vocational Qualifications, the use of competences as indicators of practitioner skills and understandings has been accepted by more than 80 per cent of national vocational areas. Initially, the design and development of these standards was the responsibility of employer-led bodies and their teams went through a laborious process of disaggregating each of the key vocational areas into units of competence, which were then broken down into defined competence statements, with the related underpinning knowledge and range (extent and context of the performance) also clearly articulated.

This process, which is shown in diagrammatic form in Table 8.3, had many critics (see, for example, Hodkinson and Issitt 1995, Ecclestone 1997, Hyland 1996), but there was a national governmental imperative to simplify vocational qualifications nationally and provide 'transparency' of assessment.

During the rapid developments which took place in the 1990s, a generally accepted definition of competence was seen as '*the ability to perform the activities within an occupation to the standards expected*', which is everything a person should do at work if they are to be effective in their job, including skills, knowledge, understanding and the ability to transfer these to

Table 8.3 The NVQ functional analysis approach to defining competence

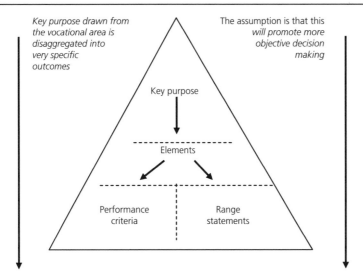

Key purpose drawn from the vocational area is disaggregated into very specific outcomes

The assumption is that this will promote more objective decision making

Key purpose

Elements

Performance criteria

Range statements

new situations, organize and plan work coping with routine and non-routine tasks, the implementation of innovation and being personally effective.

Some of the strengths and weaknesses of using competences as the basis for assessment were voiced in a useful analysis by Auerbach (1986), which is summarized in Table 8.4.

Table 8.4 Strengths and weaknesses of competence-based assessment

For – Competences provide the learner with:	Against – Competences create situations where:
explicit, predetermined outcomes.	creative, divergent and critical thinking is limited.
individualized, student-centred instruction.	assessment-centred, group processes are subverted.
the means of demonstrating skills and understandings.	there is a lack of encouragement to synthesize and generate knowledge.
a teacher who is a facilitator (humanist theory).	the measurable, observable imperative creates a positivist approach to learning (behaviourist theory).
flexible, modularized programmes.	the reductionist, disaggregation of learning can severely limit a more holistic view.
continuous assessment.	the over-concern with assessment and the necessary level of administration is restricting for teachers and learners.
a forum to demonstrate the mastery of specific performance objectives.	the demonstration of learning only through behaviour restricts the development of higher-level learning outcomes.
a process where achievements are recorded in detail.	some professional diagnostic activities cannot be expressed adequately enough.

Activity 8j For and Against Competence Approaches

Given the summary of the value of competence-based approaches in Table 8.4, analyse what you feel would be the positive and negative effects (or might be if you are not currently involved in CBET) in relation to your own learners.

8.6.5 Learner profiles and portfolios

The use of competences as an assessment vehicle is usually based around the development of a student profile or portfolio, the requirements of which will sometimes be closely prescribed by the awarding body and in other cases will be negotiated with the learner.

In those situations where a *prescribed profile* is in use, the defined learning outcomes (see also 8.6.6 below) will form the basis for discussion, negotiation and assessment and will provide a *formative* function, which allows the tutor to monitor development and identify and anticipate any problems. However, prescribed outcomes are essentially summative and in most cases, there will only be two possible outcomes: either the assessment criteria associated with the learning outcome will have been achieved (i.e. satisfactory), or it will not yet have been achieved.

In some cases a negotiated profile may be used, which is similar to the one above, but differs in that the learners play a substantial part in defining their own learning outcomes at the beginning of the programme.

A further development of the use of profiles and outcomes (which may be incorporated into either of the above systems) could be a personal development profile, which is a vehicle for *formative* assessment. Often involving self-assessment, this process may be based on logs, journals and diaries and involves the learner in reflecting on their own development against defined outcomes that have been negotiated with their tutor.

8.6.6 Learning outcomes

These days the ability to work with specific learning outcomes is a requirement at most levels of education. The awarding body may define these outcomes, or teachers involved in curriculum development may write them.

Activity 8k Criterion Referencing

Select a criterion-referenced scheme you are familiar with and analyse the outcomes defined for it. If possible suggest how these might be improved.

We have previously discussed the relative merits of learning outcomes (see 8.6.4 above), but their additional value to the learning situation is that they help:

- to clarify the learning requirements of particular modules and pathways
- students to understand what they can expect to gain from a planned learning experience and what is expected of them
- determine appropriate learning strategies
- identify appropriate forms of assessment
- make possible the accreditation of prior learning.

Structure

From a grammatical point of view, a learning outcome comprises:

a. a subject
b. an active transitive verb or verb phrase
c. an 'object' of the verb
d. a qualifying clause or phrase which provides a context or condition.

Criteria

Good learning outcomes should be:

- achievable
- measurable
- explicit
- as succinct as possible.

Examples would be:

Table 8.5 Writing good learning outcomes

Subject	Active verb or phrase	Object	Context/condition
The quantity surveyor will	be able to	accurately measure the	angle of the incline.
The drama student should	contribute effectively to	the production and performance	of at least 3 plays.
The trainee teacher	can	assess the work of her students	in a valid and reliable manner.

Obviously, it is important to select verbs that are appropriate. Bloom (1956) and his colleagues suggested three taxonomies of educational objective, and Gronlund (1985) gives examples of verbs which may be used to represent the increasing complexity of performance at each level of these domains (see also Chapter 4).

Table 8.6 Use of verbs within the three taxonomies of educational objectives

Cognitive		Affective		Psychomotor	
General objective	Illustrative verbs	General objective	Illustrative verbs	General objective	Illustrative verbs
Knows specific facts	Defines, describes, identifies, labels	Attends closely	Follows, selects, locates, replies	Perceives and attends to source	Chooses, detects, isolates, relates
Understands the meaning of material	Explains, infers, predicts, summarizes	Willingness to respond	Discusses, labels, reports, selects	Develops a set for action	Begins, reacts, responds, starts
Applies concepts and principles	Changes, discovers, manipulates, solves	Commitment to a set of values	Initiates, justifies, selects, supports	Trial and error learning	Constructs, displays, measures
Analyses relationships	Differentiates, infers, selects, separates	Organizes according to values	Defends, orders, organizes, relates	Carries our physical processes with confidence	Assembles, builds, fastens, fixes, mends, organizes
Synthesizes to form a new whole	Combines, compiles, relates, revises	Develops a life-style congruent with own value system	Acts, discriminates, proposes, revises, serves, verifies	Skilful performance	Calibrates, manipulates, works
Evaluates materials and processes	Appraises, compares, justifies, supports			Adapts skills to particular needs	Adapts, alters, changes, revises
				Creates new skills to fit new needs	Combines, designs, originates

Activity 8l Writing Learning Outcomes

Using the above guidance, try writing ten learning outcomes for a programme you are familiar with.

Obviously, a key requirement for a learning outcome is that it should be observable and measurable. Table 8.7 may help here.

Table 8.7 The use of verbs when writing observable and measurable learning outcomes

Avoid words like:	Use words like:	Avoid words like:	Use words like:
Know	State	Be interested in	Outline
Understand	Describe	Acquire the feeling for	Summarize
Really know	Explain	Be aware of	Represent graphically
Really understand	List	Believe	Compare
Be familiar with	Evaluate	Have information about	Apply
Become acquainted with	Identify	Realize the significance of	Assess
Have a good grasp of	Distinguish between	Learn the basics of	Give examples of
Appreciate	Analyse	Have a working knowledge of	Suggest reasons why

Evaluate the purpose of your assessment and the defined outcomes against the following questions:

- Are the learning outcomes compatible with those of the scheme as a whole?
- Do the learning outcomes clearly specify those objectives required for successful completion of the programme?
- Are the learning outcomes written as simple statements, comprehensive to both students and employers?
- Have the learning outcomes been expressed in cognitive, affective and psychomotor terms?
- Has the link between learning outcomes, learning strategies and the mode and method of assessment been clearly articulated?
- Does the assessment strategy for each module indicate how a valid measurement will be made of the extent to which a student has achieved the learning outcomes?

- Has a wide variety of assessment methods been used?
- Is it clear who is responsible for carrying out the assessment (tutors/peers/students)?
- Is there an appropriate balance between formative and summative assessment?
- Has consideration been given as to the approaches of norm-referenced, criterion-referenced and personal-referenced methods of assessment?
- Are appropriate criteria used to describe the important features of expected student performance within the context of the module? Is student achievement recorded against agreed criteria, contributing to student feedback and final grading?

8.7 Sufficient and fair

The design and implementation of effective assessment has always placed great demands on both teacher and student and this burden has increased in recent years as the recording and justifying of learner achievement has increasingly become a priority. In such a climate, it is essential that assessment should be **sufficient**, but not over-demanding.

Activity 8m Sufficiency in Assessment

Considering your own teaching and learning situation, think about the assessment methods which are most appropriate for your learners and your subject. Then, bearing in mind the demands on your time, suggest how you might arrive at an assessment strategy which is 'sufficient'.

Some simple ways of achieving this sufficiency are by ensuring that:

- the specification is as clear and precise as possible to ensure that the assessment design may be focused clearly on only the defined outcomes and that there is no duplication of effort.
- the time-consuming marking of 'free response' assessment is kept to a minimum by deploying objective tests where only knowledge and comprehension require testing.
- where possible *one task* is used as the basis for the assessment of a *number of defined outcomes.*
- peer, group and self-assessment are used to lighten the load for both tutors and students where appropriate.
- the timing of assessment is carefully considered in order to remove the frustrating bottle-neck created by crowded assessment schedules.

The establishment of sufficiency in assessment can also be confirmed by producing a grid of coverage. In Table 8.8 below, using a notional NVQ Care Award, the individual assessment items (in all forms) have been calculated to give an idea of syllabus coverage in terms of level, domain and content. Obviously, other criteria could be introduced to make the audit more relevant to particular programmes.

Table 8.8 Assessment coverage of NVQ care awards

NQF Level →	Level 1			Level 2			Level 3			Total items		
Domain →	Cog	Aff	P.Mtr	Cog	Aff	P.Mtr	Cog	Aff	P.Mtr	Cog	Aff	P.Mtr
Syllabus:												
Equality	4	4	-	4	4	-	4	4	-	12	12	-
Management	3	2	-	3	2	-	4	2	-	10	6	-
Communication	3	3	2	3	3	2	4	3	1	10	9	5
Services and information	2	-	-	2	-	-	3	-	-	7	-	-
Health and safety	3	3	2	4	3	2	4	3	2	11	9	6
Care	6	5	8	6	5	8	7	5	4	19	15	20
Developmental activities	3	4	4	2	4	4	2	4	4	7	12	12
Therapeutic activities	4	4	5	4	4	5	6	4	4	14	12	14
Service delivery	3	2	2	3	2	2	3	2	2	9	6	6
Total	31	27	23	31	27	23	37	27	17	99	81	63

In reality, the above distribution table may not be an accurate representation of how such a programme may be assessed, it is merely an illustration of how a balance grid (or a similar specification grid) can provide a useful audit to show if assessment is sufficient in comparison to other programmes. The important consideration is to ensure that not only is each of the domains included, but also that somewhere in our assessment processes we address each *level*. This means not just in terms of NVQ or National Qualifications Framework level, but also the *domain* level. For example, it is not sufficient for our learners to just 'know' and 'comprehend' at the lower end of Bloom's (1956) cognitive domain, when we can take them beyond to *analysing* and *evaluating*.

The establishment of *fair assessment* is a little more difficult. On the face of it, you would think that if the assessment is valid and reliable (see 8.8 below) it will automatically be fair.

However, as we have discussed in chapters 5 and 8, less confident learners may feel intimidated by the very process of assessment. Although attempts may have been made to ensure that the assessment process is 'transparent' and the requirements are clear and unambiguous, some learners who feel they are destined to failure may not have the disposition to listen or read the instructions carefully enough. When you are nervous, it is sometimes difficult to correctly interpret difficult words or remember the sequence of processes, even though to others it seems straightforward. Ensure that you repeat instructions and reassure all learners before assessment.

We have said that some learners will need more support than others during assessment, and this is outlined in the previous chapter. However, inclusiveness also places great demands on the quality of *feedback* which learners are given.

8.7.1 Feedback

Jones and Bray (1986) confirmed that feedback does assist learners unless the material is too demanding in which case feedback becomes demoralizing. Feeding back merely the grades or confirming correct answers has *little effect* on subsequent performance, while detailed factual feedback, conceptual help or feedback on strategies used is more effective. Bennett (1974) also confirms that merely ticking or giving a mark is insufficient to optimize learning. We must indicate what the student can do to *improve performance.*

Activity 8n Improving Performance

Discuss some examples from the assessment feedback which you may have given your own students and say how you might have made this more helpful in helping them to develop.

Written feedback (on free response essays and assignments) that is just confirmatory, i.e. 'you have achieved the learning outcome' is no more informative than a tick. The learner does not know from this feedback whether they have just achieved or whether they have gone well beyond the requirement. Similarly, a failure marked with a cross or a score below the required level, doesn't help the failing student to know what needs to be done to put things right. In the marking of written work, actual comments written in the margin close to the actual part of the learner's text being commented on are probably the most valuable way to move a student forward. If you can also give them examples of how they may have expressed the point more effectively, so much the better.

In addition to giving you feedback on the success of your teaching, the purpose of formative assessment is not merely to confirm that students are at the right level, but also to help them realize how they can further develop. If the assessment and subsequent feedback doesn't achieve this, then it simply isn't formative.

8.8 Validity and reliability

Two of the most important standards used to measure the methods used in assessment, evaluation and research are 'validity' and 'reliability'. Simply put, within assessment processes validity is an indication of the extent to which teachers are assessing **what they say they are assessing. Reliability** is the **level of consistency** of the adopted assessment procedures.

We will see later that these two measures have an important reciprocal relationship. First though, we need to extend further our simple definitions.

8.8.1 Validity

Although our first simple definition above holds good for assessment generally, the concept of validity may be broken down into several useful categories:

'Face' validity is the obvious first definition. This occurs when it is accepted that *on the face of it*, a chosen assessment methodology appears to have the necessary validity.

Currie (1986) goes on to present a conventional and, what is generally viewed as, an unproblematic summary of validity concepts:

Validity really has two aspects. First, is what you expect your pupils to learn and do justifiable and reasonable? Second, do the methods of assessment achieve what they set out to do?

The first part of this definition is known as *'curricular validity'* and Currie emphasizes that:

unless you have a clear idea of what are the learning outcomes you expect – and feel reasonably confident that such learning outcomes are justifiable – you will not be able to make a valid assessment.

Next Currie turns to *'construct validity'* which represents a very common view of assessment validity in that it

. . . means constructing a test or assessment . . . that tests what it sets out to test and not something else.

To illustrate this, Currie gives some useful examples of validity erosion, such as when (within an assessment of manual dexterity) listening skills or the ability to read engineering drawings (which are outside the purpose of the assessment) have a direct bearing on the result. Or, in another situation, using essay questions in a physics or history examination when the pupils have not been taught how to write a good essay answer within the subject.

Currie also points out that under this heading, norm-referenced assessment and criterion-referenced assessment (see 8.5.1 above) also have problems in relation to construct validity. The former because of the subtle influences of the discriminating processes present when we are comparing student with student and the latter because of the difficulties of devising clear, measurable criteria.

A further important consideration introduced by Currie is *retrospective and predictive validity. Retrospective validity* is mainly concerned with *content,* i.e. the teaching that has gone before and the objectives of the course. A test must ask only for what is expected and no more. For example, if a class has been taught three reasons for the First World War, it would then be invalid to ask for five reasons or give credit for them.

Predictive validity is often used in selection processes and yet, as Currie points out, 'these decisions are based on performances that may bear little resemblance to the course the student will embark upon.' A current example of this is the use of A-level results as criteria for university places, when research has not established that there is a clear correlation between performance in these examinations and subsequent performance as an undergraduate.

8.8.2 Reliability

Currie then turns to *reliability* and again she considers two aspects of this concept. The first is that reliable assessment enables the assessor to

> make reliable comparisons. The comparisons may be between the performance of different pupils (norm-related reliability) or between the pupil's attainment and the course objectives (criterion-related reliability).

The second aspect is a more common perception of the term in that reliability is seen as *consistency.* 'How far would the same test give the same result if done by the same children under the same conditions?' Currie makes the point that this is an impossible situation to achieve absolutely as there will 'always be some variables'.

Examples of such variables given by Currie are human factors in relation to the assessed (such as memory, health, the effect of environmental conditions) and the assessors (such as tiredness, prejudice, subjectivity, etc.). At this stage then, a summary of these concepts could be that:

> striving for *validity* is based on a concern to do what you *said* you intended to do *and no more.*
> establishing *reliability* is achieved through the use of a *replicable and consistent process.*

She also makes the point that the simplicity of the marking of *objective tests* will improve reliability but, where higher-level cognitive performance is being tested, will usually lead to a reduction in validity as such assessment cannot effectively test such qualities.

These comments are apt at a time when at all levels of education there is a well-established process (through the National Curriculum, QCA and the NCVQ, for example) where learning outcomes are externally devised and passed down to teachers and learners. Because such national specifications must be applicable in all relevant educational settings, the central concern is with reliability (i.e. consistency), often at the expense of validity. A reliability model may confirm that all learners are tested in the same way, but such a strategy does often involve the designers in ignoring important high-level outcomes, which are difficult to articulate and assess consistently.

Rowntree (1981) summarizes this dilemma when he points out that, because of the inherent problems of language, the wording of precise and unambiguous definitions and their later interpretation will always make the achievement of precise reliability *elusive*. Perhaps more importantly, he emphasizes that it is assessment validity which is *essential*.

To summarize, despite our best efforts, the *reliability* of assessment is always difficult to achieve consistently. However, our central concern should constantly remain focused on achieving construct validity, i.e. we actually assess only what we intended to assess.

8.9 Fitness for purpose – evaluating assessment

As we have now considered all of the main concepts of educational assessment, this is a useful point at which we can check out that our evolving design has addressed all the necessary aspects.

Activity 80 Fitness for Purpose

What criteria specific to your learning situation would you use to decide if your assessment is fit for its purpose?

Obviously, your own assessment situation will have particular assessment demands and the characteristics of your learners will often mean that there are specific outcomes you wish to achieve with them in addition to those prescribed by the awarding body. We suggest that in order to ensure that our scheme is *fit for its purpose* we must confirm that the assessment has:

- *Coverage*   That the important aspects of the curriculum will be assessed.
- *Relevance*   What we decide to assess has value and priority within the subject being studied.
- *Intention*   We are very clear about what it is we wish to assess and establish clear criteria of achievement (objectives or outcomes).
- *Balance*   Our assessment achieves a balance between the different levels of the cognitive, affective and psychomotor domains and the different parts of the syllabus.
- *Integrity*   We have let the students know the standard and criteria that they are expected to achieve.
- *Reliability*   Our methods achieve consistent results with similar groups of Learners.
- *Validity*   We are testing what we intended to test and no more.
- *Objectivity*   As far as possible we separate the interpretive process from personal feelings.

> ## Activity 8p Assessment Value
>
> Consider a group of your own learners, and summarize what you feel would be the general purpose of any assessment you may undertake relating to them. In other words, what overall value would you wish to be able to attribute to your learners as a result of the assessment?

8.10 Conclusion

Obviously, the value that we want any assessment of our learners to provide will be related to the state of their current abilities and attitudes and how these have changed since they were last assessed. However, it is probably appropriate to bring this chapter to an end by emphasizing a point we made at the beginning. Formative assessment can be a central means of motivating students and encouraging them to develop independence and learner autonomy or it can be used to encourage instrumental surface learning and learner dependence. Ecclestone (2002) warns us about sacrificing this opportunity as we seek evidence of performance through imposed summative assessment regimes designed to provide data for quality processes. We should think about the long tradition of assessment as an accepted route to learner empowerment before we continue with this route. Rowntree (1977) observes in his excellent analysis of the 'self-fulfilling prophecy' syndrome:

> For a few to emerge as outstandingly successful the majority must fail – to varying degrees. The failure may be only partial. Indeed, had the student been in a different (e.g. less selective) school or college, his performance might well have made him a success. But by comparison with those he has been led to emulate, he has fallen short . . . Unfortunately, the ethos of competitive assessment often leads the student who has failed on a few tasks (e.g. learned more slowly than other people) to feel that he has failed as a person.

We started the chapter by saying that assessment should be our first consideration when planning learning. If we articulate at this early stage what we are preparing our learners for (whether as a result of our own assessment strategies or an external imposed policy) the values we wish to endow our learners with on completion of the process will become very clear. One of those values should be to enhance the learners' view of their own self-worth and assessment should be used to encourage this learner independence, which identifies their abilities and indicates their strengths and how to build on them.

To complete this chapter, try the following activity, bearing in mind the principles and concepts we have discussed.

The *summative statement* can be taken to represent any document, certificate or diploma which a learner may take away from a programme to show what they have achieved. Naturally, they will want it to show not only what they have gained but also *how far they have travelled.* Some of these learning gains are easy to articulate, but other, perhaps more important achievements, will be difficult to express and may be specific to a particular context.

Activity 8q Summative Statement

Prepare an A4 summative report on two of your learners that provides the reader with a good understanding of how they have developed during the programme. Consider their current abilities and understandings against not only the formal assessment criteria, but also such difficult assessment areas as their social skills, their willingness to contribute to group work, what they bring to class interactions, etc. Try to choose two contrasting students for this exercise.

However, as we said at the beginning of the chapter (and at greater length in Chapter 5), the assessment process is only one aspect of the teaching and learning cycle, but because of our concern for accountability, for some learners it has taken on a whole new, more threatening dimension. In addition to measuring achievement against *externally* devised outcomes, we should also be concerned to confirm the achievement of targets, which our learners have *internally* identified for themselves. To them these attainments are an essential route to self-belief. To us they are indicators of the validity of our assessment processes.

Prescribed, observable, measurable outcomes have their place in establishing a reliable system of accreditation. However, they are only part of a complex portfolio of human attainment which should be promoted by every worthwhile educational provision. Also, it is these very predictable, imperative qualities which cause precisely defined outcomes to become repetitive and tedious. Inevitably, our current systems place the highest value on that which we can measure, and yet equal and perhaps more important qualities are ignored because they cannot be quantified. The following is a list (not definitive or in any particular order) of some of the qualities which we should find a way of acknowledging, even though we cannot precisely define them:

- trust
- empathy
- respect
- loyalty
- love
- dedication
- humour
- commitment
- enthusiasm
- tolerance
- invention
- intuition
- creativity
- responsiveness
- inspiration
- self-esteem.

A truly learner-centred assessment system should be able to acknowledge the things that we value rather than valuing only the things we can measure.

8.11 Useful publications

Black, P.J. and D. William (1998), *Inside the Black Box: Raising Standards Through Classroom Intervention.* London: BERA.
> This is one of the key studies of the damaging effect on underachieving students of summative assessment strategies allied to the irresistible school accountability juggernaut. Landmark research with significant implications.

Ecclestone, K. (1996), *How to Assess the Vocational Curriculum.* London: Kogan Page.
> Kathryn Ecclestone presents a fine review of assessment processes within vocational education, including a valuable chapter on the development of professional expertise.

Ecclestone, K. (2002), *Learning Autonomy in Post-16 Education.* London: Routledge Falmer.
> Kathryn joins Black and William in providing clear evidence of the positive effects on student emancipation of formative assessment. An important contribution to the debate.

Gipps, C.V. (1994), *Beyond Testing.* London: The Falmer Press.
> Caroline Gipps has captured the radical changes which occurred in the 1990s and their effect on assessment practices. She includes a welcome insightful chapter on the ethics of assessment.

Lloyd Jones, R. and E. Bray (1986), *Assessment from Principles to Action.* London: Macmillan.
> A very useful review of assessment concepts and principles with some helpful illustrative examples from practice.

Rowntree, D. (1981), *Assessing Students: How shall we know them?* London: Harper & Row.
> A classic of its kind from Derek Rowntree, who is one of the acknowledged experts on assessment processes and their effects on learners. A tremendous reference book, obtainable in most libraries, but now unfortunately out of print.

8.12 Useful websites

http://cms.curriculum.edu.au/assessment/default.asp
www.assessmentinst.com/
www.literacytrust.org.uk/Database/assessment.html
www.tipcet.com
www.tki.org.nz/r/assessment/one/formative_e.php
www.wncp.ca/assessment/rethink.pdf

Table 8.9 Process justifications for assessing the outcomes of learning and learners' achievements

FAQs at the stage of:	Threshold award level	Associate certificate level	Cert Ed/PGCE/Diploma level
Why do it?	Most students wish to know how successful their learning has been. It is our responsibility to ensure that the process of assessment sustains their desire to learn, rather than diminishing it. We can promote learning through assessment by ensuring that it is fair, reliable, encouraging and informative.	It is essential to establish that student learning has taken place. This knowledge helps us to establish the level that our students have achieved and to develop new learning to take them forward. We also need to establish that the learning has been understood and that they are capable of applying the knowledge gained.	There is a need to continually review the assessment process as reliability often remains elusive and validity can easily be undermined. Evaluating the role played by both the assessors and the assessed helps us to understand the effects of assessment on the learning process.
Where are we going?	A simple approach to assessment is firstly to prioritize those aspects of the subject we are teaching that we feel the learner should be able to understand or do. Ask yourself which particular skills or knowledge could be said to represent the subject. Of course, we may be teaching on a programme where the learning outcomes have already been defined by an external body. Even so, we need to appreciate why the designers believe that the identified understandings and skills are important. This is essential for planning teaching.	In every learning situation we need to develop assessment strategies, which allow students to demonstrate their knowledge and understanding. Assessment processes must be reliable and allow for the collection of valid evidence. You will need to be able to describe a range of assessment opportunities that are appropriate to your own or other programmes. We must show evidence of planning, the selection of appropriate assessment methods, recording decisions and providing supportive and instructive feedback to our students.	We wish to move towards a situation where the assessment process encourages learner autonomy through the realization that knowledge creation is valued as much as knowledge replication. Learners should have freedom to feel ownership of concepts and principles rather than automatically accepting that important knowledge lies with others. Rather than using assessment to establish conformity, we should use the process to encourage the development of informed challenges to established views and values.
How do we get there?	We need to start with the key areas of learning which either we have prioritized or an external body has defined. Our next step is to decide what evidence we need to be certain that the necessary learning of these identified areas has been achieved. Of course, teachers are busy people and so we need to ensure (where possible) that the assessment process is not too demanding of our time.	Produce an assessment scheme for your area of work, matching the assessment methods and to the stated learning outcomes and justifying the chosen strategy. Within this rationale consider the validity and reliability of the scheme. Assess your students and make and record your decisions appropriately. Explain how you might adapt your assessment methods to meet the needs of particular learners.	In these days of the dominance of centralized assessment procedures controlled by external awarding bodies, it is often difficult to develop ownership of the assessment process. However, it is important for both assessed and assessors to support a rigorous system that can withstand the pressures that funding related to student numbers, achievement and 'value added' inevitably brings.

(Continued)

Table 8.9—cont'd.

FAQs at the stage of:	Threshold award level	Associate certificate level	Cert Ed/PGCE/Diploma level
Is this the best way?	We need to be sure that we are only assessing what the learners have been told will be assessed. Efficient assessment will address several outcomes with one task.	Consider cost effectiveness, the resources available and how the assessment process may affect the learning experiences and attitudes of the students.	Evaluate the assessment process to discover not only the level of reliability and validity but also the robustness of the system in the face of external pressures.
When is the right time?	We may be constrained by dates set by external awarding bodies, external verifier visits, assessment boards, etc. However, timing is important in assessment. It is essential that the learners have time to complete the assessment task and we have time to carry out careful marking.	Consider the purpose of the assessment and how it relates to the learning experience. Check how the measurable learning outcomes relate to the key curriculum events. Confirm what the requirements are for the awarding body, the external examiners, the internal verifiers, etc.	Analyse the effect of the timing of assessment in relation to the development of student autonomy. Also reflect on the type of assessment: have you achieved an acceptable balance between formative and summative, formal and informal, reliability and validity?
Who needs to know?	Clear guidelines and accurate record keeping are essential features of effective assessment. We must ensure that the learners know what is expected of them, that we record attendance at exams, the handing in of assignments, extenuating circumstances, agreed marks, moderation, informative feedback, return dates, etc.	Confirm if the information on assessment has been recorded, stored securely and shared with colleagues and external agencies in an appropriate manner. Ensure feedback given to students is accurate and informative and will enable them to understand their performance better.	Evaluate how informed the students are in terms of their assessed performance. Have they sufficient information to know exactly why they did or didn't achieve and how to improve their performance? Alternatively, is the assessment so detailed and precise that it is encouraging student dependence?
How do we know when we've got there?	Most learners will be very aware of the strengths and weaknesses of their assessed performance and through any conventional evaluation process will let it be known if they feel that the assessment process has not been appropriate. Normal quality processes will also identify problems in terms of marking, feedback, etc.	When you have confidence that you are assessing what you intended to assess (validity) and have ensured consistency in the application of assessment processes (reliability). Moderation with colleagues, feedback from external examiners and internal verifiers and student evaluations and reviews will help in this.	You are looking for a robust, rigorous and independent assessment system which encourages the development of informed learner scepticism and student autonomy and is not compromised by the drive towards those levels of achievement or student retention which affect positions in league tables.
Has everyone had a fair chance?	We must ensure that those being assessed have been informed early in the teaching and learning process of how and when they will be assessed and that they have been prepared for it. They must know the process of informing tutors of extenuating circumstances and particular needs.	Confirm that the assessment is sufficiently flexible in design, sensitive in application and reliable in measurement to allow all students to demonstrate their current ability. Look out for ambiguity in expression, student misunderstandings and undue stress created by the assessment process.	Because assessment systems are notoriously difficult to manage and moderate consistently, an analysis of your own procedures will inevitably reveal some flaws even though they may be minor. Remember that validity is essential and reliability is always elusive.

Inherent Evaluation
Liz Mayes

9

Chapter Outline

Key Concepts

Adversarial, Controlled Response, Critical Incidents, Decision Orientated, Educational Evaluation, Fear Factor, Formative Evaluation, Free Response, Goal Orientated, Goal-Free, Illuminative, Learning Spiral, Mentor, Questionnaire Design, Rating Scale, Reasoning, Reconstructing, Reflective Paradox, Relating, Responding, Self-Evaluation, Situationalize, Student Feedback, Summative Evaluation, Transactional.

Before you begin this chapter you may wish to check the Process Justifications (Table 9.2)

9.1 Introduction

The effectiveness of the process of evaluating educational practice has always been of concern to central and local government and to managers and stakeholders within the sector, both locally and nationally. However, relatively recently the pressure for increasing openness and accountability has become much more imperative and immediate. In 1997 the New Labour Prime Minister Tony Blair's election slogan of 'Education, Education, Education', made clear their intent, but lack of success within some areas despite huge investment has lent more immediacy to the cry for accountability and evidence of progress towards the elusive goals of effective education leading to vocational expertise and high levels of employability.

The development of the 14–19 curriculum and the proposed raising of the school/college leaving age to 18 promise further funding to the new Lifelong Learning Sector, and also increasing responsibility and the demand for a willingness to demonstrate not only effective recruitment, teaching, support and assessment, but also the ability to self-evaluate with analytic thoroughness all aspects of provision. An indicator of these changing values is the prominent position which evaluation has within the newly published LLUK Standards, as compared to the previous FENTO standards which were launched as recently as 2002/3. Then evaluation of and reflection on practice appeared in the final sections of the standards. In contrast now, up front within Domain A '*Professional Values and Practice*' of the newly published LLUK Standards (see Chapter 12) are the following statements of commitment:

> *Scope: (7)* Teachers in the Lifelong Learning Sector *are committed to improving the quality of their practice.*
> *Knowledge: (4.3)* Teachers know *ways to reflect, evaluate and use research to develop own practice, and to share good practice with others.*
> *Practice: (4.3)* Teachers share *good practice with others and engage in continuing professional development through reflection, evaluation and the appropriate use of research.*

Of course, in some ways our tradition of positioning evaluation/reflection towards the end of the process is understandable because by then it is clear that we will have something substantial to reflect on and, therefore, it is wise to wait until after the event. This traditional approach to evaluation has possibly led to us treating the concept as an afterthought; something to be done at the end of a process, i.e. *summative evaluation*. While in some cases this may be appropriate, evaluation is a far more critically important and ongoing process which, if developed early enough in our practice, can help us to become more effective, reflective practitioners who are able to identify trends and influences much earlier in the process and take action to avoid potential problems (which has a lot in common with *formative evaluation* discussed in the previous chapter).

So the current view of evaluation is that it is essentially a *formative* process, which should be planned during the initial stages of curriculum development when the very process of selecting methods and approaches will automatically suggest effective ways of checking their effectiveness.

Yet, for many new teachers evaluation is often seen as a 'Do and Review' activity because they have become used to completing a range of pro forma designed to meet the requirements of their teacher education programme. As an introduction to the design of evaluation documentation try the following as our first assessment activity of this chapter.

Activity 9a Evaluating Evaluations

We have reproduced below parts of two evaluation pro forma which will give you an idea of their different styles. In particular, think about the information they are trying to elicit and the possible timing of their use. How successful do you think such styles might be, particularly in your educational context? Would the focus of the analysis and the timing affect their value?

Table 9.1 Evaluation pro forma

9.1a Summative evaluation		9.1b Formative evaluation			
In the table below, please list on the left-hand side those aspects which you feel have made this project/module/course worthwhile and on the right-hand side list those which you feel have reduced its value. Would you please also add a brief explanation for your views.		Would you please keep a log below of the various sessions which you have attended during the current programme and add your comments in the appropriate column. Try to do this concurrently while your recollections are still fresh in your memory.			
1. *Worthwhile qualities:*	*Less worthwhile qualities:*	*Session No.*	*Description:*	*Relevance:*	*Comments:*
		1.			
Explanation	*Explanation*				
		2.			

Our summary of the characteristics of the two above examples would be:

9.1a Summative Evaluation: this is partially teacher-led and partially student-centred. The format of this end-of-programme approach and the criterion 'worthwhile' have been defined by the tutor, but the responding student can identify the processes and issues to comment on under either or both headings. The strengths of this approach are that it allows a response on general as well as specific issues and it is essentially qualitative, as it is looking to the respondent to explain why.

9.1b Formative Evaluation: this teacher-led evaluation is in the form of a log and if completed properly will provide a wealth of information about each session in a programme. However, it is obviously very demanding of the student and if completed, may very well not be done properly. The descriptor for each session could be entered by the teacher before handing to the students and this could act as an *aide-memoir.*

So, the second example would provide more valuable feedback, but because it is very demanding on the students' time, may not be completed effectively for each session. However, it is still completed *after* the students have experienced the lesson and as Petty (2004) points out, '*just doing and reviewing is not enough.*'

9.2 Professional knowledge

In this chapter we will identify ways of moving on from the 'Do and Review' approach by helping you to develop the skills to reflect upon your own practice and to recognize sources you can use in order to support this process. Unfortunately, many of us automatically associate evaluation with the regular quality assurance process which took place at the end of each academic year. Students were asked to complete forms covering a range of areas for *review*. While this data may have been very useful to our institutions, there are several important factors to consider:

- Who decides on the purpose of the questionnaire?
- Who designs the form of the questionnaire?
- Were this year's results compared with previous years?
- Who would receive such a retrospective analysis?
- How will the respondent's data be used to improve provision?
- Are the responses received too late to improve the education for next year's students?
- Will the data/responses help to improve the teaching?
- If the received information indicates areas which need improving, will they be discussed with the students who have provided the data?

Unfortunately, in many cases college-wide routine evaluation data is collected and passed on for processing elsewhere. Often it is only discussed with the teacher concerned if there are problems. The responses to institutional evaluation forms will inevitably be used for a variety of purposes by any number of interested parties such as managers, funding bodies, curriculum leaders, quality departments, marketing departments, etc.

Activity 9b Improving Practice

Write a short piece in your PDJ considering if, from your experience, evaluation information provided by students is used effectively to help develop teaching and improve professional practice. Give reasons for your conclusions.

While questionnaire-based evaluation is a useful tool within colleges, it is only one of many ways to improve practice. Perhaps more important is the process of encouraging all teachers to become active, reflective practitioners. In this way the process is ongoing and integrated, and it encourages staff to become proactive and aware of all of the initiatives currently taking place. Evaluating our practice inevitably involves reflective analysis and these personal deliberations are meaningless if they remain in isolation. Validating our reflections against the knowledge of others helps to enrich our experiences and this metacognition (thinking about thinking) facilitates more accurate and wider ranging deliberations and much better informed decision making. Evaluation not only enables us to take a critical, analytical view of our practice in order to develop our professional knowledge/value system, but it also trains us to critically analyse feedback from other sources.

Experienced professionals will usually develop a particular form of knowledge which is garnered from their field of operation. This specialized knowledge will allow them to make important, complex decisions quite quickly. This is because they have deliberated about similar decisions many times before and they are able to gather all the necessary decision-making data from that particular environment in a short space of time. In fact, their reasoning within familiar contexts becomes so rapid that it is almost intuitive, and when asked to explain their decisions they often have to think carefully to identify all of the criteria they considered.

You may have found that decision making within the complex environment of the classroom is gradually becoming easier. Eventually, evaluation should become second nature, an automatic, integral part of the way you operate and a key process within your professional value base as suggested in the Professional Standards Domain A 'Professional Values and Practice'.

Activity 9c Developing Knowledge through Evaluation

Discuss in your PDJ examples of effective decision making in relation to your practice and try to identify those areas where you find the most difficulty in solving evident problems. Try to indicate how you intend to progress.

9.3 Accountability

Recent changes within the new Lifelong Learning Sector have created a situation where practitioners are not only required to be trained and qualified in their own area of specialism but also to become qualified teachers with a whole new body of theory and practice to embrace. As discussed in chapters 1 and 12, recent government changes have seen a shift in the format of this 'dual professionalism' whereby teachers need to attain and maintain a professional approach not only in their teaching role but also in their subject specialism. This professionalism requires teachers to be far more accountable through their professional body registration and the recording of Continuing Professional Development (CPD) activities in an Institute for Learning (IfL) database, not only for their area of specialism but also for their pedagogic practice.

The notion of dual professionalism encompasses CPD and addresses not only the teacher's area of subject specialism, but also the skills of teaching and developing learning. In order to maintain their professional body (IfL) registration, practitioners are required to formally record at least 30 hours' professional development annually. For many who are new to the sector the concept of professionalism, in terms of their skills, respect for materials, national regulations, etc. may already be familiar to them in the context of their own specialist area (joinery, bricklaying, hairdressing, etc.), however, the demands of teaching bring very different challenges.

The concept of accountability has moved far beyond that of being answerable to immediate superiors. Accountability within education takes place within the glare of a very public spotlight, where parents, employers and potential students are able to examine how, nationally and within local institutions, it fulfils the demanding roles of social catalyst and pathway to educational attainment. Never has organized scrutiny been so unremitting as it is now through the offices of Ofsted, the Quality Improvement Agency, the IfL and the Learning Skills Council, etc. However, some would say that these initiatives to confirm standards are a necessary step in the Lifelong Learning Sector gaining parity with the compulsory sector of educational provision and eventually also more equivalence in terms of salaries and conditions of service.

Another important step was the establishment (during the first few weeks in which he took office) by Prime Minister Gordon Brown of the new Department of Innovation, Universities and Skills. Although the term 'Skills' may at first seem like an afterthought, it is clear that the new DIUS is pursuing New Labour's view that there is a direct relationship between the performance of education and the strength of the economy, and the development of vocational skills is at the heart of their project. So, although there will be even more responsibility placed on teachers within Lifelong Learning, there is also the possibility of greater rewards. However, it is at a price, because with greater responsibility comes an increase in accountability.

At the local level, for most teachers there is already observation of their practice within their institution's quality systems. Grades are often assigned to performance and subsequent terms of employment, which can have real implications in terms of pay or promotion. Of course, teachers are not alone under this accountability spotlight and although it serves to drive up standards (as is intended) it does mean that effective evaluation has become much more of an imperative. Our skills of evaluation need to be established at an early stage to enable us to demonstrate not only a willingness to improve, but also the skills to identify where the improvement is needed. Of course, coping with these ever-increasing professional demands is sometimes very difficult, but rest assured that developing towards demonstrable quality provision will have its rewards. In this chapter we will look at a range of complementary processes to enhance our evaluative skills through reflection and the sharing of practice.

9.4 Becoming a self-evaluator

There are two basic forms of evaluation. The most obvious is evaluation carried out for a specific purpose by official assessors who could be considering the value of property or making a decision whether or not an athlete should be in an Olympic team. Both of these decision-making processes will involve the evaluators deciding on appropriate evaluation criteria which will be fair and equitable to all parties. That is because this decision making is an *external process* which must demonstrate soundness of judgement and impartiality. Very often the criteria for the second type of evaluation are not as carefully articulated, but nevertheless the judgements made can be even more crucially life-changing. Of course, we are talking about the very difficult skill of *self-evaluation*. The major problem when we are making judgements about our own performance is that we are often far too demanding and we do tend to change the criteria depending on the situation. Nevertheless, carefully considered self-evaluation is probably the very quality which has led to many wonderful achievements in every field of human endeavour. Inappropriate self-evaluation, on the other hand, has led many an intelligent person to make serious and embarrassingly mistaken judgements.

A useful guide to help in this difficult process can be to consider whether you would use the same criteria to measure the performance of a colleague in a similar situation, as you are applying to yourself. Performance as a teacher is perhaps one of the most difficult tasks to self-evaluate, because every teacher will read that situation slightly differently and will select different criteria to influence their choice of actions. Although these thoughts may not seem to be too helpful when faced with deciding your own criteria for an effective teaching performance, significant assistance is already at hand. On the board below we have scrawled the magnificent seven sources of valuable knowledge and they are all available to you right now! We will discuss each of them during this chapter.

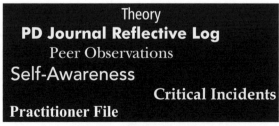

Magnificent seven board

However, you will *not* necessarily experience the above in the order presented here. When you read about them in the descriptions which follow, you will find that some are very familiar, and others you will grow to understand the value of during your programme. Separately, they will provide you with important insights into teaching in the Lifelong Learning Sector. Collectively, they will help to form an effective evaluation framework which will help to prepare you for the many competing demands that lie ahead.

9.4.1　Using theory

Our role as educators differs greatly from that of other professions, for example, nursing, medicine and law, as for many of us our professional training takes place in-post. Initially, when entering a new profession we may well turn to more experienced colleagues for advice and guidance, however the responses from busy colleagues will be mixed. Some will go out of their way to support you and provide very good advice and guidance; others may be more concerned with their own problems. Yet there is another valuable source of experience which is pertinent and easily accessed. As you will have discovered in Chapter 3, there is an existing rich body of theory about education and the ways in which people learn and it is readily available. In addition, it is also worth remembering that we do not come to this body of theory without some knowledge and perceptions of our own. Each of us, to a certain extent, naturally develop our own personal theories about how people learn and what for us represents effective teaching. Consequently, it is useful to interpret particular topics within this vast source of theory in the light of our own personal theories and experience. The process of drawing and building on such theories helps us to validate what we are doing in our everyday practice, and may well provide some insights into areas for development.

However, we are of course, discussing the achievement of the most effective ways of teaching and encouraging learning in relation to an intimidating and considerable unknown. Maybe this is an over-dramatic way of conceptualizing our relationship with a random group of learners and the potential chemistry that their group dynamics and our earnest endeavours will create. However, it is amazing to think that thousands of such interactive groups are established at the start of every college year and yet, on the whole they progress to a productive and mostly enjoyable relationship. Even so, this amazing process does inevitably involve from day one a considerable amount of trial and error. This is a salient point worth remembering: we are not discussing the evaluation of totally predictable outcomes; there is always risk. However, Petty (*ibid.*) makes it clear that the process of improving does make the risk worthwhile:

> If you don't have the occasional failure, you are not experimenting enough.

Any worthwhile development will always involve some risk, but that is a vital part of the excitement of professional practice. So too is the development of strategies to reduce any risk to a minimum by using careful evaluation processes before and after implementation. At the very heart of teaching is the difficult skill of social interaction. This can be a stimulating process, but it also means that no two sessions will ever be the same. So we are faced daily with a stimulating, unpredictable environment containing many barriers to overcome, but just as many opportunities to help learners to see their way through particular problems and discover solutions they never expected.

A relevant, suggested activity for your PDJ is provided below. (By this stage you most probably have made several entries in your Personal Development Journal, but if you haven't you might first of all read about the PDJ in Section 9.4.2, which follows.)

Activity 9d The Value of Social Interaction

Consider your Focus Learning Group (which you have hopefully used since Chapter 1) and if you can, identify the way in which the inevitable social interactions which take place within the group affect the situation and the learning taking place. Suggest also ways in which you could use these relationships to good effect during your teaching.

9.4.2 Personal development journal production

Continuing with the subject of recording and analysing teaching, we will now look at your progress with the Personal Development Journal. As you may be aware, PDJs are used on a lot of courses, especially those that combine practical skills with underpinning theory. On many post-compulsory teacher training programmes, they are used as a device to develop a *substantial narrative* based around the achievement of the Professional Standards.

Used in this way, the journal examines different aspects of our teaching and relates it to relevant theory by focusing on an area of the standards. A good example of this was perhaps during Chapter 3, when you may have started to address the standards in relation to 'Assessing Learner Needs'. For Activity 3y, you were requested to develop an informed narrative around the subject of a 'supportive learning environment' (Domain B 'Learning and Teaching', reference BP 1.1): 'Establish a purposeful learning environment where learners feel safe, secure, confident and valued' (Activity 3y.) It is possible that you first of all looked at the *Process Justification* in Chapter 3. As you know, the relevant PJ/FAQs are included at the end of chapters 3 to 9 and are at the levels of Threshold Award, Associate Certificate and Full Award to help to get you in the frame of mind for reflecting on these particular processes at a particular level. They also indicate appropriate underpinning theory to support analysis.

Some trainee teachers who have recently completed a degree course find the Personal Development Journal challenging to write. This may be because it is written in the first person, and that is considered a deadly sin in most academic writing. Most degree students are trained in objective, third-person writing and so find the change to a first-person narrative difficult. This style of writing is also very personal and so can be a challenge for students who are unused to writing about themselves.

If you haven't done it before, you will probably have found in responding to the first 'activities' in the early chapters that you have started to develop the process of *reflective narrative writing*. This is certainly not easy to do, particularly if you are new to the process. However, it is an important aspect of the evaluative process as it helps to develop the skill of translating impressions and feelings into a commentary. This move from abstract feelings and ideas to a more tangible analysis serves as a filter which removes those distracting impressions for which you can find little or no real evidence in fact. However, don't automatically discard such intuitive insights for they are often proved well-founded. You just need to bear them in mind without committing yourself to them until the evidence emerges.

You may have noticed that we have designed the 'activities' to not only address the various standards in relation to your own learning situation and learning groups but also to allow your PDJ entries to build on each other in a cyclic fashion. Basing this process on your own practice should also ensure that you will be able, in later entries, to reflect upon previous ones and enhance the learning cycle/spiral.

Your entries in the PDJ will be of two quite different types:

- There will be written responses to chapter activities which are designed to address some of the many practical issues encountered in teaching and learning. (These activities are, of course, optional.)
- On the other hand, instead of thinking about pragmatic implementation, you are encouraged to be involved in propositional thinking, i.e. theorizing about your teaching and the reason for actions and reactions you have observed from colleagues and learners.

Your Personal Development Journal should be written in the first person and should be a personal narrative account of how you have developed evidence for the areas of teaching practice covered by the journal entry. At the same time this commentary should be underpinned by references to relevant theories. This justifies your own reflections and gives you confidence in your own on-the-spot decisions and the conclusions you draw from them. At first this can be difficult, as it seems, particularly if you are used to academic writing, that the narrative style does not flow easily when written with accompanying quotations and references. The narrative style can seem self-conscious and subjective rather than objective. But, in fact, this is the basis of the best groundbreaking teacher research that is founded on teachers' personal reflections on their own practice.

9.4.3 Practitioner file

The Practitioner File is designed to record not only evidence of your assessment through teaching observations during the programme, but also the development of particular areas of interest and expertise. Whereas, in order to meet the requirements of the teaching assessment you will provide your observer with a lesson plan and rationale for each session, you will also, at other times, be generating all sorts of evidence of your developing skills as a practitioner. This may take the form of an analysis of student needs, action plans for meeting those needs, teaching materials, assessment schemes, student evaluations, etc.

The manager of the particular programme of teacher training which you are undertaking will provide you with details of how your observed teaching assessment will be carried out, however, the information you provide within this Practitioner File will support this process. We suggest that you include the records discussed below and obviously you should use any programme pro forma which is provided. However, for your convenience, appropriate blank pro forma for each of the evidence-generating activities below are provided on the **tipcet.com** website.

9.4.4 Reflective log

A way to begin this kind of writing is to complete a reflective observation that looks at a ***critical incident in your teaching from which you have learned***. The following, an actual reflection from a practitioner in post-compulsory education, may provide a useful format for your entries.

---

1. Description of the event:
(In here, write briefly what happened (use between 50 and 100 words).)

Part way through teaching a particular topic some of the students said, 'we have already done this!' I felt a sick feeling in the pit of my stomach and the desire to turn around and come in again with an alternative lesson.

---

2. Your reflections on how you dealt with the incident:
(This should be a longer account of what you did at the time to overcome the critical incident or to deal with it.)

However, this being impossible, I relied on what I know best, which is talking in a direct but empathetic way to the students. I thus elicited from them when and how they had done the topic before and how much they remembered. I also apologized and made a note on my lesson plan. I then said we could use the session for revision. I did not exactly save face but demonstrated to students that I am human and that things can be covered more than once, in a different way, and still be useful. Later, when reflecting on the event, I resolved to record in detail the incident in my self-evaluation of the session and to ask students for feedback next session on how they felt the session went, thus finding out whether they felt disadvantaged by the incident.

Activity 9e Critical Incident

Try to identify a recent critical incident (similar to the one described above) from your own practice. As our teacher says, not a 'major incident', but something that provided you with insights and probably some pleasure.

Notes on the above steps

Step 1: although only brief, this is an important step as your description of how you remember the event may be quite different to the way other witnesses remember it. The way you develop your own perception or personal construct will say a great deal about your expectations, values and purposes.

Step 2: the second half of the process is an analysis of your performance and whether you would have responded in the same way if you had been given more time to think about it. Probably, when you later look back on this section of your PDJ, you will be reassured to know that you can think 'on-your-feet'. It means you can do it again in another crucial situation.

The second step in the process is partly narrative, but also it requires you to examine the incident again in hindsight. What might have been a gut reaction at the time (and may therefore seem to be unreliable) may seem now to have been absolutely the right thing to do. You know from this that you can rely on your instincts. It is useful to discuss one of your critical incidents with colleagues or fellow students and ask for their comments on how you dealt with it, then do the same for them. Feedback like this usually reassures you that what you did was effective. Even if it was not, you survived it and with the benefit of reflective hindsight (recorded in your PDJ) will probably do it differently next time.

9.4.5 Self-awareness

As an introduction to this section, reflect for a moment on the well-known saying:

> Practice makes perfect.

This is only true when the practitioners are evaluating their performance in an effort to improve. We can all identify teachers who have delivered the same lesson many times over many years with very little improvement. In such a situation, this lack of self-awareness is potentially very damaging. Self-awareness is hugely beneficial in helping to develop the professional role. Take for example the observation that, 'we teach the way we were taught'.

For those who are new to the profession, this notion may hold some truth, and through evaluation of practice we can start to address some of the implications associated with this idea. We have already discussed how we can start to draw on other sources to inform our practice and that an awareness of our own beliefs about education and the values we hold can help us to understand why we teach the way we teach. It may even help us to recognize the foundations of what Petty (*ibid.*) describes as '*theory-in-use*'.

Some of the previous activities have asked you to 'theorize' about a lesson/session you have experienced recently and you have probably recognized that the development of these skills of *analysis and explanation* are important first steps in promoting self-awareness. Because our own theories about our teaching experiences will usually be built on the values and beliefs we hold about learning and teaching, they are inherently important to us. However, the important next step is to begin to validate these personal beliefs against a wider knowledge base.

Tann (1993) considers the concept of 'personal theories' and his belief that:

> students can be aware of their own interpretive frameworks and be able to contrast theirs and those of their peers and colleagues with those educationalists who offer their personal theories publicly, through publications or lectures.

So, although we may not always have the confidence to publicly express our personal theories, we are able to privately compare our beliefs with what Tann has called 'significant others', i.e. lecturers and authors. We are aware that contrasting our practice with that of our colleagues can provide us with valuable insights and we supplement these with views expressed by acknowledged 'authorities' and yet the benefits of doing so often remain internalized and personal.

Although the willingness to move from these private feelings and theories to a more public declaration of previously personal views is often very difficult, this step can provide such important realizations that it is worth the attempt, not only for yourself, but more crucially, for your students. Often, the most telling realization is that your views are perfectly valid and that most people are not only willing to consider them, but enjoy discussing them. The second realization often flows simply from practising the skills of justifying ideas and practices to others, and may well be the most important development in relation to self-awareness. It is during these considerations that concepts are developed and vague ideas are sharpened up and amalgamated with other perspectives.

Reflecting in this way about current practice is a vital step towards a deeper understanding of the very complex relationships which form and underpin most educational situations and relationships. By developing the skill of a sensitive externalization of important reflections, we can begin to enhance not only our own understandings, but also those of our colleagues and our learners.

9.4.6 Peer observations

This form of observation is particularly useful in helping novice teachers to evaluate their own practice and can take several forms:

1. For many new teachers, their first experience of peer observation and feedback will be the micro-teaching situation. Here, you will have the opportunity to deliver a short session to your peer group and/or tutor, within the college where the teacher training programme is being run. Sometimes it will be video-recorded in order to provide each teacher with the opportunity to see her or himself in operation. This initial session can be very traumatic, and often the initial reaction of those taking part is surprise at their accents or gestures (which they were not conscious of), rather than the quality of the teaching.
2. The second form of peer observation may take place when the novice teacher is carrying out teaching practice in a local school or college. Naturally, he or she will be visited by a tutor, who will provide feedback on the quality of the session, usually face to face, where the two parties will discuss various aspects of the taught session. The tutor will also require a lesson/session plan and often will also want to see a rationale for the chosen approach to that particular taught session. This first session is often very demanding but does have in its favour the fact that all the members are in the same boat. Various forms of feedback on the value of the session are used. This feedback allows each participant to receive a considered evaluation, either from the tutor or from colleagues. It also encourages students to develop the art of providing a sensitive evaluation to help the developmental process of colleagues.

9.4.7 Critical incidents

Most teachers have considerable pride in our profession and will point to examples of excellent teaching being carried out by colleagues, many of whom are involved in so many hours of face-to-face teaching each week that they have very little time for all the preparation, marking and administration expected in the present school, college and training environments. Even so, fellow educational professionals have offered serious criticism of the professionalism of teachers and most of this is directed at our reluctance to analyse critical incidents within our practice from a theoretical and well as a pragmatic position. Tripp (1993), made this pointed observation which still has much relevance today:

> [I]n all the major professions there is another intellectual ingredient of practice: being able to explain and thereby justify what one does through a more knowledgeable, rigorous, and academic analysis. This does not appear to be necessary in teaching.

Tripp is referring to a characteristic which other writers have also commented on, i.e. the resistance that many teachers, both experienced and novice, display towards the development of theory. Tripp also believes that teachers are reluctant to relate their experiences of teaching (and the critical incidents which happen every day and which they deal with intuitively) to any underpinning concepts or principles, or to seek justification for their actions by reference to educational research. He comments that:

> if they (the teachers) are not also able to articulate the specialist . . . knowledge or the judgements that underlie what they do, they are . . . craftspeople rather than professionals.

He argues that a more *evaluative reflection* of teaching processes would enable teachers to 'overcome their poor public image and achieve the status of a profession for their work.'

Critical incident log

The purpose of your Personal Development Journal (see 12.14.6 below) and Tripp's (*ibid.*) use of a *critical incident log* obviously have much in common. Based on his recording and analysis of critical incidents in teaching, Tripp states that teachers' work lacks public status because

> they are seen to draw on the recall of 'right answers' rather than having to use their own judgements.

Tripp recommends that teachers apply reflective analysis to a series of critical incidents during their teaching practice and their professional teaching careers in order to develop what might be called 'diagnostic teaching'. Diagnostic teaching, as defined by Tripp, is the analysis of practice in a scholarly and academic fashion to produce expert interpretations upon which to base and justify . . . professional judgements.

Tripp recommends that teachers base their journal writing around such critical incidents and goes on to define critical incidents. They are not major event or 'things', because these may be few and far between. Teachers new to reflection can then use this as an excuse not to reflect because there have been no critical incidents today. Tripp believes that *critical incidents are created*. They are produced by the 'way we look at a situation'. The incident is made critical by the 'interpretation of the significance of an event'. So any lesson can be critically analysed and a particular event made critical by our reflection on it. We need to ask not only what happened but why it happened then and with that group and what it meant for the future teaching of that particular topic. We should 'situationalize' the event and apply the question 'why' to it and then generalize it in terms of professional practice and apply relevant theories to try to make sense of the event. This means challenging the comfortable and established habitual practices we rely on in everyday teaching. Take as an example the following *critical incident* that happened to one of our teacher educators, and caused her to look beyond her routine behaviour in class and consider a new technique:

Halfway through one of her lessons with a group of trainee teachers, a student who had missed her micro-teaching assessment the previous week, by arrangement presented her prepared session to the group. It was a good, creatively managed lesson during which she asked all the students to leave their desks and bring their chairs into a large circle. The tutor also joined that circle and later confirmed that everyone liked this new layout and found that it changed completely the interactive dynamics of the group.

The tutor reported later that, 'We decided as a group to leave it that way for the rest of my session which became a much more discursive and student-led session thereafter. This layout is not something I use in my usual sessions with this group, or any other, mainly because I stick with the horseshoe layout of desks which is in place in our teaching rooms.'

(Continued)

> The student had challenged this habitual practice and had made the tutor think about the position of authority she projected to the students with her at the front, and the students behind their desks. She confessed that, 'I usually sit on my desk but had never thought to be radical enough to get rid of the desks completely. It challenged where I sit in the classroom and made me "lead from the back" and let the students manage the discussion. It was a liberating experience for me and not really a major event, just one of those nice little "happenings" we get every day in our teaching.'

Tripp maintains that teachers need to cultivate the recording of such critical incidents because analysis of them makes the important link between instinctive practice and underpinning theory and then generalizes the event into continuing professional practice. They take us out of the ordinary and make us look at the things we do every day with fresh eyes. We are, in effect, observing ourselves.

9.4.8 Reflective paradoxes

Bolton (2001), writing for student nurses who were approaching the writing of a Personal Development Journal for the first time, developed the concept of three paradoxes, which she believes lie at the heart of reflection – *letting go of certainty, looking for something when you don't know what it is, beginning to act when you don't know how to act*.

The first paradox Bolton considered, '*in order to acquire confidence you have to let go of certainty*' suggests that a confident person is more able to be flexible and creative in response to uncertain situations (see also self-concept in Chapter 5). This, of course, applies equally to teaching as to nursing. Bolton claims that at some stage

a practitioner who knows all the right answers all the time is bound to be wrong.

The paradox of deliberately moving away from familiar certainty also highlights that reflective writing is about looking beneath the everyday, accepted conventions in teaching. In some situations where you are trying to promote learner autonomy and provide motivating, creative learning experiences, the constraining nature of such a convention as 'always state learning objectives at the beginning of a session' can undermine all your efforts to encourage your learners themselves to move beyond prescription towards the excitement of knowledge creation.

Bolton's second paradox, '*looking for something when you don't know what it is*' captures a central difficulty that many learners encounter when engaging in critical reflection. The reason we usually decide to reflect on a critical incident is that we don't really understand why, what we have experienced, actually happened. We begin the reflective process believing that we can gain an insight into the unknown and fortunately our reflections often lead us to an understanding of the specifics of the situation and to a general understanding that can be applied to our teaching in the future.

The third paradox, '*beginning to act when you don't know how to act*', refers to Schon's (1987) concepts of reflection-in as well as reflection-on action. Often when teaching we realize that some aspect of our session isn't being as effective as it should be and we stop, readjust and lead the students around a 'remedial learning loop', which we develop as we speak. This surprising aspect of skilled practice is in part intuitive, but in the main it is our ability to trust our own reflections to come up with a course of action which is professional and considered, although when you begin the reflective process you have no idea what the course of action will be.

Activity 9f Reflective Paradox

Reflect on the way in which Bolton's paradox theory has applied to you and your development as a teacher. Think about the processes described above under letting go, looking for something, and beginning to act in relation to your own reflections.

These three paradoxes illustrate very well the different nature of journal writing as compared to academic essay writing and probably identify the main problems people have with beginning a reflective journal. The outcome and resulting action is unclear when you begin writing. It is the writing itself which clarifies the outcome for you, a kind of cathartic process. This is quite unlike writing a course assignment where you are certain of your outcomes before you begin to write.

9.4.9 Self-evaluation of teaching

Activity 9g Self-Evaluation of a Teaching Session

This self-evaluation should be based, where possible, on a session where there has also been an observer/assessor present.

Most teacher education courses will provide a self-evaluation pro forma, which incorporates a series of criteria for the evaluation of a session. Where the criteria are provided in this manner, it is called a controlled response evaluation. We have included an example of a completed pro forma overleaf and there is a blank copy on our website **tipcet.com** which you may download.

Try to write a lengthy reflection for each section on the pro forma, and do not avoid those areas which do not seem as significant as others in that particular session. These may just hold the key to why the session went as it did. You are reflecting on this session to complete the cycle of planning, teaching and reflection but this will also be something you can refer to again and use as a basis for future evaluations of taught sessions.

Activity 9h Controlled Response Evaluation

Our example of a completed evaluation form (overleaf) is supposedly from a Stage 2 teacher of catering (NVQ Level 1). Consider the entries and say why she may have written the responses recorded there and how they might be improved.

Obviously, a critical self-evaluation is difficult to carry out at the first attempt, especially when the event it is based on was also an observed and assessed session. The process of being observed is so stressful to student teachers that often, when they look back and try to remember the observed session, many areas are difficult to recall in detail. So inevitably, many of these reflections are vague and mostly descriptive rather than analytical. Also she has adopted a fairly defensive stance and because of this she has missed an opportunity to use the evaluation to demonstrate her clear understanding of the processes involved. Just three examples from the evaluation will help to illustrate this:

Relevance of lesson content: The content will have been included in Edna's session plan which the observer has a copy of, so little is achieved by repeating this. It would have been more helpful if Edna had said why, at this stage in their development, moving the students on to prepare scrambled eggs is appropriate progression.

Allocation of time to lesson phases: Edna could have taken this opportunity to discuss why her time allocation to different periods of the session was made and how she might improve it in future sessions.

Additional Comments: As is the case with many programme members, Edna avoided this opportunity to highlight significant events during the session and show how she understood the reason for them and what she would do about a similar event in future.

Let Edna's experience prepare you to be as analytical as possible about your observed sessions, but don't be surprised if, when you look back on this in a year's time, your reflection seem naïve. Remember, you were relatively new to self-evaluation when you wrote it, and it is surprising the progress you can make in one year.

TEACHER SELF-EVALUATION (I)

Programme member: *Edna Eccles*

College/Organization: *Northern College of Further Education*

Date: *10th January 2007*   Student group: *Catering NVQ 1*

Topic: Prepare and cook egg and batter dishes – scrambled and poached eggs

Please record your observations in response to the criteria listed on the left of the pro forma

ORGANIZATION AND SELECTION OF METHODS

Please give your post-session insights in relation to:

Meeting your perceived needs of the learners?	*I think I met the needs of the group well. Everyone seemed happy in the class.*
Your preparation of the learning environment?	*I made sure all of the resources were available and that there were sufficient so no one had to share.*
Appropriateness of your defined learning outcomes?	*The outcomes are defined in the NVQ element. They are clearly written so I needed to follow them exactly.*
Relevance of lesson content?	*The content (scrambled and poached eggs) allowed the learners to do two different methods – it is relevant to the NVQ range.*
Appropriateness of your methods in relation to student responses?	*I did this well. First of all I did a demonstration and then I talked about the science of egg cookery. Then everyone had a go and I facilitated the session. Then we all evaluated eggs and looked at what we learnt.*
Allocation of time to lesson phases?	*No problem here.*
How effective were your resources/learning aids?	*All of the pans and utensils are in a good condition. You need them to learn egg cookery. I did a handout with key points and recipies.*
Teacher/student rapport?	*We get on well and have a laugh. Just two students didn't seem to enjoy the session: always by themselves at the back.*
How students developed their learning about learning?	*We talked about what we learnt.*
The level of challenge the learners experienced?	*This was easy – everyone knows how to scramble eggs – the poaching is more tricky.*
Adaptation to the changing demands of the session?	*I didn't need to change a thing – it all went nicely to plan.*
How you modified your strategies to differentiate between learners?	*All of the learners are of the same standard – NVQ Level 1 – so we are working together from the beginning – they all have the same needs.*
Assessment of learners?	*I observed them making the egg dishes against the NCQ criteria.*
ADDITIONAL COMMENTS	None
Please give the name of the tutor who observed this session:	*Mrs Barton*

Having said that, let's now assume that a year has passed and Edna Eccles is a much more experienced, Stage 3 student. Following a recent teaching observation she has completed the less structured evaluation form overleaf (again a blank copy is available on the tipcet website). This type of evaluation form assumes that the respondent is sufficiently analytical and aware of the context to be able to identify the criteria which best represents her own developing value system.

Activity 9i Free Response Evaluation

Edna Eccles has been observed carrying out a learning review with her catering students. She has selected her own criteria to respond to with her Stage 3 self-evaluation. Consider these criteria and her responses and say what you feel about the issues she has chosen to highlight and her comments about them.

TEACHER SELF-EVALUATION (II)

Programme Member: *Edna Eccles*

College: *Northern College*

Date: *12th February 2008*   Class: *Level 3 NVQ Catering*

Subject: *SM5.3*   *Provide feedback on work performance to teams and individuals*

Observer Name: *MR Wilkinson*

Criterion One:	*Establish an effective environment for feedback.*
Response:	*We used the staff lounge and I ensured that we would not be interrupted and the phone was disconnected.*
Criterion Two:	*Encourage a positive student response to the feedback*
Response:	*Seven members of the student team attended and five of them were very positive and willing to receive feedback in an open and constructive manner.*
Criterion Three:	*Focus on specific issues.*
Response:	*All members of the team were provided with an agenda and the first item was AOB to allow them to add issues they wished to discuss.*
Criterion Four:	*Give clear examples of both negative and positive feedback.*
Response:	*Most to the feedback was positive apart from the incident of a customer complaint because of dirty cutlery and a chipped plate.*
Criterion Five:	*Be constructive – suggest ways of improving.*
Response:	*I asked the team to suggest how we could ensure that this did not happen again.*
Criterion Six:	*Negotiate appropriate responses from the team.*
Response:	*All the team agreed that the customer had every right to complain and that the problem was a group problem rather than an individual one.*
Criterion Seven:	*Negotiate appropriate responses from individuals.*
Response:	*The team themselves suggested that the solution was to check the cutlery and crockery to be used more carefully before we lay the tables and begin serving.*
Criterion Eight:	*Get team and individuals to reflect back advice given.*
Response:	*Team and individuals took turns in explaining the customer complaints procedures and how we respond according to the level of complaint.*
Criterion Nine:	*Provide structure for choice of actions.*
Response:	*Team and individuals suggested how the procedures could be improved to anticipate problems rather than wait for them to happen.*
Criterion Ten:	*Round session off in a positive manner.*
Response:	*The team were congratulated on a positive session and it was agreed that minutes of the meeting would be provided so that each of them could keep a copy in their Portfolio.*

Activity 9j Maturing Evaluation

Given Edna's development since the first evaluation in 2007, where would you place her on the Learning Spiral we discussed earlier in the chapter? Comment also on the value of the 'free response' type of evaluation.

The above evaluation shows a young teacher of catering very much in control of her environment. She has thought through the practice of reviewing learning and the principles of managing people and has organized a very effective feedback session where issues were addressed and satisfactorily solved. This shows a considerable and positive development from her first-year self-evaluations.

Before we leave the issue of self-evaluation it is worth stressing that the process is designed to establish the habit of continuous self-evaluation. A habit which will be part of the continuous improvement and development cycle which Deming (1986) said is the basis for 'delighted' customers, in this case your students and so yourself.

When you have completed your pro forma you will probably see that it required a lengthy reflection of all that happened in the session including evaluation of how you planned it and whether this was appropriate for the students and the circumstances of the session. It will not have been enough for you to recapitulate on what went well, but to examine what *did not* go as planned and to try to figure out why this was so.

This takes us back to the critical incident review and brings up an important point in the process of reflection. It is never enough to merely reassure ourselves that it was okay. As reflective practitioners we must always engage in active reflection of all our sessions, picking out the exciting and challenging incidents that make us a teacher out of the ordinary. Any teaching session has the potential for such deep reflection and should be seen as such. We are our own best observers because we are always there when we are teaching, so we should make use of ourselves as reflective self-observers and thus be continuously improving and developing through our own teaching.

9.4.10 Developing student feedback

Another important aspect of improving practice in educational settings is finding ways of getting accurate feedback from students about how they are experiencing your sessions. Many student questionnaires seem to be designed to eliminate the possibility of any detailed student comments and these are therefore not very useful in getting your students' views. This sort of questionnaire will be one which gives a series of tick box answers with one line at the end for a brief student comment. Typically, this would be given out while the teacher stands over the student and is collected in after a few minutes.

Activity 9k Circumscribed Evaluation

It is quite possible that an internal student evaluation may be influenced by a whole range of factors, such as the use of closed questions which do not allow the respondent to give a full answer, or a limited choice of options, etc. It has even been known for questionnaires to be distributed shortly before an assessment with the not so subtle implication that responses may have a bearing on the results. How can you get detach yourself from such a culture?

Naturally, the students will resent such a cynical approach to evaluation and will believe that all such evaluations in the institution are just as contrived and meaningless. There will be a feeling that it is impossible to get their view heard in such a threatening culture. When seeking student feedback, the very first thing a teacher needs to do is to find a way of overcoming the *fear factor*. The students' fear of upsetting the tutor (which may influence their assessment results), and the tutors' fear that the students are going to say something critical about the teaching which the tutor may not be equipped to deal with. We have tried to establish in this chapter the fact that reflection is not always a comfortable process and that it may bring up things which cause us extra work and some anxiety. The same is true of any evaluation process which has integrity, and what a wonderfully reassuring thing it is to have a culture which actively encourages openness and honesty.

9.4.11 Listening to students

Obviously, you need first of all to set up a meeting with your students at which you can ask them about their experiences of your course. A good way to get this started is to ask them three basic questions, which they can add to if they wish. These questions are:

1. What are the most effective parts of the course for you and why?
2. What are the least effective parts, and why?
3. What would you change about the course?

Ask the class to get into groups of about five students and leave them to discuss the questions and make notes for about 20 minutes. It is a good idea, if logistically possible, to leave the students for this time and ask one to come and get you when they have finished their discussions. Obviously, be aware of health and safety issues around leaving the group, but at least give them some space to talk without your influencing them.

Then ask each group to feedback and make your own notes of their comments. Resist the temptation to justify any negative comments, just accept them and write them down. This demonstrates to the students that you really do want to listen and to develop the course in line with their experiences. Thank the students for their frankness. It is challenging for them to feed back honestly, and they need to feel reassured that their honesty is appreciated. Such a 'listening' session is best done at the end of a module or programme, and you could possibly arrange a social event, to follow on directly after the session, where you join the students in a more relaxed atmosphere. This helps to dispel any lingering feelings of resentment or unease.

Activity 9l Listening Evaluation

Develop and implement a student-centred evaluation using an approach similar to the one outlined above and then reflect on the data you have been provided with from your students, and how this may help to improve your programme.

9.4.12 Questionnaire design

Questionnaires are, in fact, interviews by correspondence. However, you do not have the opportunity to ask supplementary questions when the answer you receive does not respond as precisely or fully to the question as you intended. For these reasons, designing a useful evaluation questionnaire is tricky. You need to reach a balance between gathering student feedback from which you can develop the course and producing a questionnaire that is not too difficult or time-consuming to analyse. Also, most people prefer a questionnaire to be anonymous so they feel able to respond honestly, but this means if there are comments that you would like to explore further, you cannot go back to that student and discuss the comments.

One approach is to give out a questionnaire as a start to course development and then hold a meeting similar to the one described in the previous section. In this way you can start discussion with a statement such as 'you raised some important issues in the student evaluation questionnaire that we would like to explore further with you.'

There are many published guides to questionnaire design, which will usually contain the following simple principles:

- keep it anonymous
- keep it short – about 10–12 questions is enough
- keep longer, individual-response questions, to the end

- try to use tick-box questions
- do not use leading questions
- do not use ambiguous questions
- do not use any unnecessary questions – what *exactly* do you want to find out?

Activity 9m Designing an Evaluation Questionnaire

Using the above guidance, design a questionnaire to obtain evaluatory, learner feedback for your own programme. Before you begin, think about how you are going to process and analyse the data. If you intend to do it manually, make sure that you leave room on the form for making notes relating to the responses received.

Also think about how and when you will administer the questionnaire. It is most effective to give it out to the group yourself and then collect it in at the end of the lesson. Although this ensures a good response rate, anonymity can be undermined if the students feel that their responses can be linked to them through your observation or by you collecting them personally for each individual. Take steps to reassure them, such as not requiring names on the forms, and either have them collected by one of the group or let them place their completed questionnaire on a pile as they leave the room.

You also need to consider the timing of the questionnaire implementation. Obviously, if you use it just before a student assessment, a possible misinterpretation by the students could be that, if they are critical, it will have a bearing on the marks they are given. It is also important to avoid administering a questionnaire in situations where the learners are feeling stressed by assessment deadlines or looming examinations. This may result in the student responses reflecting a jaded view determined by the emotional state of the students at the time.

9.5 Conclusion

As with the assessment modes discussed in the previous chapter, evaluation approaches will also adopt a particular focus depending on their purpose and the values that underpin the programme or course being evaluated. Some will be formative (i.e. where data is collected *during* the teaching) and some will be summative (data collected *after*). As we showed earlier, evaluations may be designed to gather information about *decisions* or about *goals*.

Educational evaluations may be *organization-centred* (often collecting prescribed data which is required to support quality monitoring, see Chapter 10), *tutor-centred* (where the teachers identify the criteria – we provided an example in Activity 9h), or *student-centred*.

Earlier we discussed two student self-evaluation examples in Activities 9i and 9j. In the first, the tutor provided the criteria (tutor-centred) and in the second the student wrote the criteria (student-centred). Again, where educational provision (session, module, course or programme) is being evaluated, the tutor or the student may define the criteria and, as you would expect, each focus will be different. Finally, the data collected may be *quantitative*, which provides mostly information about what has happened, or it may be *qualitative*, which would give an insight into why particular aspects did or did not find favour. Of course, when you require both types of data it can be a mixture of the two.

9.6 Useful publications

Cousins, J.B. and L.M. Earl (eds) (1995), *Participatory Evaluation in Education*. London: The Falmer Press.

A useful introduction to the notion of a partnership between teachers and administrators to bring about educational improvement. Using several case studies by actual practitioners, the book identifies principles for collaborative development.

Eisner, E.W. (1985), *The Art of Educational Evaluation*. London: The Falmer Press.

In this well-known study Elliot Eisner puts forward a strong case for focusing educational evaluation as much on the affective domain as the cognitive. His ideas have serious implications for assessment and curriculum planning.

Norris, N. (1990), *Understanding Educational Evaluation*. London: Kogan Page.

An effective overview of the range of evaluation models developed both in the USA and the UK and their relationship to applied research.

9.7 Useful websites

http://ies.ed.gov/ncee/
http://ies.ed.gov/ncee/aboutus/
www.bgci.org/education/Evaluation
www.dcu.ie/education_studies/research/cee/index.htm
www.ed.gov/offices/OUS/PES/primer1.html
www.wmich.edu/evalctr/jc/JC-Home

TABLE 9.2 Process justifications for evaluating own performance and planning future pracatice

FAQs at the level of:	Threshold award	Associate certificate	Cert. Ed./PGCE/Diploma
Why do it?	In order to improve any complex process, you have to collect information which will help you make decisions about what to change. Education is one such process, and as teachers we have the responsibility to collect data which will help us to put improvements in place. These changes are usually only small adjustments, but sometimes they are so radical that we are required to develop new courses and programmes. The same evaluation process is involved, only the scale is different.	We reflect, analyse and evaluate in order to better understand the very complex range of relationships and influences which exist within interactive situations. A reflective practitioner in the teaching context is someone who consciously examines a particular educational context in order to actively modify and improve the teaching and learning process. When analysing we theoretically break things down into their constituent parts in order to better understand the whole. We evaluate in order to measure the quality of the teaching and learning we are providing against identified criteria.	Reflection, evaluation and analysis are a range of critical processes which teachers use to better understand the teaching and learning processes. Active reflection (praxis) is the process of identifying the various elements of the learning process while they are actually changing and developing, enabling us to modify our delivery as appropriate. When evaluating, we are usually using given standards as a comparative measurement. Reflection is also often comparative but the emphasis may be on understanding rather than measuring.
Where are we going?	Continuous improvement is the goal of quality processes and evaluation strategies. To do this we collect the data we need, at times when we need it.	These critical processes lead us towards an optimum performance as teachers, which may lead to optimum achievement by the learners.	Because of the ever-changing variables within each teaching and learning situation, the reflective process is never ending. However, there is an end product, which is an autonomous, reflective learner and teacher.
How do we get there?	We arrive at a systematic improvement strategy by putting in place appropriate evaluations which collect information on the effectiveness of all aspects of our provision. Individual teachers know their own learners and learning situations best, so identification of the best ways of generating the data which will help us to optimize our provision is also up to us.	Reflect before, during and after a session and record your intuitive feelings about the different processes. Analyse the range of relationships and influences operating within your teaching context. Evaluate at different stages of provision using a range of appropriate methods against well-defined criteria. Check on the development of study skills and independence as learners.	The more involved you become in trying to understand the complexities of teaching and learning, the more you become aware of the range of subtle influences operating within the process. It may help to analyse different aspects of provision in turn. For example, learner needs, planning, delivery, assessment, etc. Look also at the less obvious aspects of learning such as student motivation and commitment, inclusion and the opportunity to interact with colleagues.
Is this the best way?	Standards are either continuously developed and sustained through internal evaluations or are decided externally and imposed. As professionals we must work towards re-establishing the former model.	Consider whether reflection is actually helpful or whether it increases anxiety. Are you looking merely for right or wrong instead of developing your own criteria for good performance within this particular context? Check that the evaluation strategies are appropriate and relevant.	Use a reflective journal to record observations and insights and student-centred as well as teacher initiated evaluations. Ensure that the evaluation process itself isn't affecting your teaching because you have become less holistic due to your concern to break everything down to allow analysis.

When is the right time?	The right time to evaluate is when things are able to be improved. In other words some form of evaluation (either formal or informal) should be ongoing, because data which can help improve provision is constantly available.	Reflection is often more meaningful when you are less tired or stressed although insights sometimes occur at surprising moments. Check the purpose of evaluation and confirm whether it is designed to modify and correct while teaching is in process (formative) or for later use to action plan improvements (summative). Ensure that key events are not being overlooked or student experiences undervalued.	Consider whether the quality of your reflection is being affected by your own expectations within a teacher education process. Does reflection seem somehow like DIY teacher training? Did you expect/hope that the course would provide more positive answers to some of the problems facing teachers? Were you hoping for a 'science' of teaching with generic methods appropriate to all situations?
Who needs to know?	Evaluations help both learners and teachers so both groups need to know about the implementation as well as the outcomes. Better still, both groups should be involved in the design, the implementation and the data analysis.	Within your particular context, you are the most important participant in the reflective process, but it is wise to check out conclusions with colleagues. Share evaluations with managers, colleagues, students and support staff. Inspectors, governors and parents may require them.	Reflections are often extremely sensitive and you may not wish to share them. However, despite the personal nature of the process you were reflecting on, it may well be that from it you develop concepts which are generic and can be shared productively with others.
How do we know when we've got there?	The concept of continuous improvement does mean that the process never ends. However, there are obviously varying degrees of improvement which are possible and when serious problems have been eradicated a level of optimum performance should be achievable which will then require periodic monitoring and adjustment.	Reflection and evaluation should lead to improvement but they are not one and the same thing. Evaluative criteria are often externally devised and related to funding and need not necessarily reflect your particular values and purposes. Reflection may lead to insights into difficulties created by the standards process itself. Teachers must balance personal values with professional roles.	As discussed earlier, there is no final destination but you will know when your reflections, evaluations and analysis are leading to important insights which are confirmed by your reading and the experiences of others. You will know when you have become the 'expert' in a particular teaching context where you understand the learners' characteristics and the range of contextual influences better than anyone else.
Has everyone had a fair chance?	Improvement in practice as a consequence of considered evaluation, will not necessarily benefit all of the learners in a given situation. We need to remain aware of the range of learner needs and ensure that we are catering for the minority as well as the majority.	Some teachers find active reflection difficult and need to develop the skill. When evaluating, we must ensure that students have an opportunity to contribute and that teachers have a say in how and when it takes place. Confirm that staff and students know what evaluation criteria and data collection methods are being used.	Sometimes, one of the difficulties faced by reflective teachers is if their analysis reveals the fact that, for one reason or another, their learners are not getting the optimum possible learning experience. You must continue (on behalf of your learners) to strive for that provision, but you also need to know why this situation has occurred.

10 Continuous Improvement

Lyn Butcher

Chapter Outline

Key Concepts

Accountability, Communication, Continuous Improvement, Contractual Obligations, Differentiation, Diversity of the Teacher's Role, Evaluation, Giving and Receiving Feedback, Inclusive Learning, Institute for Learning, Improvement, Internal/External Customers, Learning and Skills Council, Negotiation Skills, Networking, Ofsted, Professional Relationships, Quality Assurance, Quality Culture, Rapport with Learners, Referral of Learners, Reflection, Reviewing Learning.

10.1 Introduction

In this chapter we are stepping back from the organization of classroom teaching in order to take a broader perspective of the various educational processes we have discussed in earlier chapters. We are now concerned to assimilate into our practice the effective management of the overall quality of the various systems and techniques we have hopefully now put in place.

This chapter will still be concerned with each learner's individual progress at the heart of the system, but we are now focusing on the many other seemingly peripheral elements which can affect the quality of learning if they are not carefully managed. These are the less obvious responsibilities within the teacher's role such as liaison with other professionals and the maintenance of quality. Broadly, this covers effective communication, reviewing learning, working relationships and quality assurance.

With the ever-increasing diversity of the teacher's role, there is greater necessity to be aware of the link between you as the classroom teacher and the learner's whole experience within the organization. The Common Inspection Framework (CIF) requires Ofsted to inspect the whole of the learner's experience and not just classroom teaching. You need to be aware of how the organization works and your role within it, and how various systems feed into each other in order to create the learner's experience. This in turn, will help to enlighten you of the need for the sometimes-laborious paperwork which now comes with the job. As a novice teacher, your main concern will undoubtedly be with lesson preparation, delivery and marking, but from the start you will be involved in the tracking of progress, stating of outcomes and evaluation of provision – so be prepared! But rest assured – we have all been there, and in the current climate of continuous change are, in fact, still there – it is a constant learning curve for us all.

10.2 Reviewing learners

As you would expect, effective teaching inevitably means that you must consistently review your learners' progress . How and when you do this may differ from course to course, and between different organizations. However, the main principles are the same. You and your learners need to be aware of the progress being made and your organization will require you to record the outcomes of reviews as part of the quality assurance process. The Learning Skills Council (LSC) and other funding bodies will also want to check these records in order to verify the funding being provided.

You may review students as either their subject/course tutor, or as a personal tutor. As the former, you will be aware of the student's strengths and weaknesses through your teaching and assessment methods. As the latter, you will probably have to rely on information from colleagues to help gain an idea of the student's progress in a variety of subject areas. You may be the student's only tutor contact at college, or one of many. The skill comes from using (together with the student) the information gained to draw conclusions and to action plan.

Activity 10a Reviewing Learning

Try to identify some of the reasons why you might review the progress of your own learners. What would you hope to gain?

The reasons for ongoing review are many, but often it is carried out to:

- evaluate the progress learners are making
- check if the learners are on course to succeed with their studies
- identify and diagnose particular difficulties
- give the learners a platform to speak individually about their own learning
- negotiate individual targets
- discuss future aspirations
- motivate learners
- make learners feel valued
- document progress against targets
- monitor attendance, etc.

An informal review can take place at any time to meet particular student needs. However, there are usually more formal scheduled tutorial times, either at frequent intervals or at certain times of the year. It is usual to carry out initial reviews quite early in a course, perhaps immediately following induction. This enables you to check that the learner is on the right programme and to identify any specific needs which may require specialist attention. Depending on the intensity of the programme, further reviews can occur once per term, or more often. Other good times are following or during a period of industrial placement, or after assessment has taken place.

Activity 10b Types of Review

Investigate the review process in your own organization, noting the calendar of formal reviews. Collect samples of any pro forma used to 'capture' the information discussed and the action agreed. Is the process similar across the whole organization, or do different programmes/courses have different systems? For example, compare the 14–19 programme with that of adults.

Having got to know more about your establishment's approach to reviews, you now need to think about the process of carrying them out with your learners. It is possible to carry out group tutorials, but to evaluate an individual's progress you really need to talk to students on a one-to-one basis. This is easier said than done when confronted with a full class. One way to tackle the problem is to give the group a task to complete while speaking to them individually. If there is another room available (and you can trust the group to work unsupervised), it is obviously better to withdraw learners one at a time so that you can both concentrate. Another possibility is to book individual tutorials away from group sessions. This is often used with adult learners who appreciate being able to negotiate meetings at times convenient to them.

Activity 10c Interview Settings

Given that you have arranged to interview learners at particular times to carry out their reviews, discuss how you would ensure that the setting is conducive to an effective discussion?

You would prepare very much as you would for a teaching session because, during a learning review, it is equally important to create the right atmosphere in an appropriate setting. The relationship between tutor and tutee is extremely important at this time and certain values are central, especially openness, trust and confidentiality. Learners should feel safe to express their views and feelings. You need to be able to deal with potential problems in a calm and logical manner.

Just as you would carefully plan a normal lesson, so you must plan for the review. You may find it useful to draw up an 'agenda' of items to discuss, leaving room for those raised by the learner. The course leader or organization may dictate certain items.

Activity 10d Review Issues

Consider the sort of things you may discuss with your particular learners during a learning review.

Issues that may be discussed in a review include curriculum performance, work experience, attendance, attitude, discipline and rules, application for jobs or higher education, compiling profiles, personal problems, etc. You may have a list of criteria against which you need to review the student, but the trusting relationship between you makes it important that your learners are aware of these.

Give the student advance warning of any preparatory work needed on their part, i.e. what they need to bring with them. You may wish them to carry out a self-assessment prior to the meeting (see Chapter 9), to give you a base from which to start. For initial reviews, it may also be useful to use your organization's 'learner agreement' especially when talking about commitment and targets (see Chapter 6). If it is a second, or subsequent review, you should have available a copy of actions agreed at the last review – and this is a good place to start. Above all, it is essential to set the scene at the beginning – just as you would in a taught lesson.

Reviewing what the learner has achieved and agreeing sensible targets helps to aid motivation. As you progress through a formal tutorial you will need to record the information discussed. Both of you should sign and take a copy of what you agree. Targets set should be 'SMART':

- **S**pecific
- **M**easurable (for reference in the next tutorial)
- **A**ttainable
- **R**ealistic
- **T**ime related (state a date when the target is to be reached).

They should also be negotiated, as this puts more responsibility onto the learner and they are therefore more likely to be met. Targets may be curriculum related, or more general, in connection with, for example, attitude or attendance. Targets need to be in chunks of a suitable size for each individual learner – remember learners are all different and the principles of inclusive learning (Chapter 7) and differentiation (Chapter 3) should be applied here. You and the learner must monitor these targets if they are to be effective.

An example of a record of a learning review is included below, and blank pro forma are available on the associated website **tipcet.com**.

As well as target-setting, other issues may arise from the review process. You need to be prepared for learners to disclose possible problems, either academic or personal. You may not feel able to deal with these yourself and may need help from other sources. The key here is not to try to deal with issues in which you have little experience, but refer the student to specialized support.

Activity 10e Referral Agencies

Assemble a list of the range of internal and external agencies which you are currently able to use to support your learners through a formal referral system.

Some examples are: Careers Adviser, Accommodation Officer, Student Union, Study Skills, Student Counsellor, Job Centre, Youth Worker, Social Services, Citizens Advice Bureau.

Table 10.1 Learning review and action plan

Candidate:	*Barbara Gardner*
Assessor/Personal Tutor:	*Arthur Robinson*
Date and Time:	*Monday 3ʳᵈ December 2007*
Programme:	*NVQ Care Award*
Reasons for Review:	*End of term learning review*

Achievements since last review (date):   *Held on Monday 18ᵗʰ June 2007*

Assignment 4: Analysis of clinical setting. Assignment referred because, although well written, it is mostly descriptive and lacks any analysis of procedures and patient care.

Case study: Production of a client care plan well carried out according to hospital guidelines and with good insight into specific patient needs.

Unit CU7: Evidence of critical thinking about actions and applied new knowledge well to practice.

Candidate log: Little disappointing, still a tendency to focus on process with very little evidence of reflection about the procedures or the patients' reactions.

Action Agreed:

Assignment 4 to be resubmitted. To add more careful analysis of procedures, particularly the monitoring of patient care.

Candidate Log to be developed in a more reflective way and to include more detailed reflection on own professional development as a result of experience on the ward.

Agreed Completion Date:	*11ᵗʰ January 2008*
Signature of Candidate:	*BE Gardener*
Signature of Assessor/Personal Tutor:	*A Robinson*

Top copy to student, middle copy to personal tutor and bottom copy to programme coordinator.

Students should be involved in the referral process themselves and confidentiality is all important in order to maintain the trust built up between you. It is important to make the distinction between learning support and pastoral care. Pastoral care is what you will be involved in within a Personal Tutor role. This includes caring for the academic progress as well as general well-being of your learners. Learning support is where you may refer learners with specific needs, or who are struggling in a particular area of their studies – this is discussed in more detail in Chapter 7.

Whatever structure your reviews take, you must summarize the issues covered at the end – again, just like a lesson! This reinforces the key points, and allows learners to clarify anything misunderstood. Get learners to reflect the issues back to you in order to check their understanding.

Activity 10f Practical Reviews

Carry out a selection of review tutorials with different learners. Provide examples of completed tutorial log/record sheets and action plans. Include in your sample learners with differing needs and if possible, evidence of referral to more specialized support.

From the points already raised, you can see that the tutorial role is as complex as the classroom teacher role. It can often prove to be more demanding, especially if you are conducting a series of one-to-one reviews consecutively. You will probably find the first few tutorial sessions thoroughly exhausting as it takes considerably more effort to concentrate on each individual in turn than it does to teach a full class. In between teaching we are able to give a group a task to do while we gather ourselves for the next input.

With individual tutorials rest is impossible, as you must give each learner your full attention. When you get tired, you find your mind wandering onto more mundane matters and then realize that you have not been listening to your tutee. It is highly embarrassing to have to ask someone to repeat what they have said, especially if it has taken them courage to tell you something in the first place. Thankfully, it does get easier as your review skills improve and you get faster and more efficient. However, while developing this welcome expertise, ensure that you do not (because of time constraints or other pressures) succumb to the temptation to short-change your learners.

Activity 10g Identifying Skills

After looking back on the reviews you have carried out, try to identify the skills you are developing and summarize them in priority order.

Creating the appropriate atmosphere is obviously the most important competence. You may find it helpful to start the review by indulging in idle chat, asking the student how they are, what they have been doing, etc. This puts them at ease.

It is useful to refer here to the theories of Carl Rogers (1983) with regard to his 'facilitative conditions' of the 'empathy, congruence and positive reward' required within a counselling situation, but also most important in a review. Rogers states that some of the goals of being a humanistically oriented teacher are aiming 'toward a climate of trust in the classroom', 'toward a participatory mode of decision making in all aspects of learning', and 'toward helping students to prize themselves, to build their confidence and self-esteem'. All of these need to be inherent in the tutorial review.

Many other counselling skills come into play in the review situation. These include active listening (watching for verbal and non-verbal messages), attending (being there, concentrating, as described earlier), and probing (trying to gain more information). The skills of effective questioning allow us to probe students for their true feelings. Open questions give them a platform for expressing concerns. Clarifying questions check our own understanding of the facts and student feelings. Empathy helps us to convey our understanding of a student's needs back to them. Congruence allows us to negotiate plans of action that will be in agreement by both sides. Respect and trust dictate that we treat learners individually, without bias and in confidence. Some examples of the types of questions you may use are:

- **Open:**   'How do you feel you are doing on your work placement?'
                  'What do you intend to do when you leave college?'
- **Probing:**   'Tell me more about the incident with the customer.'
                  'How did you reach the conclusion in your assignment?'
                  'Give me an example of a situation in which you feel vulnerable.'
- **Clarifying:** 'So am I right in thinking…?'
                  'I think you are saying…to me; is that correct?'

Building a student's confidence and self-esteem can be facilitated through effective feedback of a learner's performance. Giving appropriate feedback is a skill that you will certainly need to develop. In these situations you will need to cope with giving negative feedback as well as positive, although all feedback should be constructive.

You may find that giving feedback is the most demanding area of reviewing learning. As mentioned earlier, you could be reviewing learners from your own course or subject, in which case the results of performance assessment will be familiar to you and you will know your learners quite well. However, you may be a Personal Tutor with many tutees from differing subject areas and information on their progress may come from a variety of sources. Giving feedback which is constructive and supportive while at the same time being accurate is a fine balancing act.

Activity 10h Good Feedback

Thinking about your own learners, summarize what you feel would be the essential qualities of good feedback to them. It will be useful to refer to this list when you undertake Activity 10i.

Commonly accepted characteristics of giving good feedback are:

- **Timing** – provide it as soon as practical and only when the student is being receptive.
- **A positive orientation** – most students respond favourably to being told that something has gone well. This will usually relax the student and they are more likely to pay attention to any negative feedback that follows.
- **Detail specific** – deal with particular incidents and avoid being too general.
- **Clear** – explain both the negative and positive comments. Clarify why something worked or did not work, instead of just saying it went well/did not go well. Give reasons.
- **Constructive** – by offering advice to help the student to move forward with their learning. Suggest what could have been done to improve the situation.
- **Tutee choice** – negotiate what you feel is an appropriate response from the student. Insistence or demand on your part may alienate the learner.
- **Tutee understanding** – get the student to reflect back your advice and suggest their own.
- **Supportive** – Do not let the recipient flounder aimlessly. They will need some structure around which to make headway.

The most difficult part of giving feedback has to be that of tackling poor performance. One effective way of doing this is to put the ball in the student's court first, by asking them how they feel they are progressing. More often than not they will identify problem areas themselves. If they do not, continue with directed questions related to more specific elements of progress. If you have criteria against which to measure, ask the learner how they feel that they have met the criteria. Obviously, this is general guidance. You may need to develop particular styles to meet different learner needs.

Activity 10i Review Evaluation

Try to accurately evaluate your own performance in tutorials against the criteria you produced for Activity 10h, above. In what areas do you need to improve? Considering the process used in your programme area or organization, how could the system be improved?

In summary, a review is a good medium to use for re-motivating learning and in turn helping to aid retention and achievement. To be effective, a review must be well planned and thorough. Certain skills of counselling need to be employed with care taken to look beyond the obvious. Feedback should be constructive and sensitive, with students fully involved. Targets should be negotiated and agreed by both parties, with regular monitoring. Records should be made of review outcomes and this feeds back into the organization's quality assurance system. Review discussions at the end, leaving the learner feeling positive. Remember, it takes time to build up the skills required to be an effective reviewer – you will not necessarily get it right first time!

10.3 Collaboration and networking

Earlier in this chapter and within previous chapters, we have emphasized that teaching should be seen as a *collaborative* activity which, naturally, involves liaison with other people in order to support learners through referral to more specialized help. This section extends on this, looking at how you will need to work collaboratively with both colleagues and external contacts, in order to coordinate all aspects of the curriculum.

Although you can often work in isolation, especially as a part-time tutor at an outreach centre, you will undoubtedly be a member of at least one team. How often you actually meet with this team will depend on the management of your organization. You may very well be a member of many teams, certainly if you work in more than one curriculum area. These teams may have conflicting demands on your time – each team wanting to make the best use of you.

In addition, the teams to which you belong may not all have been created for similar purposes. You may belong to a course team where you are all working towards delivery of an effective learning experience for students on one course. You may have the vocational area in common, but not necessarily share subject expertise. Many of the team may have worked in industry and you will all have different experiences. You may all teach the same group of students and meet to discuss planning issues, i.e. when to set assessments so that they do not clash, or to discuss how each part of the curriculum fits together. You may, on the other hand, belong to a subject team such as mathematics or information technology, or a wider curriculum team such as visual arts. You will all have the subject, or type of subject in common, but may teach on different courses and to different students. Cross-college teams will also exist, for example groups of personal tutors will meet to discuss the personal tutor curriculum. Due to the dynamic nature of post-compulsory education, more specialized project teams will be created to follow up contemporary initiatives. In addition to these teams, each organization will have management teams at a variety of levels. You will certainly be able to identify examples of these types of teams and more, within your own organization.

Activity 10j Team Membership

List the teams to which you belong both formally and informally. Summarize your role within each of these teams. Say to which teams you feel you make the most contribution and why.

As a consequence of belonging to more than one team, you may find yourself having to take on a variety of roles, some of which will be unfamiliar to you. It may now be appropriate to discuss some theory connected to the creation, structure and life of teams.

In his discussion about teamwork, Morrison (1998) gives a definition of a team as

> . . . a group of people with a common objective, whose members possess different areas of expertise, skills, personalities and abilities that complement one another, and who are committed to working together cooperatively on a common, shared task and a common purpose.

However, you may not choose to be in a particular team, and teams in education are not necessarily hand-picked for the purpose. This means that the collection of individuals may not work well together, leading to an ineffective situation. In Chapter 5 (Activity 5n) we considered Belbin's theories about the characteristics of group members and the roles they adopt.

Although you may have a tendency towards one of Belbin's characters, you will probably be comfortable in more than one of these roles. Indeed, you may take on different roles within different teams, as mentioned earlier. In theory a team will not work if it comprises too many people seeking the same role, but it does not necessarily need one of each to work – a good mix will suffice.

Other well-known related theory comes from Tuckman (1965) regarding the development of teams. This theory relates to a variety of occupations but can easily apply to education. Tuckman recognizes four stages in team development:

- **forming** – a collection of disparate individuals gather to achieve a particular task
- **storming** – they react to the task ahead and to other group members
- **norming** – they develop group cohesiveness
- **performing** – they work effectively to achieve the identified task.

Tuckman points out that it is the first three stages that will test the group's willingness and ability to direct itself collaboratively towards the agreed task. They may show their enthusiasm for the job in hand, but can become distracted as they test each other out and become orientated with other individuals as well as with the task.

Once formed, there may be many arguments, especially if progress with the task is slow. The team begins to lay down its own rules and provides a structure for completion of the task and roles are decided. The team is mature at the *performing* stage and is able to carry out the assigned tasks. However, many teams do not arrive at this stage, or do not necessarily arrive in the order stated.

Within education this is especially true, as stated by Bush and Middlewood (1997):

> [W]ith many teams consisting of a fluid mixture of full-time, part-time and temporary staff, experienced and inexperienced teachers, and professional, paraprofessional and lay members, it is reasonable to assume that team development is a fragmented, non-linear process and considerably more complex than many normative models imply.

Even with a fully mature team, there will still be ups and downs. Perhaps you can relate this theory to a team in which you belong. Within a continuous improvement culture, teams are often 'renewed' or 'reformed' as individual skills and knowledge are transferred to new projects. This process could be seen as adding a fifth stage to Tuckman's model – i.e. '*Transforming*'.

As mentioned earlier, teams in education are not always able to be hand-picked, which may lead to problems of conflict. It should, in theory, be advantageous to have a team working on a problem, but teaching has not always been seen as a teamwork activity. Teachers have historically had a good amount of autonomy and may not be open to the sharing that is required to make an effective team.

Bush and Middlewood describe the *incompatibility* between classroom teaching and teamwork by referring to an example from Clement and Staessens (1993) which compares the difference between a team of football players and a team of teachers. The footballers' central aim revolves around a team event – the football match. Conversely, the central aim of teachers is the interaction between themselves and the students in the classroom, which is *not* a team event.

Activity 10k Team Performance

Without naming people, programmes or departments, briefly discuss your experience of working in educational teams. Identify successes and those situations where agreement was difficult. Say how problems were resolved.

You may have had experience of tutors who are unwilling to contribute to a team activity (an example would be reluctance to part with material which they have developed, seeing it as their property). However, the incorporation of Further Education colleges in the early 1990s created the necessity for greater collaboration between staff because of the range of new pressures affecting colleagues. In order to survive within this highly pressured environment, the willingness to share all aspects of work with colleagues (including material preparation) is crucial. If you are willing to share responsibilities, you will often find that others are more willing to be generous towards you. With the advent of the internet, email and Virtual Learning Environments (VLEs), sharing resources has become much easier. Colleagues can share electronic resources and then adapt them easily for their own learners. It is possible to be part of a 'virtual team' and even hold meetings online or by video conferencing. It is interesting to note that, following incorporation and the onset of the culture of Total Quality

Management (TQM is discussed later in this chapter), management in colleges has leaned towards the formation of more formal teams.

Activity 10l Team Structures

Discuss how the management of your establishment is structured. Consider processes such as decision making, the devolution of responsibility, the ability to be responsive, access to information, etc.

The establishment of teams to take responsibility for particular aspects of educational provision can be extremely useful and does appear to support the empowerment ideas of Deming (see 10.6 below) However, the increase in the number of teams can cause management structures and communication processes to become more rigid at a time when flexibility and responsiveness are extremely important. If a team has a clear mandate and the ability to change things, it can become a valuable asset to a college. It is when it is formed without a clearly defined, achievable purpose and is given responsibility without authority that problems often arise.

Activity 10m Evidence of Working with Others

Collect relevant examples of memorandums, letters, emails and meeting minutes to show your involvement with colleagues, and your membership of teams. Obtain witness statements from colleagues and/or line managers regarding the contribution you make to these teams. (Your organization's performance management process and documentation may also be useful here.)

So far this section has dealt with forming and working within teams internal to the organization. Now it is necessary to move to look at the wider picture and include all contacts with whom you may come into association. This may include internal colleagues who you do not necessarily come in contact with through team meetings. These may be support staff (i.e. administrators, reprographics staff, guidance workers, caretakers, housekeepers, librarians, counsellors, etc.). All these individuals are central to the smooth running of the organization and have a huge impact on the student's total learning experience.

You will also be involved with links with external agencies, some of direct importance to your learners, and others more of a support to you as a tutor. Another consequence of the 1993 incorporation of Colleges of Further Education with its deliberate creation of a competitive culture was the gradual movement away from collaboration with colleagues in similar local institutions. This has created a greater need for teachers to belong to professional support agencies in order to maintain some contact with other practitioners, possibly in the form of subject-based associations. More recently in the 2000s, there has been a move to return to some collaboration and you may find yourself involved with contemporary initiatives in liaison with other local colleges.

A more direct connection with the students' experiences are the qualification awarding bodies, with whom you will need to keep close contact. As these award providers have responsibility for validating courses (which includes quality assurance of provision), you will be required to provide them with relevant information from time to time. Regular visits will be made by external assessors and verifiers, and you may be required to attend some awarding body training in order to run certain courses. There will be a similar relationship with higher education institutions as colleges often franchise courses from their local universities.

Add to this list your local employers who are very important contacts for three main reasons. First, your students may be on a course paid for by an employer. If you work for a business unit, they will be your main source of students and you may tailor courses especially to suit certain employees. Secondly, you may have vocational students who require periods of placement within industry. Employers can provide this experience and often furnish you with feedback on your student's progress. Lastly, it is becoming more common for tutors in Further Education to take up industrial experience themselves to keep them up to date with the outside world and hence give their courses more credibility. With the introduction of Continuing Professional Development (CPD) as a requirement to maintain qualified teacher status (see chapters 1 and 12) this may be one form of development in which you will participate.

Government agencies have an enormous impact on the day-to-day running of the whole Lifelong Learning Sector, although you may not necessarily have direct contact with them yourself. The most important one to mention here is the LSC. This is made up of a variety of people who represent local business and communities, learners who are disadvantaged, employees, young people, students with special learning needs, adult learners and individuals who face discrimination. This agency controls the planning and funding of education and training for all young people and adults, other than those in universities. Its aim is to improve the skills of England's young people and adults in order to create a competitive workforce. It also has a large part to play in the quality assurance process.

Other external contacts may include visiting speakers, suppliers of materials and resources, local secondary schools (for marketing and recruitment), advice agencies such as the careers service, centres used for outreach provision and prison education departments. Lengthy though it may be, the above is not intended to be an exhaustive list!

Organizations often describe internal and external contacts as 'stakeholders', in other words, those who have an unquestionable interest in its success. For example, students, staff, suppliers, franchise partners, parents, funding bodies and so on.

In order to help you decipher the maze of possible contacts, the following activity may help you to identify those of most importance to you at this time.

Activity 10n Stakeholder Contact

Identify the stakeholders who have a direct interest in the continuing success of your organization. Compile a list of your own internal and external contacts. (An organizational chart may help you here, or you may wish to draw up your own diagram to show the network of contacts which you maintain.) Critically analyse how these contacts directly or indirectly benefit your learners.

10.4 Communication with colleagues

Now that you are aware of your internal and external contacts, it is important to consider how you communicate with them. Within Chapter 6 we touched on communication with learners; here we will be considering complex systems or channels of communication, which need to exist to promote the smooth working of the organization.

You may have already formed some views of how communication works within your own teaching environment. In Bush and West-Burnham (1994), a chapter by Riches makes the point that unsatisfactory communication is a common complaint within organizations when he claims that:

> mistakes are often made because communication is not seen as a two-way exchange, but as a directive from above, without any consideration of those for whom the communication is intended, or of their views.

Within education, communication is made more critical due to the speed and frequency of change. In recent times, educational establishments have simultaneously had to become more efficient, complex, and aware of market forces and government legislation. Riches gives a useful classification of different spheres of communication that can be related to the educational setting:

- **Interpersonal Communication** concerns the behaviour of individual people when transferring information verbally and non-verbally.
- **Organizational Communication** appreciates the fact that all members of an organization may be sending and receiving signals simultaneously (a network).
- **Basic Mechanical aspects of Communication** identifies the use of mechanical or electronic devices to transmit and receive messages.

Person-to-person communication is obviously important in all aspects of education, but other means of communication have taken a more significant role. While memorandums and telephones used to be the main methods of communication between colleagues in different workrooms and on different sites, the popularity of electronic mail has taken over. The reasons for this are fairly obvious, and include speed of response, facility to mail more than one person at once and the ability to file and store messages for future reference. One can, however, argue that it has also removed or reduced the quality of an important aspect, i.e. personal contact.

Riches also categorizes communication flow within typical organizations as *downward*, *upward* and *horizontal*. The strongest flow is usually *downward*, from top management down through formal layers of authority. This could be via more 'static' means such as organizational rules, job specifications, or work manuals. On the other hand, it could be via more dynamic communication that changes more regularly, for example, briefings, advisory meetings, staff development sessions, in-house newsletters, etc. Communication can break down if individuals are isolated from line managers, for example when they are on different sites. Formal meetings are then necessary, and within education the timing of these is extremely complicated due to individual timetables and different patterns of working, etc. Electronic mail has partly solved this problem, but personal contact is still needed.

Effective *upward* communication (from workers to managers) depends upon the trust built between the levels and culture of the organization. *Horizontal* communication is the most frequent type within an organization, as you will often talk to work colleagues both informally and formally throughout the day. This type of communication is strongly linked to teamwork. It is also important as it bridges the gap between departments and teams.

Activity 10o Presenting your Viewpoint

Consider the processes available to you to make your voice heard. Say how your organization facilitates the participation of staff and the dissemination of views and opinions.

Barriers to organizational communication are many and varied. Inevitably there are formal and informal 'gatekeepers' who are either authorized to monitor messages or make it their business to intercept communications and to decide how much, if any, of the message to pass on. Such people are in powerful positions, which are sometimes deliberately established, but often are assumed without either full management knowledge or approval.

Another barrier can be the incorrect use of language and jargon – just as in the classroom. People who have different values can put different weight on different parts of a message as it progresses up and down the chain. A person's status can impede communication – you may not feel able to approach a senior manager for example. Failure to hear and/or interpret a message correctly could be a problem – you may hear what you want to hear.

The larger the organization, the more complex are the communication channels. Face-to-face contact may be less frequent, managers may be segregated from the staff. The further a message has to travel, the more likely it will become distorted. If you work closely together as a subject team, and are based within the same room, communication will be frequent and informal. You will keep each other up to date without the need for frequent meetings. However, with individuals increasingly having more diverse roles, teams can lose touch if care is not taken to sustain regular, formal contact. Evaluation and quality assurance can help to give your team a focus for interaction. To help you to understand the communication networks that exist within your organization, you may like to try the following activity.

Activity 10p Communication Analysis

List all the methods of communication in your organization. Comment on the effectiveness of each one. Consider the direction of the communications – are they top–down or vice versa? Suggest how you could improve the communication system to make it more effective. (You may find it helpful to draw out the communication channels in diagrammatical form.)

10.5 Quality assurance and evaluation

Even if you have not been working in education for long, you will undoubtedly have heard talk of quality processes in relation to meeting the needs of learners. The concept of quality has always been within the education system, but it is only in the past two decades that it has been transformed based on models pertaining from industry.

Although you will most likely have your own understanding of quality, it is important that we establish a precise definition here. However, defining quality is not as straightforward as it may seem. For example, the word may be used as both a noun and an adjective. The Concise Oxford Dictionary (1990) defines quality as:

- the degree of excellence of a thing
- a distinctive attribute or faculty
- a characteristic trait.

The word is often used to signify excellence in something, for example, a product or service. Within education it can be defined as 'meeting the customer requirements and expectations', but in the current competitive climate, it may also be used to describe 'exceeding customer expectations', as organizations compete for students and positions in league tables. Sallis (1996) states that:

> quality is what makes the difference between things being excellent or run of the mill. Increasingly in education, quality makes the difference between success and failure.

When providing a rationale for why an educational establishment should be involved in quality assurance Sallis classified his results into four main areas:

1. The **moral imperative**, which implies that educational establishments should provide the very best possible educational opportunities for learners – and few people in education would argue with this.
2. The **professional imperative**, closely linked to the above, implies a professional commitment to the needs of learners, which includes a duty to improve the quality of education.
3. **Competition**. Institutions need differentiation from their competitors in order to maintain a healthy supply of students.
4. The final imperative is that of **accountability**, where organizations must prove the high standards of their services within the public domain. Institutions are measured via government inspection against strict performance criteria to verify their application for funding.

You may hear the terms 'Quality Control', 'Quality Assurance', and 'Total Quality Management' used within your workplace. It may be useful to differentiate between them here. *Quality Control* is the detection and elimination of things which are not up to standard, i.e. a checking process. Government inspection is a method of quality control. External verification or moderation by Awarding Bodies is another quality control measure. *Quality Assurance* on the other hand, is a process with its aim being to prevent faults before they occur. It is about consistency, and getting things right first time. Quality Assurance aims to reduce wasted resources and unhappy customers. Your organization will more than likely have a Quality Assurance system in place. *Total Quality Management* incorporates and further develops Quality Assurance. It involves everyone in an organization being devoted to satisfying the customer's needs and is based on a culture of continuous improvement. *Quality Circles* are a direct form of employee participation in TQM. Employees are encouraged to volunteer to form teams in order to solve problems, which they themselves have identified. This gives the employee 'ownership' and as a result, greater motivation. This is in contrast to other forms of employee participation when suggestions are passed on to management for consideration, and therefore ownership lost.

The underpinning philosophy for this movement has its roots in industry, originating in the USA as far back as the 1930s. Recognized as the original quality 'guru', W. Edwards Deming, an American government statistician, demonstrated his theories as part of the American concern to revitalize Japanese industry after the end of the Second World War and the horrors of Hiroshima and Nagasaki as a consequence of the airborne attacks using atomic bombs which led to the Japanese surrender. Deming (1986) recognizes that 'quality should be aimed at the needs of the consumer, present and future', and that 'it is customers that keep a company in business'. He states that people should 'work smarter, not harder' in order to achieve an increase in productivity. Working with fellow American, Joseph Juran, Deming developed his notions of the elimination of waste and delay in production and established the first quality circles within Japanese industrial establishments. Unfortunately, these highly successful production strategies were ignored by the industrialists in the USA until the late 1970s, by which stage Japan had achieved a much larger share of the commercial market, due largely to the success of their work-based practices developed by Deming and his colleagues.

To the Japanese, the message has been simple – listen to customers and improve the methods of production and the quality of products to a high standard in order to meet their needs. Japanese managers took on board Demings suggestion that money should be invested in the 'front end' of the process to establish quality in the first place, rather than spend time and money 'checking and mending' at the end of the system. These ideas were successful first in manufacturing and then in the service industries. In the meantime the USA continued with its emphasis on maximizing outputs and profits, and, around 1980, began to realize the importance of quality principles, the relationship between the customer and the organization and the need for longer term planning.

It was not until the late 1980s that total quality began to be discussed in connection with education, beginning initially with community colleges in the USA and some UK further education colleges. This has spread to higher education and ultimately to schools.

During the 1990s there was a push for educational organizations to become accredited with a variety of quality awards. These include Investors in People, EFQM and other national quality marks, some linked to specialist areas of provision, for example, Matrix for Information Advice and Guidance and Charter Mark for Customer Care.

The LSC's 'Framework for Excellence' policy was published in June 2007 and was implemented as a pilot by some organizations within the Lifelong Learning Sector in August 2007. This is a new approach to managing performance and is driven by the LSC. The framework is based on Key Performance Indicators (KPIs) which will measure

- responsiveness – to employers and learners
- effectiveness and quality of provision
- finance – financial health; control and use of resources.

KPIs are not new to education and many organizations are now using them to set targets linked to development plans. For example, an organization may have KPIs for learner satisfaction and learner achievement. These may be benchmarked during self-assessment to data from similar organizations to give a picture of how the organization is fairing against others nationally. This new framework will eventually provide employers and learners with information on all learning providers so that a more informed choice of where to study can be made.

National Skills Academies are employer-led centres of excellence, initiated by the government to address the need for a world-class workforce. They are focused on vocational education and skills training of young people and adults in a variety of industries such as construction, financial services and manufacturing. The initiative is driven by well-known companies in each industry. In addition, Centres of Excellence in Teacher Training (CETTS) have been introduced to improve and maintain the quality of initial teacher training for the sector. All these initiatives are striving to raise and maintain quality provision – keep watching for other initiatives in the future.

All these quality systems help in the marketing of the organization and in the competition between institutions. Organizations have set up more rigorous quality assurance systems and trained staff in the quality ethos. We have been made more aware of our internal and external 'customers' and 'stakeholders' and the need for accountability through the inspection process. As Quality Assurance is proactive, it has been necessary to write detailed policies and procedures to cover all aspects of the organization's work. For example, Student and Staff Charters, Equal Opportunity and Health and Safety Policies, and Appeals Procedures as well as detailed procedures for any important organizational process. Naturally, there will also be a Quality Policy. These may all be held within some type of Quality Manual, especially if the organization is aiming for the ISO 9000 international standard. The whole vision of the organization will be explained through its 'Mission Statement'.

Activity 10q Establishment Mission

Read your establishment's 'Mission Statement' together with other policies written for your organization. See if you can identify where the principles articulated in the Mission Statement are evident in other policy statements.

Once an organization has these items in place, it is necessary to provide the means to ensure that these promises will be maintained. An example that will relate directly to you is that of schemes of work. You will need to identify the key processes, such as when and how initial and diagnostic assessment of individual needs will take place. You will also be required to show how you intend to induct students into your course, and how you will differentiate within lessons to meet all students' learning styles. Any contemporary initiatives will need to be incorporated, such as the inclusion of Information Learning Technology into the curriculum and how you will address the Literacy, Language and Numeracy (LLN) needs of your learners. This is all in addition to the more traditional information such as ensuring that you cover the syllabus, what resources you will use, and how you will assess the learners!

You will also be involved in recording learner progress and achievement. This is easier if the learners are aiming for an accredited course, but more problematical if it is non-accredited learning.

The Recognition and Recording of Progress and Achievement (RARPA) is the approach to a significant part of quality assurance for providers in the Lifelong Learning Sector for non-accredited provision. If you work in this sector, you will be involved with setting criteria for learners to achieve, showing the progress towards this and proving the learners' achievements.

As mentioned above, in order to measure whether an organization is achieving the ideals of its mission statement, it will usually draw up sets of 'Performance Indicators'. These are factors which can be used to help determine whether institutional strategic goals are being met. Examples of these indicators will be recruitment, retention and achievement targets. You may be involved with setting these for your area, but will almost certainly be involved with achieving these targets and will have key goals set via Performance Reviews with your line manager.

It is no accident that these targets are also closely linked to the funding of courses, so this information will be used by funding bodies such as the LSC. Other indicators will be linked to student satisfaction and progression, as well as the financial strength of the organization. These will all become a part of the 'Framework for Excellence' described above.

All this information is required to be maintained for inspection purposes. Each organization will have its own preferred method for this, but you will obviously need to play a part. A course or team leader may have the responsibility for maintaining the records and for reporting the information to management (upward communication). This may give you an insight into the reasons for the huge amount of administration in education today.

Activity 10r   Quality Processes

Summarize the quality procedures that influence your particular work. Identify how the data you provide feeds back to inform internal and external quality monitoring.

There are a number of ways in which quality assurance data are used to inform quality control. Quality systems need this feedback loop. Outcomes must be analysed against the overall plan. Evaluation is a key element in strategic planning for any organization, and this process should focus on the customer (students, employers, parents, etc.) and should focus on two issues. First, how far is the organization meeting the individual requirements of customers (internal and external) and how far is it meeting its strategic goals? Sallis categorizes these into immediate, short- and long-term levels of evaluation.

- **Immediate** is less formal and involves you checking on a daily or weekly (depending on regularity of contact) basis, how students are progressing. You may, for example, check that students have completed their homework or (by using questioning in class) that they can remember what was learned in the previous session.
- **Short-term** is more structured and will involve the review process described earlier in the chapter. Attainment in assessments and progress with work experience are examples. This will require recording and involves some statistical data. Its aim is to highlight any problems and to prevent students from underachieving.
- **Long-term** is an overview of progress towards strategic goals. It is mainly management-led and involves sampling of customer views on a large scale. Often this is through the use of questionnaires, but may also be via meetings with a representative sample of learners.

Data collected via this type of questionnaire will probably generate quantitative data, whereas the meetings with students may reveal qualitative information. The quantitative data will be put with other data on pass rates, retention, etc. to feed back against the performance indicators. Questionnaires will concentrate on the whole student experience as well as teaching and learning. There may well be questions linked to enrolment and recruitment, as well as refreshment and library facilities and so on.

As well as these institutionally directed questionnaires, you may find it useful to carry out your own evaluations in class which are more specifically directed at whether students are satisfied with lesson content and your own teaching style. Closed or multiple-choice questions will give you quantitative information (i.e. the 'what'), open questions will generate qualitative replies (i.e. the 'why'). The latter is of more use to you when improving your courses, the former is of more interest to management towards measurement of strategic goals. Evaluation of your own performance was discussed in more detail in Chapter 9.

Activity 10s Quantitative and Qualitative Data

Discuss the comparative value to you (when you are trying to understand your own performance as a teacher) of quantitative data (i.e. statistical information) as opposed to qualitative data (feedback on student attitudes, feelings and expectations, for example).

Quality control measures mentioned so far have concentrated on the performance of learners and the organization as a whole. However, you may be directly measured for performance, not only via any performance management system, but also via observation of your teaching. Checklists used will be linked to inspection criteria and possibly to the LLUK or other standards. You may be observed by line management and/or by peers. Expect to be graded – this will be a new dimension to you as this observation is not purely developmental as it is on teacher training programmes, but must provide some statistical data to feed into the quality assurance system. Expect to be given an action plan of points to address prior to your next observation. If you work in more than one curriculum area, you may find yourself observed on more than one occasion in the year.

Organizational self-assessment is an important part of accountability. All these measures will be used as key evidence in the reporting process. It is not just necessary to 'do', but also essential to *prove* that you 'do'.

As a result of all this measuring, institutions have had to develop more comprehensive systems for recording, storing and reporting data. Management Information Systems have to be able to report accurately to funding bodies, administer examinations information and run the payroll as well as keep management generally informed of progress towards strategic goals. The process is further complicated by the increased flexibility of certain teaching programmes, the increased number of part-time staff, and the number of interested parties to whom the organization is accountable.

Activity 10t The affect of Quality Information

Give some examples of improvements you have made to your course/subject (design, delivery and assessment) as a direct result of information gained during the quality processes. It may help to show these changes on a scheme of work. Include samples of the data used to inform the changes.

10.6 Conclusion

This chapter has aimed to show the wider aspects of the tutor's role and how factors external to the classroom can have an impact on the whole learning experience. Whatever your initial role within the Lifelong Learning Sector, you will not be able to escape the culture of constant change and accountability. We hope you can see the importance of maintaining systems of recording and evaluation, and the importance of maintaining a network of personal contacts through effective communication. Your communication skills need to be multifaceted, using different approaches with different people. You also need to respond to those within and external to your organization.

Quality assurance is important, as doing things right first time costs nothing but forward planning. Mistakes can be expensive – and there is nothing more expensive than a learner leaving education because of a bad experience – they may never feel able to return. However, as it is inevitable that you will make some mistakes, the important thing is that you learn from these.

Accept feedback on your skills willingly. Get involved, meet people, build up your own network of contacts. Say 'yes' to invitations to join new teams. Reflect on the roles you take and how the teams you are in perform. Reflect on communication channels in your organization – how easily do they flow? Reflect on the quality your students receive from you and the whole organization. Do you really listen to your students? Accept constant change as a challenge and it will not stress you – it is unlikely to go away. Rest assured, teaching in post-compulsory education will never be dull.

10.7 Useful publications

If you wish to read about the introduction of Quality Assurance to the manufacturing and service industries straight from the mouth of a quality guru, see Deming, W.E. (1986), *Out of the Crisis: Quality, Productivity and Competitive Position.* Cambridge: Cambridge University Press.

For a good, easy to read book on Total Quality Management, look at Sallis, E. (1996), *Total Quality Management in Education.* London: Kogan Page.

Morrison, K. (1998), *Management Theories for Educational Change.* London: Paul Chapman Publishing. This book talks about the quality gurus and quality awards. It also has a good chapter on teamwork.

If you want to reflect on some of the effects of incorporation of the F.E. sector, see Elliott, G. (1996), *Crisis and Change in Vocational Education and Training.* London: Jessica Kingsley. This book has a chapter on Quality Assurance which looks at how lecturers have been affected.

If you require a practical book on organizational communication, see Katz, B. (1989), *Turning Practical Communication into Business Power.* Mercury Books.

Mullins, L.J. (1999), *Management and Organisational Behaviour* (5th edn). Pearson Education Ltd. This book has a good chapter on Group Processes and Behaviour (page 483) that relates to teams and communication within an organization. It is a good all-round book if you are interested in the structure of organizations.

To find out the roles that you may play within a team, try the questionnaire in Meredith Belbin, R. (1981), *Management Teams: Why they Succeed or Fail.* Oxford: Butterworth-Heinemann.

10.8 Useful websites

For information on the 'Framework for Excellence' and 'National Skills Academies', visit **www.lsc.gov.uk** and **www.nationalskillsacademy.gov.uk**.

The EFQM Excellence Model was introduced at the beginning of 1992 as the framework for assessing organizations for the European Quality Award. For more information on this visit **www.efqm.org**.

For more information on RARPA visit **www.niace.org.uk** and **www.lsc.gov.uk**.

Try **tipcet.com** for a range of materials and suggested sources related to communication, evaluation and working in groups.

The Evolving Sector

Fred Fawbert

Key Concepts

Academic Drift, Academic/Vocational Divide, ACVEs, Casualization, Centralization, Collectivist Consensus, Commodification, Crisis in Capitalism, CTCs, De-Professionalization, De-Skilling, Economic Utility, Education Reform Act, Equality of Opportunity, Flexi-Learning, Free-Market, GNVQs, Great Debate, Hillgate Group, HMI, Industrial Lead Body, Key Stage 4, Manpower Services Commission, Market Economics, NCVQ, Neo-Conservatism, Neo-Liberal, New Right, New Labour, Ofsted, Skills, Social Welfare, Structural Reform, Structural Unemployment, Tomlinson Review, Training Agency, Utopian Planning, Vocationalism, Welfare State, YTS.

11.1 Introduction

An important aspect of being an informed professional in any field is having an awareness of not only current policies and practices, but also how these developments were brought about. Those of us in education and training also need to consider their potential effect on our colleagues, our learners and ourselves. However, before we provide a résumé of critical events in post-compulsory education, it is worth noting that the post–16 Sector has arguably been, and continues to be, the focus for more radical change than any other area of British educational provision. Although we do hope that what we report here may be an illuminating backdrop, it will inevitably be superseded by other developments, almost before the print has dried.

11.2 The political background

In her Foreword to this book, Kathryn Ecclestone welcomed the many important recent developments within the new Lifelong Learning Sector. In the past, as has been mentioned earlier in this book, we have been more used to the epithet 'Cinderella Sector'. However, given the number of names we have had, perhaps the 'evolving sector' is about right. At various times we have been known as Further Education, Post–16, Learning and Skills, Post-Compulsory and PCET. But that isn't nearly an end to it. The advent of LLUK led us to believe that we would now be the Lifelong Learning Sector, but now the recent (August 2007) splitting of the Department for Education and Skills to form two new departments has led to the creation of 'DCSF' and 'DIUS'. The compulsory sectors of primary and secondary have become the Department for Children, Schools and Families and the post-compulsory sector is now under the banner of the Department of Innovation, Universities and Skills'. We would like to think we are 'Innovation' but I suspect we are, in fact, simply 'Skills'.

This variety of titles and the final insult of what does appear to be little more than a nickname, seems to sum up one of our major dilemmas: the sector has become a catch-all for the increasing areas of provision which fall outside of the compulsory schooling and higher education remit and sometimes it is difficult for government to comprehend the full extent of college and private training provider responsibilities. So we have to accept it – 'Skills are us!'

For many of us such trivial name-calling is nothing when compared to the seismic changes we experienced in education and many other aspects of modern life, which were initiated by the world crisis in capitalism symbolized by the oil shortages of 1973. In Britain this led, among other things, to an alarming escalation in the number of young unemployed and was a period when Harold Wilson and his Labour government first publicly linked education directly to the failing economy. One of Labour's early initiatives (in response to the youth unemployment crisis) was particularly significant. In 1974, with trade union support, they established the Manpower Services Commission (MSC) under the aegis of the Department of Employment. This involvement of the DoE was, allegedly, justified because the rapidly worsening situation made it vital that urgent action should be taken and there were real fears that the then Department of Education and Science's Inspectorate (HMI) had the power to slow down or sabotage any vocational innovation. Thus began the years of progressive reduction in the power of the DES, which led to the eventual amalgamation of Employment and Education in 1995.

In retrospect, this Labour initiative set the tone for the policies of the succeeding Conservative regime, in that it marked the upsurge in government of a view that the type of general 'liberal' education being provided to the 'non-academic' stream in secondary and further education was largely inappropriate, costly and a consequence of what Martin Wiener (1985) called 'academic drift'. Although he was more concerned with undergraduate destinations, Wiener's attitude represented a perspective which found much favour with ministers who were concerned at that time about the combined power of the DES, universities and the LEAs. Wiener went on to point out that since the middle of the nineteenth century, each attempt to give greater emphasis to science and technology in schools and to install more practical and relevant curricula, had been undermined by academic values which promoted education for its own sake and continually edged out vocationally aimed initiatives. Wiener believed that this process was continued in, and indeed was led by the universities, which encouraged their best products to carry out postgraduate work and pursue academic rather than industrial or business careers.

11.3 Return to vocationalism

However, nationally during the early 1970s there was a consensus emerging which was radically different to the traditional academic preference for a broader, liberal approach to education. These changing values marked the emphatic return of government educational policy to a model that had been so dominant in Britain during the late 1800s and which focused primarily on preparing students for employment. James Callaghan, the then Labour Prime Minister, initiated what was called the 'Great Debate' with his 1976 Ruskin speech, which echoed Weiner's concerns that vocational pathways within education were being undermined for selfish purposes by academics:

> I am concerned on my journeys to find complaints from industry that new recruits from the schools sometimes do not have the basic tools to do the job that is required. I have been concerned to find that many of our best-trained students who have completed the higher levels of education at university or polytechnic have no desire or intention of joining industry. Their preferences are to stay in academic life (very pleasant I know) or to find their way into the civil service. There seems to be a need for a more technological bias in science teaching that will lead towards practical applications in industry rather than towards academic studies . . . There is no virtue in producing socially well-adjusted members of society who are unemployed because they do not have the skills.

Bash (1985), commenting on this 'fallacious and facile link between education and unemployment', was one of the many members of the academic establishment who responded to this attempt to lay at the door of education the blame for the huge problem of youth unemployment which was facing the Labour administration at that time. Bash went on to point out that unemployment was generated, not by failures of the state education system, but by shifts in the national and international economy:

> When the economy had been growing, industry had had no difficulty in providing training it considered appropriate. No matter how well educated or well trained UK school leavers had been, the 1970s and 1980s would still have been periods of massive structural unemployment . . . the possible point of application of ameliorative measures would have been the economy itself, not the education system.

There was also present at that time, within both main political parties, those who could see that a potentially expensive problem of unemployed youth could, when given the right training, provide a low-paid, flexible workforce which would not only reduce the unemployment problem, but would also provide an effective economic device that could reduce pay levels nationally.

Margaret Thatcher's arrival as Prime Minister in 1979 rapidly confirmed a much more robust challenge to the post-war consensus that had existed for over 30 years between the two main parties in government and opposition. The liberal, equality of opportunity values enshrined in the 'One-Nation' approach was abandoned and replaced by a more ideologically driven neo-liberal mindset, which has since dominated UK politics and policies for more than 20 years.

This emerging political attitude was expressed in the field of education by successive Conservative Secretaries of State for Education who turned to the 'New Right' ideas of privatization with their themes of choice, market forces and improving quality through competition. New Right pressure groups such as the Centre for Policy Studies, the National Council for Educational Standards, the Adam Smith Institute and the Institute of Economic Affairs also heavily influenced government educational thinking.

Their concepts and principles are made clear by Lawton's (1994) review of Conservative education legislation from 1979 to 1994. He identifies six clear political value positions:

- the desire for more selection
- the wish to return to more traditional curricula and teaching methods
- the desire to reduce the influence of experts and educational theory by encouraging common-sense, traditional practices
- an appeal to parental choice as a means of encouraging market forces
- a wish to reduce educational expenditure
- a process of increased centralization which had the additional purpose of reducing the power and autonomy of the LEAs.

Although there were other possible approaches to the problem of unemployment, the neo-liberal, free-market approach to economic decisions (as opposed to intervention through investment) led the Tories to target vocational training as a central solution. The Department of Employment through the MSC was used systematically during the following years as a conduit for the huge investment in the training of the young unemployed. As we will see, ultimately this elevation of the DoE and the MSC also had the effect of reducing the influence of the DES, the LEAs, the universities, polytechnics and the teachers.

This process of gradually eroding power as opposed to more direct action was probably selected because the type of aggressive legislation we saw towards the latter end of the most recent Conservative government (and since the advent in 1997 of New Labour) was just not politically viable in the early 1980s. One reason was that established power bases were too strong to be challenged, the Labour government's apprehension about HMI influence has been mentioned, but also the LEAs were sufficiently confident to challenge the DES as demonstrated by the example of Tameside who won their battle against comprehensivization in 1976. In addition, by using the MSC (on the outside), the process of destabilizing the existing system could be effected more easily. The assault was two-pronged, coming overtly from the government through pressure by politicians and less obviously through policy documents issued by the MSC.

In summary, the Conservative, neo-liberal view was that economic and political decision making and social welfare should not be subject to central management, but left to respond naturally to market competition based upon economic individualism and the privatized provision of services. They believed that theory, utopian planning, abstract ideas, generalizations and intellectuals should not be trusted as it was ideologies such as these which led to the damaging educational innovations propagated during the 1960s. In their view such initiatives as 'curriculum reform', 'relevance' and 'child-centred' education had helped to undermine traditional educational values without providing any obvious benefit to the student. They urged the government to learn the harsh lessons of this period and continue to support the principle of a strong paternalistic control promoting a disciplined society, social authoritarianism, hierarchy and subordination. They accepted that individual freedom is important, but stressed that it should be locked into acceptance of government authority.

Activity 11a Neo-Liberal Influences

Reflect on your own experience of education during the last 20 years and comment on how the above neo-liberal views and policies have influenced provision within your own particular context.

11.4 Market economics

Although within the Conservative government the views of the neo-liberal and neo-conservative factions differed on several issues, their positions on education displayed many similarities. Both were concerned with addressing the same key concerns, such as the purpose of education, the design of the curriculum and the control of the providers, e.g. schools, colleges and universities. Each agreed that powerful bureaucratic interest groups, particularly LEAs and teachers, had created a mediocre education system where underachievement and declining standards were commonplace. The Hillgate group (1987) set out to counter this perceived deterioration in educational standards through an aggressive criticism of the progressive and egalitarian views of education and supporting parental choice as a fundamental ingredient in developing an effective education system.

It is important to note that while neo-conservatism was a social doctrine, neo-liberalism was an economic one embedded in the writings of the eighteenth-century classical economist Adam Smith and the modern Austrian economist Friedrich Hayek. The conversion of many Conservative politicians to the political and economic theories of Hayek was to be one of Margaret Thatcher's most significant achievements and ultimately was the driving force of much of the educational change that followed.

Hayek appealed to conservatives because he was critical of socialism, state involvement in social welfare and of economic and social decisions being taken from a collectivist, consensus basis. Hayek had a radical alternative view that the uninhibited workings of the market provided a superior mechanism through which to structure the workings of the state. In his view, economic and political decision making and social welfare should not be subject to central management, but left to respond naturally to market competition based upon economic individualism and the privatized provision of services. Hayek considered collectivist ideas and practices as a threat to freedom and prosperity, and these sentiments were subsequently wholly supported by Thatcher and her government's policies.

Activity 11b Rejection of Collectivism

Thatcher believed that the Second World War had created an environment that encouraged the establishment of 'collectives' and that it took 30 years to reduce their influence. Obviously, she was talking primarily about trade unions, but her notions of 'individual striving' as opposed to collaborative approaches do have real implications for education. Reflect on how these political and economic views are still evident within post-compulsory education today.

Another recurring theme of Hayek's work has been that collectivist social planning is doomed to failure because society is complex and that the 'facts' that planners deal with are not concrete, but are based on human behaviour and relationships, which are unpredictable. As a consequence, in Hayek's view the free market is superior to any kind of planning for such things as full employment, a welfare state, economic targets and redistribution of income. Although Hayek's theories are highly appealing to neo-liberals, they are also fundamentally incompatible with the interventionist tendencies of the neo-conservatives. However, Thatcher managed to unite her party behind Hayek's simple philosophy that:

> the market mechanism is superior to all planning because it works automatically with a beautiful simplicity – if you leave it alone.

Hayek's economic theories are based on a deceptively simple view that we should not interfere with social institutions that have been established over time. His central example of this would be the 'market', which (in Hayek's view) is a perfect mechanism because it responds automatically to the free decisions of individuals. Hayek and his followers were opposed to economic intervention to achieve 'social justice' through a redistribution of wealth. Their key principle was that the financial rewards given to people through the operation of the market are generally a good indicator of their contribution. In other words, the efficient will prosper, while others will not. These theories heavily influenced government policy as the neo-liberals supported the importance of relying upon market forces to determine policies and provision and therefore were suspicious of the state and supported minimal government intervention.

Activity 11c Market Responses

Hayek's theories are based on a view that, as many of the variables within the economy are unpredictable and cannot be controlled, so market forces should be allowed to manage these influences. However, as we have discussed in earlier chapters, there is also a range of unpredictable variables within every educational situation. Consider how Hayek's theories translate to the classroom, and the appropriateness of educational policies based on these market principles.

One implication of the above policies was that education and other areas of public service were now seen as a commodity to be bought and sold in the marketplace. Another was that curricula within education should stress the importance of free-market ideas such as competition, choice and enterprise. Neo-conservatives, in particular those who belonged to the

Hillgate group, supported an agenda based on elitism, central control of education, a traditional curriculum and cultural heritage, all of which were viewed as crucial to social and economic well-being.

11.5 The reorientation of further education

Meanwhile, the extent of 'educational' initiatives relating to the young unemployed that were being delivered through the Department of Employment had grown rapidly since the creation of the MSC in 1974. By the mid-1980s much of the funding received by Further Education colleges was coming through the DoE. The training of the young was formalized in 1985, when the White Paper 'Education and Training for Young People' (DES 1985) recommended the establishment of the National Council for Vocational Qualifications (NCVQ) to tackle the issue of parity of esteem. The NCVQ's brief was to provide a more coherent and fair award system and they initiated the design of a national framework of vocational qualifications (NVQs). Using newly created Industrial Lead Bodies (which were heavily influenced by employers), the detailed specification of national standards of occupational competence to meet the needs of employees began in earnest (see also Chapter 10).

This framework was designed to support college, training agency and in-company-based training as part of the strategy to reduce both youth unemployment and, perhaps more importantly, the burden on the taxpayer. To this end the use of private managing agents for YTS courses based in the employers' premises, rather than FE colleges, reflected the government's preference for private enterprise and its desire to use the private sector to encourage competition and make college provision more efficient and cost-effective. The use of short-term contracts by the MSC to fund the delivery of YTS courses in further education was also intended to promote efficiency.

Activity 11d Employer Involvement in PCET

These mid-1980s initiatives to pass more responsibility for vocational education to the employers (see also the ERA below) have had variable success during the last two decades. Comment on the employer influence on post-compulsory education and training within your particular educational setting.

The process of centralizing education was finally given full rein in the 1988 Education Reform Act, which gave an unprecedented amount of control (more than 400 additional powers) to the Secretary of State for Education. Speaking against the Bill (introduced by his own party) at its second reading in the Commons, former Prime Minister Edward Heath said

> The Secretary of State has taken more powers under the Bill than any other member of the Cabinet, more than my right honourable friends the Chancellor of the Exchequer, the Secretary of State for Defence and the Secretary of State for Social Services.

The Act transferred polytechnics and major colleges of higher education out of LEA control, proposed financial delegation and self-government for LEA Colleges of Further Education and completely abolished the Inner London Education Authority.

To the government this was removing power from unrepresentative and over-bureaucratic local authorities to make services more responsive to the consumer. Many critics interpreted it as an attempt to increase the power of central government at the expense of democratically elected local councils that have dared to resist the worst excesses of Thatcherism.

The concept of City Technology Colleges (CTCs) 'responsive to the changing demands of adult and working life in an advanced industrial society' was supported. In the schools sector, the National Curriculum for the 5–16 age group was introduced with a core of maths, English and science with foundation subjects of history, geography, technology, music, art and physical education. The Secretary of State was also given the power to shape the foundation subjects by specifying attainment targets, programmes of study and assessment arrangements.

The Local Management of Schools arrangement included in the Act removed decision making from LEA members and officers and delegated it instead to governors and head-teachers. In addition, the Act contained an 'opting out' clause which allowed governors of any maintained secondary school or primary school of over 300 pupils to apply to the Secretary of State to opt out of LEA control and become a centrally funded grant-maintained school. Also 'open enrolment' to secondary schools was introduced which did away with planned admission levels (PALs) and introduced a free-market philosophy allowing parents to seek out the better schools.

On the face of it the 1988 Education Act was dedicated to market philosophy in that it sought to move the control of education from those considered to be the producers (teachers and LEAs) to those considered to be the consumers (parents and employers). Thus the intended outcome was that education should be able to deliver what the customers demands. However, this free-market approach was initiated and controlled by centralist policies concerned with establishing a more coordinated system of education and training designed to meet the challenge of foreign competition. This contradiction subsequently fuelled criticism even from the right of the Conservative party. In particular, the Institute of Economic Affairs expressed concern about educational policies which restrict the freedom of the individual to pursue his or her own ends, and which were introduced by a government acting in a restrictive, anti-market manner.

However, the Educational Reform Act, as radical as it was, didn't see an end to the centralist legislation imposed by the Conservatives. Further double-barrelled, radical legislation introduced in May 1991 marked an even more significant tightening of government control. Michael Howard, the Secretary of State for Employment presented the White Paper 'Education and Training for the 21st Century' following Kenneth Clarke, the Secretary of State for Education and Science, who had earlier presented another White Paper 'Higher Education: A New Framework'. The latter proposed legislation abolished the binary line and established a single framework for higher education that contained universities, polytechnics and colleges of higher education, together with a common funding structure administered by a Higher Education Funding Council. This White Paper emphasized that:

> by the year 2000, the government expects that approaching one in three of all 18–19 year olds will enter higher education.

Although this target was not achieved, the years since the Act have seen a massive expansion of the HE sector involving most HEIs in doubling their student numbers and some achieving three times the intake.

'Education and Training for the 21st Century' (Volumes 1 and 2) proposed the establishment of a 'new' sector of education comprising all colleges of further education and some sixth form colleges, to be under the aegis of a Central Council. Once sixth-form colleges, tertiary and FE colleges had been removed from LEA control by the Act, they went through a process of 'incorporation' that established them as self-managing institutions with a governing board (corporation) under the day-to-day control of a principal (chief executive). The majority of governors were drawn from the local business community and there was no statutory requirement for LEA involvement.

The legislation also proposed the introduction of the General National Vocational Qualification and the Further Education Funding Council was set up to finance the newly independent colleges. Their income was to be dependent on meeting set performance targets relating to recruitment, retention and achievement and if these were not met, the college would face financial penalties. The Secretary of State was given reserve powers to ensure that colleges and schools offer only NVQs to students pursuing vocations options. Colleges within the sector were formula funded using FTEs and performance indicators to arrive at the level of income.

The open enrolment provisions further promoted the notion of 'commodification' in an education 'market' by encouraging parental choice. The per capita funding arrangements meant that schools attracting more pupils received more funding, whereas those with fewer pupils got less.

The creation of grant-maintained schools and city technology colleges also increased parental power, encouraged schools towards market competition and increased the influence of the business community in educational affairs.

Even after Margaret Thatcher was replaced as Prime Minister in November 1990, liberal views on education continued to be influential. Ken Clarke, Major's first Secretary of State, reiterated that choice and competition were necessary to raise standards, a view also supported in his successor's White Paper 'Choice and Diversity' (DES 1992). The Act established Ofsted and privatized inspection teams to replace the HMI system and school league tables were introduced to aid parental choice.

It was also extremely significant that the above two 1991 White Papers were published under the logo of both the DES and the DoE and were presented jointly to the House of Commons by the Secretaries of State for Employment and Education. This strategy heralded the amalgamation of these two departments five years later and clearly confirmed that, in future, the key performance indicators for a successful education system will be full employment and a strong economy.

The 'education utility' principle, that was re-established by Callaghan in 1976 and which infers that there should be a direct correlation between investment in education and the performance of the national economy, now seems to have been firmly accepted by both major political parties.

However, these notions and the related market principles have received much opposition. Lawton (1994) argues that market choice has failed in improving educational standards and sees the market as inappropriate for the education service in principle as well as practice.

> . . . as schooling is compulsory, 'perfect competition' is completely lacking, and there is not even a price mechanism available to regulate supply and demand. It is a rigged market/non-market. We end up with the worst of both worlds – a confused mixture of compulsion and competition, with more demand for choice than can possibly be supplied. In education, the idea of a market is a non-starter; pretending that real choice exists for most parents is dishonest.

The Institute of Public Policy Research (1988) has also offered some very basic and fundamental criticisms of the prevailing view that Britain's future economic prosperity is dependent upon raising standards of reading, writing and arithmetic in schools. Although ministers have set ambitious targets to improve the literacy and numeracy of 11 year olds in the belief that this would lay the groundwork for more effective competition with the tiger economies of the Pacific rim, the IPPR has said that there was no evidence that boosting national attainment in maths or literacy would have any effect on national economic performance:

> What could be a sober and informed debate about English education is in danger of being drowned out by the simplistic and often shrill rhetoric which seems to dominate policy-making in education. Ministers are misled by the 'tyranny' of international league tables . . . but there was no correlation between positions in the international maths league and economic prosperity as measured by GNP per head. Former Eastern bloc countries such as the Czech and Slovak Republics and Bulgaria performed well in maths without reaping an economic dividend.

Activity 11e International League Tables

What is your view of IPPR's response? Do you believe that economic performance is a result of the education which workers receive?

The report went on to state that although the United States and Germany were more economically prosperous, their students were close to England's in maths results and that Britain's growth rate compared reasonably well with other countries at a similar stage of economic development.

Bailey (1989) investigated many aspects of economic utility and identified characteristics of burgeoning 'new vocationalism' which were contradictory and *undemocratic* and, although not always articulated, were nevertheless implicit within the criteria used in the criticism of education. In his view, these criticisms are, more often than not, based on invalid conceptions of the role of education and the implicit view that there is a universally accepted consensus:

> For a pupil to complain that his education is not relevant to the job he wants to do, or fails to equip him to face unemployment, is to assume that education has a proper instrumental purpose that it has failed to fulfil.
>
> For a prime minister to chide the system for failing to produce the scientists and technologists the country needs is to assume that the education system has manpower provision responsibilities that it is neglecting.
>
> For a politician to complain that the education system allows pupils to leave school with unfavourable attitudes towards wealth creation or technological growth or competition is to suggest that these are proper attitudes for an education system to foster.

Bailey believes that running through all the discussion of the economic utility model of education is an unspoken assumption that there is consensus about society, values and education. As an example he quotes a 1982 DES report, which stated:

> It has in recent years become a 'truth universally acknowledged' that education should be more closely linked to the world of work and with the country's economic performance; and there has been increasing pressure on schools to assess the relevance of their curriculum to their pupils' future working lives.

In Bailey's view, this assumed consensus is that of

> continually accepted technological change and development, strangely related to nineteenth-century conceptions of the undoubted good of 'progress', all taking place in the context of competitive free-market economy, and in a wider context of international competitive trade.

Bailey's key point is that these objectives (wealth, competition, technological change, etc.) are perceived as ends in themselves and not as a *means to an end*. He also challenges the notions that promotion of competition and technological advances are necessarily compatible or advantageous. Historically, technological advance has often led to the elimination of skills, and competition the elimination of collaborative development.

Bailey also points out that such is the pace of technological change that vocational training is often out of date by the time the trainee is admitted to the workplace. The more specific the skills, the shorter their useful life.

Also of concern is the shallow nature of the generic skills which are advocated within many vocational programmes. These are seen as often being either hopelessly vague or absolutely trivial. In Bailey's view not only is it impossible to teach skills outside of their particular context, but it is also impossible to define them in abstract or to generalize them. More importantly, Bailey sees the practice of disaggregating knowledge and understanding from the acquisition of skills as undemocratic because

> . . . only knowledge and understanding on a wide base can liberate a person from the particular restrictions of birth, social class and geography. Without such a base any choices are bound to be restricted because of the limited perspective brought to bear on them.

Bailey finishes by making the point that only a liberal education will prepare a person for the necessarily unpredictable and problematic nature of work because such an education provides an introduction to a range of cognitive perspectives and practice in creative thinking and problem solving.

Activity 11f The Importance of a Liberal Education to Working Practice

Do you agree with Bailey that the unpredictable and problematic nature of work needs the range of cognitive perspectives that only a liberal education can provide you with?

Bailey's intellectual argument may be difficult to accept within our current educational context with its predominant skills imperative allied to the urgent need to strengthen our national economy. In this context it may be useful to present an argument which uses familiar economic concepts to demonstrate how ill-informed such familiar notions of the purpose of education actually are.

The Canadian philosopher John McMurtry (1991) identified important goals, motivations, methods and quality processes which both education and the market have in common. His simple but insightful analysis of the underlying conflict between the basic principles of these two important national policies (which are often seen as being compatible) does provide us with some extremely valuable evidence of our folly in assuming that education should naturally be a servant of the economy. His contrasting findings are summarized in Table 11.1 below.

Table 11.1 John McMurtry's summary of the incompatibility of educational and market principles

Process	Principles	
	The market is about:	**Education is concerned to:**
Goals	maximizing private money profits.	advance and disseminate shared knowledge.
Motivations	satisfying whoever has the money to purchase the goods that are wanted.	develop sound understanding whether it is wanted or not.
Methods	buying and selling the goods it has to offer to anyone for whatever price that can be achieved.	never buy or sell the item it has to offer, but to require of all who would have it that they fulfil its requirements autonomously.
Quality	**Excellence can be measured by:** a. how well a product is made. b. how problem-free the product is and remains.	**Excellence can be measured by:** a. how disinterested and impartial its representations are. b. how deep and broad the problems it poses are to the one who receives it.

Activity 11g Education and the Market

Reflect on the relevance of McMurtry's views on market approaches and the relationship of education to the national economy with particular reference to your own educational situation.

Of course, the crucial implication of McMurtry's analysis is that, although teaching may be treated as a 'commodity', you cannot buy or sell *learning*. Equally important in this analysis is the fact that the creation of knowledge and its dissemination (the traditional purpose of education) is in direct opposition to the market principle that success within a competitive environment is dependent upon the 'ownership' and the *restricted distribution* of knowledge.

11.6 Tensions within PCET

During the 1990s, the government's strategy for further education was designed to increase student numbers, while simultaneously lowering funding costs. Indeed, from 1993 to 1998 student numbers in FE did increase by a third, and Smithers and Robinson (2000) note that during the same period funding in real terms *fell by 21 per cent*. As was inevitable under such a scenario, college managers were faced with extremely difficult decisions, some of which challenged their concepts of good professional practice, both in terms of educational processes and staff management. However, in order to survive within this demanding environment it has been necessary for college managers to respond quickly and effectively to the continuously imposed, central control mechanisms that have been implemented by succeeding governments. As a consequence, most post-compulsory educational organizations have had to resort to a more hierarchical management style, which has often been fairly aggressive in the way it has operated and in its relationship with staff.

As labour costs usually represent the largest outgoings of any service organization (especially in the public sector), a drive by management to promote 'greater efficiency' in order to minimize costs and maximize income became inevitable. College managers, encouraged by the College Employers' Forum (CEF) sought to replace the 'silver book' conditions for staff with college contracts that would allow for the greater 'productivity' by increasing teaching hours, reducing holiday entitlement and removing reduced class contact (RCC). Some colleges have also introduced bars within their salary scales and have replaced lecturers with assessors and facilitators on lower levels of pay and the current breadth of the LLUK Standards still reflect the numbers of 'support staff' who do not have a full teacher's role. 'Efficiency gains' have also been achieved through a general move across the sector towards 'Casualization', which has seen a decrease in the number of full-time salaried teaching staff, accompanied by a commensurate increase in hourly paid staff. In some cases these staff are employed by 'agencies'.

The ways in which learning is delivered have also allowed managers to make savings, for example a greater use of 'flexi-learning', often managed by less qualified personnel, has made possible significant reductions in class contact hours. As you would expect, all of the above management initiatives designed to enable survival under incorporation have inevitably led to claims of de-professionalization and de-skilling.

Activity 11h Changes in Employment Practice

Discuss the current relationship between management and teachers within your own situation and how this affects teaching and learner support.

Analysis by many writers including Longhurst (1996) confirmed that the market principles, together with the incorporation processes were creating antagonistic relationships between college teaching staff and managers:

> . . . the relationship between senior management and teaching staff in colleges is now one of exploitation. This is just as surely the case as in a business firm where the profits of shareholders and the large salaries of senior managers are obtained by paying other employees less that the value of the commodities they produce.

Sir William Stubbs (then plain Bill Stubbs) who was Chief Executive of the Further Education Funding Council (FEFC) had warned that the incorporation process would provide further education college managers with the opportunity to either prosper or go bankrupt and the year on year reduction in the unit of funding has undoubtedly created severe hardship for many staff and extremely difficult decisions for the executive managers of most institutions.

11.7 The advent of New Labour

Since their success in the 1997 General Election, New Labour have continued with many of the market-led policies established by their Conservative predecessors. Their justification has been that the power of the global market and their pledge to stay within the previous government's spending plans have left them with little choice but to continue with many of the Tory policies. However, some identifiable 'New Labour' policies did also emerge during the early years of government. Perhaps their most notable concern, which has immediate relevance for the post-compulsory sector, is their focus on the education of the less academic 14–19 year olds, which has been a significant educational issue with various governments since the 1960s.

While in opposition in 1996, David Blunkett, the New Labour minister, acknowledged and to some extent supported Dearing's (1996) report 'Review of Qualifications for 16–19 year olds' which identified a number of themes (i.e. low participation and achievement rates, high drop-out rates, variable standards and limited scope for broadly-based curriculum and study). Once in office, New Labour published Qualifying for Success (DfEE 1997) that built on the agenda established by Dearing and aimed to raise and widen levels of participation, retention and achievement. However, New Labour's social democratic values were evident here in their expressed intent to combat social exclusion and disaffection. Other New Labour themes, which became evident towards the millennium, were:

- social cohesion
- economic competitiveness
- up-skilling
- partnership
- widening participation
- lifelong learning.

Within three months of taking office, the £3.5 billion New Deal scheme was launched to address the continuing problem of the young unemployed (i.e. 18–24 year olds) with the Investing in Young People Strategy (IiYP) outlined in 'The Learning Age: a Renaissance for a New Britain' (DfEE 1998a). This Green Paper is aimed at increasing the number of young people achieving at qualification framework Level 2 and to ensure that all young people have the skills necessary for lifelong learning and employability.

The above paper makes clear New Labour's emphasis on the use of education and training to get people off welfare and into work and it is also evident that further education has a major role to play in helping to deliver the new government's intentions. A high profile is given to New Labour's twin aims of tackling social exclusion and up-skilling (in order to make Britain more competitive) in the significant White Paper 'Further Education for the New Millennium' (DfEE 1998b):

> The report sets out a radical vision to engage and draw back into learning those who have traditionally not taken advantage of educational opportunities – in particular, those with no or inadequate qualifications. For these people, continuing or returning to learning offers the prospect of breaking out of the cycle of economic and social exclusion.

It is also clear that the government is unhappy with the level of petty competition which existed between many colleges when they took office. Within the above paper they are urging the redevelopment of partnerships in order to achieve its defined goals and offering an implicit criticism of the wasteful Conservative reliance on competitive, market-led strategies as a means of deliberately deterring any collaboration between providers:

> We are also placing a new emphasis on partnerships within the sector, to reduce waste caused by unnecessary competition and to ensure that the sector is better placed to meet future challenges.
>
> (*ibid.*)

Activity 11i Reducing Competition

Reflect on the levels of competition and cooperation which you have experienced in your particular post-compulsory educational context and the effect these influences might have on the development and provision of teaching and learning.

However, despite New Labour's criticism of the aggressive managerialist approaches which had been encouraged by the previous administration, there has been no hint of them moving away from the outcomes-based funding and inspection procedures which have caused so much stress within colleges. Although FE funding has increased since 1997, additional money has to be 'something for something'. For example, links have to be made to raising standards, widening participation, etc., and as Smithers and Robinson have pointed out, even where improved funding is based on anticipated increases in student numbers, an efficiency gain of 1–2 per cent per year is still expected.

In order to promote further social cohesion, New Labour established a Social Exclusion Unit directly accountable to Tony Blair, then Prime Minister. The unit published their report 'Bridging the Gap: New Opportunities for 16–18 year olds not in Education, Employment or Training' (July 1999), which reported that the most potent indicator of unemployment at 21 is non-participation for six months or more between the ages of 16 and 18. A White Paper published the same year, 'Learning to Succeed: A New Framework for Post-16 Learning' (DfEE 1999) follows up this aim of persuading young people to stay in education or training until at least 18 years of age.

Tackling low education levels has always been a concern for the political left in its quest for a more egalitarian society. New Labour recognize that a lack of basic skills in numeracy and literacy has marginalized a section of society, reinforced social exclusion and has had a negative impact on the UK's competitiveness. Their policy and legislative output since coming to office has undoubtedly taken a different direction to the previous government, a change which has been positively welcomed even by some groups critical of New Labour inertia in post-compulsory education.

> NATFHE (2002) strongly support lifelong learning and the government's agenda for the new learning and skills sector – so vital to a thriving economy and inclusive and participative society.

The current government has moved away from the Tories' market-led policies to a more marked reliance on strategic planning, especially at the regional level through the Learning and Skills Councils. This more collaborative strategy, linked to a greater commitment to lifelong learning and social inclusion, represents the clearest departure from the Conservative approach. Even so, after ten years in office, many commentators are wondering whether New Labour reforms within PCET have been sufficiently robust.

Colleges are still incorporated, there has not been a departure from the policy of funding convergence, there is still widespread Casualization, there are no national conditions of service or agreed annual salary reviews for staff working in the sector. Although additional money has been provided (usually dependent on colleges meeting certain government targets) there has been little in terms of structural change. The real challenge is to reform the funding system, provide a better infrastructure and significantly improve resources in the sector.

Supporters of the government's approach would point out that the pace of change has been slow because of the problems inherited from 18 years of Tory rule, such as social exclusion and chronic underfunding. Also, trying to effect cultural change in the drive to make lifelong learning an integral part of the education system is a long-term strategy rather than a short-term aim.

11.8 Towards a 14–19 framework

However, there is definite evidence within the DfES of a will to establish equivalence of salaries and transferability of staff between the post-compulsory and compulsory sectors. This development will, of course, be expensive (as currently, further education staff are paid much less than their primary and secondary counterparts) and will certainly depend on how well PCET responds to the continuing government awareness that reforms are necessary, which since New Labour's successful re-election in 2005 has been disappointingly allied to confused strategies and often characterized by an unwillingness to take the steps necessary to reform the education and training of 14–19 year olds, which their own investigations have made abundantly clear.

In February 2002, Estelle Morris (the then Secretary of State) pointed out in her introduction to New Labour's consultation document '14–19: Extending Opportunities, Raising Standards', that at the end of 2000, only three out of four 16 to 18 year olds in England were in education and training, which was well below European and OECD average. Also, in 2001, around 5 per cent of young people did not get any GCSEs at all, and although the proportion of Year 11 students gaining five or more A to C grades at GCSE had risen dramatically since the early 1990s, it still remained at only around 50 per cent of the cohort. Perhaps what was more worrying was the fact that only 20 per cent of young people from the lower socio-economic groups go on to some form of higher education, as compared to 70 per cent from the higher socio-economic groups.

These figures are particularly significant when set against New Labour's much-publicized intention to increase and broaden participation in higher education so that (by 2010) 50 per cent of young people aged between 18 and 30 will go on to university, with access widened in particular for those whose families have no previous experience of higher education.

The authors of the Green Paper pointed out that there are many conflicting pressures on young people aged between 14 and 19 and that the price of disengagement from learning is often lifelong failure. Young people may be more autonomous and independent than were their parents and grandparents and consequently seem to demand more from their education and training. There is much evidence that they are prepared to reject what they do not like and what does not meet their immediate requirements. However, they can also find the world and their role in it more complex and confusing.

As we have pointed out in earlier chapters, between the ages of 14 and 19, young people are striving to develop and make sense of their personal, sexual and social identities. They are often demanding and assertive, and yet, because they lack self-confidence, they need our support and guidance to help them take advantage of their educational opportunities (see chapters 7 and 9). In addition, it has been shown by Hodkinson *et al.* (1996) that, despite the presence of alternative routes, once they have officially left school, young people are unlikely to change paths, and this reluctance is exacerbated by class perceptions and influences.

However, even in the face of confusing government policy, the sector has continued to develop and in particular to respond to the needs of local communities. As Smithers and Robinson (2000) point out, in many ways PCET has relished the freedom provided by incorporation, in fact

> . . . colleges currently provide for nearly 4 million students compared with 2.9 million when the sector was born. With the inclusion of the sixth-form colleges the sector now has more A level students than the schools . . . [and] continues to be the main provider for adults with 15 per cent growth over five years . . . the colleges now have more degree students than did the universities at the time of the landmark Robbins Report in 1963.

At the time of the above résumé by Smithers and Robinson, post-compulsory education was based around two major routes to qualification. On the one hand there were *vocational qualifications* (NVQs, GNVQs and Modern Apprenticeships) and on the other hand were *academic qualifications* based around A levels. This bi-partite approach had persisted even though it had been clear to practitioners that it was creating a significant academic/vocational divide. However, the 'gold-standard' of A levels remained a useful basis for selection for employers, university admission tutors and, perhaps more importantly, aspiring parents.

However, for many years there had been considerable pressure to develop a British version of the European Baccalaureate, most notably by the Further Education Unit (1983) and the London Institute for Education through the work of Hodgson and Spours (2000) and their colleagues. However, a supposed step towards this goal was to end in an embarrassing failure. Curriculum 2000 introduced Advanced Certificates in Vocational Education (ACVEs) to replace GNVQs, and this was married to a modularization of A levels to allow Advanced Subsidiary (AS) and A2 examinations, which could be combined to form A levels. To many practitioners it was so clear from the outset that the relatively easy AS level was not equivalent to half an A level and they were amazed that it should be treated as such. In their view, the AS was probably 40 per cent of an A level, and the A2 was about 60 per cent. Seizing the opportunity, many tutors encouraged students to take extra AS levels in the hope of easing their progression to university. The upshot of this confusion became evident at the time of the A-level results in 2002 when it was alleged that, in order to maintain parity of standards, the Qualifications Curriculum Authority Chief Executive personally intervened to *increase* the number of marks needed for any given grade in the A2-level examinations. Initially, there were protests from the schools where hundreds of students had been affected despite reassurances from Sir William Stubbs the QCA's chairman, that the examination was valid. The Education Secretary, Estelle Morris, appointed Mike Tomlinson to investigate the affair. He eventually found that the faults in the process could have led to an increase in the proportion of candidates gaining A levels and she later removed Sir William from his post. As expected, Stubbs blamed Morris and her Junior Minister, David Miliband, and a few weeks later Estelle Morris resigned. Eventually, it was accepted by Charles Clarke, the new Education Secretary, that a review of A levels was imperative, and Mike Tomlinson was asked to undertake what has proved to be a thankless task.

Tomlinson's review of the qualifications framework addressed the following issues:

- overcoming disengagement by young learners
- identifying the important skills and attributes which should be developed by the system
- improving the quality of learning
- promoting effective learner choice
- facilitating progression
- enhancing vocational education
- improving employer engagement.

In his eventual report, even Tomlinson, an extremely experienced educationalist, was surprised at demands which the examination and accountability processes were creating, in that there was an

> excessive burden on learners, teachers, institutions and awarding bodies from the number of examinations which many young people now take, the increasing number of examination entries and the administrative and other arrangements which support the examinations system.

The response within post-compulsory education to Tomlinson's eventual report after substantial consultation and development was mostly positive. He had indeed tackled all of the important issues in a considered and bold manner. He proposed a significant development of the 14–19 sector qualifications to allow a multi-level system of diplomas at four separate levels, which would be Entry, Foundation, Intermediate and Advanced. He suggested that there should be clear progression routes between these levels of 'holistic' learning which would counter the effects of an academic/vocational divide.

Each programme of learning would be built around a common core of study, including a personalized learning project and a focus on practical English and mathematics. Teachers would be responsible for assessments in partnership with the various awarding bodies.

Unfortunately for Tomlinson, the production of his report coincided with the 2005 General Election and almost on the eve of voting, Ruth Kelly (having replaced Charles Clarke as the Secretary of State for Education) was seemingly anxious about the effect on New Labour's marginal seats of the abandonment of A levels, and she overturned Tomlinson's potentially historic proposals and instead issued a rather shamefaced statement:

> We will not transform opportunities by abolishing what is good, what works and what is recognised by employers, universities, pupils and parents. We must build on what is good in the system and reform and replace what is not working.

Kelly instead proposed that the new programme for 14–16 year olds would include unit grades for A levels to enable universities to identify high achievers among applicants for places. There will now be a range of diplomas for the 14–19s which further education staff will have to cope with. A comment by David Bell, HMI Chief Inspector at the time of Kelly's intervention, articulates the view of many post-compulsory teachers:

> Continuing with the current GCSE and A level structure carries the risk of continuing the historic divide between academic and vocational courses, which has ill-served too many young people in the past.

Perhaps even more telling were the equally critical views from Stasz *et al.* (2004) of the Learning and Skills Research Centre:

> Issues of structure and implementation seem to be placed on a back burner while the government focuses on targets and accountability. Ironically, perhaps, this review suggests that excessive focus on qualifications may be especially counter-productive for hard-to-reach learners.

On the basis of past and present experience, by their very nature accountability systems inevitably adopt a 'reliability' approach (see Chapter 9) where the need for replication and consistency across the sector does, unfortunately, lead to the use of simplified criteria as the measurable outcomes. However, such crude measures will be significantly more inappropriate when the outcomes, which teachers must define (during their attempts to motivate traditionally reluctant learners), will tend to be short-term and unique to particular students within a specific context. Such bespoke targets have an inherent validity because they are attempting to restructure in a particular way unique and previously damaged self-concepts.

In addition, performance tables invariably lead to the identification of achievement (and underachievement) by not only the institution, but also by the department and the individual. Such strategies stimulate aggressive competition both at an institutional and an individual level, which will often have been one of the reasons why these learners withdrew from an active participation in education in the first place (see also Chapter 7).

The need for a continuation of this accountability burden has not been justified and is simply not appropriate to the very difficult task that lies ahead for PCET and may well discourage both the learner and the teacher. This long-awaited restructured Key Stage 4 had the potential to achieve so much more. As Lawton (2002) pointed out:

> The time has surely come for a clear policy on education based on cooperation not competition, social justice not selfish individualism, excellent schools for all not selection justified in terms of diversity and choice. Only then will it be possible to rely more on professional trust instead of technicist accountability.

Activity 11j Accountability Influences

Consider the above points of view related to targets and performance tables and discuss how they have affected your own teaching and the experience of your learners.

11.9 Conclusion

This chapter has been a brief résumé of changes which have taken place within post-compulsory education during the last 30 years. We have stressed throughout this book that the sector is constantly evolving and that these changes have inevitably created particular stress for both teachers and learners within the PCET/Skills/Lifelong Learning Sector.

The advent of the 14–19 curriculum promises to broaden the role of further education even more, but may also bring with it more stability and recognition for our sector. It is clear that the development of a diversified Key Stage 4 has the potential to provide appropriate progression routes for many different 14–19 learners. We will be faced with developing this diversified provision through the wide range of teaching, learning and support that such a complex and demanding innovation will require.

The twenty-first century promises a continuation of the hugely demanding process of change and innovation which the Lifelong Learning Sector has responded so well to during the last 30 years. However, there is evidence that the important work of 'Skills' (to use our new nickname) will begin to be more appropriately recognized and rewarded.

Activity 11k The 14–19 Dilemma

Write a summary in your PDJ of your views (particularly in terms of the vocational area you are teaching in) of the rejection by the government of Tomlinson's proposed abolition of A levels and the positive comments of the Foster and Leitch reports.

The government has clearly accepted that the Lifelong Learning Sector has an increasingly important role to play and this has been emphatically confirmed by both the Foster and Leitch reports in 2005. However, both warn that the workforce does need to be adequately trained, supported and rewarded if the potential is to be achieved. The attempts by LLUK and Ofsted to drive up the standards of teaching in order to make the compulsory and post-compulsory sectors more equivalent in terms of teacher preparedness have been a substantial response. However, it is clear that the new Professional Standards with their concern for Subject Mentors and 30 days CPD annually are an expensive but necessary step forward. Added to this, post-compulsory education has at last got its own professional body in the Institute for Learning, and this promises to be an ongoing catalyst for professional pride and responsibility long after the Professional Standards have become an accepted underpinning in the development of staff to meet in a rapidly developing area of responsibility, which will be increased further if the intention of raising the school leaving age to 18 is carried through.

It is clear that Gordon Brown has long since been of the view that investment in education has a direct link to the strength of the economy. This echoes the view of Tony Blair who declared on the publication of the White Paper 'Further Education: Raising Skills, Improving Life Chances' in March 2006 that FE should be a 'powerhouse of a high skills economy'.

However, even though Alison Wolf (2002) and other informed commentators do not agree with the simplistic view that there is a clear, quantifiable relationship between the performance of education and the performance of the economy, what is measurable is the significant support which our area of educational provision is at last beginning to receive in order to carry through the huge task that is needed in terms of vocational training.

11.10 Useful publications

Dale, R. (1989), *The State and Education Policy*. Buckingham: Open University Press.
Although this text is dated, Roger Dale's book remains a fine example of an analysis of the influence of government policies in shaping British educational provision. A critical introduction by Michael Apple provides an insight into how ideological stances affect objective decision making and shape policy.

Hyland, T. and B. Merrill (2003), *The Changing Face of Further Education*. London: Routledge Falmer.
Terry Hyland and Barbara Merrill have written an excellent review of the history of further education which includes an excellent chapter analysing the events which have affected the basic philosophy of the sector as a whole, and aspects of practice in particular.

Hutton, W. (1995), *The State We're In*. London: Random House UK Ltd.
Hutton, W. (1997), *The State to Come*. London: Random House UK Ltd.
In these two examinations of Tory economic policy, Will Hutton provides a searching indictment of the social effects of a free market and globalization and puts forward a strong argument for an alternative economic strategy as a basis for social justice.

Hillier, Y. (2006), *Everything You Need to Know about FE Policy*. London: Continuum International Publishing Group Ltd.
Yvonne Hillier has gathered together an excellent revue of the development of FE policy from 1940 to 2006 and examines in detail several significant reports such as 'Success for All', 'Skills for Life' and the Tomlinson Report.

Lawton, D. (1994), *The Tory Mind on Education 1979–94*. London: The Falmer Press.
As the title implies, Denis Lawton examines the values and beliefs underpinning the educational policies of the Conservative government up until 1994. Although now somewhat dated, it is extremely valuable to be able to understand the origins of many of the policies which were developed by the Tories but are still much in evidence within the present administration.

Matheson, C. and D. Matheson (2000), *Educational Issues in the Learning Age.* London: Continuum International Publishing Group Ltd.

    Catherine and David Matheson have edited a selection of papers which examine the role of education within a rapidly changing world. Education and its influence on culture, identity, society and power are considered within the context of postmodernism and globalization.

Whitty, G. (2002), *Making Sense of Educational Policy.* London: Paul Chapman Publishing.

    This excellent review by Geoff Whitty of education in relation to social theory places the policies of the New Right and New Labour within the context of significant, national educational issues and provides insightful analysis of how the different approaches to managing provision have evolved.

11.11 Useful websites

www.bcuc.ac.uk
www.FEjobs.com
www.into-Teaching.co.uk
www.Questia
www.tes.co.uk
www.tipcet.com

The LLUK Professional Standards

Fred Fawbert

Chapter Outline

Key Concepts

Access and Progression, Assessment Criteria, Credit Accumulation and Transfer, Entitlement, Equality, Examining Body, Experiential Reflections, Full and Associate Teachers, Inclusiveness, Interactive Relationship, Knowledge, Learner Autonomy, Learning Outcomes, Lifelong Learning, LLUK Standards, Mandatory Units, Pedagogy, Personal Development Journal, Post-Compulsory, Practice, Practitioner File, Professional Role, Professional Values and Practice, Professional Standards, Reflective Practice, Scope, Six Domains, Specialist Teaching and Learning, Standards, Subject Knowledge, Subject Specialist Mentor, Teacher Roles, Teacher Related Roles, Threshold Award, Units of Assessment.

12.1 The National Professional Standards Framework

Please note:

1. The LLUK Professional Standards use the description **teacher** as a generic term for teachers, tutors, trainers, lecturers and instructors in the Lifelong Learning Sector.
2. The standards also use the term **Area of Specialism** to represent the professional, vocational or subject area in which the individual has been employed to teach.
3. Not **all** standards will necessarily relate to **all** teaching roles. Rather, these role descriptions provide the basis for the development of contextualized role specifications and related units of assessment. These in turn provide benchmarks for the teacher's performance when carrying out their assigned role within the Lifelong Learning Sector.
4. As mentioned earlier, in this book we refer to **teachers** when we are talking about teacher-trainers, **students** when we are referring to trainee-teachers and **learners** when we are referring to their students.

12.2 Introduction

Following the requirements set out within the 2004 'Success for All' DfES White Paper, LLUK identified specifications, drawn from the overarching standards, for the different types of teaching role performed within the sector. These role specifications are expressed in terms of units of assessment, which clearly set out the learning outcomes and assessment criteria that teachers are expected to achieve. Units will be grouped together to make up named qualifications for specific teacher roles which will be based on rules of combination determined by LLUK. Some units within these qualifications will be mandatory and others optional, to allow for the tailoring of qualifications to suit specific roles. It will be possible for mandatory units to be contextualized, and for qualifications to contain specialist optional elements so that the qualification will be appropriate for a particular situation or role while remaining generic to the sector. Units will be available as stand-alone elements within qualifications or for use in continuing professional development (CPD) purposes, as required. Units will be set at Levels 3, 4 and 5 for most awards, in addition to Levels 6 and 7 for the professional/postgraduate awards.

12.3 The role of the Subject Mentor

One of the most important (and much discussed) requirements of the Professional Standards is that *all* students undertaking the Associate Certificate or the Full Award (Cert. Ed., PGCE or Diploma) *must* be monitored and supported by a *Subject Specialist Mentor* whose role is therefore central to the new developments in teacher education. In addition to generic teaching skills the new teacher needs the mentor to provide:

- constructive feedback on how effectively they get across their specific subject to learners
- an awareness of what is required at different levels of learning
- suggestions about how they can develop and keep up to date their own subject knowledge
- access to resources and materials for delivering their subject
- support in identifying examining body/employer requirements around their particular subject
- the opportunity to reflect on the relevant effectiveness of different ways of delivering specific areas of their subject
- encouragement to explore new information about good practice in their own area.

Both Ofsted and the LLUK have agreed that a weakness of previous teacher education for the sector has been the lack of subject specific expertise and development to guide new students in their chosen approaches, not only in relation to generic teaching, but also in teaching their specialist subject.

It is clearly difficult for teacher educators to be able to offer specific subject-based feedback and guidance to student teachers in relation to the most effective way to introduce their learners to the many subject specific skills and related knowledge during teaching across the whole of the LLS curriculum. The Subject Specialist Mentor will perform a pivotal role in the development of subject teaching and central to this responsibility will be a commitment to inclusive learning and an ability to identify possible barriers to learning and ways of ensuring full access to education for student teachers and their learners. Consequently, it is important that Subject Mentors must not only be experienced in the subject, but also the teaching of it to a range of different students and learners with differing needs. So the twin requirements of effective Subject Mentorship are inevitably, Subject Knowledge and Teaching Expertise and these should be fostered by personal qualities and interests.

The necessary skills for delivering these three areas of expertise are:

1. **Subject Knowledge**
   - a teaching qualification and understanding of Initial Teacher Training courses
   - relevant formal qualifications and relevant industrial/commercial experience
   - relevant background in subject
   - up-to-date knowledge in subject area and knowledge of industry standards
   - able to advise on planning to deliver programmes of learning to individuals and groups.
2. **Teaching Experience**
   - can be broad to include formal teaching/training and informal (e.g. apprenticeship supervision) teaching/training – but – should have included responsibility for planning learning and working in a similar environment to the mentee
   - familiar with the qualifications framework
   - acted as bridge to institutional structures and networks
   - have planned a differentiated learning experience.

3. **Personal Qualities**
   - committed to the initiation and promotion of good learning and teaching/training practice
   - committed to role of mentor and mentee
   - committed to the process of Continuing Professional Development
   - good communicator/listener
   - patient and aware of the needs of someone beginning as a teacher
   - effective organizational skills
   - flexible
   - good role model
   - openness
   - support mentee in identification of own training needs and target-setting
   - be a skilled reflective practitioner and able to share that with mentee
   - show a real commitment to the promotion of equality and inclusion.

12.4 The responsibilities of the mentor

In general the Subject Mentor will oversee the teaching of a number of student teachers in order to confirm that their understanding of their vocational subject and related professional practices is sound. They will carry our some observations, but in general their role is to monitor the development of the students' good practice in all aspects of teaching their subject specialism, and encourage in-depth self-reflection on the part of the student teacher with regard to the subject pedagogical content of the sessions they deliver and manage.

The Subject Mentor will observe some of their mentee's teaching/training sessions and these will be agreed with their teacher education team. The Subject Mentor will also be required to provide written feedback with particular reference to a particular curriculum area. The Subject Mentor will also consider, together with their mentee, the demands of the syllabus and the level and pace of learning. It will also be necessary to negotiate realistic targets with their students, agree areas for improvement, and where possible share such resources as sources of information, guidance and other supportive agencies. Finally, it will be necessary for the Subject Mentor to keep clear records of that student support which has been undertaken and responses and requests for assistance that have been received. They will liaise with the teacher educators to ensure that a holistic approach and support network is available for each student teacher.

12.5 The six domains of the professional standards

The LLUK professional standards for teachers, tutors and trainers in the Lifelong Learning Sector describe, *in generic terms*, the skills, knowledge and attributes required of those who perform the wide variety of teaching and training roles undertaken within the sector with learners and employers. Together, these will identify the components of:

- the Initial Teaching Award (passport to teaching)
- qualifications leading to Qualified Teacher Learning and Skills (QTLS) status
- other intermediate and advanced teaching qualifications.

In addition, there is a significant CPD requirement to be undertaken after certification, as the IfL expects all teachers to undertake at the very least, 30 hours' CPD per year in order to maintain their professional status.

The new overarching professional standards for teachers in the Lifelong Learning Sector are separated into six teaching domains, which are each presented under three major categories.

Table 12.1 The domains of the LLUK standards

Teaching domains:		Category descriptors:	
A	Professional values and practice	Scope	The range of responsibilities.
B	Learning and teaching		
C	Specialist learning and teaching	Knowledge	Depth and breadth of understanding of processes and
D	Planning for learning		practices used to encourage learning.
E	Assessment for learning	Practice	Learning situations capable of being addressed.
F	Access and progression		

The standards relating to each of the above six 'domains' are set out on the following pages. First of all however, it is important to point out that the LLUK Standards have essential differences to the previous FENTO Standards. The Further Education National Training Organisation defined only 26 standards together with detailed criteria which the teacher education providers could interpret to structure awards appropriate to each of the designated teaching stages – Introductory, Intermediate and Certificated. None of the criteria were optional. On the one hand, the LLUK Standards are more *prescriptive* in their specification. They have identified the six *domains* (see Table 12.1 above) which represent the key aspects of practice and then they have defined within these domains a total of no less than 183 different criteria. On the other hand, the whole range of criteria are not necessarily a prerequisite, but are to allow different teacher roles to be articulated and met at differing levels of responsibility within relevant structured teacher awards by drawing as necessary on these domains and their listed required outcomes. Each of the Domain Tables which give detailed specifications are provided below and, as you are aware, we have suggested throughout the book 170 appropriate assessment 'activities' which will help to generate evidence of achievement against most of the standards. This activity-generated evidence should be used in addition to the evidence that will be contained in the Practitioner File and the Personal Development Journal which are discussed later in this chapter (12.13 and 12.14.6). Reference to these activities is given in the right-hand column of the standards below and as you will see, often an activity will provide evidence against more than one standard.

The first domain (Table 12.2) is 'Professional Values and Practice' (below) and these 'overarching' standards are intended to support and inform all the commitments, knowledge and practice set out in the other domains. LLUK stresses that teachers should develop an awareness of these important principles in every situation they work in. Details of the other five domains are given in Tables 12.3 to 12.7 which follow.

12.6 The teacher's role and related qualifications

Because of the need to construct a flexible but clear qualifications framework which is able to accommodate the widely varying roles of teachers within the Lifelong Learning Sector, LLUK has identified *two* distinct teacher roles in the sector beyond the 'Preparing to Teach' initial award. These have been termed **teacher** roles and **teacher-related** roles. Separate qualifications are available for *both* distinct teacher roles:

1. The **teacher role** represents the full range of responsibilities performed by those who are expected to attain the status of Qualified Teacher Learning and Skills (QTLS).
2. The **teacher-related** role involves a *limited* amount of teaching responsibility and will differ between departments as the practitioners develop supporting skills appropriate to their particular context and combine these with elements of teaching. For example, supporting other teachers and trainers by coaching or supporting students in library-based study or practical activity. It is envisaged by LLUK that in the future, as teacher-related roles become more clearly defined through practice, further qualifications appropriate to such roles will be introduced. 'Mini Awards' will also be developed as necessary, to recognize specialist professional activity such as the role of *professional assessor*.

It is also intended that LLUK will work with the Qualifications Curriculum Authority (QCA) in producing the Qualifications and Credit Framework (QCF) that is unit- and credit-based. The DIUS wants the framework to be developed in order to eventually include qualifications for teachers, trainers, managers and support staff across the sector and to facilitate progression and development for staff at all levels. LLUK will ensure that this development articulates across the sector, and facilitates progression within and across sector boundaries.

The new Teacher Qualifications Framework will provide opportunities for credit accumulation and transfer (CAT), which will ensure that prior experience, achievement and qualifications are appropriately recognized by awarding institutions operating within the sector. This will enhance access to teaching and progression opportunities for those who need to take a staged approach to their career development.

Table 12.2 Domain A – standards relating to professional values and practice

Scope: Teachers in the Lifelong Learning Sector value:	Knowledge: Teachers in the Lifelong Learning Sector know and understand:	Practice: Teachers in the Lifelong Learning Sector understand that aspects of professional practice:	Chapter reference to relevant activities:
AS 1 learners, their progress and development, their learning goals and aspirations and the experience they bring to their learning.	AK 1.1 what motivates learners to learn and the importance of learners' experience and aspirations.	AP 1.1 encourage the development and progression of all learners through recognizing, valuing and responding to individual motivation, experience and aspirations.	1b, 5d–u, 6a–g, 6k, 6l, 6o, 8b, 8c, 8e, 8i, 9b, 9c, 9e, 9f, 9g, 9h, 9i, 9k, 9l, 9m, 10a–t, 11a–c, 11d–k.
AS 2 learning, its potential to benefit people emotionally, intellectually, socially and economically, and its contribution to community sustainability.	AK 2.1 ways in which learning has the potential to change lives.	AP 2.1 use opportunities to highlight the potential for learning to positively transform lives and contribute to effective citizenship.	
AS 3 equality, diversity and inclusion in relation to learners, the workforce, and the community.	AK 2.2 ways in which learning promotes the emotional, intellectual, social and economic well-being of individuals and the population as a whole.	AP 2.2 encourage learners to recognize and reflect on ways in which learning can empower them as individuals and make a difference in their communities.	
AS 4 reflection and evaluation of their own practice and their continuing professional development at teachers.	AK 3.1 issues of equality, diversity and inclusion.	AP 3.1 apply principles to evaluate and develop own practice in promoting equality and inclusive learning and engaging with diversity.	
AS 5 collaboration with other individuals, groups and/or organizations with a legitimate interest in the progress and development of the learners.	AK 4.1 principles, frameworks and theories which underpin good practice in learning and teaching.	AP 4.1 use relevant theories of learning to support the development of practice in learning and teaching.	

AS 6 teachers in the Lifelong Learning Sector are committed to the application of agreed codes of practice and the maintenance of a safe environment.

AS 7 teachers in the Lifelong Learning Sector are committed to improving the quality of their practice.

AK 4.2 the impact of own practice on individuals and their learning.

AK 4.3 ways to reflect, evaluate and use research to develop own practice, and to share good practice with others.

AK 5.1 ways to communicate and collaborate with colleagues and/or others to enhance learners' experience.

AK 5.2 the need for confidentiality, respect and trust in communicating with others about learners.

AK 6.1 relevant statutory requirements and codes of practice.

AK 6.2 ways to apply relevant statutory requirements and the underpinning principles.

AK 7.1 organizational systems and processes for recording learner information.

AK 7.2 their own role in the quality cycle.

AK 7.3 ways to implement improvements based on feedback received.

AP 4.2 reflect on and demonstrate commitment to improvement of own personal and teaching skills through regular evaluation and use of feedback.

AP 4.3 share good practice with others and engage in continuing professional development through reflection, evaluation and the appropriate use of research.

AP 5.1 communicate and collaborate with colleagues and/or others, within and outside the organization, to enhance learners' experience.

AP 5.2 communicate information and feedback about learners to others with a legitimate interest, appropriately and in a manner which encourages trust between those communicating and respects confidentiality where necessary.

AP 6.1 conform to statutory requirements and apply codes of practice.

AP 6.2 demonstrate good practice through maintaining a learning environment which conforms to statutory requirements and promotes equality, including appropriate consideration of the needs of children, young people and vulnerable adults.

AP 7.1 keep accurate records which contribute to organizational procedures.

AP 7.2 evaluate own contribution to the organization's quality cycle.

AP 7.3 use feedback to develop own practice within the organization's systems.

Table 12.3 Domain B – standards relating to learning and teaching

Scope: Teachers in the Lifelong Learning Sector know and understand (Scope targets from Domain A) plus BS commitments added below and are committed to:	Knowledge: Teachers in the Lifelong Learning Sector know and understand:	Practice: Teachers in the Lifelong Learning Sector understand that aspects of professional practice:	Chapter reference to relevant activities:
BS 1 maintaining an inclusive, equitable and motivating learning environment.	BK 1.1 ways to maintain a learning environment in which learners feel safe and supported.	BP 1.1 establish and maintain a purposeful learning environment where learners feel safe, secure, confident and valued.	2a–f, 2h–j, 3b, 3c–f, 3i, 3j, 3o, 3r–v, 5a–f, 5l–m, 6a–b, 6d–e, 6g, 6i, 6j, 6m–q, 7c, 7f, 7h, 8l, 9a, 9d–e.
BS 2 applying and developing own professional skills to enable learners to achieve their goals.	BK 1.2 ways to develop and manage behaviours which promote respect for and between others and create an equitable and inclusive learning environment.	BP 1.2 establish and maintain procedures with learners which promote and maintain appropriate behaviour, communication and respect for others, while challenging discriminatory behaviour and attitudes.	
BS 3 communicating effectively and appropriately with learners to enhance learning.	BK 1.3 ways of creating a motivating learning environment.	BP 1.3 create a motivating environment which encourages learners to reflect on, evaluate and make decisions about their learning.	
BS 4 collaboration with colleagues to support the needs of learners.	BK 2.1 principles of learning and ways to provide learning activities to meet curriculum requirements and the needs of all learners.	BP 2.1 provide learning activities which meet curriculum requirements and the needs of all learners.	
BS 5 using a range of learning resources to support learners.	BK 2.2 ways to engage, motivate and encourage active participation of learners and learner independence.	BP 2.2 use a range of effective and appropriate teaching and learning techniques to engage and motivate learners and encourage independence.	
	BK 2.3 the relevance of learning approaches, preferences and skills to learner progress.	BP 2.3 implement learning activities which develop the skills and approaches of all learners and promote learner autonomy.	

BK 2.4 flexible delivery of learning, including open and distance learning and online learning.

BK 2.5 ways of using learners' own experiences as a foundation for learning.

BK 2.6 ways to evaluate own practice in terms of efficiency and effectiveness.

BK 2.7 ways in which mentoring and/or coaching can support the development of professional skills and knowledge.

BK 3.1 effective and appropriate use of different forms of communication informed by relevant theories and principles.

BK 3.2 a range of listening and questioning techniques to support learning.

AK 7.2 their own role in the quality cycle.

AK 7.3 ways to implement improvements based on feedback received.

AP 4.3 share good practice with others and engage in continuing professional development through reflection, evaluation and the appropriate use of research.

AP 5.1 communicate and collaborate with colleagues and/or others, within and outside the organization, to enhance learners' experience.

AP 5.2 communicate information and feedback about learners to others with a legitimate interest, appropriately and in a manner which encourages trust between those communicating and respects confidentiality where necessary.

AP 6.1 conform to statutory requirements and apply codes of practice.

AP 6.2 demonstrate good practice through maintaining a learning environment which conforms to statutory requirements and promotes equality, including appropriate consideration of the needs of children, young people and vulnerable adults.

AP 7.1 keep accurate records which contribute to organizational procedures.

AP 7.2 evaluate own contribution to the organization's quality cycle.

AP 7.3 use feedback to develop own practice within the organization's systems.

Table 12.4 Domain C – Specialist learning and teaching

Scope: Teachers in the Lifelong Learning Sector know and understand (Scope targets from Domain A) plus CS commitments added below *and are committed to:*	Knowledge: Teachers in the Lifelong Learning Sector know and understand:	Practice: Teachers in the Lifelong Learning Sector understand that aspects of professional practice:	Chapter reference to relevant activities:
CS 1 understanding and keeping up to date with current knowledge in respect of own specialist area.	CK1.1 own specialist area including current developments.	CP 1.1 ensure that knowledge of own specialist area is current and appropriate to the teaching context.	2b–e, 2g, 2h, 3a, 3c, 3d, 3e, 3f, 3h–n, 3q–s, 3u, 3x, 5n, 5o, 5r, 6e, 6f, 6i, 6j, 6l, 6m, 6n, 6p, 7i, 7k, 9h, 9j.
	CK 1.2 ways in which own specialism relates to the wider social, economic and environmental context.	CP 1.2 provide opportunities for learners to understand how the specialist area relates to the wider social, economic and environmental context.	
CS 2 enthusing and motivating learners in own specialist area.	CK 2.1 ways to convey enthusiasm for own specialist area to learners.	CP 2.1 implement appropriate and innovative ways to enthuse and motivate learners about own specialist area.	
CS 3 fulfilling the statutory responsibilities associated with own specialist area of teaching.	CK 3.1 teaching and learning theories and strategies relevant to own specialist area.	CP 3.1 apply appropriate strategies and theories of teaching and learning to own specialist area.	
CS 4 developing good practice in teaching own specialist area.	CK 3.2 ways to identify individual learning in own specialist area.	CP 3.2 work with learners to address particular individual learning needs and overcome identified barriers to learning.	
BS 5 using a range of learning resources to support learners.	CK 3.3 the different ways in which language, literacy and numeracy skills are integral to learners' achievement in own specialist area.	CP 3.3 work with colleagues with relevant learner expertise to identify and address literacy, language and numeracy development in own specialist area.	

CK 3.4 the language, literacy and numeracy skills required to support own specialist teaching.

CK 3.5 ways to support learners in the use of new and emerging technologies in own specialist area.

CK 4.1 ways to keep up to date with developments in teaching in own specialist area.

CK 4.2 potential transferable skills and employment opportunities relating to own specialist area.

CP 3.4 ensure own personal skills in literacy, language and numeracy are appropriate for the effective support of learners.

CP 3.5 make appropriate use of, and promote the benefits of, new and emerging technologies.

CP 4.1 access sources for professional development in own specialist area.

CP 4.2 work with learners to identify the transferable skills they are developing, and how these might relate to employment opportunities.

Table 12.5 Domain D – Standards relating to planning for learning

Scope: Teachers in the Lifelong Learning Sector know and understand (Scope targets from Domain A) plus DS commitments added below *and are committed to:*	Knowledge: Teachers in the Lifelong Learning Sector know and understand:	Practice: Teachers in the Lifelong Learning Sector understand that aspects of professional practice:	Chapter reference to relevant activities:
DS 1 planning to promote equality, support diversity and to meet the aims and learning needs of learners.	DK 1.1 how to plan appropriate, effective, coherent and inclusive learning programmes that promote equality and engage with diversity.	DP 1.1 plan coherent and inclusive learning programmes that meet learners' needs and curriculum requirements, promote equality and engage with diversity effectively.	1a, 3f, 3h, 3l, 3m, 3n, 3p, 3q, 3r, 3t, 3u, 3w, 3x, 4a–v, 5h–k, 5s–v, 6a, 6i, 6j, 6o, 6p.
DS 2 learner participation in the planning of learning.	DK 1.2 how to plan a teaching session.	DP 1.2 plan teaching sessions which meet the aims and needs of individual learners and groups, using a variety of resources, including new and emerging technologies.	
DS 3 evaluation of own effectiveness in planning learning.	DK 1.3 strategies for flexibility in planning and delivery.	DP 1.3 prepare flexible learning session plans to adjust to the individual needs of learners.	
	DK 2.1 the importance of including learners in the planning process.	DP 2.1 plan for opportunities for learner feedback to inform planning and practice.	
	DK 2.2 ways to negotiate appropriate individual goals with learners.	DP 2.2 negotiate and record appropriate learning goals and strategies with learners.	
	DK 3.1 ways to evaluate own role and performance in planning learning.	DP 3.1 evaluate the success of planned learning activities.	
	DK 3.2 ways to evaluate own role and performance as a member of a team in planning learning.	DP 3.2 evaluate the effectiveness of own contributions to planning as a member of a team.	

Table 12.6 Domain E – Standards relating to assessment for learning

Scope: Teachers in the Lifelong Learning Sector know and understand (Scope targets from Domain A) plus ES commitments added below and are committed to:	Knowledge: Teachers in the Lifelong Learning Sector know and understand:	Practice: Teachers in the Lifelong Learning Sector understand that aspects of professional practice:	Chapter reference to relevant activities:
ES 1 designing and using assessment as a tool for learning and progression.	EK 1.1 theories and principles of assessment and the application of different forms of assessment, including initial, formative and summative assessment in teaching and learning.	EP1.1 use appropriate forms of assessment and evaluate their effectiveness in producing information useful to the teacher and the learner.	3l, 5o, 5p, 8a–j, 8m–p.
ES 2 assessing the work of learners in a fair and equitable manner.	EK 1.2 ways to devise, select, use and appraise assessment tools, including, where appropriate, those which exploit new and emerging technologies.	EP 1.2 devise, select, use and appraise assessment tools, including, where appropriate, those which exploit new and emerging technologies.	
ES 3 learner involvement and shared responsibility in the assessment process.	EK 1.3 ways to develop, establish and promote peer and self-assessment.	EP 1.3 develop, establish and promote peer and self-assessment as a tool for learning and progression.	
ES 4 using feedback as a tool for learning and progression.	EK 2.1 issues of equality and diversity in assessment.	EP 2.1 apply appropriate methods of assessment fairly and effectively.	
ES 5 working within the systems and quality requirements of the organization in relation to assessment and monitoring of learner progress.	EK 2.2 concepts of validity, reliability and sufficiency in assessment.	EP 2.2 apply appropriate assessment methods to produce valid, reliable and sufficient evidence.	
	EK 2.3 the principles of assessment design in relation to own specialist area.	EP 2.3 design appropriate assessment activities for own specialist area.	
	EK 2.4 how to work as part of a team to establish equitable assessment processes	EP 2.4 collaborate with others, as appropriate, to promote equity and consistency in assessment processes.	

(Continued)

Table 12.6—cont'd.

Scope: Teachers in the Lifelong Learning Sector know and understand (Scope targets from Domain A) plus ES commitments added below and are committed to:	Knowledge: Teachers in the Lifelong Learning Sector know and understand:	Practice: Teachers in the Lifelong Learning Sector understand that aspects of professional practice:	Chapter reference to relevant activities:
	EK 3.1 ways to establish learner involvement in and personal responsibility for assessment of their learning.	EP 3.1 ensure that learners understand, are involved and share in responsibility for assessment of their learning.	
	EK 3.2 ways to ensure access to assessment within a learning programme.	EP 3.2 ensure that access to assessment is appropriate to learner need.	
	EK 4.1 the role of feedback and questioning in assessment for learning.	EP 4.1 use assessment information to promote learning through questioning and constructive feedback, and involve learners in feedback activities.	
	EK 4.2 the role of feedback in effective evaluation and improvement of own assessment skills.	EP 4.2 use feedback to evaluate and improve own skills in assessment.	
	EK 5.1 the role of assessment and associated organizational procedures in relation to the quality cycle.	EP 5.1 contribute to the organization's quality cycle by producing accurate and standardized assessment information, and keeping appropriate records of assessment decisions and learners' progress.	
	EK 5.2 the assessment requirements of individual learning programmes and procedures for conducting and recording internal and/or external assessments.	EP 5.2 conduct and record assessments which adhere to the particular requirements of individual learning programmes and, where appropriate, external bodies.	
	EK 5.3 the necessary/appropriate assessment information to communicate to others who have a legitimate interest in learner achievement.	EP 5.5 communicate relevant assessment information to those with a legitimate interest in learner achievement, as necessary/appropriate.	

Table 12.7 Domain F – Standards relating to access and progression

Scope: Teachers in the Lifelong Learning Sector know and understand (Scope targets from Domain A) plus FS commitments added below and are committed to:	Knowledge: Teachers in the Lifelong Learning Sector know and understand:	Practice: Teachers in the Lifelong Learning Sector understand that aspects of professional practice:	Chapter reference to relevant activities:
FS 1 encouraging learners to seek initial and further learning opportunities and to use services within the organization.	FK 1.1 sources of information, advice, guidance and support to which learners might be referred.	FP 1.1 refer learners to information on potential current and future learning opportunities and appropriate specialist support services.	5d–h, 5q, 5r, 7a–l, 8e, 8i–p.
FS 2 providing support for learners within the boundaries of the teacher role.	FK 1.2 internal services which learners might access.	FP 1.2 provide learners with appropriate information about the organization and its facilities, and encourage learners to use the organization's services, as appropriate.	
FS 3 maintaining own professional knowledge in order to provide information on opportunities for progression in own specialist area.	FK 2.1 boundaries of own role in supporting learners.	FP 2.1 provide effective learning support, within the boundaries of the teaching role.	
FS 4 a multi-agency approach to supporting development and progression opportunities for learners.	FK 3.1 progression and career opportunities within own specialist area.	FP 3.1 provide general and current information about potential education, training and/or career opportunities in relation to own specialist area.	
	FK 4.1 professional specialist services available to learners and how to access them.	FP 4.1 provide general and current information about a range of relevant external services.	
	FK 4.2 processes for liaison with colleagues and other professionals to provide effective guidance and support for learners.	FP 4.2 work with colleagues to provide guidance and support for learners.	

12.7 LLUK awards and levels

Based around the above standards, LLUK have defined three stages or levels of their teacher qualifications. These are detailed below, together with a fourth which some HE institutions will add in order to continue with their previous provision, and some HEIs will be allowed to offer the first three stages at Level 3 (see also Sections 12.8 to 12.11 below).

Table 12.8 Lifelong Learning Sector awards

	HE credits	Level
Threshold Certificate: 'Preparing to Teach in the Lifelong Learning Sector' (PTLLS) is seen as a 'probationary' tool in the first year of teaching.	6	HE1/NQF4
Associate Award: 'Certificate in Teaching in the Lifelong Learning Sector'.	24	HE1/NQF4
Full Certificate/Diploma: 'Certificate in Education' or 'Diploma in Education' (LL Sector).	120	HE2/NQF4/5
Graduate Award: 'Postgraduate Cert. Ed.' or 'Professional Certificate in Education.	140	HE1/2/3/4/NQ6/7

However, it is important to point out that the above stages do not necessarily relate to length of service or the amount of teaching hours that are currently being undertaken. Our understanding of the LLUK Standards is that the level of achievement that it is necessary for a particular practitioner to attain will relate very much to that teacher's role. For example, a teacher may be full-time and have a fairly limited role that could be met by a Threshold qualification, while a part-time teacher may have a more substantial role that would require the acquisition of the Full Professional award. (See also the teacher-related role in 12.6 above.) **Note:** To gain a *LLUK endorsed* award, teaching practice must be *within a LLUK context.* Your line manager would be the appropriate person to consult about target levels and practice contexts.

In order for this programme to provide the maximum flexibility, the above LLUK Standards will form the basis of a '*spiral*' curriculum where the same elements may be visited during each of the stages: Threshold, Associate and Full Certification, each time with a more demanding level of study. The use of the *same* LLUK Domain specifications for all three stages of the programme within a spiral approach does require that the performance and knowledge criteria must *differentiate* between the stages. The outcomes for each of the defined awards are given in Sections 12.9, 12.10 and 12.11 below. We are therefore concentrating on a simple hierarchy of skills and understandings within the *Threshold* and *Associate* levels which relate to basic, fundamental teaching skills. The final level of *Full Certification* is more concerned with *evaluation and the development of the teacher as an autonomous practitioner.*

All three levels will be concerned with reflective practice, but this will become more analytical as we progress through the stages.

12.8 HE and Lifelong Learning Awards

Higher Education Institutions (HEIs) are long standing providers of teacher education for both the DCSF and the DIUS sectors and are monitored by the QAA (Quality Assurance Agency) while the teacher education provided by colleges is overseen by the QCA. Each sector has been required to incorporate the overarching LLUK Standards within their current validation frameworks in order to ensure that there will be consistency of provision across the institutions delivering teacher education for Lifelong Learning. There will be the necessary flexibility within the new framework for the provision of mandatory, optional and specialist units of assessment in order that there may be bespoke awards for particular qualifications to suit particular educational situations (see also teaching roles in 12.6 above). The QCA are also developing a Qualifications and Credit Framework which is intended to harmonize provision and to promote a valid accreditation of the experience and training which sector teachers have achieved.

Unfortunately, the QAA have made the decision to allow HEIs delivering a PGCE award to be either a ***Postgraduate*** Certificate, which would have to be equivalent to other postgraduate awards in terms of the level of study (i.e. including level M or NQF7), or they may elect

Table 12.9 Teacher education awards within the Lifelong Learning Sector

PROGRESSION ROUTES		
THRESHOLD AWARD	**ASSOCIATE TEACHER CERTIFICATE**	**DIPLOMA/PGCE** **For staff in a full teaching role**
Introductory award for all new teachers	**For regular teachers who have fewer responsibilities than those in a full teaching role**	'DIPLOMA IN TEACHING IN THE LLS (DTLLS)' or CERTIFICATE IN EDUCATION or 'POSTGRADUATE or PROFESSIONAL CERTIFICATE IN EDUCATION'
'PREPARING TO TEACH IN THE LIFELONG LEARNING SECTOR (PTLLS)'	'CERTIFICATE IN TEACHING IN THE LLS (CTLLS)'	
Pre-service, In-service, Part-time or Full-time	Pre-service, In-service, Part-time or Full-time	Pre-service, In-service, PT, Full-time
6 Level 1 HE credits or 6 level 3 or 4 NQF credits	**30 Level 2 HE Credits or 30 Level 4 or 5 NQF Credits (incorporates the 6 Credits of the Threshold Award)**	***A minimum of 120 Level 2 HE Credits or 120 Level 4/5 NQF Credits (incorporates both the Threshold and Associate Awards)***

Note: *A general tariff has been agreed, so that with whatever provider the study for the above awards is undertaken, ten hours of self or directed learning will be valued at 10 HE or NQF credits. So the Threshold Award will involve 60 hours of learning, while the Cert. Ed. will require (over two years) 1,200 hours of self or directed (taught) learning.*

to interpret PGCE to mean *Professional* Graduate Certificate in Education, which could be at the level of HE1 or NQF4. It is odd that the Qualification Assurance Agency should not have anticipated the confusion that will subsequently be created by such an arrangement. An employer receiving an application from a teacher with a PGCE may well be unsure if it is postgraduate or professional.

12.9 Threshold Award

The title of the Threshold Award is '*Preparing to Teach in the Lifelong Learning Sector (PTLLS)*' and it is rated as having six Level 1 HE credits or six Level 3 or 4 NQF credits. This is an introductory award which provides a basic minimum standard for all those entering the profession from September 2007.

12.9.1 Threshold learning outcomes

The wording of this award is slightly different at Level 4 than that used at Level 3. For example, at NQF Level 3 outcome 1.1 uses 'Explain own role' while at Level 4 (below) the outcome is expressed as 'Review own role'. This unit has five learning outcomes and the NQF Level 4 outcomes are provided for information:

The learner can

1. *Understand own role and responsibilities and boundaries of role in relation to teaching:*
    1.1 Review own role and its responsibilities, and boundaries of own role as a teacher.
    1.2 Summarize key aspects of relevant current legislative requirements and codes of practice within a specific context.
    1.3 Review other points of referral available to meet the potential needs of learners.
    1.4 Discuss issues of equality and diversity, and ways to promote inclusion.
    1.5 Justify the need for record keeping.
2. *Understand appropriate teaching and learning approaches in specialist area:*
    2.1 Identify, adapt and use relevant approaches to teaching and learning in relation to the specialist area.
    2.2 Evaluate a range of ways to embed elements of functional skills in the specialist area.
    2.3 Evaluate the teaching and learning approaches for a specific session.
3. *Demonstrate session planning skills:*
    3.1 Plan a teaching and learning session which meets the needs of individual learners.
    3.2 Evaluate how the planned session meets the needs of individual learners.
    3.3 Analyse the effectiveness of the resources for a specific session.
4. *Understand how to deliver inclusive sessions which motivate learners:*
    4.1 Analyse different ways to establish ground rules with learners which underpin appropriate behaviour and respect for others.
    4.2 Use a range of appropriate and effective teaching and learning approaches to engage and motivate learners.

    4.3 Explain and demonstrate good practice in giving feedback.

    4.4 Demonstrate good practice in giving feedback.

    4.5 Communicate appropriately and effectively with learners.

    4.6 Reflect on and evaluate the effectiveness of own teaching, making recommendations for modification as appropriate.

5. *Understand the use of different assessment methods and related record keeping:*

    5.1 Review a range of different assessment methods and approaches to record keeping.

    5.2 Evaluate the use of assessment methods in different contexts, including reference to initial assessment.

    5.3 Justify the need for record keeping in relation to assessment.

Note: *Criterion 1.1 (above) represents coverage of all six domains of the professional standards.*

12.10 Associate Teacher Certificate

The title of the Associate Teacher Award is '***Certificate in Teaching in the Lifelong Learning Sector***' (CTLLS) and is rated as 24 Level 1 HE credits or 24 Level 3 or 4 NQF credits. This is an initial award for teachers who have substantial teaching experience but have not yet gained a full teaching role and are viewed as filling an *Associate* teacher role. In such cases they will be teaching predominantly using pre-prepared teaching materials or packs which do not allow them full responsibility in the design of curriculum materials.

Or they may be teaching on a one-to-one basis, or their work may be confined to a particular level/subject/type of learner and this role does not allow them to demonstrate the full range of skills and responsibilities across a particular curriculum area. New teachers are expected to gain this basic licence to teach within five years of starting employment within the Lifelong Learning Sector. Those programme members who have already achieved the Threshold Award (see 12.9 above) will be credited with the six Level 1 credits and the development involved. The Associate Teacher Certificate is the next step and involves:

- an entry requirement of a minimum NQF (or equivalent) Level 3 qualification in their own subject specialism
- an initial assessment of literacy, numeracy and ICT needs to be addressed during the programme
- 120 hours of learning in total (at least 60 hours' guided learning and 60 hours' self-directed learning)
- Observed teaching practice
- Mentoring support.

On completion of this award the Associate Teacher will:

1. know how to carry out initial assessment in their own specialist area
2. have an understanding of the use and purpose of initial assessment
3. have an awareness of basic theories of learning and how they are applied in practice

4. have a broad understanding of the principles and practice of planning learning
5. know how to meet different learners' needs and negotiate individual learning goals
6. be able to establish and maintain a learning environment appropriate to area of expertise
7. be able to establish and maintain a learning environment appropriate to cohort
8. be able to identify key aspects of relative current legislative requirements
9. be able to establish ground rules that underpin appropriate behaviour and respect for others
10. be able to demonstrate codes of practice and principles of inclusiveness
11. know how to challenge discriminatory behaviour
12. be able to demonstrate good practice in relation to equality and respect for diversity
13. be able to select appropriate materials from the range available
14. be able to develop own materials and how to adapt them for different purposes/learners
15. be able to deliver session plans to meet the needs of individual learners
16. be able to apply appropriate teaching and learning strategies to meet individual learner needs
17. be able to ensure that all learners understand the context of the area of specialism
18. be able to develop learners' awareness of how subject specialisms can contribute to the economy/society
19. be able to facilitate opportunities for learners to use peer and/or self-assessment
20. be able to facilitate opportunities for learner feedback
21. encourage learners to reflect on own and others' performance through evaluation
22. be able to emphasize positive feedback and understand its impact on those whom it affects
23. be able to use assessment activities which produce valid, reliable and sufficient evidence
24. have a broad understanding of the principles and practice of assessment.

12.11 Diploma in Teaching – LLUK and HE

The title of the Full Teacher Award, which will be used by other than HEI providers, is the '*Diploma in Teaching in the Lifelong Learning Sector*' (DTLLS) and is usually rated at 120 Level 2/3 or 4 NQF credits. This award has long been provided by HEIs under the title '*Certificate in Education*' or the '*Postgraduate Certificate in Education*' or the '*Professional Graduate Certificate in Education*' (see 12.8 above for a further explanation) and will generally be accredited as 60 Level 1 and 60 Level 2 credits in each year of a two-year programme. However, there are inevitably other variants in the structure from the many providers of these awards.

This award is for teachers who are viewed as filling a *full teaching role* and such new teachers have up to five years to achieve the award which is equivalent to the *Certificate in Education* (the traditional teacher's award within the primary and secondary sectors). The 24 credits gained through the completion of the Associate Teacher Award (see also 12.10) will be accredited. The total of 120 credits awarded will allow the holder to progress to further qualifications (for example, BA or BEd degrees) provided by HEIs and other bodies. The full-time Cert. Ed. and PGCE will usually take one year or the part-time equivalent will take two years.

In summary, the Full Award involves:

- an entry requirement of a minimum NQF (or equivalent) Level 3 qualification in their own subject specialism
- an initial assessment of literacy, numeracy and ICT needs to be addressed during the programme

- a minimum of 1,200 hours' of learning in total (at least 600 hours' guided learning and 600 hours' self-directed learning)
- observed teaching practice
- mentoring support.

The ***DTTLS/Certificate in Education Award*** is usually taken over two consecutive years. Year 1 will involve three Level 4 modules:

1. Planning and Enabling Learning	9 credits
2. Principles and Practice of Assessment	3 credits
3. Theories and Principles for Planning and Enabling Learning	6 credits

Module One, '*Planning and Enabling Learning*' has six learning outcomes which have been expressed using slightly different nomenclature for NQF Levels 3 or 4 (e.g. the word 'Explain' at Level 3 and 'Analyse' at Level 4). The specification below represents either HE Level 1 or NQF Level 4. On completion of this award, participants will be able to:

1. *Understand ways to negotiate appropriate individual goals with learners:*
    1.1 Analyse the role of initial assessment in the learning and teaching process.
    1.2 Describe and evaluate different methods of initial assessment for use with learners.
    1.3 Evaluate ways of planning, negotiating and recording appropriate learning goals with learners.
2. *Understand how to plan for inclusive learning:*
    2.1 Establish and maintain an inclusive learning environment.
    2.2 Devise and justify a scheme of work which meets learners' needs and curriculum requirements.
    2.3 Devise and justify session plans which meet the aims and needs of individual learners and/or groups.
    2.4 Analyse ways in which session plans can be adapted to the individual needs of learners.
    2.5 Plan the appropriate use of a variety of delivery methods, justifying the choice.
    2.6 Identify and evaluate opportunities for learners to provide feedback to inform practice.
3. *Understand how to use teaching and learning strategies and resources inclusively to meet curriculum requirements:*
    3.1 Select/adapt, use and justify a range of inclusive learning activities to enthuse and motivate learners, ensuring that curriculum requirements are met.
    3.2 Analyse the strengths and limitations of a range of resources, including new and emerging technologies, showing how these resources can be used to promote equality, support diversity and contribute to effective learning.
    3.3 Identify literacy, language, numeracy and ICT skills which are integral to own specialist area, reviewing how they support learner achievement.
    3.4 Select/adapt, use and justify a range of resources to promote inclusive learning and teaching.
4. *Understand how to use a range of communication skills and methods to communicate effectively with learners and relevant parties in own organization:*
    4.1 Use and evaluate different communication methods and skills to meet the needs of learners and the organization.
    4.2 Evaluate own communication skills, identifying ways in which these could be improved, including an analysis of how barriers to effective communication might be overcome.

4.3 Identify and liaise with appropriate and relevant parties to effectively meet the needs of learners.
5. *Understand and demonstrate knowledge of the minimum core in own practice:*
    5.1 Apply minimum core specifications in literacy to improve own practice.
    5.2 Apply minimum core specifications in language to improve own practice.
    5.3 Apply minimum core specifications in mathematics to improve own practice.
    5.4 Apply minimum core specifications in ICT user skills to improve own practice.
6. *Understand how reflection, evaluation and feedback can be used to develop own good practice:*
    6.1 Use regular reflection and feedback from others, including learners, to evaluate and improve own practice, making recommendations for modification as appropriate.

Module Two, '*Principles and Practice of Assessment*' has six learning outcomes which have been expressed using slightly different nomenclature for NQF Levels 3 or 4 (e.g. the word 'Explain' at Level 3 and 'Evaluate' at Level 4). The specification below represents either HE Level 1 or NQF Level 4. On completion of this award participants will be able to

1. *Understand key concepts and principles of assessment:*
    1.1 Summarize the key concepts and principles of assessment.
2. *Understand and use different types of assessment:*
    2.1 Discuss and demonstrate how different types of assessment can be used effectively to meet the individual needs of learners.
3. *Understand the strengths and limitations of a range of assessment methods, including, as appropriate, those which exploit new and emerging technologies:*
    3.1 Evaluate a range of assessment methods with reference to the needs of particular learners and key concepts and principles of assessment.
    3.2 Use a range of assessment methods appropriately to ensure that learners produce assessment evidence that is valid, reliable, sufficient, authentic and current.
    3.3 Justify the use of peer and self-assessment to promote learner involvement and personal responsibility in the assessment of their learning.
4. *Understand the role of feedback and questioning in the assessment of learning:*
    4.1 Analyse how feedback and questioning contributes to the assessment process.
    4.2 Use feedback and questioning effectively in the assessment of learning.
5. *Understand how to monitor, assess, record and report learner progress and achievement to meet the requirements of the learning programme and the organization:*
    5.1 Review the assessment requirements and related procedures of a particular learning programme.
    5.2 Conduct and record assessments which meet the requirements of the learning programme and the organization including, where appropriate, the requirements of external bodies.
    5.3 Communicate relevant assessment information to those with a legitimate interest in learner achievement.
6. *Understand how to evaluate the effectiveness of own practice:*
    6.1 Evaluate the effectiveness of own practice taking into account the views of learners.

Module Three, '*Enabling Learning and Assessment*' has five learning outcomes which have been expressed using slightly different nomenclature for NQF Levels 3 or 4 (e.g. the word 'Explain' at Level 3 and 'Analyse' at Level 4). The specification below represents either HE Level 1 or NQF Level 4. On completion of this award participants will be able to:

1. *Understand theories, principles and applications of formal and informal assessment and their roles in learning and evaluation:*
   1.1 Analyse the application of theories and principles of assessment in relation to practice in own specialist area.
   1.2 Analyse the role of assessment and evaluation and quality processes.
2. *Understand the significance of equality and diversity issues for the assessment of learning:*
   2.1 Critically discuss the implications of equality and diversity issues in assessment for teachers and learners.
3. *Understand and demonstrate how to plan/design and conduct formal and informal assessment:*
   3.1 Plan and/or design and use assessment schemes, methods and instruments that are fair, valid, reliable, sufficient and appropriate for learners, using new and emerging technologies (where appropriate).
   3.2 Justify the selection and/or design and use of formal and informal assessment methods and tools used in own specialist area.
   3.3 Establish and maintain an appropriate environment for assessment to maximize learners opportunities for success.
   3.4 Record and report on learner progress and achievement, using organizational and/or awarding institution protocols and procedures as required.
4. *Understand and demonstrate how to give effective feedback to learners:*
   4.1 Justify and use appropriate skills and approaches in giving verbal and written feedback to learners.
   4.2 Justify and use appropriate skills and approaches to negotiate targets and strategies for improvement and success for learners.
5. *Understand and demonstrate knowledge of the minimum core literacy to improve own practice:*
   5.1 Apply minimum core specifications in own practice.
   5.2 Apply minimum core specifications in language to improve own practice.
   5.3 Apply minimum core specifications in mathematics to improve own practice.
   5.4 Apply minimum core specifications in ICT user skills to improve own practice.
6. *Understand how to evaluate and improve own assessment:*
   6.1 Evaluate and improve the design and effectiveness of formal and informal assessment practice and procedures, methods and instruments, using feedback from learners and appropriate others and referring to relevant theories of learning.
   6.2 Evaluate own approaches, strengths and development needs in relation to assessment.
   6.3 Plan and take up appropriate development opportunities to improve own practice in relation to formal and informal assessment.

The second year of the part-time award will usually consist of a further 60 credits (usually HEI Level 2/3 or 4/5 NQF), and will usually consist of three modules chosen from a list of options.

12.12 Evidence against the standards

As the LLUK units of assessment indicate, Levels 1 and 2 will involve the practical implementation of appropriate standards from each domain, whereas within Level 3 you will be considering not only the effect of the implementation, but also the external and internal influences on the chosen teaching/training methodologies and their particular context.

Levels 1 and 2 evidence will, in the main, be drawn from teaching and learning situations, involving planning, material production, administration, etc. Although Level 3 evidence will also draw heavily on practice, it will be more conceptual and will be based on more lengthy and detailed analysis of aspects of the teaching and learning process. As expected, the PDJ commentary on these processes, plus the teaching observations will provide valuable confirmatory, reflective evidence.

Common to all three levels of provision and providing the source of a wealth of appropriate evidence, are the *teaching observations*. Depending on which award is involved (see 12.8 above), a number of successful teaching observations have to be carried out in each year of the programme and these, together with the associated documentation (contained in the Practitioner File, below) will provide evidence against some of the criteria and knowledge requirements within a large percentage of the standards' outcomes.

The achievement of all of the listed standards relevant to the three awards, Threshold, Associate and Full Cert. Ed./Diploma is the aim of this programme. *The various 'activities' in each chapter, together with the practice-based work and supported by reflections within the PDJ are the means of generating evidence of achievement,* but we have avoided the 'straightjacket' of having a direct one-to-one relationship between the standards and the chapters. This would have resulted in having activities that have value only to the domain related to that chapter. This is not necessarily the most effective way to organize development, but, more importantly, many of the standards (particularly those at Common Framework Level 6 or HE Level 3) will be achieved and reinforced through several of the activities. We have called the two key documents, which we propose you use to develop appropriate evidence against the standards, the *Practitioner's File* (PF) and the *Personal Development Journal* (PDJ). Obviously each different teacher education provider will use their own titles for these documents, but we feel that the process of evidence generation will, inevitably, result in similar sorts of records. The PF is suggested as a means of collecting together experiential evidence of continuing professional development and the PDJ is an ongoing reflective commentary on this process. Details of other related useful evidential records follow below (12.13 to 12.14.6) and blank pro forma for all of these are available on the **tipcet.com** website.

12.13 Practitioner File

The Practitioner File is designed to record not only evidence of your assessment through teaching observations during the programme, but also the development of particular areas of interest and expertise. Whereas, in order to meet the requirements of the teaching assessment you will provide your observer with a lesson plan and rationale for each session you will also, at other times, be generating all sorts of evidence of your developing skills as a practitioner. These may take the form of an analysis of student needs, action plans for meeting those needs, teaching materials, assessment schemes, student evaluations, etc.

The manager of the particular programme of teacher training which you are undertaking will provide you with details of how your observed teaching assessment will be carried out. The information you provide within this Practitioner File will support this process. We suggest that you include the records discussed below and obviously you should use any programme pro forma which is provided. However, for your convenience, appropriate blank pro forma for each of the evidence-generating activities below are provided on the **tipcet.com** website.

12.14 Teaching Log

This is intended to be a record of all the teaching you carry out during the programme. LLUK have a requirement that you achieve 30 hours' teaching practice during Stages 1 and 2 and a further 120 hours during Stage 3 (150 hours in total). In general, a simple one-line record of the different teaching commitments will be sufficient. In order to register the achievement of an endorsed award with IfL, teaching must be carried out within a Further Education context. You may, if you wish, insert a copy of your contract and refer to it on the Teaching Log pro forma. This will eliminate the need to complete the pro forma in detail. You may need to get these entries confirmed by a signature.

12.14.1 Session plan

Your programme manager will have provided you with the requirements of each Teaching Observation and inevitably this will involve developing a session plan. This process is discussed in detail in Chapter 4 and again, if required, a blank pro forma is available on the **tipcet.com** website.

12.14.2 Rationale

Often an observer will ask you to justify the approach you are taking when teaching a particular class. This rationale may contain such considerations as reflections on learner characteristics and needs, the learning environment, and a justification for your selection of defined learning outcomes, teaching methods, principles of learning, use of resources, assessment and evaluation, etc. You may add some reflections on how earlier teaching sessions (perhaps with the same group of students) have affected your chosen approach. It is useful if each observation is developmental (i.e. building on earlier observations) and is used (at least in part) to address related criteria within one or more of the domains defined within the LLUK Standards.

12.14.3 Generic self-evaluation schedule

A retrospective analysis of your teaching session is a valuable form of evidence in relation to the LLUK Standards as it allows you to establish your own ability to identify the successful and less-successful aspects of the observed session and any other examples of your teaching. This schedule should be completed shortly after the teaching session while all of the subtle details are still fresh in your memory. If possible you should discuss your completed self-evaluation with your observer, and relate it to your own rationale for the session and to the observer's written report. Further details and examples are contained in Chapter 9.

12.14.4 Specific self-evaluation schedule

As you progress to CF Level 6/HE3, for example, instead of using the above (12.14.3) pro forma (which provides you with the evaluation criteria) you may wish to define your own criteria so that your analysis may focus more precisely on what you perceive to be the most significant characteristics (strengths and weaknesses) of your teaching performance. This evaluation pro forma, which is also discussed in Chapter 10, allows you to define the ten most appropriate criteria and then to add your response.

12.14.5 Progress summary

It is suggested that these pro forma should be completed with your observer during the debriefing after each Teaching Observation. It is intended to record your progressive development during teaching practice throughout the programme. The strengths and areas for improvement identified during previous observations should inform the selection, planning and delivery of subsequent observed sessions. For example, if in the first observed session a weakness is identified in the design and use of learning aids, the debriefing should include action planning to address the weakness. Ideally, the next observed session should include an opportunity to demonstrate significant improvement in this respect. Each observed session should consciously have built into it at least one aspect which differs from earlier observations and there should be clear evidence of progression. Observed sessions in particular should demonstrate an awareness of differentiation between students in the group, including techniques for catering for different levels of ability and interest. There should also be evidence of the purposeful use of group activities.

Note: Your observer may respond to the evidence you provide against criteria and knowledge goals in a particular domain (as shown on your Lesson Plan and Rationale) and will confirm those which have been met in the appropriate column of the Progress Summary.

12.14.6 Personal development journal

Whereas the *Practitioner File* (above) is clearly designed to record each stage of your *practical* development as a teacher, the purpose of the activities in the *Personal Development Journal* is the continued development of your cognitive skills through *reflective* practice.

The purpose of reflection is to learn from experience in order to modify and develop strategies and principles for future action and to increase awareness of the actual learning process itself. Teachers who evaluate and plan in this manner not only improve their own performance but also, in doing so, create a responsive and supportive learning environment which, in turn, will help their own students to become independent, aware and able to **learn** *about their own learning* (meta-learning) and to begin to take responsibility for it. These themes are developed in Chapter 2, 'Reflections in the Personal Development Journal' and in Chapter 9 we provide further guidance.

Completing the Personal Development Journal
Please Note: *Chapter 9 also contains further guidance on completing the PDJ.*

The purpose of the PDJ is the production of a reflective commentary to accompany the various types of evidence that will be presented for the accreditation of the LLUK Standards against an appropriate award.

As you know, the standards are structured around the six domains of the teaching and training developmental process and within these areas are defined the standards relating to *Scope, Knowledge and Practice*. For the sake of clarity, these overarching concerns have been disaggregated from the six domains (which are discussed in chapters 3 to 10) into related performance criteria and these are detailed in Tables 1.3 to 1.9 above.

These criteria and specifications are used as guidelines to inform the gathering of evidence against each of the broad areas of competence. So, to repeat, the central activity of our accreditation procedure is to address these defined standards with evidence which meets the *majority* of the criteria and their related specific and generic knowledge requirements. If you find it impossible to address any of the criteria, you should provide within your PDJ a written justification which explains why that criterion is not appropriate within your teaching situation.

The domain specifications (which begin with Domain A) are addressed within chapters 3 to 10 which have been designed to facilitate the process of identifying the relevant practical and theoretical activities which are the core of teaching and training and which should be the basis of the presented evidence and related reflections. It may also be useful to consider the *Process Justifications* which are also described in Section 12.14.9 below.

12.14.7 The assessment process

It is important that assessment is not viewed as a series of independent tasks but should be considered as a whole and as an integral part of the learning process. One piece of evidence, such as an entry in the PDJ, a completed 'activity' from chapters 3 to 10, a teaching observation or an academic assignment, will be relevant to more than one standard. In fact, most of the forms of assessment are, or can be designed to be, relevant to all of the standards. When gathering evidence, care should be taken to cross-reference each item of evidence to the standards to which it refers.

12.14.8 Sources of evidence

Evidence may be derived from:

- *Observation of performance.* For a HE 1/2, CF 4/5 (DTLLS), Certificate in Education, PGCE award you must undertake a minimum of 120 hours teaching practice and a number of these sessions will be observed. The evidence from these observations may address any of the six domains of practice.
- *Product evidence.* This may consist of documentation produced as a natural part of a teacher's normal work and could include schemes of work, learning resources, assessment records, etc. In addition to routine documentation, within the Practitioner File, there are optional pro forma available. By using these, programme members may produce appropriate and useful additional documentation such as Rationales, Progress Summaries, Lesson Plans, PDJ entries and so on.
- *Evaluation reports.* It is suggested that programme members carry out a self-evaluation of their observed teaching sessions. You may also draw on evaluations you carry out as part of your organization's quality systems and within the PDJ you should also evaluate other aspects of your work in order to produce the necessary evidence.
- *Witness testimony.* Evidence from others may be produced as a result of direct observation of performance (for example, teaching observation). In addition, experienced colleagues (such as your Subject Mentor) may well provide testimony of performance during collaborative or team teaching exercises.
- *Evidence of knowledge and understanding.* A wide range of knowledge and understanding is required to achieve the standards for teaching and learning within post-compulsory education. Confirmation that teachers have such knowledge may be inferred in part from their performance. This however, will not always be sufficient and other assessment will be required. For example, the chapter-based activities and assignments, the entries in the PDJ, and questioning during observed teaching.

12.14.9 Process justifications

Within the six domains of practice identified within the LLUK Standards (see 12.5 above) differing levels of performance are implicit. At the end of each of the key chapters there is a *Process Justification Table* which is a considered assessment of the differing levels of performance implied within the specifications for each award (i.e. Threshold, Associate and Full Certificate/Diploma) for incorporating the standards into your practice. This analysis also suggests the kind of teaching and learning activities you may use to generate evidence appropriate to that stage/level and how you might reflect on the various types of evidence you have produced in order to demonstrate wider reading and underpinning specific and generic knowledge.

12.14.10 Structured tasks

Rather than relying only on personal reflections as the basis of your journal of evidence, you may wish (with your Programme Leader's permission) to use the more prescriptive *structured tasks* encompassed within the 'activities' contained in all of the key area chapters (i.e. chapters 3 to 10) as a means of generating all or part of your evidence against the standards.

12.14.11 Experiential reflections

(See also 12.14.6)

The PDJ is an individual reflection on teaching and learning experiences, which may take many forms. You may wish to analyse recent events, you may like to articulate a problem-solving process you have recently been involved with, or you could evaluate aspects of practice. Also within each of the previous chapters there are specific 'activities' which suggest a range of different reflections on aspects of practice. These reflections should be carried out in your PDJ so that you build up a developmental log during your teacher education programme. Remembering that it is meant to be *personal*, most reflections will take one of two basic forms:

> *Experiential:* Descriptive, setting the teaching/training in context and providing detail of the various activities.
>
> *Theoretical:* Analysing the process and offering justifications, explanations, evaluations and action plans. Initially, it is expected that your journal entries will, in the main, be descriptions of the practical teaching you are involved with. For example, your Practitioner File may well contain the necessary details about a planned observed session, such as completed session plans which will provide an outline of your intended teaching and also rationales which will give a justification for your chosen approach and methodology. You may also wish to add in the PDJ a commentary on your experiences not only in the classroom, but also within the teacher education course. Reflect on the preparations you made, completing the documentation, implementing your chosen teaching method, being observed, completing the evaluation sheets, etc. Try to give an insight into what you value about the process and the aspects which are less than helpful, but keep in mind the need to generate evidence against the knowledge requirements and to show wider reading.

However, as valuable as it will be, it is also important that you should begin to go beyond such a review of practical activities and begin to conceptualize and analyse your work in order to meet the specific and generic knowledge requirements of the LLUK Standards. Try to include in your commentary views on principles and concepts, and show some familiarity with related theory in order to maximize the value of this evidence.

12.14.12 Further progression

Finally, just a reminder that, difficult as it may have been, achieving your DTLLS, Certificate in Education or PGCE should not mark the end of your professional development. Most universities and many colleges provide further Continuing Professional Development programmes to help you meet your IfL CPD requirement.

Typically, these will be relevant, one-year Foundation Degrees, two-year BA Degrees or Masters programmes. It would be a shame to let the developmental momentum you have built up slip away!

Bibliography

Armitage, A., R. Bryant, R. Dunnill, K. Flanagan, D. Hayes, A. Hudson, J. Kent, S. Lawes and M. Renwick (1999), *Teaching and Training in Post-Compulsory Education*. Buckingham: Open University Press.

Auerbach, E.R. (1986), 'Competency-based ESL: One step forward or two steps back'. *TESOL Quarterly*, 20, 3, 411–29.

Ausubel, D. and R.C. Andersson (1965), *Readings in the Psychology of Cognition*. New York: Holt, Rinehart & Winston.

Bailey, C. (1989), 'The Challenge of Economic Utility', in B. Cosin, M. Flude and M. Hales (eds). *Work and Equality*, Buckingham: Open University Press.

Bain, J., R. Ballantyne, J. Packer and C. Mills (1999), 'Understanding journal writing to enhance student teachers' reflectivity during field experience placements'. *Teachers and Teaching: Theory and Practice*, 5, 1, 23–32.

Ballantyne, R. and J. Packer (1995), 'Making connections: using student journals as a teaching/learning aid'. *HERDSA Gold Guide*, No. 2 (Canberra).

Bandura, A. and R.H. Walters (1963), *Social Learning and Personality Development*. New York: Holt, Rinehart & Winston.

Bash, L. (1985), *Urban Schooling; Theory and Practice*. Buckingham: Open University Press.

Belbin, M.R. (1981), *Management Teams. Why they Succeed or Fail*. Oxford: Butterworth-Heinemann.

Berryman, J. (1991), *Psychology and You*. London: British Psychological Society.

Bigge, M.L. (1982), *Learning Theories for Teachers*. New York: Harper & Row.

Black, P.J. and D. William (1998), *Inside the Black Box: Raising Standards through Classroom Intervention*. London: BERA.

Bloom, B.S. (ed.) (1956), *Taxonomy of Educational Objectives: Handbook 1, Cognitive Domain*. London: Longman.

Bolton, G. (2001), *Reflective Practice: Writing and Professional Development*. London: Paul Chapman Publishing.

Boud, D., R. Keogh and D. Walker (1985), 'Promoting Reflection in Learning', in D. Boud, R. Keogh and D. Walker (1985), *Reflection: Turning Experience into Practice*. London: Kogan Page.

Bruner, J. (1966), *Towards a Theory of Instruction*. Cambridge, MA: Harvard University Press.

Burns, R. (1982), *Self-Concept Development and Education*. London: Holt, Rinehart & Winston.

Bush, T. and D. Middlewood (eds) (1997), *Managing People in Education*. London: Paul Chapman Publishing.

Bush, T. and J. West-Burnham (1994), *The Principles of Educational Management*. London: Longman Group UK Ltd.

Buzan, T. (1993), The Mind Map Book: *Radiant Thinking*. London: BBC Books.

Calderhead, J. (1988), *Teachers' Professional Learning*. Philadelphia: Falmer Press.

Calderhead, J. and P. Gates (eds) (1993), *Conceptualising Reflection in Teacher Development*. London: Falmer Press.

Callaghan, J. (1976), *Speech at Ruskin College, 22 October 1976. Times Educational Supplement*.

Carr, W. (1995), *For Education: Towards Critical Educational Inquiry*. Buckingham: Open University Press.

Castling, A. (1996), *Competence-Based Teaching and Training*. London: Macmillan.

Clement, M. and K. Staessens (1993), 'School Culture, School Improvement and Teacher Development'. *Teaching and Teacher Education*, 16, 1, 81–101.

Coffield, F., D. Moseley, E. Hall and K. Ecclestone (2004), *Learning Styles for Post 16 Learners – What Do We Know?* London: L.S.R.C.

Cohen, L. and L. Manion (1989), *Research Methods in Education*. London: Routledge.

Cooley, C.H. (1912), *Human Nature and Social Order*. New York: Scribners.

Cotton, A. (ed) (1998), *Thinking about Teaching*. London: Hodder & Stroughton.

Coulthard, M. (1992), *Advances in Spoken Discourse Analysis*. London: Routledge.

Cousins, J.B. and L.M. Earl (eds) (1995), *Participatory Evaluation in Education*. London: The Falmer Press.

Currie, R. (1986), 'Validity and Reliability', in R.L. Jones and E. Bray (eds), *Assessment from Principles to Action*. London: Macmillan.

Daines, J. and B. Graham (1997), *Adult Learning, Adult Teaching*. Nottingham: Continuing Education Press.

Dart, B. and J. Clarke (1991), 'Helping students become better learners: A case study in teacher education'. *Higher Education*, 22, 317–35.

Dale, R. (1989), *The State and Education Policy*. Buckingham: Open University Press.

Deming, W.E. (1986), *Out of the Crisis: Quality, Productivity and Competitive Position*. Cambridge: Cambridge University Press.

Dewey, J. (1916), *Democracy and Education*. Chicago: Free Press.

Dewey, J. (1933), *How we think: A Restatement of the Relation of Reflective Thinking to the Educative Process*. Chicago: Henry Regnery.

Dewey, J. (1938), *Experience and Education*. London: Collier Macmillan Publishers.

DES (1985), *Education and Training for Young People*. London: HMSO.

DfEE (1998a), *The Learning Age: A Renaissance for a New Britain*. London: HMSO.

DfEE (1999), *Learning to Succeed: A New Framework for Post-16 Learning*. London: HMSO.

DfEE (2002), *14–19: Extending Opportunities: Raising Standards*. London: HMSO.

DfES (2004), *Success for All*. London: HMSO.

DfES (2004), *Equipping Our Teachers for the Future: Reforming Initial Teacher Training for the Learning and Skills Sector*. London: HMSO.

DfES (2005), *Every Child Matters*. London: HMSO.

DfES (2005), *Further Education: Raising Skills, Improving Life Chances*. London: HMSO.

DfES (2006), *Youth Matters; Next Steps*. London: HMSO.

DfES (2006), *Prosperity for all in the Global Economy: World Class Skills, (Lord Leitch Report)*. London: HMSO.

Douglas, S. (1992), 'Notes toward a history of media audiences', *Radical History Review*, 54, 127–38.

Dryden, G. and J. Vos (1994), *The Learning Revolution*. Aylesbury: Accelerated Learning Systems.

Ecclestone, K. (1996), *How to Assess the Vocational Curriculum*. London: Kogan Page.

Ecclestone, K. (1997), 'Energising or enervating: implications of NVQs in professional development'. *Journal of Vocational Education and Training*, 49, 1, 65–79.

Ecclestone, K. (2002), *Learning Autonomy in Post-16 Education*. London: Routledge Falmer.

Eisner, E.W. (1985), *The Art of Educational Evaluation*. London: The Falmer Press.

Eldridge, W.D. (1983), 'The use of personal logs to assist clinical students in understanding and integrating theories of counselling intervention'. *Instructional Science*, 12, 279–83.

Elliott, G. (1996), *Crisis and Change in Vocational Education and Training*. London: Jessica Kingsley Publishers.

Fairclough, N. (1989), *Language and Power*. Harlow: Longman.

Fawbert, F.P. (1987), *Using Video in Training*. Carnforth, UK: Parthenon Publishing.

Festinger, L. (1957), *A Theory of Cognitive Dissonance*. New York: Paperback (Trade Paper).

Flavell, John H. (1979), 'Metacognition and Cognitive Monitoring: A New Area of Cognitive Development Inquiry' *American Psychologist*, Vol. 34, p. 906.

Freire, P. (2000), *Pedagogy of the Oppressed* (30th Anniversary Edition). London: Continuum International Publishing.

Further Education Unit (FEU 1983), *A Basis for Choice*. Blagdon: FEU.

Gagne, R.M. (1985), *The Conditions of Learning*. New York: Holt, Rinehart & Winston.

Gardner, H. (1993), *Multiple Intelligences: The Theory in Practice*. New York: Basic Books.

Gibbs, G. (1988), *Learning by Doing*. London: FEU.

Gillespie, H., H. Boulton, J. Hramiak and R. Williamson (2007), *Learning and Teaching with Virtual Learning Environments*. Poole: Learning Matters.

Gregorc, A. (1984), *An Adult's Guide to Style*. New York: Harper & Row.

Gronlund, N. (1985), *Stating Behavioural Objectives for Classroom Instruction*. New York: Macmillan.

Hackman, J.R. and C.G. Morris (1978), 'Group process and group effectiveness: a reappraisal', in L. Berkowitz (ed.), *Group Processes*. New York: Academic Press.

Halliday, M.A.K. (1978), *Language as a Social Semiotic: Social Interpretation of Language and Meaning*. London: Arnold.

Hettich, P. (1990), 'Journal writing: Old fare or nouvelle cuisine?'. *Teaching of Psychology*, 17, 36–9.

Hill, C. (2003), *Teaching Using Information and Learning Technology in Further Education*. Poole: Learning Matters.

Hillier, Y. (2006), *Everything You Need to Know about FE Policy*. London: Continuum International Publishing Group Ltd.

Hodkinson, P. and Issitt, M. (1995), 'Competence, professionalism and vocational education and training,' in Hodkinson, P. and Issitt, M. (eds), *The challenge of competence*. London: Cassell.

Hodkinson, P., A. Sparkes and H. Hodkinson (1996), *Triumphs and Tears: Young People, Markets and the Transition from School to Work*. London: David Fulton.

Honey, P. and A. Mumford (1982), *The Manual of Learning Styles*. Maidenhead: Peter Honey.

Hutton, W. (1995), *The State We're In*. London: Random House UK Ltd.

Hutton, W. (1997), *The State to Come*. London: Random House UK Ltd.

Hyland, T. (1993), 'Professional development and competence-based education'. *British Journal of Education Studies*, Vol. 19, No. 1, 123–32.

Hyland, T (1996), 'Professionalism, ethics and work-based learning'. *British Journal of Education Studies*, 44, 2, 168–80.

Hyland, T. and B. Merrill (2003), *The Changing Face of Further Education*. London: Routledge Falmer.

IPPR (1988), *Educational Attainment – A Comparative Study*. London: Institute for Public Policy Research.

James, W. (1890), *Principles of Psychology*. New York: Holt, Rinehart & Winston.

Jarvis, P., J. Holford and C. Griffin (1999), *The Theory and Practice of Learning*. London: Kogan Page.

Johnson, D.W. and Johnson, R.T. (1979), 'Conflict in the Classroom: Controversy and Learning'. *Review of Educational Research*, 49 (1), 51–70.

Johnson, D.W. and Johnson, R.T. (1990), *Cooperation and Competition: Theory and Research*. Edina, Minn.: Interaction Book Company.

Jones, R.L. and E. Bray (1986), *Assessment: From Principles to Action*. London: Macmillan.

Katz, B. (1989), *Turning Practical Communication into Business Power*. London: Mercury Books.

Kelly, G. (1955), *The Psychology of Personal Constructs*, Vols, I and II. New York: W.W. Norton.

Kelly, G. (1979), in Bannister and Fransella (eds) (1970), *Inquiring Man: The Theory of Personal Constructs*. Harmondsworth: Penguin.

Kelly, R. (2005), *Harnessing Technology*. London: DfES.

Kemmis, S. (1985), 'Action research and the politics of reflection', in D. Boud, R. Keogh and D. Walker (eds), *Reflection: Turning Experience into Practice*. London: Kogan Page.

Knowles, M. (1970), *Self-Directed Learning: A Guide for Learners and Teachers*, Chicago: Association Press.

Knowles, M. (1984), *The Adult Learner: A Neglected Species (3rd edn)*. Houston: Gulf Publishing.

Kolb, D.A. (1984), *Experiential Learning – Experience as the Source of Learning and Development*. Englewood Cliffs, New Jersey: Prentice Hall.

Krathwohl, D.R. (1964), *Taxonomy of Educational Objectives: Handbook II, Affective Domain*. New York: David McKay.

Kyriacou, C. (1998), *Essential Teaching Skills*. Gloucester: Stanley Thornes.

Landeen, J., C. Byrne and B. Brown (1992), 'Journal keeping as an educational strategy in teaching psychiatric nursing'. *Journal of Advanced Nurnsing*, 17, 347–55.

Laurillard, D. (2002), *Rethinking University Teaching: A Conversational Framework for the Effective Use of Learning Technologies*. London: Routledge Falmer.

Lave, J. and E. Wenger (1991), *Situated Learning: Legitimate Peripheral Participation (Learning in Doing: Social, Cognitive and Computational Perspectives)*. Cambridge: Cambridge University Press.

Lawton, D. (1994), *Education and Politics in the 1990s*. London: The Falmer Press.

Lawton, D. (1994), *The Tory Mind on Education 1979–94*. London: The Falmer Press.

Lawton, D. (2002), 'Towards a 14 to 19 Framework'. *Forum*, 44, 2.

Leary, M. (1981), 'Working with biography,' in T. Boydell and M. Pedler (eds), *Management Self-Development: Concepts and Practices*. Aldershot: Gower.

Leitch, S. (2005), *Skills in the UK: The Long-Term Challenge*. Interim Report, www.dfes.gov.uk.

Lewin, K. (1951), *Field Theory in Social Sciences*. New York, Harper & Row.

Marton, F., D. Hounsell and N. Entwistle (1984), *The Experience of Learning*. Edinburgh: Scottish Academic Press.

Maslow, A.H. (1970), *Motivation and Personality*. New York: Harper & Row.

Matheson, C. and D. Matheson (2000), *Educational Issues in the Learning Age*. London: Continuum International Publishing Group Ltd.

McAllister, M. (1996), 'Learning contracts: an Australian experience'. *Nurse Education Today*, Vol. 16, 199–205.

McMurtry, J. (1991), 'Education and the market model'. *Journal of Philosophy of Education*, 25, 2.

Mead, G.H. (1934), *Mind, Self and Society*. Chicago: University of Chicago Press.

Minton, D. (1991), *Teaching Skills in Further and Adult Education*. London: City and Guilds/Macmillan Publishing.

Moon, J. (1999), *Reflection in Learning and Professional Development: Theory and Practice*. London: Kogan Page.

Moon, J. (1999), *Learning Journals: A Handbook for Academics, Students and Professional Development*. London: Kogan Page.

Morrison, K. (1998), *Management Theories for Educational Change*. London: Paul Chapman Publishing Ltd.

Mullins, L.J. (1999), *Management and Organisational Behaviour (5th Edition)*. London: Pearson Education Limited.

Norris, N. (1990), *Understanding Educational Evaluation*. London: Kogan Page.

Novak, Joseph D. (1983), 'The Use of Concept Mapping and Knowledge Vee Mapping with Junior High School Science Students', *Science Education*, Vol. 67, pp. 625–45, Oct 1983

Office for Standards in Education (Ofsted) (2003), *The Initial Training of Further Education Teachers: A Survey*. London: HMSO.

Parker, S. (1997), *Reflective Teaching in the Postmodern World: A manifesto for Education in Postmodernity*. Buckingham: Open University Press.

Pask, G. (1976), 'Styles and strategies of learning'. *British Journal of Educational Psychology*, 5, 128–48.

Perry, W.G. (1970), *Forms of Intellectual and Ethical Development in College Years*. New York: Holt, Rinehart and Winston.

Petty, G. (2004), *Teaching Today*. Cheltenham: Nelson Thornes.

Reece, I. and Walker, S. (2007), *Teaching, Training and Learning – A Practical Approach (fifth edition)*. Sunderland: Business Education Publishers Ltd.

Revans, R. (1980), *Action Learning: New Techniques for Management*. London: Bland and Briggs.

Robson, J. (1998), 'Profession in crisis: status, culture and identity in the further education college'. *Journal of Vocational Education and Training*, 50, (4), 585–607.

Rogers, A. (1994), *Teaching Adults*. Buckingham: Open University Press.

Rogers, C. (1980), *A Way of Being*. New York: Houghton Miffin.

Rogers, C. (1983), *Freedom to Learn for the 80s*. Columbus: Merrill.

Rowntree, D. (1981), *Assessing Students: How shall we know them?* London: Harper & Row.

Sallis, E. (1996), *Total Quality Management in Education*. London: Kogan Page.

Salmon, G. (2002), *E-Moderating: The Key to Teaching and Learning Online*. London: Routledge Falmer.

Salmon, G. (2000), *E-tivities: The Key to Active Online Learning*. London: Routledge Falmer.

Sanders, P. (1996), *First Steps in Counselling*. London: PCCS Books.

Schon, D. (1987), *Educating the Reflective Practitioner*. San Francisco: Jossey-Bass Publishers.

Shaffer, D. (1999), *Developmental Psychology (5th edn)*. New York: Brooks/Cole.

Skinner, B.F. (1938), *The Behaviour of Organisms: an Experimental Analysis*. London: Routledge and Kegan Paul.

Stasz, C., Hayward, G., Oh, S. and Wright, S. (2004), *Outcomes and Processes in Vocational Learning: A review of the Literature*, London: Learning and Skills Research Centre.

Stenhouse, L. (1975), *An Introduction to Curriculum Research and Development*, London: Heinemann.

Stevens, J. and D. (2001), *Web-based Learning*. London: Kogan Page.

Stoker, D. (1994), 'Teaching and Learning in Practice'. *Nursing Times*, 2, 65–73.

Tann, S. (1993), 'Eliciting Student Teachers' Personal Theories', in J. Calderhead and P. Gates (eds), *Conceptualising Reflection in Teacher Development*. London: Falmer Press.

Thorne, K. (2002), *Blended Learning: How to Integrate Online and Traditional Learning*. London: Kogan Page.

Tuckman, B.W. (1965), 'Developmental Sequence in Small Groups'. *Psychological Bulletin*, 63, 6, 384–99.

Tyler, R. (1949), *Basic Principles of Curriculum Instruction*. Chicago: University of Chicago Press.

Usher, R.S. (1985), 'Beyond the anecdotal: adult learning and the use of experience'. *Studies in the Education of Adults*, 17, 59–75.

Wagenaar, T.C. (1984), 'Using student journals in sociology courses'. *Teaching Sociology*,11, 419–37.

Walkin, L. (1990), *Teaching and Learning in Further and Adult Education*. Gloucester: Stanley Thornes.

Whitty, G. (2002), *Making Sense of Educational Policy*. London: Paul Chapman Publishing.

Wiener, M. (1985), *English Culture and the Decline of the Industrial Spirit*. Harmondsworth: Penguin.

Wolf, A. (2002), *Does Education Matter?* Harmondsworth: Penguin.

Yinger, R.J. and C.M. Clark (1981), *Reflective Journal Writing: Theory and Practice*, Occasional Paper No. 50. The Institute for Research on Teaching, Michigan State University.

Zeichner, K.M. (1992), 'Conceptions of reflective teaching in contemporary US teacher education program reforms' in L. Valli (ed.), *Reflective Teacher Education*. Albany: New York State University Press.

Index